The CONTEMPORARY SUPERINTENDENT

D1200115

Edited by

Lars G. Björk • Theodore J. Kowalski

The
CONTEMPORARY SUPERINTENDENT
Preparation, Practice, and Development

Bruce G. Barnett • Tricia Browne-Ferrigno • C. Cryss Brunner

Bonnie C. Fusarelli • Lance D. Fusarelli • Thomas E. Glass

Margaret Grogan • D. Keith Gurley • John L. Keedy

George J. Petersen • Juanita Cleaver Simmons • Michelle D. Young

CORWIN PRESS
A SAGE Publications Company
Thousand Oaks, California

Copyright © 2005 by Corwin Press.

All rights reserved. When forms and sample documents are included, their use is authorized only by educators, local school sites, and/or noncommercial entities who have purchased the book. Except for that usage, no part of this book may be reproduced or utilized in any form or by any means, electronic or mechanical, including photocopying, recording, or by any information storage and retrieval system, without permission in writing from the publisher.

For information:

Corwin Press
A Sage Publications Company
2455 Teller Road
Thousand Oaks, California 91320
www.corwinpress.com

Sage Publications Ltd.
1 Oliver's Yard
55 City Road
London EC1Y 1SP
United Kingdom

Sage Publications India Pvt. Ltd.
B-42, Panchsheel Enclave
Post Box 4109
New Delhi 110 017 India

Printed in the United States of America

Library of Congress Cataloging-in-Publication Data

The contemporary superintendent: Preparation, practice, and development / [edited by] Lars G. Björk, Theodore J. Kowalski.
        p. cm.
Includes bibliographical references and index.
ISBN 1-4129-1326-8 (cloth)—ISBN 1-4129-1327-6 (pbk.)
    1. School superintendents—United States. 2. School management and organization—United States. 3. Educational leadership—United States. I. Björk, Lars G. II. Kowalski, Theodore J.
LB2831.72.C68 2005
371.2′011—dc22

                                                        2005003265
This book is printed on acid-free paper.

05   06   07   08   09   10   9   8   7   6   5   4   3   2   1

Acquisitions Editor:	Elizabeth Brenkus
Editorial Assistant:	Candice L. Ling
Production Editor:	Melanie Birdsall
Copy Editor:	Nancy Sixsmith, Freelance Editorial Services
Typesetter:	C&M Digitals (P) Ltd.
Proofreader:	Cheryl Rivard
Indexer:	Sheila Bodell
Cover Designer:	Anthony Paular

Contents

Preface

Widespread concern for the quality of public education during the past two decades has launched the most intense, comprehensive, and sustained effort to improve education in American history. During the past decade, the scope, complexity, and intensity of reforms have increased interest in large-scale, systemic reform. As a consequence, superintendents are being viewed as pivotal actors in the algorithm of school improvement and student success. Questions about the relevance and efficacy of superintendent preparation and professional development programs provided grist for widely divergent views of how the next generation of superintendents should be prepared. On the one hand, national commissions, task force reports, and nationwide studies of the superintendency have called for greater alignment of preparation with the changing realities of practice. On the other hand, some critics have called for deregulating the field and abandoning the notion of administrator licensure altogether. Over the past several decades, nearly one-third of the states have either rescinded licensing requirements for school district superintendents or have created loopholes allowing persons without a license to hold this important position.

This book provides a scholarly and objective analysis of issues surrounding the role of superintendents. Past, present, and future practices are examined; traditional preparation is critiqued from several perspectives; and recommendations grounded in the realities of present and emerging practice are recommended. The argument is made that both preparation and licensing standards need to be strengthened to ensure effective future leadership and to ensure that the steadily expanding body of knowledge about high-performing districts and educational excellence are infused. The book has been written at an especially propitious time given the dissimilar reform initiatives surrounding this pivotal position.

The content has been developed over a three-year period from a series of scholarly papers presented primarily at the annual meetings of the American Educational Research Association and the University Council for Educational Administration. All the papers were subjected to blind peer review.

About the Editors

 **Lars G. Björk** is an associate professor in the Department of Administration and Supervision at the University of Kentucky, codirector of the University Council for Educational Administration's Joint Program Center for the Study of the Superintendency, and a senior associate editor of *Educational Administration Quarterly*. He has co-edited several books, including *Higher Education Research and Public Policy* (1988); *Minorities in Higher Education* (1994); and *The New Superintendency: Advances in Research and Theories of School Management and Educational Policy* (2001); and has coauthored *The Study of the American Superintendency 2000: A Look at the Superintendent of Education in the New Millennium* (2000) and *The Superintendent as CEO: Standards-Based Performance* (2005).

 **Theodore J. Kowalski** is the Kuntz Family Chair in Educational Administration at the University of Dayton. A former superintendent and college of education dean, he is the author of numerous books and articles, including two books on the superintendency: *Keepers of the Flame: Contemporary Urban Superintendents* (Corwin, 1995) and *The School Superintendent: Theory, Practice, and Cases* (Merrill, Prentice Hall, 1999). He is the editor of the *Journal of School Public Relations* and was editor of the yearbook of the National Council of Professors of Educational Administration.

About the Contributors

Bruce G. Barnett is a professor in the Department of Educational and Leadership Studies at the University of Texas, San Antonio. His work focuses on forging alliances with educational organizations, particularly the creation of school-university partnership programs for developing aspiring school leaders that emphasize mentoring, peer coaching, student cohorts, learning communities, instructional leadership, and moral dimensions of leadership. He coauthored *Developing Educational Leaders, A Working Model: The Learning Community in Action* (2002); *Restructuring Student Learning* (1996); *The TQE Principal: A Transformed Leader* (1994); and *The Moral Imperatives of Leadership: A Focus on Human Decency* (1991).

Tricia Browne-Ferrigno is an assistant professor in the Department of Administration and Supervision at the University of Kentucky and is an associate editor for *Educational Administration Quarterly*. She currently directs a multiyear, federally funded advanced leadership development project for school administrators in Pike County School District in eastern Kentucky. Her research includes longitudinal influences and effectiveness of preservice preparation and inservice professional development on the practice of educational leaders, effects of learning in cohorts, and policy influences on public education improvement. Her work has been published in *Educational Administration Quarterly*, *Journal of School Leadership*, and the *NCPEA Yearbook*.

C. Cryss Brunner is an associate professor in the Department of Educational Policy and Administration at the University of Minnesota and is joint director of the UCEA Joint Program Center for the Study of the Superintendency. Her research on women, power, the superintendency, and the gap between public schools and their communities has appeared in journals such as the *Educational Administration Quarterly*, *Educational Policy*, *Journal for a Just and Caring Education*, *Journal of Educational Administration*, *Policy Studies Journal*, *School Administrator*, *Educational Considerations*, *Urban Education*, *Contemporary Education*, and *Journal of School Leadership*. In addition to one sole-authored book, *Principles of Power: Women Superintendents and the Riddle of the Heart* (2000), she has edited one, *Sacred Dreams: Women* *and the Superintendency* (1999), and coedited one with Lars Björk, *The New Superintendency* (2001). She is one of the coauthors of the *American Association of School Administrators' Ten-Year Study of the School Superintendency* (2000). With Margaret Grogan, she has just completed a national study (2003) of all women superintendents and central office administrators, funded by the American Association of School Administrators (AASA). Brunner is the 1996–97 recipient of the National Academy of Education's Spencer Fellowship for her work on the relationship between superintendents' conceptions of power and decision-making processes. She is the 1998 recipient of the University Council for Educational Administration's Jack Culbertson Award for her outstanding contributions to the field as a junior professor.

Bonnie C. Fusarelli is an assistant professor in the Department of Educational Research, Leadership, and Policy at North Carolina State University. She is author of 20 articles on school leadership and recently coedited the *Politics of Education Yearbook* (2004). She has two forthcoming books: *Communicating With the Public in Education* (with Bruce S. Cooper and Steven D'Agostino) and *The Rising State: How State Power Is Transforming Our Nation's Schools* (with Lance D. Fusarelli and Bruce S. Cooper).

Lance D. Fusarelli is associate professor and program coordinator of the Educational Leadership Programs in the Department of Educational Research, Leadership, and Policy at North Carolina State University. He is the author of two books, an edited volume, and 30 articles, many on school leadership. He is the author of *The Political Dynamics of School Choice* (2003) and coauthored *Better Policies, Better Schools: Theories and Applications* (2003). He recently coedited *The Promises and Perils Facing Today's School Superintendent* (2002). His recent work focuses on the occupational satisfaction, job perceptions, and mobility of superintendents nationwide.

Thomas E. Glass is professor of Education Leadership at the University of Memphis. He is the coauthor of the 2000 AASA Ten Year Study of the Superintendency and authored the 1990 Ten Year Study. He has served as a superintendent and has been a consultant to superintendent organizations and public school districts across the nation.

Margaret Grogan is currently professor and chair, Department of Educational Leadership and Policy Analysis, University of Missouri–Columbia. She edits a series on Women in Leadership for SUNY Press. Her current research focuses on the superintendency, the moral and ethical dimensions of leadership, and women in leadership. Recent publications include a chapter in the NSSE Yearbook, 2002, "Shifts in the Discourse Defining the Superintendency: Historical and Current Foundations of the Position," with Cryss Brunner and Lars Björk; and, with Dick Andrews, a recent *Educational Administration Quarterly* article, "Defining Preparation and Professional Development for the Future" (2002). She has just published a new book with Daniel Duke, Pam Tucker, and Walt Heinecke: *Educational Leadership in an Age of Accountability* (2003).

D. Keith Gurley is an elementary principal near Kansas City, Missouri. He has previously served in the education field as elementary and middle school principal, assistant superintendent in several school districts in Kansas, and as assistant professor in educational leadership at the University of Kentucky. He has conducted research in the principalship, superintendent induction, and professional learning communities.

John L. Keedy is a professor at the University of Louisville and has served as a principal and a central office administrator. He has published in the *Canadian Administrator, Journal of Educational Administration, Teaching and Teaching Education, Journal of Educational Research, Journal of School Leadership,* and *Theory Into Practice,* among others. His research interests include studying norms within institutional settings, school reform, and— recently—the superintendency. His teaching interests include qualitative research methods, organizational theory, and action research for school administrators.

George J. Petersen is an associate professor of educational leadership at California Polytechnic State University in San Luis Obispo, California. His research focuses on the district superintendent and school board relationship, and the influence of that relationship on the development of policy, board decision making, and instructional leadership. His work in this area has been published in *Educational Administration Quarterly, Journal of School Leadership, Journal of Educational Administration, Journal of Law and Education, Education Policy Analysis Archives,* and *Educational Leadership Review.* He has a forthcoming book (with Lance Fusarelli), *The District Superintendent and School Board Relationship: Trends in Policy Development and Implementation.*

Juanita Cleaver Simmons is currently an assistant professor in the Department of Educational Leadership and Policy Analysis, University of Missouri–Columbia. She is coordinator of the Masters Learning and Instruction courses. Her current research focuses on urban student achievement and the impact of gender and race bias on student social and academic success. She has several years' experience in urban public school administration and has worked at state and national levels.

Michelle D. Young is the executive director of the University Council for Educational Administration and is a faculty member in Educational Leadership and Policy Analysis at the University of Missouri–Columbia. She serves on the Editorial Board of the *Educational Administration Quarterly, Educational Administration Abstracts,* and *Education and Urban Society.* She also serves on the National Advisory Board for ERIC, the Wallace–Reader's Digest Funds LEADERS Count Advisory Committee, the National Policy Board for Educational Administration, and the National Commission for the Advancement of Educational Leadership Preparation. Her scholarship focuses on how school leaders and school policies can ensure equitable and quality experiences for all students and adults who learn and work in schools. She is the recipient of the William J. Davis award for the most outstanding article published in a volume of the *Educational Administration Quarterly*. Her work has also been published in the *Review of Educational Research, Educational Researcher, American Educational Research Journal, Journal of School Leadership,* and *International Journal of Qualitative Studies in Education,* among other publications.

1

Evolution of the School District Superintendent Position

Theodore J. Kowalski

Normative role expectations for local school district superintendents have evolved over the past 150 years, incrementally becoming more extensive, complex, and demanding. By the 1980s, 82% of the states had promulgated laws or policies that required officeholders to complete a prescribed program of graduate study and subsequently obtain a state-issued license (or certificate) to practice. All but three of these states specified courses that had to be completed, and somewhat surprisingly, only 25 states identified "classroom teaching experience" as a license requirement (Baptist, 1989). More recently, Feistritzer (2003) reported that although 41 states continue to require preparation and licensing for superintendents, more than half of these states (54%) issue either waivers or emergency certificates to individuals who do not meet the prescribed qualifications. In addition, 15 of the 41 states (37%) allow or sanction alternative routes to licensure. Overall, the trend has been toward rescinding requirements for this key position, as evidenced by radical policy decisions such as in Tennessee, in which the only remaining requirement for being a superintendent is a bachelor's degree (Kowalski & Glass, 2002).

In truth, superintendent preparation and licensing have been contentious issues since the position's inception. Latent concerns were rekindled during the 1980s as issues of governance emerged in relation to the national school reform movement. Critics of the status quo, however, continue to vehemently disagree over needed policy revisions. In one camp are those advocating strengthening requirements; virtually all these individuals come from within the profession. Their recommendations have ranged from eliminating weak programs (e.g., Clark, 1989) to establishing a national preparation curriculum (e.g., Kowalski, 1999) to placing greater emphasis on instructional leadership (e.g., Murphy, 1994). In the other camp are those advocating the deregulation of preparation and licensing; virtually all these individuals come from outside the profession. Their most recent attack is found in the publication *Better Leaders for America's Schools: A Manifesto*, published by the Broad Foundation and the Thomas B. Fordham Institute (2003). The document, which mainly presents opinions and anecdotal evidence, refers to university-based preparation programs and state licensing standards as meaningless hoops, hurdles, and regulatory hassles. The authors declare, "For aspiring superintendents, we believe that the states should require only a college education and a careful background check" (p. 31).

Clearly, no issue is currently more crucial to the future of the position of school district superintendent than the battle being fought over professional preparation and state licensing. The intent of licensing professionals is to protect society and not the licensee. Consequently, a decision to deregulate a profession should not be made solely in political arenas in which self- and group interests are more likely to outweigh societal interests. This chapter is grounded in the belief that persons within a profession, regardless of their personal views, have a responsibility to ensure that policy debates of this magnitude will be objective and empirically based. As a first step toward meeting this obligation, the content of this chapter traces the evolution of the superintendency in the context of five role conceptualizations. The intent is to demonstrate the depth and complexity of the position's knowledge base. In addition, the argument is made that future policy decisions will be enlightened if role conceptualizations are considered and critiqued in relation to the nature of local school districts, minority practitioner perspectives (both gender and race), and traditional approaches to professional preparation.

EVOLUTION OF SUPERINTENDENT ROLES

The position of school district superintendent was created during the late 1830s; by 1850, 13 large city school systems already employed an administrator in this capacity. By most accounts, the very first district superintendents were appointed in Buffalo, New York, and Louisville, Kentucky

(Grieder, Pierce, & Jordan, 1969). By 1900, most city school districts had established this position. The need for school systems to have a top executive stemmed from a myriad of conditions including the development of larger city school districts, the consolidation of rural school districts, an expanded state curriculum, the passage of compulsory attendance laws, demands for increased accountability, and efficiency expectations (Kowalski, 2003a).

Petersen and Barnett (2003) note that there are some discrepancies in historical, accounts, and they attribute this variance to three conditions: the use of different literature sources, differing interpretations of historical accounts, and the analytical approaches used. Although some scholars (e.g., Tyack & Hansot, 1982) relied on a developmental approach (based on the premise that the superintendent's role matured over time), others (Callahan, 1966) employed a discursive analysis (relying on rhetoric and writings to determine role expectations). Noting the use of these two distinctively different approaches, Brunner, Grogan, and Björk (2002) concluded that the discursive approach resulted in a greater number of developmental stages.

There is some dispute over the earliest role conceptualization of the district superintendent. Carter and Cunningham (1997) and Petersen and Barnett (2003), for example, identify it as being a school board's clerk. This role, thought to exist for several decades prior to 1850, was predicated on the belief that big-city school boards were reluctant to relinquish power, so they relegated their superintendents to performing simple clerical and practical tasks. This role proved to be temporary, a condition that might explain why some historians (e.g., Callahan, 1966) did not view it as relevant to modern practice.

Five role conceptualizations are addressed in this chapter to demonstrate how the position of district superintendent evolved and to show why none has become irrelevant to modern practice. The first four—teacher-scholar, manager, democratic leader, and applied social scientist—were described by Callahan (1966); the fifth, communicator, was depicted by Kowalski (2001, 2003b). In practice, neatly separating them is virtually impossible because they often overlap. Nevertheless, they provide an essential framework for understanding the complexity of the position and the knowledge and skills required for effective practice.

Superintendent as Teacher-Scholar

From the time when the position was created until the first decade of the twentieth century, the primary foci of district superintendents were implementing a state curriculum and supervising teachers. The *common school movement* was intended to assimilate students into American culture by having public schools deliver a set of uniform subjects and courses—a strategy that required centralized control and standardization. State, county, and district superintendents were assigned to oversee the process (Kowalski, 1999).

After the Civil War, rapidly developing urban school systems established normative standards for public elementary and secondary education, and their superintendents were viewed as master teachers (Callahan, 1962). They devoted much of their time to supervising instruction and ensuring curricular uniformity (Spring, 1994). They frequently authored professional journal articles about philosophy, history, and pedagogy (Cuban, 1988), and some subsequently became state superintendents, professors, and college presidents (Petersen & Barnett, 2003). The characterization of superintendent as teacher-scholar was summarized in an 1890 report on urban superintendents:

> It must be made his recognized duty to train teachers and inspire them with high ideals; to revise the course of study when new light shows that improvement is possible; to see that pupils and teachers are supplied with needed appliances for the best possible work; to devise rational methods of promoting pupils. (Cuban, 1976, p. 16)

During the late 1800s and early 1900s, superintendents were the most influential members of the National Education Association. They never viewed themselves as being separated from the teaching profession. Management functions were often assumed by school board members or relegated to subordinates because the superintendents did not want to be viewed publicly as either managers or politicians. They often hid behind a cloak of professionalism, especially when they encountered ambitious mayors and city council members who wanted to usurp their authority (Callahan, 1966).

The conceptualization of the district superintendent as teacher-scholar began to wane circa 1910, but it never became irrelevant; emphasis on instructional leadership fluctuated throughout the past century. Summarizing the literature on this topic, Petersen and Barnett (2003) pointed out that the concept of superintendent as instructional leader has been challenged for various reasons that range from politics to position instability to school board member expectations. Research findings on the superintendent's influence over educational outcomes have been mixed. For instance, Zigarelli (1996) used data from the National Education Longitude Study for 1988, 1990, and 1992 to conclude that the evidence did not support a claim that the relationships between district administrators and schools improved instruction. Studies having a broader perspective of superintendent influence usually paint a different picture. After examining seven of them (Bredesen, 1996; Coleman & LaRocque, 1990; Herman, 1990; Morgan & Petersen, 2002; Murphy & Hallinger, 1986; Petersen, 2002; Peterson, Murphy, & Hallinger, 1987), Petersen and Barnett (2003) concluded that superintendents "can influence the views of school board members and others by articulating and demonstrating involvement, a sincere interest in the technical core of curriculum and instruction and viewing it as their primary responsibility" (p. 15).

Today, differences of opinion about superintendents being instructional leaders are evident in inconsistent state policies for professional preparation and licensure. Nearly one-third of the states have either eliminated the superintendent's license or allow alternative routes to obtaining it. Deregulation of licensing and preparation is grounded in the belief that being a professional educator is an inconsequential criterion that discourages highly effective business, political, and military leaders from becoming superintendents (Broad Foundation & Thomas B. Fordham Institute, 2003). Ironically, this myopic policy position comes at a time when national and state reform initiatives are increasing accountability standards for student performance. Björk (1993) noted that superintendents indirectly influence instruction through functions such as staff selection, principal supervision, and budgeting—decisions that often are undervalued with respect to overall effectiveness. Currently, state deregulation and district decentralization continue to heighten expectations that superintendents can recommend policy and develop rules that will increase educational productivity (Kowalski, 2001).

Superintendent as Manager

As early as 1890, reservations were being expressed about the ability of traditional superintendents to administer large city districts. These concerns focused primarily on a perceived lack of managerial knowledge and skills. As Cuban (1976) noted, heated debates were waged on this topic and "the lines of argument crystallized over whether the functions of a big-city superintendent should be separated into two distinct jobs, i.e., business manager and superintendent of instruction" (p. 17). Qualms about managerial competencies intensified as America began its transition from an agrarian to an industrial society. New factories sparked a demographic chain reaction, first producing urbanization and then large school systems. In this context, school board members focused more directly and intensely on resource management. They and other political elites began demanding that superintendents infuse the tenets of classical theory and scientific management, perceived then to be the successful underpinnings of the Industrial Revolution, into school administration (Callahan, 1962). By 1920, the role transformation had been officially completed; superintendents were expected to be scientific managers—individuals who could improve operations by concentrating on time and efficiency (Tyack & Hansot, 1982).

From approximately 1900 to 1920, leading education scholars, including Ellwood Cubberly, George Strayer, and Franklin Bobbitt, joined political elites in demanding that school administrators learn and apply the principles of scientific management (Cronin, 1973). The mounting pressures for this role transformation prompted officials at several leading universities to offer courses and subsequently graduate degrees in school management. Simultaneously, prominent superintendents were reevaluating the merits of protecting their public image as professional educators. Many decided that relinquishing this persona was necessary if policymakers and the general public were to accept the contention that administrative work had become separate from and more important than teaching (Thomas & Moran, 1992).

Opposition to the refashioning of superintendents into industrial managers came from two opposing groups. On the one hand, many mayors, city council members, and other political bosses feared that casting superintendents as managers would increase the stature, influence, and power of this position (Callahan, 1962).[1] On the other hand, some leading education scholars opposed the management conceptualization because they thought it was counterproductive to the principle of local control. More precisely, they feared that business and government power elites would act in concert with superintendent-managers to seize control of public education, thus diminishing participatory democracy (Glass, 2003).

In his book *Education and Cult of Efficiency*, historian Raymond Callahan (1962) chronicled how and why the infusion of business values into educational philosophy and the role transformation of superintendents became inextricably intertwined. Judging these conditions to be detrimental to the nation, he concluded that both contemporary social forces and the collusion of leading big-city superintendents were responsible for them. He was especially harsh in his assessment of the superintendents, concluding that they lacked conviction and courage. He then labeled them *dupes:* powerless and vulnerable pawns who were unwilling to defend their profession or their organizations. His analysis, referred to as the *Thesis of Vulnerability*, has been widely accepted by many but not all education scholars (Eaton, 1990). Burroughs (1974) and Tyack (1974), for example, disagreed with Callahan. They characterized the same superintendents as cunning, intelligent, political pragmatists who merely responded to the societal realities imbued in their work context. Thomas and Moran (1992) offered a third point of view: They posited that these administrators were opportunists who had embraced classical theory and scientific management because it expanded their legitimate power base.

Although historians have disagreed about motives, they concur that management became the dominant role expectation for school superintendents in the early 1900s. Budget development and administration, standardization of operation, personnel management, and facility management were the first tasks they assumed (Callahan, 1962). By 1930, however, the still relatively new business manager conceptualization was being subjected to intense criticism. The great economic stock market crash and subsequent depression tarnished much of the glitter that the captains of industry had acquired during the Industrial Revolution. Some prominent superintendents who were previously praised for emulating industrial managers were now being disparaged. In addition, many local school district patrons were overtly protesting the level of power that administrators had acquired; most felt disenfranchised by the bureaucratic structure that had been imposed on their local districts (Kowalski, 2003a). In the midst of this dissatisfaction, leading progressive educators, such as George Sylvester Counts, intensified their criticisms, arguing that business values imposed on public education were incongruous with the core political values of a democratic society (Van Til, 1971).[2]

Studying the evolution of the managerial role, Thomas Glass (2003) observed that both context and district size have been critical issues. He noted that the work of a superintendent in a small-enrollment rural district was quite dissimilar from the work of a superintendent in a large-enrollment urban district. Consequently, he cautioned that generalizations about managerial responsibilities are typically precarious. Management, and especially fiscal management, has been stressed heavily in small districts in which superintendents often have little or no support staff. In these settings, a superintendent manages the largest transportation program and food service program in the community.

Even though the degree of emphasis placed on management has fluctuated, the importance of the role is rarely questioned. Experienced practitioners recognize that many of their leadership attributes become insignificant when budgets are not balanced, school facilities are deemed not to be safe, and personnel problems routinely result in litigation. Superintendents in larger-enrollment and more affluent districts often can relegate managerial responsibilities to their staff, but even those able to do so are held accountable for efficient and productive operations (Kowalski, 1999). Commenting about contemporary school administration, John Kotter, Harvard Business School Professor, noted that superintendents must be both effective leaders and effective managers. As all organizations move toward decentralization and democratization, the demands placed on chief executives, including district superintendents, increase. Correspondingly, the minimum levels of knowledge and skills escalate (Bencivenga, 2002). Professor Kotter's observations illuminate the reality that the challenge facing today's superintendent is not choosing between leadership and management; it is establishing equilibrium between these two essential roles.

Superintendent as Democratic Leader

The role of democratic leader is often equated with *statesmanship*. Björk and Gurley (2003) traced the origins of statesmanship from Plato to Alexander Hamilton. Plato believed that a statesman acted unilaterally and paternalistically to control and direct critical societal functions.

Hamilton viewed a statesman as a true politician who juggled the interests of the common people and the interests of the economic elite while remaining an aristocrat. Callahan's (1966) conception of the superintendent as statesman was probably not in total agreement with either of these perspectives. His historical analysis of the period between 1930 and the mid-1950s is centered primarily on political leadership in a democratic context. After studying these perspectives, Björk and Gurley (2003) concluded that the term *statesman* "is not and may never have been an appropriate role conceptualization for the American superintendency, inasmuch as the role has never been about a stately, patriarch ubiquitously and benevolently guiding school systems single-handedly" (p. 35). Instead of statesman, they viewed this superintendent role as one of an astute political strategist.

The democratic leader characterization is anchored in both philosophical and political realities. In the 1930s, scarce fiscal resources forced school officials to engage more directly in political activity, especially in relation to lobbying state legislatures. Previously, the behavior of highly political superintendents was regarded as unprofessional (Björk & Lindle, 2001; Kowalski, 1995). But such convictions faded when it became apparent that public schools had to compete with other governmental services to acquire state funding. At approximately the same time, a cadre of prominent education professors was continuing its efforts to restore participatory democracy in local districts. One of the most vocal members in this group was Ernest Melby, a former dean of education at Northwestern University and New York University (Callahan, 1966). Melby (1955) believed that the infusion of business values had led superintendents to become less reliant on their greatest resource: the community. He warned administrators about the dangers of insulating themselves from the public and urged superintendents instead to "release the creative capacities of individuals" and "mobilize the educational resources of communities" (p. 250). In essence, democratic leaders were expected to galvanize policymakers, employees, and other taxpayers to support the district's initiatives (Howlett, 1993).

By the mid-1950s, the idea of having superintendents engage in democratic administration also met with disfavor. Detractors argued that the concept was overly idealistic and insufficiently attentive to realities of practice. They believed that democratic administration as it had been characterized produced problems for organizations and those who embraced it. In their eyes, everyday problems of superintendents were economic, social, and political; and knowledge and skills, not philosophy, were necessary to solve them (Kowalski, 1999). Although the ideal of democratic administration became less prominent after the 1950s, it never died. Over the past 20 years, it has reemerged, not only in public education but also in all types of organizations, largely because of a mix of changing values and economic realities. In the case of public education, scholars (e.g., Hanson, 2003; Wirt & Kirst, 2001) recognize that even the best education policies usually prove to be ineffective when they are unacceptable to the public. Policy and politics are inextricably joined in a democracy, a reality that promotes democratic administration. Perhaps more so now than in the past, ideological and moral differences among community factions require facilitation and conflict management (Keedy & Björk, 2002).

Superintendent as Applied Social Scientist

As with earlier role conceptualizations, the view of superintendent as applied social scientist was forged by a mix of societal and professional forces. Callahan (1966) identified the following four as the most influential:

- *Growing dissatisfaction with democratic leadership after World War II.* As previously noted, the concept of democratic leadership came under attack by those who perceived it to be overly idealistic. These detractors thought that shared authority and decision making exacerbated political, social, and economic problems rather than solving them.
- *Rapid development of the social sciences in the late 1940s and early 1950s.* The social sciences were being developed rapidly during this era. The seminal book *Toward a Theory of Action* (Parsons & Shils, 1951) exemplified this fact. Many scholars concluded that the social sciences were at the core of administrative work, including practice in districts and schools.
- *Support from the Kellogg Foundation.* During the 1950s, the Foundation provided more than $7 million in grants, primarily to eight major universities to support the research of school administration professors in the area of the social sciences.
- *A resurgence of criticisms of public education in the 1950s.* Changes in role conceptualizations were fueled by public dissatisfaction, and the image of superintendent as applied social scientist was no exception. During this era, however, the displeasure related to emerging social and political concerns. The end of school desegregation seemed apparent, families were leaving cities to move to new suburbs, the first wave of post-World War II baby boomers was entering public education, and the escalating cold war with the Soviet Union intensified national defense concerns. Such issues presented unique challenges to public elementary and secondary education, and many policymakers and public opinion shapers concluded that local district superintendents were not prepared to deal with them.

At least two other factors now appear to have been equally influential. Circa 1955, efforts to make school administration an established academic discipline equal to business management and public administration were intensifying (Culbertson, 1981). Redefining administrators as applied social scientists and infusing the social sciences into the curriculum for preparing school administrators were viewed as positive steps toward that goal (Crowson & McPherson, 1987). Second, prior to the 1950s, the practice of administration focused largely on internal operations, but systems theory was gradually employed to demonstrate how external legal, political, social, and economic systems affected organizations (Getzels, 1977). School administration professors concluded that such theoretical constructs were equally essential for their students.

The model of superintendent as social scientist encouraged professors and practitioners to emphasize empiricism, predictability, and scientific certainty in their research and practice (Cooper & Boyd, 1987). The intent was to rewrite the normative standards for practice; superintendents in the future were expected to apply scientific inquiry to the problems and decisions that permeated their practice. The study of theory was at the core of this normative transition, as evidenced by the changes in school administration textbooks. Those written prior to 1950 never mentioned theory, but virtually none written after 1950 omitted theory (Getzels, 1977). By the 1970s, the behavioral sciences became thoroughly integrated into school administration literature, including primary textbooks (Johnson & Fusarelli, 2003).

Similarities between the onset of the management role and the onset of the applied social scientist role are striking. In both instances, public dissatisfaction was atypically high, school administration professors were seeking to elevate their profession's status, and administration was described as being distinctively different from and more demanding than teaching (Kowalski, 2003a). Consequently, it is not surprising that both roles were subjected to similar criticisms. Depicting superintendents as experts unavoidably resurrects fundamental questions about the incompatibility of professionalism and democracy. How much power should superintendents possess? Can professionalism and democracy coexist in the administration of a public agency? In truth, public administration differs from other forms of administration in that professional knowledge is applied in highly political contexts and is subject to political scrutiny (Wirt & Kirst, 2001). Clearly, then, vulnerability to public contempt increases when superintendents act unilaterally or devalue public opinion (Kowalski, 1999).

Although emphasis on the behavioral sciences lessened after 1980, research and theories from constituent disciplines had already become embedded in school administration's knowledge base. Addressing the role in more recent times, Fusarelli and Fusarelli (2003) identified school reform and the quest for social justice as relevant issues. In the former, superintendents are expected to have the expertise necessary to research deficiencies and to recommend policy to ameliorate them. This expertise includes the ability to reshape institutional cultures that deter positive change. In the latter, superintendents are expected to have the expertise necessary to deal with social and institutional ills such as poverty, racism, gender discrimination, crime, and violence. Both expectations require knowledge and skills from various social science disciplines. Examples include psychology, sociology, anthropology, economics, and criminology. Moreover, superintendents are expected to conduct and utilize research in dealing with these issues.

Superintendent as Communicator

The ever-prescient Peter Drucker (1999) labeled the new era of organizations the Information Age: What matters in times of unremitting global competition and availability of huge amounts of information are the skills of accessing and processing information and making decisions based on that information. As early as the late 1970s, Lipinski (1978) and other scholars predicted that technology would move society away from a manufacturing base to an information base. *A Nation at Risk* (National Commission on Excellence in Education, 1983) sounded an alarm that public schools were not sufficiently performance-driven with respect to preparing students to be competitive in a global economy. America's public schools have always been expected to be efficient institutions, and computers exacerbated that anticipation (Kearsley, 1990). Dyrli and Kinnaman (1994), for instance, argued that technology could increase productivity through increased processing speed, greater memory capacity, miniaturization, decreased cost, and increased ease of use. Media reports on international comparisons, however, suggested that American public schools had become neither more efficient nor more productive (Bracey, 2003).

Historically, communication in school administration has been treated as a skill—that is, something one does well when assuming a role. Consequently, skills tend to be role-specific; the nature of the skill is shaped by the role characterization. As an example, appropriate managerial behavior and appropriate political behavior have been dissimilar. Today, however, such variations are no longer encouraged. Normative communicative behavior specifies two-way, symmetrical interactions for all school administrators. As a result, communication should no longer be viewed as a variable skill but rather as a pervasive role characterization (Kowalski, 2005).

The view of superintendent as communicator emerged in conjunction with America's transition from a manufacturing society (Kowalski, 2001). Communicative expectations for administrators reflect a confluence of reform initiatives and the social environment in which they are being pursued. Virtually every major school improvement concept and strategy encourages superintendents to work collaboratively with principals, teachers, parents, and other taxpayers to build and pursue collective visions. Yet many districts and schools retain cultures that promote work isolation (teachers and administrators working individually and in seclusion) (Gideon, 2002) and closed organizational climates (administrators attempting to avoid community interventions) (Blase & Anderson, 1995).

Since the early 1990s, policy analysts (e.g., Bauman, 1996; Fullan, 1996; Hess, 1998) have concluded that meaningful school reform requires revising institutional climates, including organizational structure and culture. In addition, current reform efforts are largely predicated on the conviction that restructuring complex institutions necessitates a social systems perspective (Chance & Björk, 2004; Murphy, 1991; Schein, 1996). "Systemic thinking requires us to accept that the way social systems are put together has independent effects on the way people behave, what they learn, and how they learn what they learn" (Schlechty, 1997, p. 134). In this vein, the nature of public schools is influenced by human transactions occurring within and outside the formal organization—exchanges often conducted in the midst of fundamental philosophical differences (Keedy & Björk, 2002). Restructuring proposals that ignore the ubiquitous nature of political disagreements almost always fail, either because key implementers and stakeholders are excluded from visioning and planning or because the values and beliefs expressed in the reforms are incongruous with prevailing institutional culture (Kowalski, 1997; Schlechty, 1997).

Many scholars (e.g., Henkin, 1993; Murphy, 1994) believe that school improvement needs to be pursued locally and that superintendents must be key figures in the process. This assignment, though, is highly intimidating for many superintendents for one or more of the following reasons:

- Topics that inevitably produce substantial conflict must be discussed openly and candidly with groups inside and outside the organization (Carlson, 1996).
- Often administrators either have been socialized to believe that conflict is counterproductive or they feel insecure managing it (Kowalski, 2003b).
- Many educators are dubious about reform, having experienced a myriad of change failures during their careers (Sarason, 1996). Even new teachers and administrators often come to accept things as they are (Streitmatter, 1994).

Despite these obstacles, superintendents must realize that they are unlikely to achieve true school restructuring unless they identify and challenge what individuals and groups truly believe and value about education (Trimble, 1996) and how they promote and accept change (Leithwood, Jantzi, & Fernandez, 1994). Increasingly, scholars are concluding that communication and culture are inextricably linked. For example, Conrad (1994) wrote, "Cultures are communicative creations. They emerge and are sustained by the communicative acts of all employees, not just the conscious persuasive strategies of upper management. Cultures do not exist separately from people communicating with one another" (p. 27). Although organizational research typically has categorized culture as a causal variable and communication as an intervening variable (Wert-Gray, Center, Brashers, & Meyers, 1991), the relationship between the two is more likely reciprocal (Kowalski, 1998). Axley (1996), for instance, wrote the following about interdependence: "Communication gives rise to culture, which gives rise to communication, which perpetuates culture" (p. 153). In this vein, communication is a process through which organizational members express their collective inclination to coordinate beliefs, behaviors, and attitudes. In schools, communication gives meaning to work and forges perceptions of reality. As such, culture influences communicative behavior, and communicative behavior is instrumental to building, maintaining, and changing culture (Kowalski, 1998).

In the case of local school districts, normative communicative behavior is shaped largely by two realities: the need for superintendents to assume leadership in the process of school restructuring (Björk, 2001; Murphy, 1994) and the need for them to change school culture as part of the restructuring process (Heckman, 1993; Kowalski, 2000).

A nexus between effective practice and communication skills is not unique to education; recent studies of business executives revealed that most who found themselves under attack were ineffective communicators (Perina, 2002). In the case of district superintendents, the role of effective communicator is framed by relatively new expectations that have become apparent since the early 1980s. Examples include engaging others in open political dialogue, facilitating the creation of shared visions, building a positive school district image, gaining community support for change, providing an essential framework for information management, providing marketing programs, and keeping the public informed about education (Kowalski, 2004). As communities become increasingly diverse, superintendents also have the responsibility of building more inclusive cultures (Riehl, 2000).

CONCLUDING COMMENTS

One overarching objective of this book is to enlighten decisions that affect the preparation and licensing of school superintendents. Although historical accounts of the five role conceptualizations provide a framework for this objective, they do not speak to current and future relevancy. These perspectives and implications for required knowledge and skills are examined in Chapters 5–9 of this book. The authors of these chapters also consider organizational context using the following typology of local school districts:

- *Urban.* Districts located in major cities with populations of at least 100,000
- *County.* Districts serving an entire county that include heterogeneous geographic areas (e.g., a mix of small cities and rural areas or a large city and suburbs)
- *Suburban.* Districts surrounding major urban areas

- *Cities and towns.* Districts located in cities and towns with populations of fewer than 100,000
- *Rural.* Districts comprised primarily of nonresidential areas

The purpose of addressing context is to make distinctions in role expectations based on the nature of a superintendent's workplace. Management responsibilities in rural and urban districts, for example, are almost always dissimilar.

Chapters 10 and 11 of this book provide critiques of the five role characterizations. The first explores female perspectives and the second explores the perspectives of people of color. Since its inception, the district superintendency has been overwhelmingly occupied by white males (Glass, Björk, & Brunner, 2000). The research agenda has also had a decidedly male perspective (Björk, 2000; Shakeshaft, 1989). The writings of scholars who have studied the experiences of women and racial minorities in the superintendency (e.g., Brunner, 1998; Grogan, 1999) at the very least raise the possibility that historical accounts of role expectations have not addressed diversity. Therefore, the intent of these two chapters is to determine the extent to which each characterization has been, is, and will be gender- and race-neutral. In addition, the authors offer perspectives about how gender and race could or should influence professional preparation.

NOTES

1. By exhibiting management competency, the superintendents could argue that their organizations should be free of political interference from other government agencies. If successful, their added power could be expressed through activities such as employment decisions, awarding contracts, and doling out favors to segments of the community.

2. To this day, many individuals confuse criticisms of the core values of classical theory with the function of management. Counts (1952), for example, viewed management as essential in all large organizations. His criticisms circa 1930 did not focus on superintendents performing management functions; instead, they pertained to the concentration of power in the hands of superintendents and political elites. He believed that the application of classical theory in public organizations was detrimental because it eradicated or diminished public participation. Consequently, it is important to distinguish between management as a function and scientific management as a philosophy.

REFERENCES

Axley, S. R. (1996). *Communication at work: Management and the communication-intensive organization.* Westport, CT: Quorum Books.

Baptist, B. J. (1989). *State certification requirements for school superintendents. Improving the preparation of school administrators. Notes on reform No. 7.* (ERIC Document Reproduction Service No. ED 318 107)

Bauman, P. C. (1996). *Governing education: Public sector reform or privatization.* Boston: Allyn & Bacon.

Bencivenga, J. (2002). John Kotter on leadership, management and change. *School Administrator, 59*(2), 36–40.

Björk, L. G. (1993). Effective schools—effective superintendents: The emerging instructional leadership role. *Journal of School Leadership, 3*(3), 246–259.

Björk, L. G. (2000). Introduction: Women in the superintendency—Advances in research and theory. *Educational Administration Quarterly, 36*(1), 5–17.

Björk, L. G. (2001). Institutional barriers to educational reform: A superintendent's role in district decentralization. In C. C. Brunner & L. G. Björk (Eds.), *The new superintendency* (pp. 205–228). New York: JAI.

Björk, L. G., & Gurley, D. K. (2003). *Superintendent as educational statesman.* Paper presented at the annual meeting of the American Educational Research Association, Chicago.

Björk, L. G., & Lindle, J. C. (2001). Superintendents and interest groups. *Educational Policy, 15*(1), 76–91.

Blase, J., & Anderson, G. (1995). *The micropolitics of educational leadership: From control to empowerment.* New York: Teachers College Press.

Bracey, G. W. (2003). PIRLS before the press. *Phi Delta Kappan, 84,* 795.

Bredesen, P. V. (1996). Superintendents' roles in curriculum development and instructional leadership: Instructional visionaries, collaborators, supporters, and delegators. *Journal of School Leadership, 6*(3), 243–264.

Broad Foundation & Thomas B. Fordham Institute. (2003). *Better leaders for America's schools: A manifesto.* Los Angeles: Authors.

Brunner, C. C. (1998). Women superintendents: Strategies for success. *Journal of Educational Administration, 36*(2), 160–182.

Brunner, C. C., Grogan, M., & Björk, L. G. (2002). Shifts in the discourse defining the super-intendency: Historical and current foundations of the position. In J. Murphy (Ed.), *The educational leadership challenge: Redefining leadership for the 21st century* (pp. 211–238). Chicago: The University of Chicago Press.

Burroughs, W. A. (1974). *Cities and schools in the gilded age.* Port Washington, NY: Kennikat.

Callahan, R. E. (1962). *Education and the cult of efficiency: A study of the social forces that have shaped the administration of public schools.* Chicago: University of Chicago Press.

Callahan, R. E. (1966). *The superintendent of schools: A historical analysis.* (ERIC Document Reproduction Service No. ED 0104 410)

Carlson, R. V. (1996). *Reframing and reform: Perspectives on organization, leadership, and school change.* New York: Longman.

Carter, G. R., & Cunningham, W. G. (1997). *The American school superintendent: Leading in an age of pressures.* San Francisco: Jossey-Bass.

Chance, P. L., & Björk, L. G. (2004). The social dimensions of public relations. In T. J. Kowalski (Ed.), *Public relations in schools* (3rd ed.) (pp. 125–148). Upper Saddle River, NJ: Merrill, Prentice Hall.

Clark, D. L. (1989). Time to say enough! *Agenda: Newsletter of the National Policy Board for Educational Administration, 1*(1), 1, 4–5.

Coleman, P., & LaRocque, L. (1990). *Struggling to be good enough: Administrative practices and district ethos.* London: Falmer.

Conrad, C. (1994). *Strategic organizational communication: Toward the twenty-first century* (3rd ed.). Fort Worth, TX: Harcourt Brace College Publishers.

Cooper, B. S., & Boyd, W. L. (1987). The evolution of training for school administrators. In J. Murphy & P. Hallinger (Eds.), *Approaches to administrative training in education* (pp. 3–27). Albany: State University of New York Press.

Counts, G. S. (1952). *Education and American civilization.* New York: Teachers College Press.

Cronin, J. M. (1973). *The control of urban schools: Perspective on the power of educational reform-ers.* New York: Free Press.

Crowson, R. L., & McPherson, R. B. (1987). The legacy of the theory movement: Learning from the new tradition. In J. Murphy & P. Hallinger (Eds.), *Approaches to administrative training in education* (pp. 45–64). Albany: State University of New York Press.

Cuban, L. (1976). *The urban school superintendent: A century and a half of change.* Bloomington, IN: Phi Delta Kappa Educational Foundation.

Cuban, L. (1988). How schools change reforms: Redefining reform success and failure. *Teachers College Record, 99*(3), 453–477.

Culbertson, J. A. (1981). Antecedents of the theory movement. *Educational Administration Quarterly, 17*(1), 25–47.

Drucker, P. F. (1999). *Management challenges for the 21st century.* New York: HarperCollins.

Dyrli, O. E., & Kinnaman, D. E. (1994). Preparing for the integration of emerging technologies. *Technology and Learning, 14*(9), 92, 94, 96, 98, 100.

Eaton, W. E. (1990). The vulnerability of school superintendents: The thesis reconsidered. In W. E. Eaton (Ed.), *Shaping the superintendency: A reexamination of Callahan and the cult of efficiency* (pp. 11–35). New York: Teachers College Press.

Feistritzer, E. M. (2003). Certification of public-school administrators: A summary of state practices. In *Better leaders for America's schools: A manifesto* (pp. 67–76). Los Angeles: Broad Foundation & Thomas B. Fordham Institute.

Fullan, M. G. (1996). Turning systemic thinking on its head. *Phi Delta Kappan, 77*(6), 420–423.

Fusarelli, B. C., & Fusarelli, L. D. (2003, November). *Preparing future superintendents to be applied social scientists.* Paper presented at the annual conference of the University Council for Educational Administration, Portland, Oregon.

Getzels, J. W. (1977). Educational administration twenty years later, 1954–1974. In L. Cunningham, W. Hack, & R. Nystrand (Eds.), *Educational administration: The developing decades* (pp. 3–24). Berkeley, CA: McCutchan.

Gideon, B. H. (2002). Structuring schools for teacher collaboration. *Education Digest, 68*(2), 30–34.

Glass, T. E. (2003). *The superintendency: A managerial imperative?* Paper presented at the annual meeting of the American Educational Research Association, Chicago.

Glass, T. E., Björk, L. G., & Brunner, C. C. (2000). *The American school superintendent: 2000.* Arlington, VA: American Association of School Administrators.

Grieder, C., Pierce, T. M., & Jordan, K. F. (1969). *Public school administration* (3rd ed.). New York: Ronald Press.

Grogan, M. (1999). Equity/equality issues of gender, race, and class. *Educational Administration Quarterly, 35*(4), 518–536.

Hanson, E. M. (2003). *Educational administration and organizational behavior* (6th ed.). Boston: Allyn & Bacon.

Heckman, P. E. (1993). School restructuring in practice: Reckoning with the culture of school. *International Journal of Educational Reform, 2*(3), 263–272.

Henkin, A. B. (1993). Social skills of superintendents: A leadership requisite in restructured schools. *Educational Research Quarterly, 16*(4), 15–30.

Herman, J. L. (1990). *Instructional leadership skills and competencies of public school superintendents: Implications of preparation programs in a climate of shared governance.* (ERIC Document Reproduction Service No. ED 328 980)

Hess, F. M. (1998). The urban reform paradox. *American School Board Journal, 185*(2), 24–27.

Howlett, P. (1993). The politics of school leaders, past and future. *Education Digest, 58*(9), 18–21.

Johnson, B. C., & Fusarelli, L. D. (2003, April). *Superintendent as social scientist.* Paper presented at the annual meeting of the American Educational Research Association, Chicago.

Kearsley, G. (1990). *Computers for educational administration.* Norwood, NJ: Ablex.

Keedy, J. L., & Björk, L. G. (2002). Superintendents and local boards and the potential for community polarization: The call for use of political strategist skills. In B. Cooper & L. D. Fusarelli (Eds.), *The promises and perils facing today's school superintendent* (pp. 103–128). Lanham, MD: Scarecrow Education.

Kowalski, T. J. (1995). *Keepers of the flame: Contemporary urban superintendents.* Thousand Oaks, CA: Corwin.

Kowalski, T. J. (1997). School reform, community education, and the problem of institutional culture. *Community Education Journal, 25*(3–4), 5–8.

Kowalski, T. J. (1998). The role of communication in providing leadership for school reform. *Mid-Western Educational Researcher, 11*(1), 32–40.

Kowalski, T. J. (1999). *The school superintendent: Theory, practice, and cases.* Upper Saddle River, NJ: Merrill, Prentice Hall.

Kowalski, T. J. (2000). Cultural change paradigms and administrator communication. *Contemporary Education, 71*(2), 5–10.

Kowalski, T. J. (2001). The future of local school governance: Implications for board members and superintendents. In C. Brunner & L. G. Björk (Eds.), *The new superintendency* (pp. 183–201). Oxford, UK: JAI, Elsevier Science.

Kowalski, T. J. (2003a). *Contemporary school administration* (2nd ed.). Boston: Allyn & Bacon.

Kowalski, T. J. (2003b, April). *The superintendent as communicator.* Paper presented at the annual meeting of the American Educational Research Association, Chicago.

Kowalski, T. J. (2004). School public relations: A new agenda. In T. J. Kowalski (Ed.), *Public relations in schools* (3rd ed.) (pp. 3–29). Upper Saddle River, NJ: Merrill, Prentice Hall.

Kowalski, T. J. (2005). Evolution of the school superintendent communicator. *Journal of Communication Education.*

Kowalski, T. J., & Glass, T. E. (2002). Preparing superintendents in the 21st century. In B. Cooper & L. D. Fusarelli (Eds.), *The promises and perils facing today's school superintendent* (pp. 41–60). Lanham, MD. Scarecrow Education.

Leithwood, K., Jantzi, D., & Fernandez, A. (1994). Transformational leadership and teachers' commitment to change. In J. Murphy & K. S. Louis (Eds.), *Reshaping the principalship* (pp. 77–98). Thousand Oaks, CA: Corwin.

Lipinski, A. J. (1978). Communicating the future. *Futures, 19*(2), 126–127.

Melby, E. O. (1955). *Administering community education.* Englewood Cliffs, NJ: Prentice Hall.

Morgan, C., & Petersen, G. J. (2002). The superintendent's role in leading academically effective school districts. In B. S. Cooper & L. D. Fusarelli (Eds.), *The promise and perils of the modern superintendency* (pp. 175–196). Lanham, MD: Scarecrow Press.

Murphy, J. (1991). *Restructuring schools.* New York: Teachers College Press.

Murphy, J. (1994). The changing role of the superintendency in restructuring districts in Kentucky. *School Effectiveness and School Improvement, 5*(4), 349–375.

Murphy, J., & Hallinger, P. (1986). The superintendent as instructional leader: Findings from effective school districts. *Journal of Educational Administration, 24*(2), 213–236.

National Commission on Excellence in Education. (1983). *A nation at risk: Imperative for reform.* Washington, DC: U.S. Government Printing Office.

Parsons, T., & Shils, E. A. (Eds.) (1951). *Toward a general theory of action.* Cambridge, MA: Harvard University Press.

Perina, K. (2002). When CEOs self-destruct. *Psychology Today, 35*(5), 16.

Petersen, G. J. (2002). Singing the same tune: Principals' and school board members' perceptions of the superintendent's role in curricular and instructional leadership. *Journal of Educational Administration 40*(2), 158–171.

Petersen, G. J., & Barnett, B. G. (2003, April). *The superintendent as instructional leader: History, evolution and future of the role.* Paper presented at the annual meeting of the American Educational Research Association, Chicago.

Peterson, K. D., Murphy, J., & Hallinger, P. (1987). Superintendents' perceptions of the control and coordination of the technical core in effective school districts. *Educational Administration Quarterly, 23*(1), 79–95.

Riehl, C. (2000). The principal's role in creating inclusive schools for diverse students: A review of normative, empirical, and critical literature on the practice of educational administration. *Review of Educational Research, 70*(1), 55–81.

Sarason, S. B. (1996). *Revisiting the culture of the school and the problem of change.* New York: Teachers College Press.

Schein, E. H. (1996). Culture: The missing concept in organization studies. *Administrative Science Quarterly, 41*(2), 229–240.

Schlechty, P. C. (1997). *Inventing better schools.* San Francisco: Jossey-Bass.

Shakeshaft, C. (1989). The gender gap in research in educational administration. *Educational Administration Quarterly, 25*(4), 324–337.

Spring, J. H. (1994). *The American school, 1642–1993* (3rd ed.). New York: McGraw-Hill.

Streitmatter, J. (1994). *Toward gender equity in the classroom: Everyday teachers' beliefs and practices.* Albany: State University of New York Press.

Thomas, W. B., & Moran, K. J. (1992). Reconsidering the power of the superintendent in the progressive period. *American Educational Research Journal, 29*(1), 22–50.

Trimble, K. (1996). Building a learning community. *Equity and Excellence in Education, 29*(1), 37–40.

Tyack, D. (1974). The "One Best System": A historical analysis. In H. Walberg & A. Kopan (Eds.), *Rethinking urban education* (pp. 231–246). San Francisco: Jossey-Bass.

Tyack, D., & Hansot, E. (1982). *Managers of virtue: Public school leadership in America, 1820–1980.* New York: Basic Books.

Van Til, W. (1971). Prologue: Is progressive education obsolete? In W. Van Til (Ed.), *Curriculum: Quest for relevance* (pp. 9–17). Boston: Houghton Mifflin.

Wert-Gray, S., Center, C., Brashers, D. E., & Meyers, R. A. (1991). Research topics and methodological orientations in organizational communication: A decade of review. *Communication Studies, 42*(2), 141–154.

Wirt, F. M., & Kirst, M. W. (2001). *The political dynamics of American education* (2nd ed.). Berkeley, CA: McCutchan.

Zigarelli, M. A. (1996). An empirical test of conclusions from effective schools research. *Journal of Educational Research, 90*(2), 103–110.

2

Characteristics of American School Superintendents

Lars G. Björk, Thomas E. Glass, and C. Cryss Brunner

During the past several decades, widespread concern for the condition of education and the economy launched and sustained what arguably is the most intense effort to reform public education in recent history. For more than two decades (1983–2005), national commission and task force reports examined the condition of American public education, heightened expectations for schooling, and called for improving instruction as well as fundamentally altering the manner in which schools are organized, administered, and governed. Recommendations for improvement that stimulated reform initiatives launched by state legislatures, education agencies, and districts not only challenged conventional assumptions about the nature of schooling but also increased awareness of the importance of school and district leadership. During the early 1990s, interest in large-scale systemic reform also heightened interest in the role of superintendents. Although they are viewed as essential to launching and sustaining improvement initiatives, the scope, intensity, and complexity of changes increased demands on superintendents (Brunner, Grogan, & Björk, 2002) and concurrently raised concerns about how they are being changed as well as the need to change.

Some of the most important resources available to national, state, and local education policymakers, researchers, and superintendents interested in tracking changes, understanding problems, and framing solutions are the American Association of School Administrators' (AASA) 10-year reports.

Beginning in 1923, the National Education Association's (NEA) Department of Superintendence conducted the first in a series of nationwide studies of superintendents that has continued each decade throughout the twentieth century. *The Study of the American School Superintendency 2000: A Look at the Superintendent of Education in the New Millennium* (Glass, Björk, & Brunner, 2000) is the most recent in this tradition of longitudinal studies. Although this and previous 10-year reports provide credible information about men in the profession, information on women in the superintendency are derived by disaggregating their responses (294) from the total (2,262) number of surveys returned. This approach can lead to a less-than-thorough understanding of the characteristics and perspectives of women in the superintendency. Recently, C. Cryss Brunner and Margaret Grogan completed an important and indeed historic initiative, *The 2003 Study of Women Superintendents and Women Central Office Administrators,* funded by AASA. Brunner and Grogan (2005) used the same survey instrument developed for the most recent AASA 10-year study (Glass et al., 2000) and included additional open-ended questions to gain greater insight into important issues facing these superintendents. As a consequence, data from these two studies not only can be compared but can together provide definitive national data sets that are indispensable to scholars, practitioners, and policymakers. Selected findings relating to how women perceive and enact the five role configurations that are addressed in this volume are reported in Chapter 10, "Women Superintendents and Role Conception: (Un)Troubling the Norms."

Empirical data from the most recent 10-year study (Glass et al., 2000) provide a wide array of current information on the superintendency, including demographic characteristics; search and selection patterns; role expectations; age; career patterns; tenure, turnover, and attrition rates; school board relationships; and opinions on important problems facing the field. These data are discussed in Chapter 2. Findings on professional preparation and the relationship among community power, the school board's political configurations, and superintendents' preferred administrative style and mentoring are reported in Chapters 3 and 7 of this volume. In addition, Brunner and Grogan (2005) discuss recent findings on women in the superintendency in Chapter 10 of this volume.

SUPERINTENDENT SEARCH AND SELECTION PROCESSES

Superintendent search and selection processes vary considerably by district size. The most prevalent method (54%), however, is for a local school board to form its own committee and designate several of its members to work with district staff that help manage the process. They draw up a job description for board review; once approved, it is forwarded to universities and state administrator associations and is published in newspapers. In small districts, selected board members work with staff to organize and review applications to screen applicants and decide which candidates it will invite for interviews before a committee meeting of the whole board is called. A majority (76%) of very small school districts, however, act as their own search agents, managing the processes from beginning to end. Nearly half (46%) of very large districts, however, tend to hire private search firms or the state school boards association to conduct the superintendent search. A number of search firms are owned and staffed by retired superintendents who established excellent reputations in the field during their careers. Occasionally, professors of educational administration also work as consultants for private search firms or the state school boards association. Fees charged by private search firms and associations usually are dictated by the size of the district, the number of services required, and whether the search is restricted to local candidates or is national in scope. Because the search process is highly complex and fraught with legal ramifications, most agencies, consultants, and state school board associations provide some inservice training for board members in how to conduct a superintendent search and selection process (Glass et al., 2000).

The idea that superintendents are selected because of their personal qualities and characteristics has been a significant part of how individuals view superintendent search and selection processes. For example, two-thirds of superintendents sampled in Glass's study (1992) indicated that they were hired because of "personal characteristics" (including the image they projected or a role model they presented during the interview process) combined with information that search committee members gleaned through contacts with their counterparts and knowledgeable citizens in the candidates' districts. These search and selection approaches seemed to diminish in importance over the next several decades. By 1992, only 39% of superintendents said they were hired because of personal qualities and characteristics; however, it remained relatively unchanged, increasing to only 40% by 2000 (Glass et al., 2000). This may reflect radically changing demands on districts' chief executive officers' (CEOs) need for more stringent selection criteria, and the "maturing" of the profession (see Table 2.1). Data also indicate that this might not be the perspective of superintendents in very small districts, in which they are more likely to attribute personal characteristics as the reason they were hired (Glass et al., 2000).

The superintendency is a position fraught with a wide range of problems. As a consequence, local boards of education seek to hire superintendents who are viewed as change agents capable of improving learning and teaching, increasing management efficiency, and effectively responding to community demands. Glass et al. (2000) report that 26% of superintendents are hired to serve as change agents. Expectations to serve as change

Table 2.1 Reasons Given by Superintendents for Their Selection to Current Position

Reason for Selection	Group A >25,000 Pupils No.	%	Group B 3,000–24,999 Pupils No.	%	Group C 300–2,999 Pupils No.	%	Group D <300 Pupils No.	%	National Unweighted Profile No.	%
Personal Characteristics	30	31.9	204	37.5	554	41.3	105	42.0	893	40.1
Change Agent	27	28.7	157	28.9	341	25.4	62	24.8	587	26.3
Maintain Status Quo	1	1.1	4	.7	22	1.6	6	2.4	33	1.5
Instructional Leader	30	31.9	157	28.9	330	24.6	57	22.8	574	25.8
No Particular Reason	1	1.1	9	1.7	39	2.9	13	5.2	62	2.8
Not Sure	5	5.3	13	2.4	55	4.1	7	2.8	80	3.6
Total	94	100.0	544	100.0	1,341	100.0	250	100.0	2,229	100.0

SOURCE: Glass, T. E., Björk, L. G., & Brunner, C. C. (2000). *The study of the American superintendency: A look at the superintendent in the new millennium.* AASA. Used with permission of American Association of School Administrators.

agents appear fairly uniform across all districts, ranging from 29% for superintendents in large urban districts to 25% for superintendents in very small rural districts. An examination of five role expectations provides a comprehensive view of what superintendents expect their work will entail after they are hired.

Superintendent Role Expectations

As discussed by Kowalski in Chapter 1, Callahan (1966) identified four stages in the evolution of the American superintendency (1865–1966) that describe distinct role conceptualizations. These stages include (1) *teacher-scholar* (1850–1900), (2) *business manager* (1900–1930), (3) *educational states-man* (1930–1950), and (4) *social scientist* (1950–1967). In addition, Kowalski (2003) posits that a fifth role conceptualization, *communicator,* is needed to describe how superintendents enacted their role over the course of history (1850–2003). Kowalski and Björk (2004) and Kowalski (2005) investigated these role conceptualizations. These role configurations will be discussed to ascertain relevance in contemporary district settings.

Teacher-Scholar

From the mid-1880s until the first decade of the twentieth century, superintendents' work was primarily focused on implementing a state curriculum and supervising teachers. They were viewed as "master" teachers and intellectual leaders in larger districts (Callahan, 1962; Petersen & Barnett, 2005). Although their educational leadership role waned after 1910, it did not become totally irrelevant. Rather, over the following decades, expectations that superintendents should provide oversight of district academic affairs fluctuated in importance. During recent decades, widespread interests in school reform heightened expectations that district CEOs provide the visionary leadership and expertise to improve student academic performance. The AASA report (Glass et al., 2000) found that the teacher-scholar role remains highly relevant. For example, more than 40% of all superintendents surveyed indicated that the school board's primary expectation of them was to serve as an educational leader. This role expectation was more pronounced (48%) in larger districts serving more than 25,000 students (48%) and in those serving between 3,000 and 24,999 students (51%). It appears that school board expectations for superintendents to serve as educational leaders vary by gender. For example, 51% of females and 38% of males indicate that this role is their most important responsibility. In addition, slightly more than one-quarter of superintendents (26%) indicated they were expected to serve as an instructional leader. This responsibility typically involves working closely with other administrators and teachers to improve learning and teaching in the district. Furthermore, functions associated with their role as an educational leader are directly related to significant challenges facing their districts, including assessing and testing learner outcomes (ranked second), dealing with demands for new ways of teaching or operating educational programs (ranked fourth), and coping with changing priorities in the curriculum (ranked fifth). These data suggest that the superintendent as educational leader and teacher-scholar (Callahan, 1962) remains highly relevant (Kowalski & Björk, 2004).

Business Manager

As the size of districts increased during the latter part of the nineteenth century, questions were raised about whether superintendents had the knowledge and skills to competently manage the affairs of large urban school districts (Cuban, 1976; Kowalski, 1999). After the turn of the century, however, superintendents were assigned management duties that included budget development, administrative oversight of operations, and personnel and facility management. Although support for superintendents to serve as business managers diminished after the 1929 stock market crash, most realized the need for competent district management—a perspective that became deeply embedded in the culture of school administration (Kowalski, 1999) and remains a highly relevant aspect of superintendents' work (Kowalski & Glass, 2002). For example, more than one-third (36%) of the superintendents indicated that a primary expectation of the board was to be a managerial leader (Glass et al., 2000). A very large percentage identified three serious management-related problems facing them: (1) lack of adequate financial resources (97%), (2) accountability (88%), and (3) compliance with state and federal mandates (82%). These critical management issues suggest the continued importance of this aspect of the superintendent role (Kowalski & Björk, 2004).

Educational Statesman

This role conceptualization is anchored in American political philosophy and the political realities of superintendents' work (Björk & Gurley, 2005). During education's formative years, the profession eschewed political involvement by superintendents (Björk & Lindle, 2001; Kowalski, 1995). During the 1930s, however, these convictions were set aside as expectations mounted for school and district administrators to serve as lobbyists and political strategists, and to successfully compete for scarce resources. Melby (1955), Callahan (1962), and Howlett (1993) endorsed the idea of democratic administration and viewed local communities as an important resource that could be mobilized to galvanize support for district initiatives. Although the notion of superintendents serving as democratic leaders fell from favor in the 1950s (Kowalski, 1999), emerging circumstances in the coming decades supported recognition that superintendents needed to function as democratic leaders (Björk & Gurley, 2005).

The role of superintendents as democratic leaders is defined by the realities rather than the rhetoric of practice. For example, Glass et al. (2000) found that 58% of superintendents said that community-based interest groups attempted to influence board decisions. This was even more pronounced in large school districts that serve more than 25,000 students, in which more than 90% of superintendents indicated that interest groups' influence was prevalent. In addition, nearly 13% of superintendents indicated that the board's primary role expectation for them was to serve as a democratic or political leader. Furthermore, 83% of superintendents said that the administrator-board relationship (e.g., micropolitics) was a serious problem. Evidence suggests that role expectations for superintendents to serve as democratic leaders are important in district organizational and community contexts (Kowalski & Björk, 2004).

Social Scientist

The notion of superintendent as applied social scientist was influenced by a wide range of factors (Callahan, 1966; Fusarelli & Fusarelli, 2005; Kowalski & Björk, 2004), including attempts by educational administration programs to gain acceptance by social science disciplines (Culbertson, 1981), the need to understand school districts as complex systems (Getzels, 1977), and achieving social justice for children (Fusarelli & Fusarelli, 2005). Recent education reform reports and the NCLB Act underscore the importance of superintendents' instructional leadership role to ensure that all children learn and improve their life chances. Glass et al. (2000) found that 26% of superintendents were hired to serve as instructional leaders and 26% were hired to serve as change agents. Once on the job, 40% viewed instructional leadership as a key role expectation. In addition, negative effects of social factors on student academic performance require that superintendents be at the forefront of ensuring that schools are simultaneously socially just, democratic, and productive learning environments (Fusarelli & Fusarelli, 2005; Goldring & Greenfield, 2002; Sergiovanni, 1992; Starratt, 1991).

Communicator

School boards expect superintendents to effectively communicate with a wide range of constituents, subordinates, and colleagues in launching and sustaining district reform initiatives (Kowalski & Keedy, 2005). As Kowalski (1998) notes, superintendents' normative communicative behavior is influenced by several realities of practice: (a) the need for them to provide leadership in improving learning and teaching, (b) the need for them to alter district cultures as part of improving schooling, and (c) the need to access and use relevant information to solve problems of practice. Glass et al. (2000) found that nearly all superintendents (95%) said that they were the board's primary conduit of information about district and community matters. In addition, a majority of superintendents indicated that they communicated regularly with parents and other community citizens in (a) setting district objectives and priorities (69%), (b) strategic planning (61%), (c) fundraising (60%), and (d) program and curriculum decisions (60%). In addition, modern technologies enhance the quality of their communication (Kowalski & Keedy, 2005).

Superintendent–School Board Relations

Working relationships and lines of authority between school boards and superintendents have changed over the past century. Before 1900, superintendents were viewed as supervisors and administrators responsible for carrying out board of education policies. After the turn of the century, however, many superintendents advocated the adoption of business ideology and management models, advancing the idea that CEOs should be highly trained professionals who make administrative decisions. During the era of scientific management that pressed for increased efficiency (1900–1930), superintendents in large urban districts argued persuasively for the adoption of a quasi-corporate board model of district governance. Later, during the 1940s, superintendents and boards bifurcated work into two principal domains of responsibility. Boards interacted with community interest groups in shaping education policy, and administrators made decisions and ensured that policies were carried out (Tyack & Hansot, 1982). This bifurcation of responsibilities fits the apolitical disposition of the profession. Unfortunately, boards failed to understand the demarcation of roles, and tensions emerged. Although tensions between board members and superintendents are common, most do not seriously interfere with district operations.

Role conflict, however, can result in superintendent turnover (McCurdy, 1992). A study of school boards by the Institute for Educational Leadership (IEL) in 1986 characterized the school board as an institution in trouble. Findings from the IEL study identified considerable support for the traditional role of the school board as a grassroots community institution. It also identified serious levels of community apathy and lack of knowledge about what school board members do and the challenges they face (IEL, 1986). In a follow-up report, IEL (Danzberger, Kirst, & Usdan, 1992) declared that school board governance needed drastic reforms to improve board performance. They recommended higher levels of collaboration between superintendents and boards as well as viewing policy and decision making as a shared responsibility. Findings from AASA's 10-year studies suggest that this may be unfolding in many districts. For example, in the 1992 study (Glass, 1992), 29% of superintendents overall said they viewed the initiation of district policy as a shared responsibility with the board. In 2000, however, 37% of superintendents indicated that this was the case in their districts. Shared responsibility for policy and decision making occurs less frequently in the larger districts because they tend to have more board members serving on standing committees that examine issues and recommend policies to the whole board. In smaller districts, however, boards tend to work and make decisions as one body. Superintendents in districts serving fewer than 3,000 students report that they initiate policy 50% of the time, as compared with their counterparts in larger districts with enrollments greater than 25,000 students who take the lead in policy making only 20% of the time (Glass et al., 2000). Goodman, Fulbright, and Zimmerman (1997) note that this collaborative theme was advanced by the Educational Research Service, which heightened interest in creating governance teams capable of improving student achievement.

Superintendent Career Patterns

During recent years, scholars studying the characteristics of American superintendents (Brunner & Grogan, 2005; Hodgkinson & Montenegro, 1999; Johnson, 1996; Kowalski, 1995) report findings that are generally consistent with those reported by Glass et al. (2000) in AASA's most recent 10-year study. Between 1950 and 2003, the median age of superintendents was approximately 50 years of age. This finding is understandable in view of typical superintendent career patterns that involve moving through the chairs and gaining experience as educators, managers, and leaders. Although few individuals preparing to enter the education profession intend to become a superintendent, data identified two distinct career paths. The most common path traveled by superintendents (48.5%) was from teacher to assistant principal or principal to central office administrator to superintendent. This career path is most prevalent among superintendents in districts serving more than 25,000 students and in districts with 3,000–24,999 students. The next most common route followed by aspiring superintendents (31.2%) was that from teacher to assistant principal or principal to superintendent. This pattern appears to be most common in districts serving fewer than 2,999 students as well as in very small districts with fewer than 300 students (see Table 2.2). The latter finding is reasonable because very small districts have a paucity of central office staff positions that might provide midcareer stepping-stones to the superintendency. In addition, data indicate that the career path for males tends to be through the high school principalship. Although the work of superintendents and principals is qualitatively different, common wisdom in the field holds that they both require skills in managing large staffs, understanding the complexity of education organizations, and honing their skills in working with citizens, parents, and community interest groups.

Table 2.2 Career Paths of Superintendents

Career Path	Group A (>25,000 Pupils)		Group B (3,000–24,999 Pupils)		Group C (300–2,999 Pupils)		Group D (<300 Pupils)		National (Unweighted Profile)	
	No.	%	No.	%	No.	%	No.	%	No.	%
Teacher, Principal, and Central Office	65	68.4	322	59.0	624	46.4	74	29.5	1,085	48.5
Principal and Central Office	3	3.2	11	2.0	20	1.5	2	0.8	36	1.6
Teacher and Central Office	11	11.6	84	15.4	89	6.6	13	5.2	197	8.8
Teacher and Principal	6	6.3	83	15.2	488	36.3	121	48.2	698	31.2
Central Office Only	1	1.1	11	2.0	8	0.6	6	2.4	26	1.2
Principal Only	0	0.0	4	0.7	24	1.8	4	1.6	32	1.4
Teacher Only	1	1.1	3	0.5	27	2.0	18	7.2	49	2.2
Other	8	8.4	28	5.1	65	4.8	13	5.2	114	5.1
Total	95	1,00.0	546	100.0	1,345	100.0	251	100.0	2,237	100.0

SOURCE: Björk, L. G., Keedy, J. L., & Gurley, D. K. (2003). Career patterns of American superintendents. *Journal of School Leadership, 13*(4), page 421. Used with permission.

A comparison of findings from Glass et al. (2000) and the previous 10-year study (Glass, 1992) indicates that aspiring superintendents are spending more time moving through "the chairs" before becoming CEOs. Increasing licensure and experience requirements as well as part-time and evening graduate school work (McCarthy, 1999) can contribute to increased time in the "chairs." Typically, superintendents begin their career paths as a teacher at age 23. Then, after 8 years of teaching, a significant majority (84%) then attain a position as either an assistant principal or principal between the ages of 25–35. Some (9%) then move to a central office staff position in their late 30s. In most instances, individuals make decisions to become a superintendent when they are midcareer, typically while they are serving as an assistant principal or principal. Glass et al. (2000) found that on average, superintendents spent a little more than a year in obtaining their first superintendency after becoming certified and actively seeking a position. Most entered the superintendency in their early to mid-40s, serving in this position in 2–3 districts spanning between 15–18 years. They spent an average of nearly 7 years in each school district. In addition, findings also indicate that 56% of superintendents served in only one district, suggesting a substantial influx of new CEOs. Glass et al. (2000) also found that although 88% of superintendents spent their education careers in one state, more than 68% of superintendents surveyed were hired from outside of their present district, influencing perceptions of impermanence and the transitory nature of the position.

Another interesting finding by Glass et al. (2000) is that superintendent career patterns are changing. For example, in 1971, 46.5% of all superintendents in small rural districts with enrollments of fewer than 300 students were under the age of 40. Glass (1992) observed that only 17% of superintendents began their careers in small districts before moving up the ladder to larger suburban districts that are more adequately financed and offer higher salaries and benefits. The same trend appears to be unfolding in districts of 300–2,999 students. In 1971, 22% of superintendents in these districts were under age 40; however, by 1992 only 8% and then by 2000 only 2% of superintendents reflected these characteristics. These data suggest that experienced superintendents are remaining in small to medium-sized districts.

CHARACTERISTICS OF WOMEN SUPERINTENDENTS

The percentage of women in the superintendency has varied considerably during the past century. For example, Blount (1998) reports that in 1910, 8.9% of school superintendents were women, which didn't increase to 11% until 1930. By 1950, it declined to 9% and then to 6.7% by 1952. In 1971, it declined to 1.3% and in 1982 stagnated at 1.2%. Explanations for this decline vary. During the first half of the twentieth century, school consolidation reduced the number of small and rural districts, many of which had women superintendents (Glass, 1992). The effects of consolidation, unfair search processes, and discriminatory hiring practices (Tallerico, 2000) contributed to a precipitous decline in the number of women superintendents in the nation (Glass et al., 2000). Chase and Bell (1990) found that search firms and boards of education serve as gatekeepers of the superintendency, and even if they can be "positively disposed toward women as education leaders," "supportive of women in leadership positions," and "helpful to individual women" (p. 174), they have not altered practices that privilege white males in hiring (Tallerico, 2000). Thus they continue to dominate the profession (Chase & Bell, 1990; Tallerico, 2000; Young, 1999).

By 1992, the number of women in the superintendency increased to 6.6% and then moved upward to 13.2% by 2000—the highest level achieved during the past 90 years (Glass et al., 2000). The majority (68%) of women superintendents held positions in rural or suburban districts serving fewer than 2,999 students (see Table 2.3). The greatest gains for women in the superintendency between 1992–2000 were in suburban or urban districts serving between 3,000–24,999 students, increasing from 5% to 14%. Growth in the percentage of women in the superintendency over the past several decades might emanate from the growing consciousness for ensuring equitable treatment in search and selection processes. Both Tallerico (2000) and Kamler and Shakeshaft (1999) note that when search consultants are proactive in recruiting women, help to educate boards of education about their strengths as district leaders, and advocate for fair search and selection processes, a greater number of women are hired as CEOs. In addition, when women who aspire to the superintendency are part of university professor, superintendent, and board of education networks, they are more likely to learn about district vacancies.

It also should be noted that the majority (71%) of women superintendents in 2000 were employed under their first contract. In addition, 58% indicated that they had served as a superintendent for fewer than 5 years. These data indicate that the progress of women in the profession is recent. Although this progress is praiseworthy, women continue to be noticeably underrepresented in a profession in which they hold a majority of teaching and administrative positions. The extraordinary disparity between men and women in the superintendency is paradoxical. Women account for 65% of teachers, 43% of principals (Kamler & Shakeshaft, 1999), 57% of central office administrators, and 33% of the assistant and associate superintendent positions in schools and districts (Hodgkinson & Montenegro, 1999, pp. 113–115). Although women have been making notable progress in most levels of the public school system during the past decade, their nominal representation at the most senior levels of district leadership structures, such as the high school principalship, assistant and

Table 2.3   Gender of Superintendents by District Size

| Gender | Group A >25,000 Pupils | | Group B 3,000–24,999 Pupils | | Group C 300–2,999 Pupils | | Group D <300 Pupils | | National Unweighted Profile | |
	No.	%	No.	%	No.	%	No.	%	No.	%
Male	79	83.2	469	85.9	1,191	88.9	199	79.3	1,938	86.8
Female	16	16.8	77	14.1	149	11.1	52	20.7	294	13.2
Total	95	4.2	546	24.4	1,340	6.0	251	11.2	2,232	100.0

SOURCE: Björk, L. G., Keedy, J. L., & Gurley, D. K. (2003). Career patterns of American superintendents. *Journal of School Leadership, 13*(4), page 421. Used with permission.

associate superintendent, and superintendent, is conspicuous (Hodgkinson & Montenegro, 1999). An analysis of the education workforce study conducted by Skrla (1999) indicates that the likelihood of a male teacher becoming a superintendent is 1 in 43; however, for female teachers, it is 1 in 825. Concisely, men were 20 times more likely than women to move from the classroom to the superintendency. According to the U.S. Census Bureau, the superintendency is the most male-dominated of any profession in the United States. Unless circumstances are radically changed, that will remain the case during the coming decades.

Career Paths of Women Superintendents

Survey data indicated that men and women differ in their respective career experiences that lead to the superintendency. Women more often reported having served as elementary teachers, district coordinators, assistant superintendents, and high school teachers, respectively; men indicated at least one or more years' experience as high school teachers, junior high or middle school teachers, assistant superintendents, and directors or coordinators, respectively (Brunner, 2000). Brunner, citing Edson's (1995) longitudinal study (1981–1995), noted that females who aspired to the principalship were much more successful in obtaining elementary principalships than they were in gaining secondary principalships. Brunner confirmed Edson's findings when she reported that nearly three times as many males (51%) than females (18.5%) have served as high school principals. In addition, nearly twice as many female (55.6%) as male (28.7%) superintendents have served as district coordinators and assistant superintendents.

Glass et al. (2000) found that the career patterns of women in the superintendency differed from men in that they were less inclined to follow the prevalent career path from teacher to principal before becoming a superintendent. Rather, they tended to move from the classroom to a central office position that emphasized curriculum and instruction, bypassing the principalship, before becoming a superintendent. As a consequence, however, women were less likely to gain experiences in finance, administration, and community relations (which were considered by 80% of superintendents as keys to succeeding as CEOs). These experiences align with the most difficult problems rank ordered by superintendents, including financial issues (35%), community pressure (17%), understanding board roles (16.5%), and avoiding mismanagement (10%).

CHARACTERISTICS OF SUPERINTENDENTS OF COLOR

Information about people of color serving in the superintendency (1930s–1950s) suggests that their presence was low and that they largely served in southern districts in which there was a high percentage of African American students (AASA, 1983; Collier, 1987). Recent studies of Hispanic Americans in school administration (Ortiz, 1998) expanded our understanding of diversity among CEOs. In addition, AASA's report *Women and Racial Minority Representation in School Administration* (1993) noted that superintendents of color tended to serve in communities with a significant minority population. For example, in AASA's 10-year study, Cunningham and Hentges (1982) reported that in 1980, only 2% of superintendents were people of color. By 1990, the percentage increased to a little more than 3% (Jones & Montenegro, 1990). Glass et al. (2000) indicated that by 1993, nearly 4% of superintendents were people of color, but nearly half of them (46%) served large urban districts with more than 50,000 students. In addition, disaggregating descriptive data typically reported under a single "minority" heading enabled them to report that 5.1% of superintendents in the United States were people of color, including 2.2% African American, 1.4% Hispanic American, 0.8% Native American, 0.2% Asian American, and 0.5% Other. A majority of the 5.1% of the nation's superintendents of color serve in large/urban or small town/rural districts. More than 50% of superintendents of color serve in districts with 3,000 or more students, and 23% are CEOs in districts with enrollments larger than 25,000 students (see Table 2.4).

Although the percentage of superintendents that are people of color increased by 31% since 1982, there are still relatively few individuals of color in the school leadership "pipeline." As a consequence, there is concern that their representation in the CEO ranks might plateau or precipitously decline (Björk, 1996). Hodgkinson and Montenegro (1999) cogently argue that increasing the percentage of superintendents of color in the future will depend on whether the field can successfully compete with other better-paying professions and increase the number of minority teachers, principals, and central office staff in the "pipeline." The near absence of people of color in the superintendency is conspicuous and is unquestionably one of the most significant problems facing the field and the nation.

Career Paths of Superintendents of Color

Although there is a paucity of nationwide empirical studies that focus exclusively on individuals of color in the superintendency, aggregated data under a "minority" category are admittedly problematic. Recent work by Brunner and Grogan (2005) rectify this gap by providing a more complete picture of diversity in the field. Glass et al. (2000) found that career patterns of superintendents of color differ from their Caucasian colleagues. For example, although nearly 80% of white superintendents started their administrative careers as an assistant principal or principal, only 65% of individuals of color took this career path. Rather, superintendents of color generally

Table 2.4 Persons of Color in the Superintendency by District Size

Race	Group A >25,000 Pupils		Group B 3,000–24,999 Pupils		Group C 300–2,999 Pupils		Group D <300 Pupils		National Unweighted Profile	
	No.	%	No.	%	No.	%	No.	%	No.	%
White	73	76.8	508	93.4	1,289	96.4	242	97.2	2,112	94.9
Black	14	14.7	22	3.9	14	1.0	0	0.0	50	2.2
Asian	0	0.0	3	0.6	2	0.1	0	0.0	5	0.2
Native American	0	0.0	2	0.4	12	0.9	4	1.6	18	0.8
Other	1	1.1	0	0.0	9	0.7	1	0.4	11	0.5
Total	95	4.3	544	24.5	1,339	60.1	249	11.1	2,227	100.0

SOURCE: Björk, L. G., Keedy, J. L., & Gurley, D. K. (2003). Career patterns of American superintendents. *Journal of School Leadership, 13*(4), page 421. Used with permission.

began their careers as central office staff members in categorically funded programs rather than as school administrators. More than 52% of persons of color follow the path of teacher, principal, central office staffer, and then superintendent. More specifically, 22% of persons of color began their administrative careers as program directors or coordinators, in comparison with 13% of their white counterparts.

SUPERINTENDENCY: A MATURING PROFESSION

Over the past century, the age of superintendents has increased. For example, the 1923 AASA study indicates that the median age of superintendents was 43.1 years and then hovered at about 48 to 50 years between 1950 and 1992. The most recent AASA 10-year study reports that the median age of superintendents increased to 52.5, which is the oldest recorded median age during the twentieth century (Glass et al., 2000), as shown in Figure 2.1 and Table 2.5. Changes were most noticeable in several district types. For example, in 1992, nearly 40% of superintendents serving in districts with student enrollments of more than 25,000 students were under age 50. By 2000, however, only 20% of those districts had superintendents under that age. In 1992, 59% of superintendents from districts with fewer than 300 students were less than 50 years old. In 2000, however, only 48% of superintendents in these districts were under age 50 (see Figure 2.1).

Figure 2.1   Median Age of Superintendents, 1923 to 2000

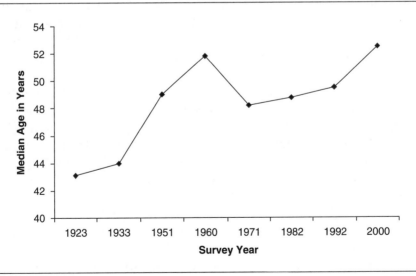

SOURCE: Björk, L. G., Keedy, J. L., & Gurley, D. K. (2003). Career patterns of American superintendents. *Journal of School Leadership, 13*(4).

Furthermore, in 1992, only 29% of superintendents serving in urban districts with enrollments of more than 25,000 students were over the age of 55; whereas in 2000, nearly 50% were above that age (see Table 2.5). Although there are few individuals in the superintendency that are over the age of 60, their numbers are increasing in very large districts with student enrollments of more than 25,000, as well as in very small districts serving fewer than 300 students. In 1992, only 10% of superintendents over the age of 60 served in large urban districts; whereas in 2000, nearly 16% held positions in these districts. During the same period, those over 60 years of age serving in districts with fewer than 300 students increased from nearly 5% to nearly 9%. Two-thirds (66%) of the women superintendents surveyed included in AASA's most recent 10-year study were between the ages of 46 and 55, slightly younger than the national average (Glass et al., 2000).

Early Retirement: Examining the Issue and Analyzing the Data

Although many state legislatures created retirement programs offering inducements for early retirement at age 55 to reduce expenditures, many policy analysts were concerned that it would have secondary consequences (i.e., trigger a precipitous decline in the number of practicing superintendents by 2005). These concerns, coupled with claims that the job is no longer "doable," have provided grist for strident claims that superintendents are leaving the profession faster than they can be replaced (Brockett, 1996). Most calculations of attrition rates of superintendents tend to be overly simplistic, so calculations often exaggerate the problem—for several reasons. First, superintendents who leave their positions or retire become part of a "left-the-profession" statistic, regardless of whether they are hired by another district in the same state, "retire" and then work on a temporary contract basis, or accept a position in another state to build up additional retirement benefits (i.e., become "double-dippers"). Unfortunately, the field does not track these data, so we do not have an accurate picture of superintendent movement and attrition. Second, when a superintendent leaves the district, the position is typically filled by an experienced superintendent from another district in the state—not unlike the game of Musical Chairs. Although a relatively small percentage of superintendents actually exit the profession, those calculating attrition rates tend to count only the number of superintendent vacancies, leading to inflated reports of those CEOs leaving the profession (Björk & Glass, 2003).

Glass et al. (2000), however, argue that the probability of a worst-case scenario actually taking form is highly unlikely. They found that most superintendents in the nation are at a midpoint in their careers. The median age of superintendents increased from 48.5 to 52.5 between 1992–2000, which suggests that most entered the profession later in their careers than previously. In addition, they served an average of 8.5 years in

Table 2.5 Percentage of Superintendents in Age Groups by District Size: Comparisons, 1971 Through 2000

Age Group	Group A >25,000 Pupils				Group B 3,000–24,999 Pupils				Group C 300–2,999 Pupils				Group D <300 Pupils			
	1971	1982	1992	2000	1971	1982	1992	2000	1971	1982	1992	2000	1971	1982	1992	2000
Under 40	3.6	4.5	1.4	0.0	7.1	6.3	3.3	0.7	21.5	14.8	8.1	2.7	46.5	35.3	17.0	6.4
40–44	13.9	13.4	10.4	4.2	22.2	13.8	15.3	4.6	23.5	18.2	21.6	7.1	11.3	16.1	24.5	10.9
45–49	19.0	21.4	28.5	15.8	20.9	22.1	28.9	24.0	15.6	21.6	28.1	25.7	14.1	14.7	17.8	30.2
50–54	19.0	25.0	26.4	30.5	21.8	30.3	27.1	41.9	15.2	22.3	22.2	37.7	2.8	19.2	21.7	24.6
55–59	10.7	27.7	18.7	33.7	16.7	20.8	18.7	20.5	15.9	18.1	15.5	19.0	8.5	8.5	14.2	19.0
Over 60	24.8	7.2	10.4	15.8	11.3	6.8	6.8	8.3	8.3	4.9	4.5	7.0	16.9	6.2	4.8	8.9

SOURCE: Björk, L. G., Keedy, J. L., & Gurley, D. K. (2003). Career patterns of American superintendents. *Journal of School Leadership, 13*(4), page 421. Used with permission.

careers that typically span 15–18 years in 2–3 districts (Glass, 1992; Björk & Glass, 2003). These data led the researchers to conclude that the predicted massive exodus of superintendents in the coming decade will probably not occur. Björk and Glass (2003) provide a prudent estimate of annual attrition at a 6% to 7% rate for the nation's 12,604 superintendents. These calculations suggest that nearly 8,000 new superintendents will have to enter the profession during the coming decade (2000–2010). This attrition rate has remained relatively constant since the end of World War II. Thus, claims of a crisis in the superintendency are grossly exaggerated.

Examining the Purported "Crisis" in the Superintendency

Reports on increasing board conflict, projected retirements of high school principals who serve as a pipeline into the superintendency, declining tenure rates, and low quality of applicant pools contributed to a perception that the superintendency was facing a serious crisis (Cooper, Fusarelli, & Carella, 2000; Education Research Service, 1998; National Association of Elementary and Secondary Principals, 1998; United States Department of Labor, 2000). The perception of low tenure rates has persisted since the early1990s when the average tenure of district CEOs serving in large urban districts was reported as being 2.5 years (Rist, 1991). Although empirical evidence indicates that it applied only to a limited number of large urban school districts, it was generalized to all superintendents and eventually became regarded as fact (Council of Great City Schools, 1999; Glass, 1992; Kowalski, 1995; Renchler, 1992; McKay & Grady, 1994). Although Glass (1992) notes that tenure rates vary across districts, he found that the national average of superintendent tenure in the nation was 6.5 years. Factors contributing to superintendents' turnover rates range from board conflict and instability in very large urban districts to very small districts serving as entry-level positions that are vacated when opportunities in larger and better-financed districts emerge. For example, superintendents in very large urban and very small rural districts had the shortest tenure rate: between 1 and 3 years. Superintendents serving in districts with enrollments of between 300–3,000 students had the longest tenure rate: 7 years. Notwithstanding evidence to the contrary, many believed that average tenure of superintendents was 2 to 3 years, thus lending credibility to popular fiction (Kowalski, 2003).

Authors contributing to a special issue of the *Journal of School Leadership* (2003), "Superintendent Shortage: Reality or Myth," provide a coherent and empirically based discussion of the nature and scope of the superintendent shortage issue. For example:

- Glass and Björk observe considerable dissonance between school board presidents who are highly satisfied with their superintendents and pronouncements made by leaders in professional associations, private sector search firms, and state education agencies that the quality of superintendents is declining. They identified a substantial number of school boards that had three or more CEOs in a 10-year period—a condition they characterized as "churning." In these instances, the boards' inability to retain superintendents is not a problem caused by a shortage of superintendents as much as it is by school board instability. They contend that reformers not only have misidentified the issue but also are asking policymakers to solve the wrong problem.

- Björk, Keedy, and Gurley examine trend data from the previous four AASA 10-year studies and found that the average tenure of superintendents has ranged from 5.6 years to the current mean of between 6 and 7 years over the 1971–2000 span of time. In addition, they note that the superintendent attrition rate has on average been about 8% per year since the end of the 1950s. Thus, when reports suggest that 80% of superintendents will leave the profession in the next decade, it is the norm rather than an exception (i.e., a crisis). They also report that superintendents enter the profession later in their careers, enjoy a longer average tenure in office, and retire from the profession later than during previous decades. These data refute anecdotal evidence of the existence of a crisis on a national scale.
- Kowalski directly refutes the notion of a widespread claim that a national crisis in the superintendency exists. Using highly credible economic models that define occupational shortages, he asserts that self-interested groups of school boards and superintendents are perpetuating the myth that a shortage exists. Using 10-year AASA study data and findings from a seminal study by Cooper, Fusarelli, and Carella (2000), Kowalski demonstrates that superintendents' tenure, rather than declining, has increased over the past 30 years. He contends that a shortage is confined to large, inner-city districts and to small and rural districts.
- Cooper, Fusarelli, and Carella examined recent national data from the *Superintendents' Professional Expectations and Advancement Review Survey* (2000) and found that most superintendents indicated that they were pleased with their present positions and had an average tenure of slightly more than 7 years in the current position.
- Analyzing national- and state-level data to determine superintendent longevity, Natkin, Cooper, Alborano, Padilla, and Ghosh (2003) found that superintendent tenure has not changed significantly since 1975, averaging 6–7 years. They conclude that the "revolving-door" syndrome, often used to characterize the profession as a profession, is a myth.
- Tallerico examined supply-and-demand issues in the superintendency and concludes that some policies might unintentionally contribute to the misperception of an oversupply of candidates (e.g., teachers gaining administrator certification with no intention of

pursuing such positions) and to the speculation that teachers are opting out of practice because the job is "undoable." She also notes that some practices, including valuing predominately male administrator qualities (e.g., control, power, hierarchy) over female values (e.g., collaboration, shared problem solving), can contribute to the superintendency shortage because women are not obtaining these top jobs at the rate commensurate to that of white men.

This set of empirically based examinations of the issue of superintendent shortage points out that a widespread shortage does not exist. It is situational and is caused by a wide range of factors, including the low representation of women and people of color in the profession, financial exigency, school board instability and "churning," and entry-level status of very small rural districts.

Although it is evident that the crisis in the superintendency is more a myth than a reality in the United States, it does not mean that some districts do not have a difficult time attracting and retaining CEOs. These circumstances, however, are viewed as situational and require a wide array of informed solutions rather than broad-based policy intervention.

CONCLUSION

Policymakers, professional associations, practitioners, and professors share the common ground of preparing the next generation of district leaders to confront the problems facing American public education. To succeed in this endeavor, they must also share an appreciation for empirical evidence and understand how it can contribute to improving the discourse on educational policies and effectiveness of decision making. Understanding the characteristics and issues facing superintendents is a small but nonetheless important aspect of achieving this objective. These and other empirical findings by scholars in the field hopefully will help refute misleading and often self-serving pronouncements as well as contribute to useful public policies. Data also should be used to identify promising areas for changing present professional preparation and development approaches, not only for identifying tasks, issues, and responsibilities faced by superintendents but also for identifying distinct differences in district contexts that impact superintendents' work.

REFERENCES

American Association of School Administrators. (1983). *Perspectives on racial minority women school administrators.* Alexandria, VA: Author.
American Association of School Administrators. (1993). *Women and racial minority representation in school administration.* Alexandria, VA: Author.

Björk, L. G. (1996). The revisionists' critique of the education reform reports. *Journal of School Leadership, 6*(3), 290–315.

Björk, L. G., & Glass, T. E. (2003). The superintendent shortage: Findings from research on school board presidents. *Journal of School Leadership, 13*(3), 264–287.

Björk, L. G., & Gurley, D. K. (2005). Superintendent as educational statesman and political strategist. In L. G. Björk & T. J. Kowalski (Eds.), *The contemporary superintendent: Preparation, practice, and development.* Thousand Oaks, CA: Corwin.

Björk, L. G., & Keedy, J. L. (2003). Superintendent shortage: Reality or myth. *Journal of School Leadership, 13*(3, 4).

Björk, L. G., Keedy, J. L., & Gurley, D. K. (2003). Career patterns of American superintendents. *Journal of School Leadership, 13*(4).

Björk, L. G., & Lindle, J. C. (2001). Superintendents and interest groups. *Educational Policy, 15*(1), 76–91.

Blount, J. M. (1998). *Destined to rule the schools: Women and the superintendency, 1873–1995.* Albany: State University of New York Press.

Brockett, D. (1996). Boards find fewer superintendent candidates. *School Board News, 16*(10), 1.

Brunner, C. C. (2000). Female superintendents. In T. E. Glass, L. G. Björk, & C. C. Brunner, *The study of the American superintendency 2000: A look at the superintendent in the new millennium.* Arlington, VA: American Association of School Administrators.

Brunner, C. C., & Grogan, M. (2005). Women superintendents and role conception: (Un)Troubling the norms. In L. G. Björk & T. J. Kowalski (Eds.), *School district superintendents: Role expectations, professional preparation, development, and licensing.* Thousand Oaks, CA: Corwin.

Brunner, C. C., Grogan, M., & Björk, L. G. (2002). Shifts in the discourse defining the superintendency: Historical and current foundations of the position. In J. Murphy (Ed.), *The educational leadership challenge: Redefining leadership for the 21st century* (pp. 211–238). Chicago: University of Chicago Press.

Callahan, R. E. (1962). *Education and the cult of efficiency: A study of the social forces that have shaped the administration of public schools.* Chicago: University of Chicago Press.

Callahan, R. E. (1966). *The superintendent of schools: A historical analysis.* (ERIC Document Reproduction Service No. ED 0104 410)

Chase, S., & Bell, C. (1990). Ideology, discourse, and gender: How gatekeepers talk about women school superintendents. *Social Problems, 37,* 163–177.

Collier, V. (1987). *Identification of skills perceived by Texas superintendents as necessary for successful job performance.* Unpublished doctoral dissertation, University of Texas, Austin.

Cooper, B. S., Fusarelli, L. D., & Carella, V. A. (2000). *Career crisis in the superintendency? The results of a national survey.* Arlington VA: American Association of School Administrators.

Council of Great City Schools. (1999). *Urban school superintendents: Characteristics, tenure, and salary.* Retrieved June 23, 2004, from http://wwwcgsc.org/reports/home/superintendents.htm

Cuban, L. (1976). *The urban school superintendent: A century and a half of change.* Bloomington, IN: Phi Delta Kappa Educational Foundation.

Culbertson, J. A. (1981). Antecedents of the theory movement. *Educational Administration Quarterly, 17*(1), 25–47.

Cunningham, L., & Hentges, J. (1982). *The American school superintendency 1982: A summary report.* Arlington, VA: American Association of School Administrators.

Danzberger, J. P., Kirst, M. W., & Usdan, M. D. (1992). *Governing public schools: new times, new requirement.* Washington, DC: Institute for Educational Leadership.

Edson, S. (1995). Ten years later: Too little too late? In D. Dunlap & P. Schumuck (Eds.), *Women leading in education* (pp. 36–48). Albany: SUNY Press.

Educational Research Service. (1998). *Is there a shortage of qualified candidates for openings in the principalship?* Retrieved April 20, 2001, from www.naesp.org/misc/shortage.htm

Fusarelli, B. C. & Fusarelli, L. D. (2005). Reconceptualizing the superintendency: Superintendents as social scientists and social activists. In L. G. Björk & T. J. Kowalski (Eds.), *The contemporary superintendent: Preparation, practice, and development*. Thousand Oaks, CA: Corwin.

Getzels, J. W. (1977). Educational administration twenty years later, 1954–1974. In L. Cunningham, W. Hack, & R. Nystrand (Eds.), *Educational administration: The developing decades* (pp. 3–24). Berkeley, CA: McCutchan.

Glass, T. E. (1992). *The study of the American school superintendency: America's education leaders in a time of reform*. Arlington, VA: American Association of School Administrators.

Glass, T. E., Björk, L. G., & Brunner, C. C. (2000). *The study of the American superintendency 2000: A look at the superintendent in the new millennium*. Arlington, VA: American Association of School Administrators, and Lanham, MD: Scarecrow Press.

Goldring, E., & Greenfield, W. (2002). Understanding the evolving concept of leadership in education: Roles, expectations, and dilemmas. In J. Murphy (Ed.), *The educational leadership challenge: Redefining leadership for the 21st century* (pp. 1–19). Chicago: University of Chicago Press.

Goodman, R., Fulbright, L., & Zimmerman, W., Jr. (1997). *Getting there from here: School board-superintendent collaboration: Creating a school governance team capable of raising student achievement*. Arlington, VA: Educational Research Service.

Hodgkinson, H., & Montenegro, X. (1999). *The U.S. school superintendent: The invisible CEO*. Washington, DC: Institute for Educational Leadership.

Howlett, P. (1993). The politics of school leaders, past and future. *Education Digest, 58*(9), 18–21.

Institute for Educational Leadership. (1986). *Strengthening grassroots leadership*. Washington, DC: Author.

Johnson, S. M. (1996). Leading to change: The challenge of the new superintendency. San Francisco: Jossey-Bass.

Jones, E., & Montenegro, X. (1990). *Women and minorities in school administration*. Arlington, VA: American Association of School Administrators.

Kamler, E., & Shakeshaft, C. (1999). The role of search consultants in the career path of women superintendents. In C. C. Brunner (Ed.), *Sacred dreams: Women and the superintendency* (pp. 51–62). Albany: SUNY Press.

Kowalski, T. J. (1995). *Keepers of the flame: Contemporary urban superintendents*. Thousand Oaks, CA: Corwin.

Kowalski, T. J. (1998). The role of communication in providing leadership for school reform. *Mid-Western Educational Researcher, 11*(1), 32–40.

Kowalski, T. J. (1999). *The school superintendent: Theory, practice, and cases*. Upper Saddle River, NJ: Merrill, Prentice Hall.

Kowalski, T. J. (2003). Superintendent shortage: The wrong problem and the wrong solutions. *Journal of School Leadership, 13*(3), 288–303.

Kowalski, T. J. (2005). Evolution of the school district superintendent position. In L. G. Björk & T. J. Kowalski (Eds.), *The contemporary superintendent: Preparation, practice, and development*. Thousand Oaks, CA: Corwin.

Kowalski, T. J., & Björk, L. G. (2004). *Role expectations of the district superintendent: Implications for deregulating preparation and licensing*. Unpublished manuscript, University of Dayton.

Kowalski, T. J., & Glass, T. E. (2002). Preparing superintendents in the 21st century. In B. Cooper & L. D. Fusarelli (Eds.), *The promises and perils facing today's school superintendent* (pp. 41–60). Lanham, MD. Scarecrow Press.

Kowalski, T. J., & Keedy, J. L. (2005). Preparing superintendents to be effective communicators. In L. G. Björk & T. J. Kowalski (Eds.), *The contemporary superintendent: Preparation, practice, and development*. Thousand Oaks, CA: Corwin.

McCarthy, M. (1999). The evolution of educational leadership preparation programs. In L. Murphy & K. S. Louis, *Handbook of research on educational administration* (2nd ed.), (pp. 119–139). San Francisco: Jossey-Bass.

McCurdy, D. (1992). *Superintendent and school board relations.* Arlington, VA: American Association of School Administrators.

McKay, J., & Grady, M. (1994). Turnover at the top. *Executive Educator, 16,* 37–38.

Melby, E. O. (1955). *Administering community education.* Englewood Cliffs, NJ: Prentice Hall.

National Association of Elementary and Secondary Principals. (1998). Over fifty-percent of the principals in America will retire in the next ten years. *Principal, 70*(4), 65.

Natkin, G., Cooper, B., Alborano, J., Padilla, A., & Ghosh, S. (2003). Predicting and modeling superintendent turnover. *Journal of School Leadership, 13*(3), 328–346.

Ortiz, F. (1998, April). *Who controls succession in the superintendency? A minority perspective.* Paper presented at the annual meeting of the American Educational Research Association, San Diego, CA.

Petersen, G. J., & Barnett, B. (2005). Superintendent as instructional leader: Current practice, future conceptualizations, and implications for preparation. In L. G. Björk & T. J. Kowalski (Eds.), *The contemporary superintendent: Preparation, practice, and development.* Thousand Oaks, CA: Corwin.

Renchler, R. (1992). Urban superintendent turnover: The need for stability. *Urban Superintendents' Sounding Board, 1*(1), 1–2.

Rist, M. (1991, December). Race, politics, and policies rip into the urban superintendency. *Executive Educator, 12*(12), 12–14.

Sergiovanni, T. J. (1992). *Moral leadership: Getting to the heart of school improvement.* San Francisco: Jossey-Bass.

Skrla, L. (1999, April). *Femininity/masculinity: Hegemonic normalizations in the public school superintendency.* Paper presented at the annual meeting of the American Educational Research Association, Montreal.

Starratt, R. K. (1991). Building an ethical school: A theory for practice in educational leadership. *Educational Administration Quarterly, 27*(2), 185–202.

Tallerico, M. (2000). Gaining access to the superintendency: Headhunting, gender, and color. *Educational Administration Quarterly, 36*(1), 18–43.

Tallerico, M. (2003). Policy, structural, and school board influences on superintendent supply and demand. *Journal of School Leadership, 13*(3), 347–364.

Tyack, D., & Hansot, E. (1982). *Managers of virtue: Public school leadership in America, 1820–1980.* New York: Basic Books.

U.S. Department of Labor. (2000). *Occupational outlook handbook, 2000–2001 edition (Bulletin 2520).* Washington, DC: U.S. Government Printing Office.

Young, M. (1999, April). *The leadership crisis in Iowa.* Paper presented at the annual meeting of the American Educational Research Association, Montreal, Canada.

3

National Education Reform Reports

Implications for Professional Preparation and Development

Lars G. Björk, Theodore J. Kowalski,
and Michelle D. Young

During the past 50 years (1954–2003), decisions handed down by the U.S. Supreme Court and legislation enacted by Congress and the states launched two separate yet related initiatives that fundamentally changed the nature of schooling in the United States. The first initiative ensured equal access to public education to a wide range of students, particularly to those who had been poorly served by the system during previous decades. The second initiative focused on excellence, ensuring the quality of instruction for all children. During the past two decades (1983–2003), dramatic changes in society raised concerns about the condition of education, particularly with regard to the viability of the nation's economic and democratic system of government. National commissions and task forces were assembled to scrutinize public schools. Their reports were highly critical of the condition of education in the nation and provided grist for protracted debates on the purpose, nature, and direction of public education well into the twenty-first century. So the nation launched what is arguably the most intense and unrelenting effort to reform public education in American history.

Although most commission report recommendations released during the first two waves of educational reform (1983–1989) focused on the need to increase accountability, enhance student learning, improve curricula, and strengthen teaching, several acknowledged that principals and superintendents were central to successful school improvement (American Association of Colleges of Teacher Education, 1988; Björk, 1993; Björk, 1996; Carnegie Forum on Education and the Economy, 1986; Holmes Group, 1986). Several national commissions and task forces on educational administration were convened to scrutinize the nature and condition of university-based professional preparation programs. Although educational administration reports were highly critical of conventional practices, they outlined a set of reforms directed toward recentering the field. These reports made several key observations and recommendations. They noted that recent changes in the nature and direction of school reform eclipsed management-focused professional preparation programs that aligned with administrators' work during previous decades. Reports also concluded that inasmuch as reform initiatives were changing schools, educational administration had to be realigned to fit new circumstances, which would involve adopting work-embedded preparation approaches as well as performance-based assessment to ensure that aspiring school and district leaders could successfully perform job requirements. Over the past two decades (1983–2003), continuous calls for reform and threats of losing accreditation have helped leverage changes that are strengthening the professional preparation enterprise and eliminating weak programs (Björk, 1996, 2001; Murphy & Forsyth, 1999). Although the profession has mapped out a hopeful journey, hard work still remains.

NATIONAL EDUCATION COMMISSION AND TASK FORCE REPORTS

Although serious efforts to correct school deficiencies began in the late 1970s (Firestone, 1990), the release of A Nation at Risk in 1983 launched an era of educational reform in the United States that was unprecedented in its magnitude, duration, and intensity. Although the content and claims made within the A Nation at Risk document were disputed, the media coverage of this publication facilitated the development of a public perception that not only had our nation's schools failed children, but this failure had precipitated the nation's economic decline. This perception stimulated calls for investigating public school effectiveness.

Analysts concur that educational reform reports were released in three successive waves and reflected separate yet related themes (Bacharach,

1990; Firestone, Fuhrman, & Kirst, 1990; Lane & Epps, 1992; Murphy, 1990). The first swell of educational reform reports (1983–1986) commenced with the release of *A Nation at Risk* in 1983, which was followed in rapid succession by similar documents, including *Making the Grade* (1983), *High School* (1983), *Action for Excellence* (1983), and *Educating Americans for the 21st Century* (1983) (Björk, 1996). These first-wave reports called for improving student test scores, assessing schoolwide performance and tracking progress, increasing graduation requirements, lengthening the school day and year, and increasing the rigor of teacher licensure requirements. Many states promulgated legislation that focused on increasing school accountability and regulatory controls that often reached into the classroom. These initiatives shifted policy making from districts to state levels of government, constrained the district role in policy making, expanded the size of district bureaucracies, and increased the workload of superintendents, principals, and teachers (Björk, 1996).

Although a wide array of recommendations was offered by the authors of second-wave reports (1986–1989), an analysis of five of them—*A Nation Prepared* (1986), *Tomorrow's Teachers* (1986), *Time for Results* (1986), *Investing in Our Children* (1985), and *Children in Need* (1987)—revealed recurring themes. First, they concluded that standards-based assessment systems should be implemented for the purpose of holding schools accountable for improving student test scores. Second, they recommended placing greater emphasis on higher-order thinking skills, problem solving, computer competency, and cooperative learning. Third, they reported that national demographic trends and circumstances of children living in poverty had important implications for education. Fourth, they presented a compelling case for radically redesigning teaching and learning processes to better serve all children, particularly those viewed as "at risk" (Murphy, 1990). Fifth, the reports concluded that rigid bureaucratic structures and regulatory controls had a stultifying effect on schools contributing to low academic performance and high student failure rates. The reports recommended decentralizing decision making and adopting site-based management (SBM) approaches as a way to increase teacher participation and nurture professionalism (Björk, 1996).

Authors of the third-wave (1989–2003) reports were highly critical of previous solution-driven commission recommendations (Peterson & Finn, 1985; Clark & Astuto, 1994) that placed greater emphasis on organizational and professional issues rather than on the well-being of students and student learning. Prominent reports released during the third wave included *Beyond Rhetoric: A New American Agenda for Children and Families* (1991), *Turning Points* (1989), *Visions of a Better Way: A Black Appraisal of Public Schooling* (1989), *Education That Works: An Action Plan for the Education of Minorities* (1990), *National Excellence: A Case for Developing America's Talent*, released in November 1993, and *Great Transitions* (1995). Authors of these reports offered two canons for authentic reform. First, efforts to improve education had to focus on children and learning rather than on organizational structures or teacher professionalism. Second, providing support to families was viewed as essential to enhancing children's capacity to learn as was fundamentally redesigning schools to serve as the hub of integrated service systems (Murphy, 1990, p. 29). Many of these concepts were subsequently embodied in Professional Development Schools, Cities in Schools, Sizer's Coalition of Essential Schools, and Comer's School Development Programs (Fullan, 1993).

Several recent reform initiatives—including *America 2000: An Education Strategy* (1991), *Goals 2000: Educate America Act* (1994), and the No Child Left Behind Act (NCLB, 2002)—reflect earlier commission report themes. These national initiatives were accompanied by media fanfare that attracted the notice of policy elites and raised concerns among a wide range of school practitioners, state education leaders, and scholars. For the most part, they affirm that demographic changes occurring in society have significant implications. For schools, they acknowledge the importance of strengthening teaching to enhance student learning—particularly with children viewed as being at risk—and they suggest that leadership is central to the success of school improvement. Although the NCLB eventually gained bipartisan support, conservative and progressive factions in Congress were sharply divided over the issue of funding adequacy. Conservatives believed that a combination of modest federal support, reallocation of state education appropriations, and judicious use of existing district resources would adequately fund NCLB mandates.

Progressives agreed that the intent of NCLB is laudable in that it is directed toward ensuring that all children learn, particularly subgroups (e.g., African Americans, Hispanic Americans, and Native Americans, as well as students with disabilities, low income, and limited English-proficient students) that have been least well served by schools in the past. These progressives, however, were highly critical of several features including arbitrary growth targets and narrow definitions of which content areas are important (e.g., reading, language, and math). Linn (2003) and Stecher & Hamilton (2002) found that this orientation skews instruction away from other areas (e.g., history, science, and the arts). In some states, such as Kentucky, NCLB is undermining systemic reform initiatives that arguably set the standard for school improvement in the nation for more than a decade. In addition, analysts concur that the process used under NCLB to rate school performance, which involves multiple targets, is problematic. For example, if a school meets only 9 out of 10 federal targets, it is identified it as a "failing school"! Furthermore, the act fails to acknowledge research findings that point to a strong relationship between the effects of poverty and children's capacity to learn, resulting in low student achievement that limits life chances (Björk, 1996). Rather than addressing or ameliorating the underlying problem (i.e., poverty), the federal government has chosen to hold school districts responsible for ensuring that low socioeconomic status

(SES) students perform at high academic levels. In addition, some analysts suggest that sweeping NCLB requirements eclipse the Tenth Amendment ("Reserve Clause") of the U.S. Constitution that makes education the responsibility of state governments. This intrusive behavior might well lead to states' resistance and legal challenges to the federal government's far-reaching authority for education expressed in NCLB (Sergiovanni, Kelleher, McCarthy & Wirt, 2004). It is not surprising that progressives characterize NCLB as the largest underfunded federal education mandate in American history. In addition, observers note that NCLB legislation has been criticized by conservatives who argue that it contradicts fundamental tenets of Republican ideology that calls for a limited role of the federal government in general, and intruding into state affairs in particular. Nearly 30 years after Ronald Reagan called for a limited federal role in education and pressed Congress to shift responsibility from the federal to state governments, the present Bush administration is reversing course and recentralizing control over public education. This shift has drawn strong criticism from progressive Democrats as well as the more conservative factions within the Republican Party.

Although the federal government requires NCLB to be fully in place during the next several years, states are finding it uncommonly difficult to meet increasing performance demands and to fulfill all provisions by 2014 without being sanctioned. Some view these mandates as unattainable and the outcome a foregone conclusion. For example, state efforts to implement the act expeditiously are being compromised by economic decline, increasing tax cuts, and rising budget deficits. In addition, certain provisions of NCLB appear harsh. For example, if a school fails to make required progress after two years, it is labeled "in need of improvement." Students are given the option to transfer to a higher-performing school, and the students' home districts are required to provide transportation. This provision remains in effect throughout a multiyear period of corrective action. In year three, the school must offer low-performing students additional help such as tutoring. In year four, the school must adopt one of six corrective options (including implementing a new curriculum, replacing teachers, accepting outside help, and extending the school day and year). In year five, the school must develop an alternative-governance structure that can mean replacing all or most of the teachers and administrators or allowing the state to assume control of the school. In year six, alternative-governance plans must take effect. Although analysts concur that NCLB is heightening attention to glaring inequities in district funding and student performance, many speculate that it might be less about helping all children learn than about declaring that American public schools have failed the nation's children and the economy. It thus provides some segments of the Republican Party with an opportunity to proffer school vouchers as an alternative way to fund "public" education (Björk, 1996, 2001; Björk & Keedy, 2002).

EDUCATION ADMINISTRATION COMMISSION REPORTS AND RECOMMENDATIONS FOR REFORM

Although most educational reform reports released during the past several decades (1983–2003) underscore the importance of strengthening school curriculum, teaching, and learning for all children, Peterson and Finn (1985) commented that "at a time when the nation is deeply concerned about the performance of its schools, and near-to-obsessed with the credentials and careers of those who teach in them, scant attention has been paid to the preparation and qualifications of those who lead them" (p. 42). The notion that school leaders are key to the success of reform initiatives was subsequently affirmed by several commission reports released by the Carnegie Forum on Education and the Economy (1986), the Holmes Group (1986), the American Association of Colleges of Teacher Education (1988), and the National Commission for the Advancement of Educational Leadership Preparation (Young, 2002a). Serious questions were raised about the condition and viability of university-based professional preparation (Björk, 2001).

Several national commissions and task forces examined the nature of leadership and university-based leadership preparation programs between 1986 and 2003. They were instrumental in shedding light on the way demands for reform were altering the nature and direction of preparation programs. Their recommendations laid the foundation for a continuing national debate among scholars, association executives, policymakers, and practitioners on how the roles of principals and superintendents are changing or might change (Crowson, 1988). Importantly, they helped frame recommendations regarding how the next generation of aspiring principals and superintendents should be identified, recruited, and prepared. Although most reports did not distinguish between pre- and inservice training or view professional learning as a career-long continuum, analysts concur that commission recommendations are highly relevant to both. Five key recommendations emerged from educational administration reform reports:

- Strengthening field connections
- Revising course content
- Modifying instructional strategies
- Providing work-embedded instruction
- Recruiting student cohorts

Although the reports recognized the importance of university-based preparation programs, they noted that changing school contexts required parallel changes in university-based professional preparation programs and offered constructive criticism directed toward improving rather than eliminating them.

The National Commission on Excellence in Educational Administration (NCEEA) (NCEEA, 1987) recognized the importance of university-based preparation programs, but saw the need for strengthening field connections. Two years later, the National Policy Board for Educational Administration (NPBEA) (NPBEA, 1989) proposed that university-based programs adopt the notion of work-embedded learning and create partnership sites with school districts for clinical experiences, field residencies, principal apprenticeship programs, and action research. A decade later, the National Commission for the Advancement of Educational Leadership Preparation (NCAELP) reinforced the need for stronger field connections, pointing out that effective preparation programs tend to involve practitioners in their programs by inviting them to be members of program advisory boards and by involving them in the planning of programs and courses, delivery of courses, and supervision of field experiences.

Several national commission reports (NCEEA, 1987; NPBEA, 1989; Young, 2002a) recommended that revising course content and course sequences was at the center of developing a coherent work-embedded curriculum. In addition, the Danforth Foundation (1987) recommended that programs shift away from conventional emphasis on school management to an emphasis on leadership that reflects emerging work in decentralized systems characterized by shared governance, participatory decision making, and school-based councils. The NCAELP recommended that programs be anchored to leadership that is focused on supporting student learning (Young, 2002a). These reports were consistent in emphasizing that principals and superintendents were central to the success of school reform, and as expectations for enhancing students' learning increased, the notion of leadership for learning evolved. Embedded within the concept "leadership for learning" is the expectation that school and district leaders have a working knowledge of learning, teaching, curriculum construction, and alignment (Björk, 1993; Cambron-McCabe, 1993; Murphy, 1993).

McCarthy et al. (1988) persuasively argued that reconfiguring educational administration programs, linking with the field of practice, and aligning course content with practice were the field's most crucial needs. Moreover, they viewed these changes as essential to making other program changes such as changes in instructional strategies. The importance of modifying instructional strategies was emphasized in several reform reports released during the mid-1980s and more recently by NCAELP. These reports not only underscored the importance of modifying instructional strategies but also called for a shared responsibility for professional preparation and greater school-university cooperation in integrating academic and clinical experiences (AACTE, 1988; NASSP, 1985; NCEEA, 1987; Young, 2002a). Convincing theoretical and empirical evidence supports the use of active learning including simulations, case studies, practice-based and problem-based learning, collaborative action research (Milstein & Associates, 1993), integration of formal and experiential knowledge (Björk, 1999), and using more student-oriented rather than professor-centered instructional strategies. In addition, Bridges and Hallinger (1991, 1992) and

Murphy (1990) underscore the value of orienting curriculum more explicitly toward problems of practice, employing reality-oriented instructional formats, and using performance-based assessments. These strategies not only increase program relevance but also contribute to ending "isolated, passive, and sterile knowledge acquisition" (Prestine, 1992, pp. 2–3).

The notion of integrating instruction and clinical experiences not only is a crucial facet of enhancing the effectiveness of professional preparation programs but also is central to bridging the gap between the academic and practice arms of the profession (Björk, 1999, 2000; Griffiths, 1988; Murphy, 1990). According to Ashe, Haubner, and Troisi (1991), work-embedded learning is common ground for school-university partnerships, is aligned with principles of optimum adult learning, and integrates the acquisition of professional and craft knowledge that contributes to higher levels of application and skill transference across school settings.

Finally, the notion of recruiting student cohorts into educational preparation programs is recommended by several national commission reports. Arguably, these strategies can help identify and attract the "best and brightest" candidates as well as contribute to creating highly favorable environments that enhance learning and development. These recommendations are directed toward increasing entrance requirements to ensure that aspiring school and district leaders have an understanding of instruction, possess strong analytical abilities, and demonstrate a potential for leadership.

Reform reports also draw attention to the need to ensure that cohorts reflect diverse ethnic, racial, and gender differences in our society (NPBEA, 1989; AACTE, 1988) and underscore the importance of using a range of ways for identifying and recruiting the next generation of aspiring school and district leaders (Young, 2002a). Carver (1988) suggests that school-university collaboration is one of the most productive approaches to recruiting highly qualified aspiring principals and superintendents and has an added benefit of nurturing a sense of shared responsibility and commitment among institutional partners. After being nominated, however, programs can find it useful to have candidates go through a series of assessments to help identify strengths and weaknesses, weed out less-promising individuals, and plan experiences for those who are enrolled.

Several prominent themes permeating reports released by national commissions and task forces over the past two decades have influenced efforts to recenter the field and restructure professional preparation programs. First, the idea that principals and superintendents are key to the success of school reform underscored the importance of balancing management and transformational leadership roles. Second, the notion of leadership for learning heightened attention to student achievement. Third, the call for using empirical evidence in decision making also applies to efforts directed toward shifting efforts to reconfiguring university-based professional preparation programs from rhetoric to reasoned action.

THE ROLE OF PROFESSIONAL ASSOCIATIONS IN PREPARATION PROGRAM REFORM

Although critics have indicted professor-oriented associations for disregarding the changing nature of leadership in schools and districts and endorsing conventional university-based professional preparation programs, there is overwhelming evidence to the contrary. In fact, the two professor-oriented associations, the University Council for Educational Administration (UCEA) and the National Council of Professors of Educational Administration (NCPEA), have been at the forefront of restructuring professional preparation programs over the past two decades. For example, in the late 1980s, the UCEA, a consortium of universities in the United States and Canada, sponsored the NCEEA and released *Leaders for America's Schools* (1987), which unambiguously called for increasing the quality, rigor, and relevancy of university-based educational administration programs and recommended closing 300 of the 500 programs in the nation that did not meet high standards. The NCEEA report also recommended that programs should bridge the gap between the preparation and practice by forging partnerships among universities, districts, and professional and professor associations that share a common interest in reconfiguring professional preparation programs. Two of the most significant recommendations included acknowledging the need to adopt work-embedded learning models and sharing responsibility for preparation with school districts.

In 1988, the UCEA played a key role in founding the NPBEA. Its founding was a significant turning point in unifying the profession after several decades of disjointed activities (Murphy & Forsyth, 1999). It also enabled the field to speak with a unified and authoritative voice on policy issues associated with professional preparation, served as an advocacy group for improving preparation and practice, and promised to monitor changes. One of NPBEA's first published reports, *Improving the Preparation of School Administrators: An Agenda for Reform* (NPBEA, 1989), called for eliminating weak educational administration programs, strengthening those remaining, and reducing student-faculty ratios. It also recommended that the licensing credential for school administrators be the practitioner-oriented doctorate (Ed.D.).

Several years later, the NCPEA joined the policy board. Together, the UCEA and the NCPEA worked with other professional organizations on the policy board to improve the preparation of educational leaders. In 1993, the NPBEA released *Principals for Our Changing Schools*, which identified the knowledge and skills needed by school leaders and was used as a template for enhancing the quality of educational administration program content, relevance, and pedagogy. In 1996, the National Council for the Accreditation of Colleges of Teacher Education (NCATE) adopted these guidelines for the review of educational administration programs and in 1997 began using them in colleges of education under their purview. Two years later, in 1999, the NPBEA explored the idea of creating the American Board for Leadership in Education (ABLE). The mission of the ABLE was to create a rigorous and relevant set of performance-based certification standards based on what leaders needed to know and do and offer a national board certification similar to the National Board for Professional Teaching Standard's national board certification for teachers. Under the ABLE, national board certification would encompass several levels ranging from novice to distinguished and included specialty area endorsements. It was viewed not as displacing state licensure prerogatives but as offering an opportunity to earn a more prestigious and rigorous national licensure. This strategy has proven highly successful in the medical field, in which physicians receive specialty board certification after completing medical school and multiyear residency and internship experiences.

In 2000, the American Education Research Association (AERA), in collaboration with UCEA and the Laboratory for Student Success (LSS) at Temple University, formed a task force called Developing Research in Educational Leadership and charged it with responsibility for promoting and encouraging high-quality research in educational leadership. Three years later, it released its report, *What We Know About Successful School Leadership* (Leithwood & Riehl, 2003), which reviewed research findings and summarized what we know about effective leadership related to instructional improvement as well as implications for current practice and the preparation of aspiring leaders. The report provides policymakers, practitioners, and professors with empirical evidence on how school and district leaders can directly and indirectly influence student achievement.

The task force report affirms that demographic changes, expanding cultural differences and variance in socioeconomic status, a widening spectrum of learner disabilities and capacities, curriculum standards, and achievement benchmarks are changing the landscape of learning, teaching, and leadership in public schools. It also makes a compelling case for recentering the work of practitioners to improve learning and teaching and to realign university-based professional preparation to be consistent with these new demands.

The report provides empirical evidence that supports five ways in which leaders can positively influence student learning. First, successful school leaders can positively affect student learning by distributing leadership; enacting moral, instructional, and transformational leadership roles; and establishing high academic expectations. Second, successful leaders can identify a core set of leadership practices that have shown to be successful across educational contexts including setting directions, building the capacity of school staff, and developing the organization. Third, successful school leaders can view accountability as both challenges and opportunities to align changing practices with school contexts and needs. Fourth, successful leaders can approach the education of diverse groups of students by developing a better understanding of community contexts and examining prevailing school practices. Fifth, successful school leaders can help nurture the educational culture of families by building trust, improving communication, providing parents with the knowledge and resources needed to help their children succeed, and improving school practices. Empirical evidence of successful school leadership delineated in the report *What We Know About Successful School Leadership* (Leithwood & Riehl, 2003) provides a useful framework for improving practice and reconfiguring how the next generation of school and district leaders are identified, recruited, prepared, hired, and evaluated.

The UCEA launched a concurrent effort to examine implications of changing school and district practices for university-based professional preparation programs. During the fall of 2000, this organization convened a blue-ribbon panel of scholars, practitioners, policy analysts, and representatives of national education organizations to establish the NCAELP to "examine and improve the quality of educational leadership in the United States" (Young, 2002b, p. 4). The commission reviewed recommendations of previous commissions and task forces including the work of the NCEEA (1987), the NPBEA (1989), the NCATE (1987), and the Council of Chief State School Officers (CCSSO) Interstate School Leadership Licensure Consortium (ISLLC) (1996). The first meeting of the NCAELP was cosponsored by the UCEA, the NPBEA, and the Johnson Foundation. The meeting was convened at the Wingspread Conference Center during the spring of 2001, and discussions centered on how to restructure the work of university-based professional preparation programs to prepare learner-focused leaders (Young, 2002b).

The NCAELP identified seven essential themes for restructuring university-based professional preparation programs:

- The recentering and reculturing of the profession must be guided by concern for improving student learning.
- Universities and school districts must share responsibility for professional preparation.
- Leadership standards should be used to bring coherence to program content, measuring effectiveness and separating exceptional from weak programs.
- Research findings should inform efforts to redesign next-generation preparation strategies.
- Leadership standards also should be used to guide professional development activities directed toward building the capacity of veteran leaders to improve student learning.
- Preservice and inservice leadership preparation should be viewed as parts of a cohesive system designed to improve student learning.
- Transforming professional preparation programs will require immediate and proactive engagement of both the academic and political communities (Young, 2002b).

In sum, the NCAELP recommendations outline the direction and nature of changes needed to align university-based leadership preparation with the changes taking place in schools.

INSTITUTIONAL ACCREDITATION AND STANDARDS-BASED LICENSURE

Recognizing the merits of establishing criteria for licensure, professional associations took the lead in aligning changes taking place in schools and administrators' work with professional licensure. These initiatives provided frameworks for standards-based licensure, preparation, and the evaluation of principals and superintendents over the past several decades. During the early 1980s, the American Association of School Administrators (AASA) convened superintendents and professors of educational administration and asked them to define a set of performance-based goals, competencies, and skills relevant to chief executive officers (CEOs) and to formulate recommendations for improving professional preparation of aspiring district leaders delineated in its report, *Guidelines for the Preparation of School Administrators* (Hoyle, 1982). Subsequently, the AASA funded a number of studies intended to validate the skills enumerated in its report, and these studies served as the basis for formulating eight performance goals intended to improve practice. These performance-based standards and indicators were described in *Skills for Successful School Leaders* (Hoyle, English, & Steffy, (1985). The eight standards included (1) designing, implementing, and evaluating school climate; (2) building support for schools; (3) developing school curricula; (4) conveying instructional management; (5) evaluating staff; (6) developing staff; (7) allocating resources, and (8) engaging in research, evaluation, and planning. The 1990 edition explored how these standards could be used to improve the preparation of aspiring superintendents, guide professional development activities, and provide a framework for performance-based state licensure.

The Commission on Standards for the Superintendency was formed by the AASA during the early 1990s. Its membership included executives from the AASA, the NPBEA, superintendents, professors of educational administration, and a consultant from Educational Leadership Services. The purpose of the commission was to develop a set of professional standards that integrated professional knowledge and research findings on executive leadership performance, as well as competencies and skills needed to effectively work in changing public school contexts. These standards refined and expanded efforts of the previous commission and formulated a set of recommendations delineated in *Skills for Successful School Leaders* (Hoyle, English, & Steffy, 1990). Consistent with previous initiatives, they were directed toward strengthening practice, improving inservice professional development programs, providing guidelines for hiring and evaluating superintendents, restructuring preservice preparation programs, and framing state-level professional licensure. The AASA's *Professional Standards for the Superintendency* (Hoyle, 1993) and the Commission on Standards for the Superintendency created eight professional standards or performance goals. They include (1) leadership and district culture, (2) policy and governance, (3) communications and community relations, (4) organizational management, (5) curriculum planning and development, (6) instructional management, (7) human resources management, and (8) values and ethics of leadership.

Over the past two decades (1983–2003), these efforts have contributed to moving the superintendency toward standards-based preparation, development, and licensure (Hoyle, 1993; Hoyle, Björk, Collier, & Glass, 2004; Hoyle, English, & Steffy, 1985, 1990, 1998). Second, these initiatives signaled a shift away from simply acquiring knowledge as measured by university graduate degrees to performance-based assessment of an individual's competency to serve as a district CEO. Third, these eight standards might be viewed as a picket fence framework for vertically aligning knowledge acquisition and performance activities across several horizontal levels, including preservice preparation, practice, and professional development. Moreover, the AASA's standards-based performance, preparation, and licensure initiative influenced other association efforts, including those launched by the NPBEA and the CCSSO, which launched similar standards-based initiatives.

In 1994, the CCSSO formed the ISLLC to develop a set of national licensure standards intended to shift preparation and practice away from management toward leadership and to recenter the field to focus on the importance of improving student learning. Those promulgating the ISLLC standards also intended them to be used as a template for improving the content, pedagogy, and clinical experiences of principal preparation programs. More specifically, the six ISLLC standards included (1) building a shared vision, (2) creating a culture of learning, (3) ensuring safe and productive learning environments, (4) working together with parents and community citizens, (5) working in a fair and ethical manner, and (6) understanding broad socioeconomic, legal, political, and cultural contexts in which schools are embedded. The central themes of the ISLLC standards included acquiring knowledge, enhancing practice, improving schooling through reflective practice, and demonstrating their capacity to effectively lead schools.

During 1998, the ISLLC addressed the issue of how to relicense veteran administrators. The ISLLC developed the Collaborative Professional Development Process for School Leaders (CPDP) that is a work-embedded and performance-based professional growth process. In an effort to emphasize the importance of applying knowledge to improving practice, in 1999 the ISLLC and the Educational Testing Service (ETS) designed a professional licensure portfolio that calls for candidates to demonstrate proficiency in applying ISLLC standards to practice. The ISLLC Assessment Portfolio is used as a foundation for initial standards-based licensure as well as for relicensing veteran school leaders. In addition, the School Leaders Licensure Assessment (SLLA), a performance-based assessment instrument based on the ISLLC standards, was developed by the ETS for use in combination with other methods to certify individuals for initial principal licensure.

NATIONAL STANDARDS-BASED ACCREDITATION AND STATE PROGRAM APPROVAL PROCESSES

The accreditation process is defined and administered by the profession and reifies its commitment to developing, validating, and enforcing mutually agreed-upon standards of quality. As Wise (1992) notes, the accreditation process serves as a cornerstone of the professions and ensures that academic programs "modify their requirements to reflect changes in knowledge and practice generally accepted in the field" (p. 12). Accreditation standards convey expectations of quality, whereas the accreditation process provides assurances of integrity and serves as a criterion for awarding state and federal funds (Kaplin, 1982; Millard, 1983).

The nation's preoccupation with educational reform, accountability, and assessment increased pressure on voluntary accreditation associations to provide the public with assurances of institutional quality. Widespread adoption of the ISLLC standards by states in large measure influenced the nature and direction of NCATE, National Association of State Directors of Teacher Education and Certification (NASDTEC), and Educational Leadership Constituent Council (ELCC) reviews of professional preparation programs. Analysts, scholars, and practitioners concur that one of the most significant changes in administrator certification during the past several decades is widespread abandonment of conventional course-driven certification in favor of standards- and performance-based licensure (Björk, 2001; Björk & Larson, 1994; Hart & Pounder, 1999; Murphy & Forsyth, 1999; Sergiovanni, Kelleher, McCarthy, & Wirt, 2004).

Although some view these regulatory initiatives as an unprecedented challenge to institutions of higher education, colleges of education, educational leadership programs, officials, and reformers assert that compliance with new accreditation standards will help to achieve two important goals: strengthening professional preparation and eliminating weak programs. These initiatives are directed toward recentering the field to focus on enhancing student learning, embedding professional learning in work contexts, and underscoring the importance of demonstrating the capacity to apply knowledge to improving education.

The importance of standards-based performance expectations for licensure, certification, and accreditation that are coherently related was articulated in the report *What Matters Most: Teaching for America's Future* (1996) released by the National Commission on Teaching and America's

Future (NCTAF). In referring to licensure, certification, and accreditation as "the three-legged stool of teacher quality" (p. 29), the report unambiguously claims that although these three factors are related, they are distinctly different. In general, the term *licensure* refers to a permit issued by states that allows an individual to enter a profession and practice. Contrary to popular belief, a license is not a contract between the holder and issuer (i.e., a property right), so the issuer typically has a legal right to alter requirements for, to suspend, or to revoke a license (Kowalski, 2003). Although the terms *licensing* and *certification* have often been used interchangeably in education (Hart & Pounder, 1999), the latter has a different meaning in most professions. Certification usually connotes a higher level of competence in a given area in which a person is licensed to practice, and it is granted within the profession—not by the state (Kowalski, 2003). True certification within the education profession has not been common. The Association of School Business Officials (ASBO) has offered several levels of professional certification for its members, and the National Board for Professional Teaching Standards (NBPTS) offers national certification for teachers. Although the NPBEA has tried to establish national certification for educational leaders, to date no national certification for superintendents has been established (Kowalski, 1999).

NATIONAL ASSOCIATION OF STATE DIRECTORS OF TEACHER EDUCATION AND CERTIFICATION (NASDTEC)

The NASDTEC, an organization dedicated to licensing well-prepared educators for our nation's schools, represents professional standards boards, commissions, and state departments of education in all 50 states, the District of Columbia, the Department of Defense Dependent Schools, the U.S. Territories, New Zealand, and British Columbia, which are responsible for the preparation, licensure, and discipline of educational personnel. Although NASDTEC serves its members in many ways, the organization is perhaps best known for its work in the areas of licensure and standards.

NASDTEC's manual on state licensure is a commonly used resource for state and national leaders. The manual provides an overview of all certification and licensure policies in each of the 50 United States. Moreover, NASDTEC makes use of this information in its efforts to promote the mobility of educators across the country by administering the interstate contract, identifying ways to eliminate the barriers to reciprocity, adopting common language for educator certification, and standardizing teacher education program graduates reports (NASDTEC, 2004).

Although the NASDTEC is not an accrediting agency, it develops standards for use by state departments of education or professional standards boards when conducting periodic reviews and approving professional preparation programs for educators. It also strives to improve licensure and certification requirements across states by facilitating professional mobility through reciprocity agreements (interstate certification contracts), advocating criminal background checks, and maintaining data in the Educator Identification Clearinghouse for disciplinary actions taken against educators and criminal convictions (Hart & Pounder, 1999).

As with most regulatory agency standards related to educational leadership that have lagged behind rather than preceded educational reform activities, regulatory changes adopted by NASDTEC for approving educational administration programs have followed national reform initiatives. For example, they have adopted authentic standards for accreditation and program approval that are tied to knowledge, skills, and pedagogy identified by professional associations as being relevant to the actual work of school and district leaders in assessing program quality and student performance.

NASDTEC functions through a committee structure, with regional representation on each of five committees: an executive committee, an interstate committee, a professional practice committee, a professional preparation and continuing development committee, and an ad hoc committee. Of particular interest to this chapter, the Professional Preparation and Continuing Development Committee holds that performance-based educator preparation is best suited to improve PK–12 student learning, and that performance-based standards should be used to build rigorous, high-quality educator preparation programs. NASDTEC's professional preparation and continuing development committee works to convince states to adopt, adapt, or develop performance-based standards as a part of educator preparation program approval.

NATIONAL COUNCIL FOR ACCREDITATION OF TEACHER EDUCATION (NCATE) ACCREDITATION

Concern that accreditation standards have not remained relevant to the changing nature of practice have also led to calls for reform. For example, during the mid-1970s, NCATE was challenged to reform its standards when the AACTE (AACTE, 1983) released its report, *A Proposed Accreditation System: An Alternative to the Current NCATE System*. This report reiterated concerns raised previously, including ambiguous standards, uneven application of NCATE standards, redundant review processes, failure to ascertain the viability of institutional governance systems for the School Personnel Preparation programs, inability to rate the importance of different standards, and the tendency to create biases against certain types of institutions. In addition, it recommended ways to improve the NCATE accreditation system, cautioning that failure to act over the next five years might lead to formation of an alternative national accrediting association (Gollnick & Kunkel, 1986; Scannell, Gardner, Olsen, Sullivan, & Wisniewski, 1983). The report included several key recommendations, including creating a centralized governance system to coordinate activities of teacher education "units" and focusing accreditation criteria and institutional reviews on school personnel preparation programs as a whole rather than on discrete programs within an institution (Gideonse, 1990; Gollnick & Kunkel, 1986; Scannel, Gardner, Olsen, Sullivan, & Wisniewski, 1983).

During the most recent education reform era, the fact that accreditation was critical to the survival and credibility of university-based professional preparation programs became evident (Gideonse, 1990). As public demands for accountability increased, the professions were compelled to promulgate new accreditation standards governing the quality of postsecondary professional preparation programs. Consequently, accreditation standards became inextricably entwined with notions of quality control and quality assurance, and university-based professional preparation programs responded by modifying organizational structures, program content, and instructional processes (Björk & Larson, 1994; Wise, 1992; Young, Chambers, Kells, & Associates, 1983). In a larger sense, national accreditation of postsecondary education programs became as much a necessity as it did a mark of prestige for those institutions that achieved and maintained rigorous national standards.

In response to criticism within the accreditation community and increasing pressure to improve schooling, the NCATE (1990) affirmed that its central purpose was to encourage teacher-training institutions to meet rigorous academic standards of excellence in professional education and implemented several changes in accreditation criteria and procedures. First, it called for improved academic content-area preparation of teachers entering the field. Second, NCATE standards that went into effect in 1986 mandated a uniform and cohesive governance system for school personnel preparation programs. Third, the NCATE focused on the "unit" (i.e., departments, colleges, and schools of education) for initial or continuing institutional reviews and accreditation (Björk & Larson, 1994; Gollnick & Kunkel, 1986; Hart & Pounder, 1999; Millard, 1983; Murphy & Forsyth, 1999; NCEE, 1983). The NCATE responded to criticisms and shaped its mission to effectively encompass evaluation, accountability, and proactive improvement of the education unit and professional preparation programs. More recently, the NCATE published its *NCATE 2000* document, which outlined a new direction for the accreditation of colleges and schools of education. The new direction focused program reviews on results (i.e., how well graduates are prepared to perform in the workplace). Thus NCATE standards were reframed to increase focus on how well candidates were prepared rather than how they were prepared. Contemporaneously, the NCATE required that all specialized professional associations (SPAs) standards also focus on outcomes and performances.

As the intensity of educational reform increased during the past decade, the NCATE increased collaboration with other agencies, including the NPBEA and the NASDTEC, to "ensure that accreditation, licensure, and advanced certification standards are compatible" (Hart & Pounder, 1999, p. 136). The NCATE collaboration led to the development of the ELCC (which will be discussed next) as well as the NCATE partnership agreements with the states. Although the nature of NCATE partnerships differs by state, most partnerships involve the use of NCATE standards as the basis for unit and (in some cases) SPA reviews as well as joint program-approval accreditation site visits.

EDUCATIONAL LEADERSHIP CONSTITUENT COUNCIL (ELCC) STANDARDS FOR ADVANCED PROGRAMS IN EDUCATIONAL LEADERSHIP

Collaboration between the NCATE and the NPBEA, as described previously, led to the development of the ELCC. In 1995, four organizations from the NPBEA—the AASA, the Association for Supervision and Curriculum Development (ASCD), the National Association of Elementary School Principals (NAESP), and the National Association of Secondary School Principals (NASSP)—volunteered to form and fund the ELCC, which provides the NCATE's review of educational leadership programs.

To assist in this effort, the NPBEA created and supported two working groups to develop a common set of guidelines for the NCATE accreditation review of advanced programs in educational leadership. This occurred first in 1993–1995 and then again in 2000–2001. In both cases, the purpose of developing these guidelines was to provide a common set of criteria for preparing candidates for educational leadership positions.

In 1995, the NCATE approved the first set of standards, titled *Guidelines for Advanced Programs in Educational Leadership.* These standards focused on requisite knowledge, skills, and leadership characteristics viewed as central to developing and sustaining learner-centered schools. They included (a) strategic leadership, (b) instructional leadership, (c) organizational leadership, (d) political-community leadership, and (e) the internship. The strategic leadership standard focused on understanding educational contexts, articulating the purpose of schooling, possessing the capacity to develop a shared vision, using data and information to frame and solve problems, exercising leadership to accomplish common goals, and acting in an ethical manner. The instructional leadership standard encompassed knowledge and skills central to collaboratively designing learner-centered curricula and instructional programs, nurturing school cultures, assessing outcomes and using data to align professional development to improve student learning, and providing a wide range of services to families and students that enhances learning. The organizational leadership standard was directed toward understanding and building the capacity of the organization to support learning and teaching. The political-community leadership standard accentuated the need to understand constitutional, statutory, and regulatory provisions, and policies that ground schools as political systems and proscribe their work. Notions of social and organizational justice ground ethical behaviors and beliefs in democratic participation, citizen involvement, communication, and relations with local communities.

The internship standard addressed the long-held belief by practitioners and professors that work-embedded learning is essential to synthesizing knowledge to improving practice. This internship is characterized as either a concurrent or capstone school-embedded learning experience that takes place over an extended period of time and is collaboratively guided by professors and practitioners. Even if the NCATE held that the internship optimally should be a yearlong, full-time experience, it acknowledged that few aspiring principals or superintendents have the luxury of completing such a requirement without substantial financial support. Unfortunately, few states and still fewer districts have provided financial assistance for full-time internships (Björk, 2001).

The NCATE's shift in focus in 2000 necessitated the revision of standards for the review of advanced programs in educational leadership. As a result, a second working group representing the NPBEA member organizations was created. At the same time that the new working group was being appointed, standards developed by the ISLLC were being adopted or adapted by a large number of states for the licensure of school and school system leaders. As a result, it was decided that the ISLLC standards should be used as criteria for the new results-focused NCATE/ELCC standards.

The new *Standards for Advanced Programs in Educational Leadership* are stated as candidate proficiencies because program assessment by the ELCC is designed to focus on results criteria. The new standards focus on six areas of candidate competency and the internship. The seven standards are the following:

- *Standard 1.0.* Candidates who complete the program are educational leaders who have the knowledge and ability to promote the success of all students by facilitating the development, articulation, implementation, and stewardship of a school or district vision of learning supported by the school community.

- *Standard 2.0.* Candidates who complete the program are educational leaders who have the knowledge and ability to promote the success of all students by promoting a positive school culture, providing an effective instructional program, applying best practice to student learning, and designing comprehensive professional growth plans for staff.

- *Standard 3.0.* Candidates who complete the program are educational leaders who have the knowledge and ability to promote the success of all students by managing the organization, operations, and resources in a way that promotes a safe, efficient, and effective learning environment.

- *Standard 4.0.* Candidates who complete the program are educational leaders who have the knowledge and ability to promote the success of all students by collaborating with families and other community members, responding to diverse community interests and needs, and mobilizing community resources.

- *Standard 5.0.* Candidates who complete the program are educational leaders who have the knowledge and ability to promote the success of all students by acting fairly, with integrity and in an ethical manner.

- *Standard 6.0.* Candidates who complete the program are educational leaders who have the knowledge and ability to promote the success of all students by understanding, responding to, and influencing the larger political, social, economic, legal, and cultural context.

- *Standard 7.0.* Internship. The internship provides significant opportunities for candidates to synthesize and apply the knowledge and practice and develop the skills identified in Standards 1–6 through substantial, sustained, standards-based work in real settings, planned and guided cooperatively by the institution and school district personnel for graduate credit (NPBEA, 2002).

A complete copy of these standards and standards' rubrics are available on the NCATE Web site under "Program Standards" for the ELCC. According to the NPBEA, several significant changes differentiate these standards from previous standards:

- The knowledge, skills, and concepts are viewed holistically. They are generic and integrated for all school leaders, although the emphasis of each might shift for the various leadership roles.
- The standards reflect an emphasis on program outcome effectiveness rather than being limited to numeric computations of courses and printed reports of content offered.
- Program reports require evidence of knowledge and skills learned and applied in simulated and real contexts rather than solely exhibits of content offered.
- Program reports will be examined by teams of reviewers composed of university professors and district administrators or school-level administrators, depending upon the program.
- An internship component is required in all programs.
- For the first time in the review process, institutions are required to submit evidence of candidate and program assessments aligned with the standards and provide evidence of overall program outcome effectiveness to demonstrate program quality (NPBEA, 2002, pp. 13–14).

ELCC reviews are conducted within NCATE institutions that offer postbaccalaureate programs to prepare superintendents, principals, curriculum directors, or supervisors at the master's, post-master's, specialist, or doctorate degree levels. At the present time, the review process is managed by four educational organizations that work together to strengthen educational leadership programs: the ASCD, the NAESP, the NASSP, and the NPBEA.[1] However, member organizations of the NPBEA are considering changing the organizational base of the ELCC. There are several reasons for this. First, until recently, the ELCC had no representation from higher education. Faculty members from educational leadership have raised concerns about this lack of representation for several years. In response, when the NPBEA replaced the AASA on the ELCC, it appointed the UCEA to represent both the NPBEA and higher education on the ELCC. Second, the withdrawal of the AASA from the ELCC had fiscal implications for the ELCC that the NPBEA has been asked to help address. Third, the NCATE is currently in the process of redesigning the way that SPA reviews are conducted. The NCATE plans to centralize the management of the SPA review process. This organizational change will require leadership of the ELCC and the NPBEA to rethink and revise the role that the ELCC has played with regard to NCATE/ELCC program reviews.

CONCLUSION

National educational reform initiatives and the adoption of standards-based licensure, certification, and accreditation frameworks are significant in time, place, and purpose. They emerged in response to widespread public demand for school reform and succeeded because of the unprecedented willingness of a wide range of practitioner and university associations to find common ground and purpose. In combination, these separate yet related licensure, certification, and accreditation initiatives support leveraging changes in practice, reconfiguring principal and superintendent preparation programs, and bringing coherence to professional development.

Several key concepts emerged from commission and task force reports that hold considerable promise for fundamentally altering the way the next generation of school and district leaders are prepared, including (a) recentering the field to focus on improving student learning, (b) viewing schools as political entities embedded in local communities, (c) restructuring schools to achieve social and organizational justice, (d) sharing responsibility for professional preparation with school districts, (e) situating learning in work contexts, (f) orienting curriculum explicitly toward problems of practice, (g) using reality-oriented instructional formats, (h) adopting student-centered rather than professor-centered instructional approaches, (i) convening aspiring school and district leaders into cohorts to function as communities of learners, and (j) employing performance-based assessment strategies to ensure that candidates can perform competently. These recommendations are unambiguously directed toward ending "isolated, passive, and sterile knowledge acquisition" (Prestine, 1992, pp. 2–3) that has characterized university-based educational administration during past decades and adopting hands-on and proactive application of knowledge that will exemplify programs in the future. At this juncture, the field of educational administration has developed a coherent template for recentering the field and radically changing professional preparation. These initiatives should be guided by sound theoretical and empirical evidence, however.

NOTE

1. Although the AASA was one of the founding members of the ELCC, the AASA recently discontinued its support of the NCATE, the NPBEA, and the ELCC.

REFERENCES

American Association of Colleges of Teacher Education. (1983). *A proposed accreditation system: An alternative to the current NCATE system.* Washington, DC: Author.

American Association of Colleges of Teacher Education. (1988). *School leadership preparation: A preface to action.* Washington, DC: Author.

Ashe, J., Haubner, J., & Troisi, N. (1991, September). University preparation of principals: The New York study. *NASSP Bulletin, 75*(536), 145–150.

Bacharach, S. (Ed.). (1990). *Educational reform: Making sense of it all.* Boston: Allyn & Bacon.

Björk, L. G. (1993). Effective schools—effective superintendents: The emerging instructional leadership role. *Journal of School Leadership, 3,* 246–259.

Björk, L. G. (1996). The revisionists' critique of the education reform reports. *Journal of School Leadership, 6,* 290–315.

Björk, L. G. (1999, April). *Integrating formal and experiential knowledge: A superintendent preparation model.* Paper presented at the annual meeting of the American Educational Research Association, Montreal.

Björk, L. G. (2000). Professional preparation and training. In T. E. Glass, L. G. Björk, & C. C. Brunner. *The study of the American superintendency 2000: A look at the superintendent in the new millennium* (pp. 127–166). Arlington, VA: American Association of School Administrators.

Björk, L. G. (2001). Preparing the next generation of superintendents: Integrating formal and experiential knowledge. In C. C. Brunner & L. G. Björk (Eds.), *The new superintendency: Advances in research and theories of school management and educational policy* (pp. 19–54). Greenwich, CT: JAI Press.

Björk, L. G., & Keedy, J. L. (2002, Winter). Decentralization and school council empowerment in Kentucky: Implications for community relations. *School Public Relations Journal 23*(1), 30–44.

Björk, L. G., & Larson, P. (1994). NCATE accreditation: A force for change in university governance structures. *People and Education, 2*(3), 353–374.

Bridges, E., & Hallinger, P. (1991). Problem-based learning: A promising approach for preparing educational administrators. *UCEA Review, 23*(3), 3–6.

Bridges, E., & Hallinger, P. (1992). *Problem-based learning for administrators.* Eugene, OR: ERIC/CEM.

Cambron-McCabe, N. (1993). Leadership for democratic authority. In J. Murphy (Ed.), *Preparing tomorrow's leaders: Alternative designs* (pp. 157–176). University Park, PA: University Council for Educational Administration.

Carnegie Council for Adolescent Development. (1989). *Turning points.* Washington, DC: Author.

Carnegie Council on Adolescent Development. (1995). *Great transitions: Preparing adolescents for a new century.* Washington, DC: Author.

Carnegie Forum on Education and the Economy: Task Force on Teaching as a Profession. (1986). *A nation prepared: Teachers for the 21st century.* Washington, DC: Author.

Carver, F. D. (1988, June). *The evaluation of the study of educational administration.* Paper presented at the EAAA Allerton House Conference, University of Illinois, Urbana-Champaign.

Clark, D., & Astuto, T. (1994). Redirecting reform: Challenges to popular assumptions about teachers and students. *Phi Delta Kappan, 75*(7), 512–520.

Commission on Policy for Racial Justice of the Joint Center for Political Studies. (1989). *Visions of a better way: A black appraisal of public schooling.* Washington, DC: Joint Policy Center for Political Studies.

Commission on Precollege Education in Mathematics, Science, and Technology. (1983). *Educating Americans for the 21st century.* Washington, DC: National Science Foundation.

Committee for Economic Development. (1985). *Investing in our children.* New York: Author.

Committee for Economic Development. (1987). *Children in need.* New York: Author.

Council of Chief State School Officers. (1996). *Interstate school leaders licensure consortium: Standards for school leaders.* Washington, DC: Author.

Crowson, R. L. (1988). Editors introduction. *Peabody Journal of Education, 65*(4), 1–8.

Danforth Foundation. (1987). *Program for the preparation of school principals (DPPSP).* St. Louis, MO: Author.

Firestone, W. A. (1990). Continuity and incrementalism after all: State responses to the excellence movement. In J. Murphy (Ed.), *The educational reform movement of the 1980's: Perspectives and cases* (pp. 143–166). Berkeley, CA: McCutchan.

Firestone, W. A., Fuhrman, S., & Kirst, M. W. (1990). An overview of educational reform since 1983. In J. Murphy (Ed.), *The reform of American public education during the 1980's: Perspectives and cases.* (pp. 349–364) Berkeley, CA: McCutchan.

Foster, W. (1986). *Paradigms and promises: New approaches to educational administration.* Buffalo, NY: Prometheus.

Fullan, M. (1993). *Change forces: Probing the depths of educational reform.* London: Falmer.

Gideonse, H. (1990, March). *The redesign of NCATE 1980–1986.* Unpublished paper, University of Cincinnati.

Gollnick, D., & Kunkel, R. (1986). The reform of national accreditation. *Phi Delta Kappan, 68*(4), 310–312.

Griffiths, D. E. (1988). *Educational administration: Reform PDQ or RIP* (Occasional paper #8312). Tempe, AZ: University Council for Educational Administration.

Hart, A., & Pounder, D. (1999). Reinventing preparation programs: A decade of activities. In J. Murphy & P. Forsyth (Eds.), *Educational administration: A decade of reform* (pp. 115–151). Thousand Oaks, CA: Corwin.

Holmes Group. (1986). *Tomorrow's teachers.* East Lansing, MI: Author.

Hoyle, J. (1982). *Guidelines for the preparation of school administrators* (2nd ed.). Arlington, VA: American Association of School Administrators.

Hoyle, J. (1993). *Professional standards for the superintendency.* Arlington, VA: American Association of School Administrators.

Hoyle, J., Björk, L. G., Collier, V., & Glass, T. E. (2004). *The superintendent as CEO: Standards-based performance.* Thousand Oaks, CA: Corwin.

Hoyle, J., English, F., & Steffy, B. (1985). *Skills for successful school leaders: Why are some administrators more successful than others?* Arlington, VA: American Association of School Administrators.

Hoyle, J., English, F., & Steffy, B. (1990*). Skills for successful school leaders: Why are some administrators more successful than others?* (2nd ed.). Arlington, VA: American Association of School Administrators.

Hoyle, J., English, F., & Steffy, B. (1998). *Skills for successful 21st century leaders: Standards for peak performers.* Arlington, VA: American Association of School Administrators.

Kaplin, W. (1982). Accrediting agencies' legal responsibilities in pursuit of the public interest. Washington, DC: Council on Postsecondary Education.

Kowalski, T. J. (1999). *The school superintendent: Theory, practice, and cases.* Upper Saddle River, NJ: Merrill, Prentice Hall.

Kowalski, T. J. (2003). *Contemporary school administration: An introduction* (2nd ed.). Boston: Allyn & Bacon.

Lane, J., & Epps, E. (Eds.). (1992). *Restructuring schools: Problems and prospects.* Berkeley, CA: McCutchan.

Leithwood, K., & Riehl, C. (2003). *What we know about successful school leadership.* Philadelphia: Laboratory for Student Success, Temple University.

Linn, R. (2003). Accountability: Responsibility and reasonable expectations. *Educational Researcher, 32*(7), 3–13.

McCarthy, M., Kuh, G., Newell, L., & Iacona, C. (1988). *Under scrutiny: The educational administration professorate.* Tempe, AZ: University Council for Educational Administration.

Millard, R. (1983). Accreditation. *New Dimensions in Higher Education, 11*(43), 9–27.

Milstein & Associates (1993). *Changing the way we prepare educational leaders: The Danforth experience.* Thousand Oaks, CA: Corwin.

Murphy, J. (1990). The reform of school administration: Pressures and calls for change. In J. Murphy (Ed.), *The reform of American public education in the 1980's: Perspectives and cases.* Berkeley, CA: McCuthan.

Murphy, J. (Ed.). (1993). *Preparing tomorrow's school leaders: Alternative designs.* University Park, PA: UCEA.

Murphy, J., & Forsyth, P. (Eds.). (1999). *Educational administration: A decade of reform.* Thousand Oaks, CA: Corwin.

National Association of Secondary School Principals. (1985). *Performance-based preparation of principals: A framework for improvement.* Reston, VA: Author.

National Association of State Directors of Teacher Education and Certification. (2004). *About NASDTEC.* Retrieved June 21, 2004, from http://www.nasdtec.org/about.tpl

National Commission on Children. (1991). *Beyond rhetoric: A new American agenda for children and families.* Washington, DC: Author.

National Commission on Excellence in Education. (1983). *A nation at risk: The imperative for educational reform.* Washington, DC: Author.

National Commission on Excellence in Educational Administration. (1987). *Leaders for America's schools.* Tempe, AZ: University Council for Educational Administration.

National Commission on Teaching for America's Future. (1996). *What matters most: Teaching for America's future.* New York: Author.

National Council for Accreditation of Teacher Education. (1987). *NCATE standards, procedures, and policies for the accreditation of professional education units: The accreditation of professional education units for the preparation of professional school personnel at basic and advanced levels.* Washington, DC: Author.

National Council for Accreditation of Teacher Education. (1990, January). *NCATE standards, procedures, and policies for the accreditation of professional education units: The accreditation of professional accreditation units for the preparation of school personnel at basic and advanced levels.* Washington, DC: Author.

National Council for Accreditation of Teacher Education. (1995). *NCATE guidelines for advanced programs in educational leadership.* Washington, DC: Author.

National Council for Accreditation of Teacher Education. (2000). *NCATE 2000 accreditation standards.* Washington, DC: Author.

National Governors' Association. (1986). *Time for results: The governors' 1991 report on education.* Washington, DC: Author.

National Policy Board for Educational Administration. (1989). *Improving the preparation of school administrators: An agenda for reform.* Charlottesville, VA: Author.

National Policy Board for Educational Administration. (1993). *Principals for our changing schools.* Charlottesville, VA: Author.

National Policy Board for Educational Administration. (2002). *Instructions to implement standards for advanced programs in educational leadership.* Charlottesville, VA: Author.

National Science Board. (1983). *Educating Americans for the 21st century.* Washington, DC: National Science Foundation.

Peterson, K. D., & Finn, C. E. (1985, Spring). Principals, superintendents, and administrator's art. *The Public Interest, 79,* 42–62.

Prestine, N. (1992). Preparation of school leaders can emphasize learning in context. *Leadership and Learning, 4*(2), 2–3.

Quality Education for Minorities Project. (1990). *Education that works: An action plan for the education of minorities.* Cambridge: Massachusetts Institute of Technology.

Scannel, D., Gardner, W., Olsen, H., Sullivan, C., & Wisniewski, R. (1983). *A proposed accreditation system: An alternative to the current NCATE system.* Washington, DC: AACTE's Committee on Accreditation Alternatives, American Association of Colleges of Teacher Education.

Sergiovanni, T., Kelleher, P., McCarthy, M., & Wirt, F. (2004). *Educational governance and administration* (5th ed.). Boston: Allyn & Bacon.

Stecher, B., & Hamilton, L. (2002). Putting theory to the test: Systems of educational accountability should be held accountable. *Rand Review, 26*(1), 16–23.

Task Force on Education for Economic Growth. (1983). *Action for excellence.* Denver: Education Commission of the States, Carnegie Forum on Education and the Economy.

Twentieth Century Task Force on Federal Educational Policy. (1983). *Making the grade.* New York: Twentieth Century Fund.

U.S. Congress. (March, 1994). *Goals 2000: Educate America Act* (PL 103-227). Washington, DC: Author.

U.S. Department of Education. (1991). *America 2000: An education strategy.* Washington, DC: Author.

U.S. Department of Education. (1993). *National excellence: A case for developing America's talent.* Washington, DC: Author.

Wise, A. (1992). The case for restructuring teacher preparation. In L. Darling-Hammond (1992), *Excellence in teacher education: Helping teachers develop learning-centered schools* (pp. 179–201). Washington, DC: National Education Association.

Young, K., Chambers, C., Kells, H., & Associates. (1983). *Understanding accreditation.* San Francisco: Jossey-Bass.

Young, M. D. (2002a). *National commission for the advancement of educational leadership preparation: Ensuring the university's capacity to ensure learning-focused leadership.* Columbia, MO: UCEA.

Young, M. D. (2002b). From the director . . . NCAELP convenes. *UCEA Review, 43*(2), 4–5.

Learning Theory and Research

A Framework for Changing Superintendent Preparation and Development

Lars G. Björk, Theodore J. Kowalski,
and Tricia Browne-Ferrigno

During the past several decades (1983–2005), changes in the nature of superintendents' work have stimulated calls for altering how the next generation of CEOs are identified, prepared, hired, and evaluated (Björk, 2001a, 2001b). National commission and task force reports on the condition and adequacy of university-based professional preparation programs and standards-based licensure initiatives promulgated by professional associations and research findings provide a framework for discussing promising new directions for professional preparation. The notion of aligning professional preparation with emerging realities of practice, principles of adult learning, and acquisition of professional and craft knowledge not only underscores the importance of moving instruction out of the classroom and into work-embedded contexts (Björk, 2001b) but also affirms the relevance of the American Association of School Administrators

(AASA) and the Interstate School Leadership Licensure Consortium (ISLLC) licensure standards. Although the reports recognized the importance of university-based preparation programs, they noted that changing school contexts required parallel changes in university-based professional preparation programs and offered constructive criticism directed toward improving rather than eliminating them.

Recent analyses of National Commission and task force reports discussed in Chapter 3 (Björk, Kowalski, & Young, 2005) identify major themes that help frame the challenge of reconfiguring superintendent preparation: (a) recentering and reculturing the profession to ensure that student learning is enhanced; (b) strengthening field connections; (c) sharing responsibility among key stakeholders including universities, state departments of education, associations, and school districts; (d) identifying and recruiting highly qualified individuals; (e) revising and aligning course content with emerging leadership roles; (f) using leadership standards and indicators to help assess school leaders' effectiveness as well as differentiating exceptional and unacceptable professional preparation programs; (g) modifying instructional strategies to reflect how adults acquire professional and craft knowledge (i.e., work-embedded and problem-based learning; student cohorts); (h) employing leadership standards to determine whether or not professional development programs enhance leadership skills and influence student learning and success; (i) viewing preservice and inservice learning as a coherent system focused on improving schools and student learning; and (j) proactively engaging in political and policy-making processes to ensure that parents and citizens have a voice in how to best serve the interests of children in their respective communities. These themes provide a template for reframing how superintendents are prepared and underscore the importance of developing strategies based on theories and research findings on adult learning.

ROLE EXPECTATIONS OF THE DISTRICT SUPERINTENDENT AND LICENSURE STANDARDS

Roles assumed by district superintendents have been evolving for more than 100 years in response to the increasing complexity and changing nature of the work. State policies requiring these administrators to complete a prescribed program of professional studies to obtain a license to practice recognize the need to provide assurances of quality (Wise, 1992; Young, Chambers, Kells, & Associates, 1983) to protect the public and students' interests in schools (Ashbaugh & Kasten, 1992). Although policymakers assumed that individuals holding an administrator certificate were qualified to manage and lead schools and districts (Young, Petersen, & Short, 2002), the publication *A Nation at Risk* (NCEE, 1983) heightened concern for the quality of public education and raised questions about the role of principals and superintendents in educational reform, as well as their qualifications to manage and lead schools and districts (Björk, 2001b).

Since the mid-1980s, two conflicting views on the relevance of professional preparation and standards-based licensure have emerged. The first, articulated primarily by critics from within the academy, supports reforms to make preparation and licensing more practice-based and rigorous (Cooper, Fusarelli, Jackson, & Poster, 2002; Murphy, 1994). The second, voiced primarily by critics from outside the profession, advances the notion that deregulating preparation and licensing would enhance local school boards' options of employing executives from outside of education (Broad Foundation & Thomas B. Fordham Institute, 2003; Hess, 2003). The latter position is a byproduct of the intense criticism of public education made by political and business elites (Kowalski, 1999) and has resulted in modest success in deregulating state licensure requirements. For example, after two decades, 9 states no longer require superintendents to possess a license, and among the remaining 41 states, 21 have provisions allowing waivers or emergency certificates to be issued. Moreover, 15 states allow or sanction alternative routes to licensure (i.e., other than university-based study) (Feistritzer, 2003). The most recent call for deregulation is found in the publication *Better Leaders for America's Schools: A Manifesto*, issued by the Broad Foundation and Thomas B. Fordham Institute in May, 2003. The *Manifesto* presents three central themes: (1) University-based preparation programs and state licensing standards are meaningless hoops, hurdles, and regulatory hassles; (2) many prominent business executives and retired senior military officers are willing to serve as superintendents if they can circumvent these pointless requirements; and (3) efforts to improve public schools have failed largely because of ineffective leadership (Kowalski & Björk, 2005). At this juncture, when policymakers are being asked to choose between deregulation and reforming professional preparation programs, a sound understanding of problems affecting the superintendency and the knowledge and skills needed to be a CEO would be prudent.

Knowledge and Skills Required of Superintendents

An analysis of the types of knowledge and skills required of superintendents is essential for evaluating the merits of deregulating requirements for entering the position as well as guiding the work of those committed to improving university-based superintendent-preparation programs. Three steps are used to analyze the relevance of knowledge and skills needed by superintendents. First, an historical analysis of the development of superintendency over the past century was carried out to clarify primary role conceptualizations. Five role conceptualizations emerged from a review of the literature. The first four were identified by Callahan (1966) and the fifth was identified by Kowalski (2001; 2003): (1) *teacher-scholar* (1850 to early 1900s), (2) *organizational manager* (early 1900s to 1930); (3) *democratic leader* (1930 to mid-1950s), (4) *applied social scientist* (mid-1950s to mid-1970s), and (5) *communicator* (mid-1970s to present). Second, the role conceptions' validity was tested against data from *The Study of the American Superintendency 2000: A Look at the Superintendent of Education in the New Millennium* (Glass, Björk, & Brunner, 2000). Next, the knowledge base associated with these five role conceptualizations was compared with two primary superintendent licensure standard documents, *Professional Standards for the Superintendency* developed under the auspices of the AASA (Hoyle, 1993) and the *Interstate School Leaders Licensure Consortium: (ISLLC) Standards for School Leaders* (1996). The purpose of this analysis was to determine whether or not primary role conceptualizations are accurately reflected in required standards-based knowledge and skills.

Superintendents' Role as Teacher-Scholar

Between the mid-1800s and the early 1900s, district superintendents were primarily responsible for implementing a state curriculum composed of a set of uniform subjects and courses and supervising teachers. At this juncture, their role was rather narrow and can best be characterized as being "master" teachers whose primary responsibility was for maintaining centralized control of district curriculum and instruction (Spring, 1994). Throughout this period, they were often viewed as intellectual leaders in communities (Callahan, 1962) who authored professional journal articles about philosophy, history, and pedagogy (Cuban, 1988); and in some instances, they eventually became state superintendents, professors, and college presidents (Petersen & Barnett, 2003). After 1910, however, the role of superintendents as teacher-scholars receded as other aspects of their roles increased in importance. As noted by Petersen and Barnett (in Chapter 5) and Björk (2001b), recent school reform initiatives heightened expectations that these CEOs should serve as instructional leaders to enhance the academic achievement of all children. Expectations for superintendents to serve as teacher-scholars were discussed in AASA's most recent 10-year report (Glass et al., 2000) and were found to be of considerable relevance to present practice. For example, more than 40% of superintendents said that their school board's primary expectation of them was to serve as an educational leader. Furthermore, functions associated with the teacher-scholar role conceptualization also were prominent in the listing of superintendents' greatest challenges: (a) Assessing and testing learner outcomes was ranked second overall, (b) dealing with demands for new ways of teaching or operating educational programs ranked fourth, and (c) coping with changing priorities in curriculum ranked fifth. As a whole, these outcomes indicate that functions associated with the teacher-scholar role remain germane to superintendents' present work.

Superintendents' Role as Organizational Manager

As the size and complexity of urban schools increased during the late nineteenth century, discussions that schools did not operate as efficiently as successful businesses (Kowalski, 1999) fueled concerns about the perceived lack of superintendents' managerial knowledge and skills (Cuban, 1976, p. 17). During the early decades of the twentieth century, Cubberly, Strayer, and Bobbitt persuasively argued for adoption of scientific management by public school administrators (as cited in Cronin, 1973). As a consequence, two concurrent initiatives were launched that had a lasting effect on the superintendency. First, prominent universities started offering management courses. Second, many urban superintendents attempted to persuade the general public and policymakers that their work had changed dramatically, becoming more managerial in nature and thus distinct and more important than teaching (Thomas & Moran, 1992). As discussed by Kowalski in Chapter 1, primary management responsibilities assigned to superintendents during this period included budget development and administration, standardization of administrative operation, personnel management, and facility management. Although support for the organizational manager conceptualization diminished during the late 1920s, these functions became embedded in the culture of administration. Throughout the twentieth century, educators and policymakers accepted the premise that superintendents had to be effective managers (Johnson, 1996; Kowalski, 1999). According to Glass et al. (2000), superintendents' management functions are important influences in defining this dimension of their role conceptualization. For example, slightly more than one-third (36%) of the superintendents responding to the AASA survey (Glass, Björk, & Brunner, 2000) reported that their respective boards' primary expectation of them was to be an organizational manager. Nearly all of them cited three management-related problems as being serious: (a) the lack of adequate financial resources (97%), (b) accountability (88%), and (c) compliance with state and federal mandates (82%). These findings suggest that superintendents' role conceptualization as manager remains highly relevant to present practice.

Superintendents' Role as Democratic Leader

The role conceptualization of superintendent as democratic leader is anchored in both notions of participatory democracy and political realities of community ownership of public schools. As noted by Björk and Gurley in Chapter 7, the history of American schooling provides ample evidence that local citizens viewed schools as being within their community's domain of responsibility (Cremin, 1951; Tyack & Hansot, 1982). Throughout this formative period of education (Brunner, Grogan, & Björk, 2002), superintendents' involvement in political affairs was regarded as inappropriate and unprofessional (Björk & Lindle, 2001; Kowalski, 1995). During and following the Depression of the 1930s, however, schools were forced to compete for increasingly scarce resources while concurrently trying to restore democracy in urban, bureaucratic school districts (Callahan, 1966; Melby, 1955). Both tasks required the political acuity needed to secure education's fair share of public resources; galvanize policymakers, employees, taxpayers, and parents to support these initiatives; and serve as democratic statesmen by strengthening democratic processes (Howlett, 1993). By the mid-1950s, the notion of superintendents enacting democratic administrations was displaced by the economic and political problems faced by superintendents (Björk & Gurley, 2003). The intensity of political activity increased during the next five decades (1955–2005) as demographic changes accelerated, concerns for the condition of schooling were heightened, and demands for participation in decision- and policy-making venues increased. As Björk and Gurley observe, the political role of superintendents is largely defined by the realities of practice and thus "to be 'above politics' is to be outside of reality" (Johnson, 1996, p. 153). Glass et al. (2000) found that 58% of the responding superintendents acknowledged that community pressure groups have influenced board decisions. Additionally, 83% of superintendents identified administrator-board relations (micropolitics) as one of the most serious problems they faced. Collectively, these outcomes demonstrate that working with the board and public remains a primary role expectation of district CEOs.

Superintendents' Role as Applied Social Scientists

Superintendents' acceptance of the applied social scientist role was influenced by several factors, including the realization that internal public school operations and productivity were influenced by external legal, political, social, and economic systems (Getzels, 1977). Furthermore, Culbertson (1981) notes that efforts to make school administration an academic discipline during the mid-1950s infused the social sciences into professional preparation programs, thus redefining the role of school and district administrators (Crowson & McPherson, 1987). This conceptualization of superintendents emphasized theory (i.e., empiricism, predictability, and scientific certainty) in its research and practice (Cooper & Boyd, 1987) and changed the normative standards for practice. Kowalski in Chapter 1 and Fusarelli and Fusarelli in Chapter 8 point out that superintendents were expected to apply knowledge of the social sciences, use scientific inquiry methods to understand and solve problems that permeated their practice, and be cast as "experts," possessing a cogent knowledge essential to eradicating social injustices in public institutions (Johnson & Fusarelli, 2003).

Glass et al. (2000) found that 40% indicated that the board's primary role expectation was for a superintendent to serve as an educational leader, which included being knowledgeable about assessment and testing, as well as developing strategies for improving curriculum, teaching, and learning. As social factors became entwined with improving student learning, a profoundly different reality of work emerged. To successfully address these issues, superintendents must draw upon the social sciences to understand differing needs and values, expertly disaggregate student test data, be proficient in analyzing the causes of social and learning problems, and be proactive in building political coalitions in support of socially just organizational policies and practices in districts. In these circumstances, instructional and political leadership is a moral enterprise, and superintendents must play a key role in guiding schools in achieving a socially just and democratic society (Fusarelli & Fusarelli, 2005; Goldring & Greenfield, 2002; Sergiovanni, 1991; Starratt, 1991).

Superintendents' Role as Communicator

The role of superintendent as communicator, discussed by Kowalski and Keedy in Chapter 9, emerged as the American economy evolved from a manufacturing to an information-based society (Kowalski, 2001). Expectations of superintendents to be skilled at communicating with professionals in the district and community citizens reflected a confluence of recent education reform initiatives and the changing social contexts in which they were being pursued. With few exceptions, every school improvement proposal called upon school and district administrators to work collaboratively to build and pursue a common community vision for education. Although prevailing belief systems viewed community interventions as being less productive (Blase & Anderson, 1995) than working in isolation (Gideon, 2002), most policy analysts have concluded that meaningful school reform requires changing the underlying values and beliefs of educators (Bauman, 1996) and changing how they are organized, managed, and governed (Björk, 2001b; Chance & Björk, 2004). Schlechty (1997) noted that "systemic thinking requires us to accept that the way social systems are put together has independent effects on the way people behave, what they learn, and how they learn what they learn" (p. 134). Many communication scholars have concluded that organizational culture and communication patterns are inexorably related and reciprocal (Axley, 1996; Conrad, 1994; Wert-Gray, Center, Brashers, & Meyers, 1991). In this regard, culture influences communication, and in turn, communication contributes to building, maintaining, and changing culture (Kowalski, 1998; 2005). Superintendents' communicator role is influenced by two conditions: first, the need to restructure school cultures; second, the need to access and use information in a timely manner to solve problems of practice (Björk, 2001b; Heckman, 1993; Kowalski, 2000; Murphy, 1994). In addition, the frequency, intensity, and quality of communication have been enhanced by modern technologies (Kowalski & Keedy, 2005). Glass et al. (2000) found that nearly all superintendents (95%) acknowledged that they were the board's primary source of information, and a majority reported having engaged regularly in communication-intensive interactions with parents and other citizens.

It is apparent that the five role conceptualizations of superintendents are supported and validated by historical evidence and recent research findings. As a consequence, they constitute a highly relevant composite of contemporary practice. Taken as a whole, they provide adequate rebuttal to the *Manifesto*'s claim that the knowledge base that undergirds university-based professional preparation is irrelevant to the position.

REQUIRED KNOWLEDGE AND SKILLS IN RELATION TO CURRENT LICENSURE STANDARDS

Descriptions of the five conceptualizations were used to identify the knowledge and skills required for each role (Table 4.1). These data suggest that whereas certain knowledge and skills cut across all conceptualizations, other expertise is role-specific. Collectively, however, pertinent knowledge and skills provide a relevant mosaic of the position's knowledge base.

Table 4.1   Knowledge and Skills Associated With Superintendent Role Conceptualizations

Role	Pertinent Knowledge and Skills
Teacher-Scholar	Pedagogy; educational psychology; curriculum; instructional supervision; staff development; educational philosophy
Manager	Law; personnel administration; finance/budgeting; facility development/maintenance; collective bargaining/contract maintenance; public relations
Democratic Leader	Community relations; collaborative decision making; politics
Applied Social Scientist	Quantitative and qualitative research; behavioral sciences
Communicator	Verbal communication; written communication; listening; public speaking; media relations
Multirole*	Motivation; organizational theory; organizational change and development; leadership theory; ethical/moral administration; technology and its applications; diversity/multiculturalism; human relations

*This category includes knowledge and skills pertinent to all or nearly all roles.

Two standards documents, one developed by AASA and the other by ISSLC, have been used as professional preparation and licensing standards since the mid-1990s. The former includes eight superintendent-specific standards affirmed by Hoyle, Björk, Collier, and Glass (2004); the latter includes six generic standards applicable to all administrative positions. Standards from both documents are listed in Appendix A. Because these standards provide a framework for preparation and licensing, there is a general consensus that they accurately reflect and validate normative superintendent role expectations.

One alternative for examining claims that the knowledge base for the superintendency is questionable or invalid is to compare information presented in Table 4.1 with the two sets of prevailing licensure standards. If the accepted knowledge base for the superintendency is not relevant, the comparison should make an incongruity apparent. To determine congruence, role conception congruence in Table 4.1 was interfaced with the AASA and ISLLC *Standards;* comparison results are displayed in Table 4.2. Analysis reveals that every knowledge base component identified in Table 4.1 is addressed in at least one standard in both documents. Moreover, no standard addresses a knowledge or skill not found in Table 4.1.

This analysis supports widespread belief that knowledge and skills essential to the five role conceptualizations are integral parts of the professional knowledge base, are relevant to contemporary practice, and validate AASA and ISLLC *Standards* for professional licensure.

RESTRUCTURING PROFESSIONAL PREPARATION PROGRAMS

Over the past 20 years (1983–2003), national commission and task force reports convened by federal agencies, foundations, and professional associations have acknowledged that changes in how schools and districts are organized, managed, and governed will require significant changes in the nature of leadership. These changes require preparation programs to align their work with the new realities of practice. Several themes cut across educational administration reports that suggest important directions for reconfiguring how the next generation of superintendents is identified and prepared and how veteran CEOs enhance their knowledge and skills. First, the growing public demand for participation in governance and decision making enhances the value of democratic leaders who have the knowledge and skills to engage staff, parents, and community citizens in open discourse. Second, recentering the field to focus on enhancing the capacity of all children to achieve at high levels of competence requires school and district leaders to become knowledgeable about learning, teaching, and curriculum. Third, the reality of educational accountability requires considerable knowledge of testing, data analysis, and interpretation to successfully sustain enduring efforts to improve schooling. Fourth,

Table 4.2   Interface of Knowledge and Skills and the AASA and ISLLC
Standards

Pertinent Knowledge/Skills	AASA	ISLLC
Teacher-Scholar		
Pedagogy	6	2
Educational psychology	6	2
Curriculum	5	2
Instructional supervision	6	2, 5
Staff development	6, 7	2
Educational philosophy/history	2	5
Manager		
School law	2, 4, 7	3, 6
Personnel administration	7	3
Finance/budgeting	4	3
Facility development/maintenance	4	3
Collective bargaining/contract maintenance	4, 7	3, 5
Public relations	3, 4	3, 6
Democratic Leader		
Community relations	3	1, 4, 6
Collaborative decision making	1, 2	1, 4
Politics	1, 2, 8	1, 6
Governance	2	6
Applied Social Scientist		
Quantitative and qualitative research	4, 5	1
Behavioral sciences	1, 8	4, 6
Measurement and evaluation	5, 6	2
Communicator		
Verbal communication	3	1, 4, 6
Written communication	3	1, 4, 6
Media relations	3, 8	6
Listening	3	1, 6
Public speaking	3	1, 6
*Multirole**		
Motivation	5, 6, 7	2
Organizational theory	1, 2, 7	1, 2, 5
Organizational change and development	1	1, 4, 6
Leadership theory	1	1, 2, 5
Ethical/moral administration	8	5
Technology and its applications	3, 4, 6	2, 3
Diversity/multiculturalism	1, 3, 8	1, 2, 4

NOTE: Numbers in the AASA and ISLLC columns refer to the *Standards* number. See
Chapter 4 Appendix for reference.

*This category includes knowledge and skills pertinent to all or nearly all roles.

data from accountability testing and data from empirical research provide templates for program and policy initiatives that require school leaders to be skilled in communicating and persuading a wide array of individuals, interest groups, and factions that undertaking reforms are in the best interest of the community. Fifth, accomplishing real systemic change demands transformational leadership skills that involve actively engaging others in accomplishing mutual purposes. To successfully recenter and reculture districts, the next generation of superintendents must possess a breadth and depth of knowledge about human behavior, communication, and politics; tacit knowledge of how organizations work; and acuity for understanding the importance of socially just schools and serving as moral leaders (Björk, Kowalski, & Young, 2005).

In addition, report recommendations for changing the scope and direction of university-based professional preparation programs provide a template for action. Commission and task force recommendations concur that school districts and universities should share responsibility for preparing leaders; programs should be standards-based, and full-time internships should be the norm rather than the exception; highly qualified individuals should be recruited and selected into programs; aspiring administrators should be organized in cohorts, and learning should be reality-based, problem-oriented, and work embedded so that content reflects the realities of practice; and instruction should be student-centered rather than professor-centered, thus reconfiguring university-based superintendent-preparation programs (Björk, Kowalski, & Young, 2005).

CHARACTERISTICS OF UNIVERSITY-BASED SUPERINTENDENT-PREPARATION PROGRAMS

The history of educational administration programs is brief and less well-defined in comparison with the professions of law, medicine, and dentistry (Achilles, 1994; McCarthy, 1999), which have national associations that influence uniformity and rigor with regard to program standards, content, instructional processes, and state licensing. Most educational administration programs have a common core of management-oriented courses (e.g., personnel, law, facilities, and finance), as well as discipline-based academic offerings (e.g., from sociology, political science, economics, and so on) (Murphy, 1999a, 1999b). However, they are inadequately linked to the realities of practice (Calabrese & Straut, 1999; Milstein, Bobroff, & Restine, 1991; Murphy, 1992). Although the work of superintendents is qualitatively different than principals, the preparation of CEOs tends to be extensions of principal-oriented programs.

Although there are some similarities across superintendent programs, they vary considerably across states and institutions with regard to subject content, pedagogy, degree of difficulty, and inclusion of field experiences. The practicum or internship, if required at all, is neither comprehensive nor demanding (Murphy, 1990b, 1992) and not aligned with the acquisition of professional knowledge.

In most instances, student enrollments in superintendent-preparation programs tend to be low, courses are housed in departments that have few faculty (2%) whose primary area of specialization is the superintendency, and programs tend to be scattered across a wide range of institutions (McCarthy, Kuh, & Beckman, 1997). As a consequence, either retired or practicing superintendents often serve as adjuncts to deliver most courses. Individuals enter the superintendency primarily through completing administrator certification or academic degree programs and pass required state licensure examinations. Preparation and licensure tend to be protracted over several years and serve midcareer professionals who are in their mid-30s to mid-40s, are married, and have job and family commitments that preclude full-time study (Calabrese & Straut, 1999). These circumstances typically produce part-time, commuter students who pursue certification and graduate degrees during evenings and in summer school. In their recent study, Glass et al. (2000) found that only 8% of superintendents reported that the master's degree was the highest graduate preparation they attained. A higher percentage of superintendents, however, earned a master's degree plus additional coursework (24%), a specialist degree (22%), or a doctoral degree (45%). Over the past 30 years, superintendents have earned graduate degrees at an increasingly higher rate. Unfortunately, the majority (62%) of superintendents completed their degree and/ or licensure requirements more than 11 years previously, which was well before the educational reform movement placed new demands on schools and districts.

The mosaic of needed improvements in superintendent preparation is influenced by a number of interconnected lines toward reform. First, an expanding body of research on effective superintendents and effective school systems beginning in the 1980s (Hallinger & Murphy, 1982; Murphy & Hallinger, 1986, 1988; Peterson, Murphy, & Hallinger, 1987) and continuing in the 1990s (Hightower et al., 2003) provides extensive evidence about how superintendents create high-performing districts that enhance students' academic performance (Murphy & Datnow, 2002).

Second, changing demographics and community contexts have been relentlessly influencing the structure of educational organizations, functions of school districts, and the nature of leadership. As demands for participation in governance and decision making expanded, attention shifted away from the primacy of schools and districts in decision and policy making toward parent and citizen involvement. Thus, as the structure of organizations is recast from the tenets of hierarchy to principles of community (Murphy, 1991), the role of the district superintendent is changing dramatically (Murphy, 1994, 1999a).

Third, although not without notable strengths (Glass et al., 2000), preparation programs for superintendents are plagued with a number of problems. Many of these stem from the unwillingness or inability of preparation programs to reshape them in light of the knowledge previously discussed, including research on effective superintendents as well as scholarship on the changing expectations and demands on organizations and leadership during recent years. Other concerns arise from problems within the inner workings of these programs, including well-documented weaknesses in (a) how candidates are identified and selected into programs, (b) what core content is included and how instruction is delivered, and (c) how mastery of professional and craft knowledge to which they have been exposed is assessed (McCarthy, 1999; Murphy, 1992, 1999b). In light of this evolving understanding about how superintendents promote high-performing organizations and nurture educational excellence for all children, the need to strengthen how the next generation of school and district leaders is prepared makes it an especially propitious moment for action. An examination of research findings and best practices can provide a framework for undertaking changes that align professional preparation programs with the emerging realities of practice.

Superintendents' Evaluation of Their University-Based Professional Preparation Programs

Over the past several decades (1977–2005), critics presented an unrelenting stream of anecdotal stories about dissatisfaction among administrators with their university-based licensure and graduate degree programs and argued that they should either be radically reformed or eliminated. Glass et al. (2000) identified a serious inconsistency, however, between critics' assertions that superintendents were dissatisfied with their preparation and empirical evidence spanning nearly two decades (1982–2000) in which a majority of superintendents regarded their programs favorably. For example, Cunningham and Hentges (1982) found that more than 70% of superintendents viewed their preparation as either "excellent" or "good." Five years later, a study conducted by the National Center for Educational Information (1987, cited in Glass, 1992) found that superintendents were generally pleased with their university-based preparation. Furthermore, Chapman's (1997) study of beginning superintendents found that 87% rated their university-based preparation programs as "excellent" or "good." Although the quality of instruction was rated high, superintendents indicated that they would have benefited from more "hands-on" field experiences.

A retrospective analysis of AASA's last three 10-year studies of the American superintendency might help shed some light on how superintendents view their experiences in university-based educational administration as well as their program's strengths and weaknesses. For example, the first AASA report (Cunningham & Hentges, 1982) indicated that more than 74% of respondents rated their program as either "excellent" (27%) or "good" (47%). The second AASA report (Glass, 1992) also asked respondents to evaluate their university-based preparation program. In that survey, 73% of superintendents regarded their experiences as being either "excellent" (26%) or "good" (47%). Only 22% indicated that their experience was "fair," and fewer than 5% percent rated their university-based preparation as "poor." The third AASA report (Glass et al., 2000) found that superintendents held similar views as those reported in the two previous studies. More than 73% indicated their preparation program as being "excellent" (26%) or "good" (47%). Again, only 22% viewed their experience as "fair," whereas fewer than 4% said it was "poor." In addition, the 2000 study also found that 78% of superintendents receiving their highest degree within the past five years rated their programs more favorably than those who had completed their licensure or degree requirements earlier.

An examination of these reports also identified several weaknesses in preparation programs that have persisted over time. The four most prominent identified in the 2000 study include (1) the lack of hands-on application (20%), (2) inadequate access to technology (19%), (3) failure to link content to practice (17%), and (4) too much emphasis on professors' personal experiences (14%). A review of research findings spanning nearly two decades (1982–2000) suggests that although superintendents expressed a need for more relevant, hands-on, field-based experiences, the majority of superintendents were satisfied with their preparation. This directly contradicts critics' claims that university-based preparation programs are widely regarded by practitioners as being ineffective (Björk, 2000).

Superintendents' Tacit Knowledge

One of the most important aspects of gaining hands-on experience is learning about how organizations work and how administration is done. During the past decade, researchers have made significant contributions to understanding how high-performing CEOs acquire tacit knowledge and how it contributes to successful leadership practices (Björk, 2002). Polyani's (1967) philosophical discussion of personal or tacit knowledge explores how individuals unconsciously acquire understanding through reflection on experience. Two decades later, empirical studies conducted by Reber (1989) affirmed that tacit knowledge is acquired through direct experience, and Argyris (1999) notes that acquisition of tacit knowledge is central to changing behavior to achieve organizational objectives. Nestor-Baker and Hoy (2001), citing Sternberg (1990), identify persistent themes in the early literature on the nature of intelligence that influenced more recent attempts to define, investigate, and apply the notion of tacit knowledge or practical intelligence in real-world settings (Sternberg, 1996; Wagoner, 1987).

Definitions of practical intelligence emphasize the capacity to learn from experience, to adapt and shape one's environment, to have the acuity to retrieve and synthesize knowledge at abstract levels, and to solve problems of practice (Nestor-Baker & Hoy, 2001, p. 88). Thus, practical intelligence, rather than placing primary emphasis on the acquisition of formal knowledge (i.e., "knowing about" administration), is concerned with "knowing for" improving practice (Björk, Lindle, & Van Meter, 1999). The notion of "knowing for" improving practice is also described by Nestor-Baker and Hoy as "knowing how" to do administration. In sum, tacit knowledge or practical intelligence is related to unconsciously acquiring an understanding of how organizations work and using it in solving problems of practice. In applying the notion of tacit knowledge to the study of the superintendency, Nestor-Baker and Hoy note that it "can have negative as well as positive consequences, especially when such action becomes self-reinforcing of the status quo and prevents inquiry into inconsistencies" (p. 87). In this regard, those who structure opportunities for work-embedded learning should stress linking aspiring superintendents with exemplary CEOs.

In the study of tacit knowledge, researchers make a distinction between academic and practical intelligence. They note that academic intelligence is characterized by acquisition and facile use of formal (academic) knowledge that is often measured by IQ tests. Practical intelligence, on the other hand, refers to gaining and using tacit knowledge. Neisser (1976), and later Wagoner and Sternberg (1985), identify differences between the kinds of problems found on IQ tests that are used by schools and those found in everyday life. The principal difference between academic and practical problems is presented in Figure 4.1. In general, academic problems tend to be clearly defined, are typically formulated by others, have full information, involve limited strategies for obtaining a solution, have one correct solution, and are disconnected from work experiences. Practical problems, on the other hand, are loosely defined, not formulated by others, have limited information, involve a wide range of acceptable solutions, and are embedded in practice.

Figure 4.1   Differences Between Academic and Practical Problems

Academic Problems	Practical Problems
Clearly defined	Loosely defined
Formulated by others	Unformulated by others
Full information provided	Little information available
Limited strategies for obtaining a solution to a problem	Multiple strategies for obtaining problem solutions
One correct solution	Multiple correct solutions
Disconnected from work experience	Embedded in work experience

SOURCE: Adapted from Wagoner & Carter (1996), p. 449.

The distinction between academic and practical problems is manifested in differing views of managerial problem solving (Wagoner & Carter, 1996). The field of management is split between those who view managers as rational technicians whose job it is largely to apply the principles of management science to the marketplace and those who view managers as craftspersons or artists whose practice is not reducible into scientific principles. Although tacit knowledge pertains to job-related activities, it relates more to understanding how distinct aspects of work are intertwined. In other words, tacit knowledge is related to understanding how the whole system works. In this regard, tacit knowledge has three primary characteristics: (1) It is related to knowing how to do things, (2) it is relevant to the attainment of practical goals, and (3) it is typically acquired in work contexts through reflective processes. In sum, tacit knowledge is related to competent performance of real-world tasks and achieving personal goals (Sternberg, 1996).

During the past decade, research on tacit knowledge has been conducted by Sternberg and his colleagues (Sternberg, Wagoner, & Okagaki, 1993; Sternberg et al., 2000) across a variety of populations, occupations, age levels, and work settings. For example, research on tacit knowledge has been conducted within the legal profession (Marchant & Robinson, 1999), the military (Horvath, Williams, Forsyth, Sweeney, Sternberg, & McNally, 1994; Sternberg, Wagoner, Williams, & Horvath, 1995), medicine (Patel, Arocha, & Kaufman, 1999), sales (Wagoner, Sujan, Sujan, Rashotte, & Sternberg, 1999), management (Argyris, 1999; Hatsopoulis & Hatsopoulis, 1999), and the superintendency (Nestor-Baker & Hoy, 2001). Recognizing that tacit knowledge can enhance successful performance is heightening interest in finding ways to measure how much tacit knowledge individuals possess relative to measures of achievement as well as how it is acquired and used. Understanding how high-performing executives acquire and use tacit knowledge is informed by two significant findings.

First, tacit knowledge was found to relate to experience in a specific domain. And those working at different levels in the same organization acquire and use different types of tacit knowledge. In other words, the tacit knowledge acquired by principals about how school organizations work is significantly different from the superintendents' understanding of how districts function. In addition, those with less experience in a given domain (school or district) tend to exhibit lower tacit knowledge scores. Sternberg et al. (1993) also note that those with more experience in those circumstances record higher tacit knowledge scores. They also found that the number of years of experience is less important to an individual's success than what an individual learns from the experience.

Second, measures of tacit knowledge are predictive of future performance (Sternberg et al., 1993).

Although those in the military, medicine, law, business, and educational administration are interested in how to increase the amount of tacit knowledge that individuals possess through preparation and development activities, researchers discovered that tacit knowledge is also acquired through indirect means. Patel et al. (1999) found that for the most part, professionals acquire tacit knowledge after they have completed formal preparation. Reber (1989) found that tacit knowledge contributes to organizational innovation and that it is primarily acquired through socialization processes (i.e., subconsciously and without the direct assistance of others or through reflective processes). Wagoner and Sternberg (1985) contend that although competence in the workplace is highly dependent on tacit knowledge, just because it is not openly expressed or stated does not imply that it can't be articulated or taught. Researchers acknowledge that tacit knowledge is acquired in work settings, is practical rather than academic, and is informal rather than formal, and thus tends to be ill suited to the direct instruction typical of preservice and professional development programs. These findings suggest that increasing an individual's tacit knowledge (practical intelligence) will require working directly with exemplary CEOs, participating in high-risk activities, and engaging in reflective processes that are characteristics of exemplary superintendent internship programs.

STRATEGIES FOR RECONFIGURING SUPERINTENDENT-PREPARATION PROGRAMS

Integrating the acquisition of professional and craft knowledge in work settings requires fundamentally altering how professional preparation is organized, sequenced, and situated. National commission and task force report recommendations provide a template for change and outline a set of useful learning strategies.

University-District Partnerships: Shared Preparation Responsibilities

Viewing administrator preparation as a shared university-district responsibility is not unprecedented in the history of the profession (Björk, 2001b; Murphy, 1990a). A wide range of partnerships, collaborations, coalitions, consortia, and networks have been effective as a means for increasing the rigor and relevancy of initial preservice leadership preparation and continuing inservice programs. These strategies are grounded in the belief that when working collaboratively, university and district partners possess the basic building blocks for recasting institutional roles, changing conventional administrative practices, and enhancing leadership preparation.

The role of universities is to transmit formalized knowledge and long-standing professional culture from one generation to the next, cultivate the intellect and develop analytic skills of aspirants, and contribute to building and enhancing the professions—including medicine, dentistry, law, business, and educational administration. In doing so, universities have exhibited a comparative advantage over other organizations primarily for three reasons: (1) their capacity to sustain a core of expert faculty committed to teaching, learning, and public service; (2) their ability to offer academic degrees that have broad-based legitimacy; and (3) their stability needed to ensure continuity in professional preparation over time. School districts, professional associations, state education agencies, and private sector organizations often lack these critical elements and tend to be more susceptible to changing political priorities, unpredictable markets, uncertain revenue streams, and challenges to program validity. Despite the comparative advantages of universities with respect to other providers, March (1974, 1978) observes that attempts by institutions of higher education to apply knowledge to improving practice without involving school districts have been unremarkable. Sergiovanni (1989) refers to this as "neglect of practical intelligence" (p. 17), characterizes it as a significant weakness, and persuasively argues for expanding work-embedded learning and performance-based assessment. Although finding a way to link the academic and practice arms of the profession has been a conundrum in the past (Farquhar, 1977; Milstein, Bobroff, & Restine, 1991; Murphy, 1992; Newell, 1952), both universities and districts might benefit by sharing responsibility in the future.

Although gaining hands-on, work-embedded experience is indispensable to increasing the relevance of professional preparation programs, superintendents value the professional knowledge acquired in university-based preparation programs (Glass et al., 2000). Yet superintendents also must have practical skills gained in authentic work settings to properly manage districts, continually ensure that all children learn, and appropriately address concerns of parents, citizens, and policymakers (Carter & Cunningham, 1997). In these instances, superintendents receive unambiguous feedback that allows them to make straightforward inferences about whether or not their actions had a desired effect.

On the other hand, superintendents are often faced with solving non-routine, complex educational, managerial, and political problems. When events occur infrequently or extend over time, feedback can be ambiguous, so attempting to understand events from a limited number of subjective experiences might be ill-advised (Leithwood & Steinbach, 1992). In these instances, superintendents must have a broad knowledge about the root causes of problems, analytical skills, and solution strategies learned in university settings. Because superintendents' work is both routine and nonroutine (Leithwood, 1995a), placing exclusive emphasis on either the acquisition of formal knowledge in university settings or the craft knowledge in district "grow-your-own" programs fails to prepare individuals to face the complex problems facing contemporary schools and districts (Björk, 2001b). Although Culbertson (1981) acknowledges the importance of contextually relevant, work-embedded learning, we need to develop a thorough understanding of these concepts and other best practices in educational administrator preparation and how they can enhance professional preparation.

Superintendent Selection: Cohort Participation

Several national commission reports recommended that programs end self-selection processes and move toward recruiting students in collaboration with school districts and forming learning cohorts as a way to attract and develop highly committed and talented aspiring administrators (American Association of Colleges of Teacher Education [AACTE], 1988; National Policy Board for Educational Administration [NPBEA], 1989). In addition, they also emphasize the need to increase admission requirements and performance standards to ensure that aspiring school and district leaders possess strong analytical abilities, high administrative potential, and demonstrated knowledge of communities, democratic processes, and instructional and learning processes (AASA, 1960; Browne-Ferrigno & Shoho, 2004; Stout, 1973; Young et al., 2002). Because many influential business and political leaders are agitating to eliminate state licensure requirements (Broad Foundation & Thomas B. Fordham Institute, 2003), Usdan (2002) asserts that the "field of educational leadership preparation desperately needs to be transformed as expeditiously as possible" (p. 306), particularly with regard to who enters preparation programs. Superintendents play critical roles in the success of school system enterprises; hence, the selection of new entrants must be conducted carefully and through collaboration between universities and districts. Additionally, although recommendations for improving administrator preparation stress the importance of using a variety of means for identifying and recruiting aspiring school and district leaders, they emphasize the need for cohorts to reflect diverse ethnic, racial, and gender differences in society (AACTE, 1988; NPBEA, 1989).

Research findings indicate that the "closed cohort" (Basom, Yerkes, Norris, & Barnett, 1995, p. 7) model contributes to improving the quality of instruction, cultivates a sense of community among students and faculty that positively influences students' academic performance, enhances persistence, increases commitment to learning, and supports reflective thinking processes (Barnett, Basom, Yerkes, & Norris, 2000; Browne-Ferrigno & Muth, 2003; Hill, 1995). Closed cohorts of learners also provide excellent opportunities for aspiring educational leaders to learn and practice skills in collective goal setting, community building, conflict resolution, and culture management (Geltner, 1994; McCarthy, 1999; Milstein & Krueger, 1997). Barnett & Muse (1993) found that cohort members tend to demand more from faculty and professional development providers, challenge conventional instructional approaches, and create tension between faculty and students when the relevance of course content is questioned. Findings suggest that cohorts contribute to more dynamic learning environments that are more student-centered and -directed and provide altering patterns of interaction between learners and instructors, making them more collegial.

University-district collaboration in recruitment is important for increasing mutual commitment, motivating individuals to actively engage in professional development, and establishing a sense of shared responsibility among cohort members (Carver, 1988). Admitting students to licensure and graduate degree programs in cohort groups is an important structural change that provides continuity and support for students involved in long-term field experiences. This approach appears to be a growing practice in university settings. For example, Norton (1999) found that 50% of the institutions in the University Council for Educational Administration (UCEA) used cohorts at the master's degree level and 80% used them at the doctoral degree level. More recently, in a study that sampled a broader range of institutions, McCarthy, Kuh, and Beckman (1997) found that 50% of the students in Ed.D. programs and 25% of students in Ph.D. and master's degree programs were enrolled in cohorts (Björk, 2001b). However, simply using the cohort model does not guarantee positive results: Instructors and cohort participants must work together to create dynamic, risk-safe learning environments (Browne-Ferrigno & Muth, 2003). More importantly, although cohorts are now used more extensively in administrator preparation, little empirical evidence is available about the influence of cohort participation on later professional practice (Browne-Ferrigno, Barnett, & Muth, 2003; Muth & Barnett, 2001).

Work-Embedded Learning: Superintendent Practicum and Internship

As the size and complexity of schools and districts increased during the early twentieth century, the preparation of school and district administrators shifted from workplace apprenticeships focused on "learning by doing" and directed by those who were acknowledged experts to universities that focused on abstract analysis guided by professors. A basic assumption of university-based preparation programs is that knowledge, concepts, skills, and strategies learned in classroom settings are readily transferred and applied to unfamiliar problems in work situations (Hoberman & Mailick, 1994). Findings from empirical studies, however, suggest that this may not be the case. There is equally convincing evidence that the converse is also true: Knowledge, skills, and strategies gained through classroom learning or field-based experiences are not readily transferred to other work settings (Calabrese & Straut, 1999; Resnick, 1986). Moreover, Carraher, Carraher and Schliemann (1985) found that few individuals were successful in solving comparable problems in other circumstances when presented differently. Findings from situated learning research, however, suggest that professional knowledge acquired concurrent with performing related work tends to enhance meaning, retrieval, and transference to new situations (Bridges & Hallinger, 1992). Thus, integrating the acquisition of formal and craft knowledge within a work context can increase both learning and transfer (Singley & Anderson, 1989).

Both Lewin (1951) and Dewey (1974) were strong proponents of learning in context. Rather than treating formal knowledge (theory) and practice (craft knowledge) as separate domains, they viewed them as complementary dimensions of continuous learning. They hypothesized that reinforcing or changing behavior is most likely to occur when it is linked to work. They also note that learning can be enhanced when individuals engage in repeated cycles of abstract learning, proposing how concepts learned may be applied in practice, observing and using them in practice, obtaining feedback, and finally reflecting on their actions. This approach is similar to Bridges' and Hallinger's (1991, 1992) problem-based learning and posits that individuals acquire professional knowledge (theory) before they practice. In other words, professional knowledge helps practitioners to understand problem situations, encode it in a context modeled on practice, and then reflect on the information learned through observing consequences of their actions. They also note that reflective processes provide intentional redundancy that enhances memory and information retrieval.

Although critics often view formal knowledge as irrelevant to practice, Brown, Collins, and Duguid (1989) point out that theories are practical and relevant in that they are based on empirical observations of how individuals work and learn in organizations, so they facilitate the interpretation of events, planning, and implementation strategies. Thus, the common assumption that formal knowledge (theories) and experiential knowledge (practice) are distinctly separate domains is a conspicuous oversimplification of complex learning processes (Björk, 2001b).

Those responsible for superintendent preparation recognize that doing the same things in the same way will not produce different results. They also acknowledge that producing different outcomes will require reconfiguring superintendent preparation and reconnecting the academic and practice arms of the profession. Although most scholars and practitioners agree that knowledge and practice are central to successful skill transfer, preservice professional preparation and inservice development programs tend to either situate learning in classrooms or immerse it in immediate work contexts. A more powerful strategy is to integrate the acquisition of professional knowledge in work settings (Tan, 1989). Although national commission reports, professional associations, and research findings concur that the acquisition of professional knowledge in work-embedded settings is the cornerstone of rebuilding professional preparation programs, illustrating how these several dimensions are complementary is useful.

A comparison of ineffective and effective learning strategies (Figure 4.2) juxtaposes instructional practices and outcomes of conventional and emergent superintendent-preparation programs. The characteristics of effective instructional practices used in restructured educational administration programs (a) emphasize learner-focused inquiry, (b) stress the importance of work-embedded learning, (c) integrate professional and craft knowledge, (d) emphasize relational and systems thinking, and (e) demand that problem-solving activities be informed by research findings and the professional knowledge base. The success of these new instructional practices is dependent upon the success of situating learning in work-embedded, district contexts. Reformers concur that the task of restructuring superintendent-preparation programs involves identifying where knowledge and practice align and splicing them together to enhance learning and work performance.

Superintendent Practicum

Widely ranging opinions are touted regarding whether superintendent practica should be a sheltered experience or an opportunity to participate in actual "high-risk" work (Björk, 2001b). Schön (1992) posits that the purpose of engaging in field-based learning experiences is to "represent essential features of a practice to be learned while enabling students to experience at low risk, vary the pace and focus of the work, and go back to do things over when it seems useful to do so" (p. 179). However, Hoberman and Mailick (1994) assert that the absence of risk can diminish rich opportunities for work-embedded learning. They argue that field-based learning settings should reflect a full range of complex social, economic, and political circumstances that enable and constrain administrator action. In their view, work-embedded learning should involve actual, rather than sheltered, activities that have real consequences for the district and the learner.

Although professional literature and research findings indicate that work-embedded learning should be the core of professional preparation because field-based learning experiences provide powerful ways for aspirants to acquire professional and craft knowledge, student characteristics limit participation. As noted previously, the vast majority of aspiring superintendents attend preparation programs on a part-time basis (McCarthy, 1999). Program participants usually work full-time in midlevel administrative positions and have family obligations that limit their time for learning. Further, lack of external financial support from states and districts precludes participation in extensive full-time, field-based activities.

Superintendent Internship

Internships are recommended as a means for promoting the professional development and socialization of aspirants into a particular community of practice (Argyris & Schön, 1974; Brown & Duguid, 1991; Lave & Wenger, 1991). Hence, while serving as an intern in authentic settings

Figure 4.2 A Comparison of Ineffective and Effective Learning in Traditional and Emerging School District and Superintendent Professional Preparation Programs

Characteristics of Ineffective Learning	Characteristics of Traditional District Organization	Characteristics of Traditional Educational Administration Programs	Characteristics of Effective Learning	Characteristics of Districts as Learning Organizations	Characteristics of Restructured Educational Administration Programs
1. Low transfer	Bureaucratic, narrow definition of tasks and jobs	Instructor-focused, knowledge transfer, emphasis on formal knowledge	1. High transfer	Continuous learning, common vision, self-organizing	Learner-focused, inquiry-oriented, problem-based, field-based
2. Passive learning	Hierarchical arrangement of work, tight supervision, limited worker discretion	Lecture method, concepts taught independent of school contexts	2. Active learning, contextual relevance, problem-based, experiential feedback	Shared decision making and governance, expert knowledge valued	Active learning, integration of formal and clinical experience
3. Strengthen stimulus-response linkages	Preference for the one best answer (way), limited scope of problems and solutions	Break down learning into component parts, strengthen stimulus-response relationships, repetitive learning, reward the one correct answer	3. Strengthen holistic understanding, relationships, search for meaning and sense making	Collective search for problems and solutions	Teach for holistic understanding, constructed knowledge, systems thinking
4. Emphasis on correct answer	Task completion	Emphasis on formal knowledge	4. Emphasis on multiple perspectives and solution strategies	Improve performance	Emphasis on multiple problem-solving strategies
5. Fragmented and decontextualized learning	Short-term task focus, independent of school context	Separation of school-university responsibility for preparing aspiring administrators, course/credit/certification-driven	5. Holistic understanding, integrated systems thinking, context dependent	Long-term perspective, capacity-building orientation	Shared school-university responsibility for preparing aspiring school leaders, context-rich, performance-based

SOURCE: Adapted from Björk (2001b) p. 40, and Berryman, S., & Bailey, T. (1992). *The double helix of education and the economy.* New York: Institute for Education and the Economy, Teachers College, Columbia University.

under the guidance of veteran practitioners, an aspiring superintendent has opportunities to integrate new theories into new practices. Over time, "an intern's theory-in-use becomes aligned with the intern's 'espoused theory' and can be shaped through appropriately guided coaching experience and [ultimately] translated into a theory of practice" (Calabrese & Straut, 1999, p. 402). Through well-designed and -implemented internships, aspiring educational administrators have a "practice ground" (p. 403) that provides opportunities to close the gap between theory and practice. One goal of internships is to assist aspirants to transition from an entry level of competence to a basic before assuming full responsibilities as a certified administrator. Thus, throughout the internship experiences, the aspirant must be an active participant in authentic work responsibilities that require complex problem identification, responsible action to solve the problem, and then reflection upon the outcome of actions taken (Bridges & Hallinger, 1997; Calabrese & Straut, 1999; Schön, 1987).

Internships provide three critically important components of experiential introduction into administrator practice (Murphy, 1992). First, the intern is immersed peripherally into the requisite roles, responsibilities, professional talks, and time requirements of authentic practice. Second, the intern can practice administrative tasks without having full responsibility or accountability for outcomes. And third, the intern has opportunities to observe veteran administrators at work and develop professional relationships that can lead to permanent placement as an administrator. The key to successful field-based experiences—whether part-time clinical practica or full-time internships—is leadership mentoring that supports role socialization for aspirants, fosters professional development for aspiring and practicing administrators alike, and expands leadership capacity building throughout the organization (Browne-Ferrigno & Muth, 2004).

Peer Mentoring: Leadership Capacity Building

Mentoring is a critical aspect of most professional socialization processes and places stewardship for learning crafts of administration and leadership in the hands of veterans who are recognized for their expertise and skills at coaching aspiring members (Beyu & Holmes, 1992; Head & Gray, 1988). Hoberman and Mailick (1994) found that mentoring is essential to the success of work-embedded learning in medical residencies and judicial clerkships. The most recent AASA 10-year study (Glass et al., 2000) reported that mentoring in the profession is a widespread practice. For example, 66% of the responding superintendents had served as mentors to peers, and 78% of that group reported that they had been mentored without regard to district size, age, race, or gender. Glass et al. (2000) found that a larger percentage of CEOs are presently serving as mentors than was the case during previous decades when the first two large-scale studies were conducted. In addition, they reported that a greater percentage of women superintendents (71%) had mentors than did their male counterparts (56%). Furthermore, the percentage of women who reported having mentors increased from 59% in 1992 to 71% in 2000. In addition, a greater percentage of superintendents of color (90%) reported serving as a mentor than did their white colleagues (77%). These data support the contention that mentoring is an inherent, long-standing aspect of the profession.

Superintendents typically mentor colleagues by serving as role models, sharing information, providing feedback, offering insights, and helping to guide reflective practice (Björk, 1999, 2001b). The amount, immediacy, and quality of feedback provided by mentors are directly related to learning and skill transfer. For example, Joyce and Showers (1983) and Joyce (1987) note that mentoring increases learning. When professionals attend staff development sessions to acquire a new skill and the training emphasizes passively learning underlying concepts or theory, only 5% of what is learned is subsequently transferred into practice. When learning theory is coupled with observing demonstration of a related skill, individuals can transfer 10% of what was learned into practice. However, the percentage of transfer increases to 20% when individuals learn about a theory, observe the skill using the theory being demonstrated, and then immediately practice the skill. When feedback by instructors is added to the theory, demonstration, or practice continuum, 25% of the new skill is potentially transferred to practice. Feedback in this context, however, is limited to a literal description of activities and outcomes without opportunity for evaluation, analysis, or reflection. When mentoring is added to this learning sequence (i.e., observation, demonstration, and practice), the percent skill transfer increases to 90% (Figure 4.3).

Unfortunately, most preservice preparation and staff development training programs tend to "include only theory and demonstration with some token practice. Almost none include feedback much less [mentoring] on a regular, systematic basis" (Gottsman, 2000, p. 22).

Mentoring can be a powerful way to augment learning and skill-transference to practice and sustains arguments that work-embedded learning is a central concept to professional learning—provided certain conditions are met (Browne-Ferrigno & Muth, 2004). Mentoring experiences for aspiring administrators need to have clearly defined purposes and goals for all involved participants. Aspiring administrators who enter into mentoring relationships with veteran practitioners must understand their roles as field-based experiential learners, take appropriate risks without debilitating fear of reproach, and assume responsibilities for their own actions and professional growth. Likewise, mentors must be carefully selected and trained to ensure that interactions and relationships with aspiring administrators are mutually beneficial to them as well. Effective mentors must be available to provide constructive guidance, be willing to engage in reflective dialogue, and be able to communicate honestly and openly about their expectations and their actions. Additionally, mentors of

Figure 4.3   Stages of Learning, Mentoring, and Skill Transfer

Stages of Adult Learning	Stages of Mentoring	Amount of Skill Transfer to Work Situations
Abstract Learning	Theory	5%
Proposing Application of Ideas	Theory and Practice	10%
Observing Practice Gaining Work Experience	Theory, Practice, and Demonstration	20%
Obtaining Feedback	Theory, Practice, Demonstration, and Feedback	25%
Reflecting on Actions	Theory, Practice, Demonstration, Feedback, and Mentoring	90%

SOURCE: Björk, L. G., & Keedy, J. (2001). Changing social context of education in the United States: Social justice and the superintendency, *Journal of In-service Education, 27*(3), pp. 405-428. Based on Bridges & Hallinger (1992); Dewey (1974); Gottsman (2000); Joyce (1987); Joyce & Showers (1983).

aspiring administrators need to be not only well respected by their colleagues, highly effective in their own practice, and innovative in their leadership but must also be skilled at providing appropriate levels of oversight and independence (Browne-Ferrigno & Muth, 2004). Through intensive and extensive interaction with new entrants to the community of practice, mentoring also provides ongoing professional development for veteran practitioners, thus steadily improving role performance for all (Lave & Wenger, 1991; Wenger, 1998).

Professional Reflection: Continuous Professional Development

The primary challenge of professional preparation and staff development programs is to build the capacity of aspiring and veteran superintendents into becoming expert problem solvers in key work areas. Schwab (1964) suggests that theories of practice confirm that expert problem solvers use "a variety of theories of action both to guide interpretations of problems and to magnify and diversify what may be a potential solution to a problem" (p. 63). In addition, Berliner (1986) notes that experts tend to use professional and abstract knowledge more frequently than those concerned only with superficial aspects of problems. Furthermore, Berleiter and Scardamalia (1986) add that expert problem solvers develop and use abstract categories and general principles of action more frequently and identify patterns more quickly than others viewed as being less adept.

When comparing the capacity of expert with nonexpert problem solvers in handling unstructured problems, Leithwood and Stager (1989) found that experts (a) are inclined to be very explicit about their assumptions with regard to the hypothetical nature of problems presented, (b) quickly grasp indirect implications of problems presented, (c) readily apply problem-solving principles, (d) commit more time framing the problem, and (e) gather more information relevant to the issue and solution strategy options. In sum, superintendents confronted with complex problems and turbulent environments either must have or must develop the capacity to serve as expert problem solvers.

Developing the capacity of aspiring and veteran superintendents to make sense of ambiguous, complex, and unique problems (Leithwood & Stager, 1989) and then move toward appropriate solution strategies can be greatly enhanced by reflective thinking. Although some professional preparation programs use reflective journals as part of practicum, internship, and staff development experiences, this technique has not been effective in changing aspiring or veteran superintendents' behavior. Short and Rinehart (1993) offer recommendations for altering administrator behavior through reflective thinking processes that involve six steps: (1) Describe a problem faced by superintendents, (2) reflect on how they view the problem, (3) propose alternative solutions and delineate possible consequences, (4) list criteria for satisfactory resolution, (5) articulate the reasons for choosing the alternative solution, and (6) think about what was learned from this particular problem solving activity. Short and Rinehart (1993) found that using these sequential activities helped develop the capacity for reflective thinking and contributed to expert problem identification, decision making, and problem solving. They also noted that interaction with mentors enhanced individuals' capacity for reflective thinking and expert problem solving.

CONCLUSION

Public demand for educational reform not only heightened awareness of the role of superintendents in sustaining systemic reform initiatives but also raised concerns about how the next generation of district leaders are identified, recruited, prepared, selected, evaluated, and retained over time (Björk, 2001a). These circumstances supported unambiguous recommendations from national commissions and task forces that the academic and practice arms of the profession share responsibility for preparation. Although collaboration is highly desirable and can create circumstances that greatly enhance student learning, collaboration across institutional boundaries is often difficult to establish and maintain (Cibulka & Kritek, 1996; Sirotnik & Goodlad, 1988). The call for collaboration, however, has stimulated the creation of a broad array of university-district partnerships, coalitions, consortia, and networks (McCarthy, Kuh, & Beckman, 1997; Norton, 1999) that involve professional preparation of school and district administrators, curriculum design, and course content development. Although schools and universities can mutually benefit from modifying conventional practices to increase the relevancy of leadership-preparation programs, accruing real dividends will depend on radically redefining the respective roles of institutional partners.

Although researchers have found that learning—situated in work contexts—enhances knowledge acquisition and retention and skill transfer, field-based educational administration and professional development programs remain an exception rather than a rule. Three main factors limit the capability of educational administration departments to adopt field-based, work-embedded programs. First, conventional classroom-based instruction is less labor-intensive and less costly than field-based programs. Second, university reward structures tend to value securing external grants, research, and publishing rather than field-related instruction, mentoring, and coaching. Finally, district and state funds are rarely provided to support individuals who pursue superintendency licensure or internships. Although national commission recommendations, research findings, and recent performance-based licensure standards and program-accreditation standards call for fundamental changes in preparation programs toward collaborative field-based, work-embedded models, without political will and financial commitment by states, districts, and universities, these needed innovations will languish until the next round of national commission reports calls our attention to what many in the field presently regard as a blinding flash of the obvious.

APPENDIX

Superintendent-Preparation/Licensing Standards

American Association of School Administrators (focused specifically on superintendents)

Standard 1. Leadership and district culture

Standard 2. Policy and governance

Standard 3. Communications and community relations

Standard 4. Organizational management

Standard 5. Curriculum planning and development

Standard 6. Instructional management

Standard 7. Human resources management

Standard 8. Values and ethics of leadership

Interstate School Leadership Licensure Consortium (focused on all school administrators)

Standard 1. A school administrator is an educational leader who promotes the success of all students by facilitating the development, articulation, implementation, and stewardship of a vision of learning that is shared and supported by the school community.

Standard 2. A school administrator is an educational leader who promotes the success of all students by advocating, nurturing, and sustaining a school culture and instructional program conducive to student learning and staff professional growth.

Standard 3. A school administrator is an educational leader who promotes the success of all students by ensuring management of the organization, operations, and resources for a safe, efficient, and effective learning environment.

Standard 4. A school administrator is an educational leader who promotes the success of all students by collaborating with families and community members, responding to diverse community interests and needs, and mobilizing community resources.

Standard 5. A school administrator is an educational leader who promotes the success of all students by acting with integrity, fairness, and in an ethical manner.

Standard 6. A school administrator is an educational leader who promotes the success of all students by understanding, responding to, and influencing the larger political, social, economic, legal, and cultural context.

REFERENCES

Achilles, C. M. (1994). Searching for the golden fleece: The epic struggle continues. *Educational Administration Quarterly, 30*(1), 6–26.

American Association of Colleges of Teacher Education. (1988). *School leadership preparation: A preface to action.* Washington, DC: Author.

American Association of School Administrators. (1960). *Professional administrators for America's schools* (38th AASA Yearbook). Washington, DC: National Educational Administration.

Argyris, C. (1999). Tacit knowledge in management. In R. J. Sternberg & J. Horvath (Eds.), *Tacit knowledge in professional practice: Researcher and practitioner perspectives* (pp. 123–140). Mahwah, NJ: Lawrence Erlbaum.

Argyris, C., & Schön, D. (1974). *Theory in practice: Increasing professional effectiveness.* San Francisco: Jossey-Bass.

Ashbaugh, C., & Kasten, K. (1992). *The licensure of school administrators: Policy and practice.* Washington, DC: American Association of Colleges for Teacher Education.

Axley, S. R. (1996). *Communication at work: Management and the communication-intensive organization.* Westport, CT: Quorum Books.

Barnett, B. G., Basom, M., Yerkes, D., & Norris, C. (2000). Cohorts in educational leadership programs: Benefits, difficulties, and the potential for developing school leaders. *Educational Administration Quarterly, 36*(2), 255–282.

Barnett, B. G., & Muse, I. (1993). Cohort groups in educational administration. *Journal of School Leadership, 3,* 400–415.

Basom, M., Yerkes, D., Norris, C., & Barnett, B. G. (1995). *Exploring cohorts: Effects on principals and leadership practice.* St. Louis: Evaluative report supported through mini-grant from the Danforth Foundation.

Bauman, P. C. (1996). *Governing education. Public sector reform or privatization.* Boston: Allyn & Bacon.

Berleiter, C., & Scardamalia, M. (1986). Educational relevance of the study of expertise. *Interchange, 17,* 10–24.

Berliner, D. (1986). In pursuit of the expert pedagogue. *Educational Researcher, 15*(7), 5–3.

Beyu, T. M., & Holmes, C. T. (Eds.). (1992). *Mentoring: Contemporary principles and issues.* Reston, VA: Association of Teacher Educators.

Björk, L. G. (1999, April). *Integrating formal and experiential knowledge: A superintendent preparation model.* Paper presented at the annual meeting of the American Educational Research Association, Montreal.

Björk, L. G. (2000). Professional preparation and training. In T. Glass, L. Björk, & C. C. Brunner, *The study of the American superintendency 2000: A look at the superintendent in the new millennium* (pp. 127-166). Arlington, VA: American Association of School Administrators.

Björk, L. G. (2001a). Institutional barriers to educational reform: A superintendent's role in district decentralization. In C. C. Brunner & L. G. Björk (Eds.), *The new superintendency* (pp. 205–228). Oxford, England: JAI, Elsevier Science.

Björk, L. G. (2001b). Preparing the next generation of superintendents: Integrating formal and experiential knowledge. In C. C. Brunner, & L. G. Björk (Eds.). *The new superintendency: Advances in research and theories of school management and educational policy* (pp. 19–54). Greenwich, CT: JAI Press.

Björk, L. G. (2002, February). *Tacit knowledge: How successful superintendents improve student learning.* Featured presentation on Successful Superintendents: What It Takes to Move School Systems Toward Improved Student Achievement. Paper presented at the National Conference on Education, American Association of School Administrators, San Diego, CA.

Björk, L. G., & Gurley, D. K. (2003). *Superintendent as educational statesman.* Paper presented at the annual meeting of the American Educational Research Association, Chicago.

Björk, L. G., Kowalski, T. J., & Young, M. D. (2005). National education reform reports: Implications for professional preparation and development. In L. G. Björk & T. J. Kowalski (Eds.), *The contemporary superintendent: Preparation, practice, and development.* Thousand Oaks, CA: Corwin.

Björk, L. G., & Lindle, J. C. (2001). Superintendents and interest groups. *Educational Policy, 15*(1), 76–91.

Björk, L. G., Lindle, J. C., & Van Meter, E. (1999). A summing up. *Educational Administration Quarterly, 35*(4), 658–664.

Blase, J., & Anderson, G. (1995). *The micropolitics of educational leadership: From control to empowerment.* New York: Teachers College Press.

Bridges, E., & Hallinger, P. (1991). Problem-based learning: A promising approach for preparing educational administrators. *UCEA Review, 23*(3), 3–6.

Bridges, E., & Hallinger, P. (1992). *Problem-based learning for administrators.* Eugene, OR: ERIC/CEM.

Bridges, E., & Hallinger, P. (1997). Using problem-based learning to prepare educational leaders. *Peabody Journal of Education, 72*(2), 131–146.

Broad Foundation & Thomas B. Fordham Institute. (2003). *Better leaders for America's schools: A manifesto.* Los Angeles: Authors.

Brown, J. S., Collins, S., & Duguid, P. (1989). Situated cognition and the culture of learning. *Educational Researcher, 18*(1), 32–42.

Brown, J. S., & Duguid, P. (1991). Organizational learning and communities of practice: Toward a unified view of working, learning and innovation. *Organizational Science, 2*(1), 40–57.

Browne-Ferrigno, T., Barnett, B. G., & Muth, R. (2003). Cohort program effectiveness: A call for a national research agenda. In F. C. Lunenburg & C. S. Carr (Eds.), *Shaping the future: Policy, partnerships, and emerging perspectives* (pp. 274–290). 11th Annual Yearbook of the National Council of Professors of Educational Administration. Lanham, MD: Scarecrow Education.

Browne-Ferrigno, T., & Muth, R. (2003). Effects of cohorts on learners. *Journal of School Leadership, 13*(6), 621–643.

Browne-Ferrigno, T., & Muth, R. (2004). Leadership mentoring in clinical practice: Role socialization, professional development, and capacity building. *Educational Administration Quarterly.*

Browne-Ferrigno, T., & Shoho, A. (2004). Careful selection of aspiring principals: An exploratory analysis of leadership preparation program admission practices. In C. Carr & C. Fulmer (Eds.), *Educational leadership: Knowing the way, showing the way, going the way* (pp. 172–189). 12th Annual Yearbook of the National Council of Professors of Educational Administration. Lanham, MD: Scarecrow Education.

Brunner, C., Grogan, M. & Björk, L. (2002). Shifts in the discourse defining the superintendency: Historical and current foundations of the position. In J. Murphy (Ed.), *The educational leadership challenge: Redefining leadership for the 21st century. Ninety-ninth yearbook of the National Society for the Study of Education (NSSE)* (pp. 211-238). Chicago: University of Chicago.

Calabrese, R. L., & Straut, D. (1999). Reconstructing the internship. *Journal of School Leadership, 9,* 400–421.

Callahan, R. E. (1962). *Education and the cult of efficiency: A study of the social forces that have shaped the administration of public schools.* Chicago: University of Chicago Press.

Callahan, R. E. (1966). *The superintendent of schools: A historical analysis.* (ERIC Document Reproduction Service No. ED 0104 410)

Carraher, T., Carraher, D., & Schliemann, A. (1985). Mathematics in the streets and in schools. *British Journal of Developmental Psychology, 3,* 21–29.

Carter, G. R., & Cunningham, W. G. (1997). *The American school superintendent: Leading in an age of pressures.* San Francisco: Jossey-Bass.

Carver, F. D. (1988, June). *The evaluation of the study of educational administration.* Paper presented at the EAAA Allerton House Conference, University of Illinois at Urbana-Champaign.

Chance, P. L., & Björk, L. G. (2004). The social dimensions of public relations. In T. J. Kowalski (Ed.), *Public relations in schools* (3rd ed.) (pp. 125–148). Upper Saddle River, NJ: Merrill, Prentice Hall.

Chapman, C. H. (1997). *Becoming a superintendent: Challenges of school district leadership.* Upper Saddle River, NJ: Merrill, Prentice Hall.

Cibulka, J., & Kritek, W. (1996). *Coordination among schools, families, and communities: Prospects for educational reform.* Albany: State University of New York Press.

Conrad, C. (1994). *Strategic organizational communication: Toward the twenty-first century* (3rd ed.). Fort Worth, TX: Harcourt Brace.

Cooper, B. S., & Boyd, W. L. (1987). The evolution of training for school administrators. In J. Murphy & P. Hallinger (Eds.), *Approaches to administrative training in education* (pp. 3–27). Albany: State University of New York Press.

Cooper, B. S., Fusarelli, L. D., Jackson, B. L., & Poster, J. (2002). Is "superintendent preparation" an oxymoron? Analyzing changes in programs, certification, and control. *Leadership and Policy in Schools, 1*(3), 242–255.

Cremin, L. A. (1951). *American common school: An historical conception.* New York: Columbia University Teachers College.

Cronin, J. M. (1973). *The control of urban schools: Perspective on the power of educational reformers.* New York: Free Press.

Crowson, R. L., & McPherson, R. B. (1987). The legacy of the theory movement: Learning from the new tradition. In J. Murphy & P. Hallinger (Eds.), *Approaches to administrative training in education* (pp. 45–64). Albany: State University of New York Press.

Cuban, L. (1976). *The urban school superintendent: A century and a half of change.* Bloomington, IN: Phi Delta Kappa Educational Foundation.

Cuban, L. (1988). How schools change reforms: Redefining reform success and failure. *Teachers College Record, 99*(3), 453–477.

Culbertson, J. A. (1981). Antecedents of the theory movement. *Educational Administration Quarterly, 17*(1), 25–47.

Cunningham, L., & Hentges, J. (1982). *The American school superintendency 1982: A summary report.* Arlington, VA: American Association of School Administrators.

Dewey, J. (1974). *John Dewey on education: Selected writings.* R. D. Archambault (Ed.). Chicago: University of Chicago Press.

Farquhar, R. H. (1977). Preparatory programs in educational administration. In L. L. Cunningham, W. G. Hack, & R. O. Nystrand (Eds.), *Educational administration: The developing decades* (pp. 329–357). Berkeley, CA: McCutchan.

Feistritzer, E. (2003). *Certification of public-school administrators.* Washington, DC: National Center for Education Information.

Fusarelli, B. C., & Fusarelli, L. D. (2005). Reconceptualizing the superintendency: Superintendents as social scientists and social activists. In L. G. Björk & T. J. Kowalski (Eds.), *The contemporary superintendent: Preparation, practice, and development.* Thousand Oaks, CA: Corwin.

Geltner, B. B. (1994). *The poser of structural and symbolic redesign: Creating a collaborative learning community in higher education.* Ypsilanti: Eastern Michigan University. (ERIC Document Reproduction Service No. ED 374 757)

Getzels, J. W. (1977). Educational administration twenty years later, 1954–1974. In L. Cunningham, W. Hack, & R. Nystrand (Eds.), *Educational administration: The developing decades* (pp. 3–24). Berkeley, CA: McCutchan.

Gideon, B. H. (2002). Structuring schools for teacher collaboration. *Education Digest, 68*(2), 30–34.

Glass, T. E. (1992). *The study of the American school superintendency 1992: America's education leaders in a time of reform.* Arlington, VA: American Association of School Administrators.

Glass, T. E., Björk, L. G., & Brunner, C. C. (2000). *The 2000 study of the American school superintendency: A look at the superintendent of education in the new millennium.* Arlington, VA: American Association of School Administrators.

Goldring, E., & Greenfield, W. (2002). Understanding the evolving concept of leadership in education: Roles, expectations, and dilemmas. In J. Murphy (Ed.), *The educational leadership challenge: Redefining leadership for the 21st century* (pp. 1–19). Chicago: University of Chicago Press.

Gottsman, B. (2000). *Peer coaching for effectiveness* (2nd ed.). Lanham, MD: Scarecrow Press.

Hallinger, P., & Murphy, J. (1982). The superintendent's role in promoting instructional leadership. *Administrator's Notebook, 30*(6), 1–4.

Hatsopoulis, N., & Hatsopoulis, G. (1999). The role of tacit knowledge in management. In R. Sternberg & J. Horvath (Eds.), *Tacit knowledge in professional practice: Researcher and practitioner perspectives* (pp. 141–152). Mahwah, NJ: Lawrence Erlbaum.

Head, F., & Gray, M. (1988). The legacy of mentor: Insights into Western history, literature and the media. *International Journal of Mentoring, 2*(2), 26–33.

Heckman, P. E. (1993). School restructuring in practice: Reckoning with the culture of school. *International Journal of Educational Reform, 2*(3), 263–272.

Hess, F. M. (2003). Lifting the barrier. *Education Next, 3*(4), 12–19.

Hightower, A. M., Knapp, M. S., Marsh, J. A., & McLaughlin, M. W. (2003). *School districts and instructional renewal.* New York: Teachers College Press.

Hill, M. S. (1995). Educational leadership cohort models: Changing the talk to change the walk. *Planning and Changing, 26*(3/4), 179–189.

Hoberman, S., & Mailick, S. (1994). Some learning theory. In S. Hoberman & S. Mailick (Eds.), *Professional education in the United States: Experiential learning, issues and prospects* (pp. 19–26). Westport, CT: Praeger.

Horvath, J., Williams, W., Forsyth, G., Sweeney, P., Sternberg, R., & McNally, J. (1994). *Tacit knowledge in military leadership: A review of the literature.* Technical Report 1017. Alexandria, VA: United States Army Research Institute for the Behavioral and Social Sciences.

Howlett, P. (1993). The politics of school leaders, past and future. *Education Digest, 58*(9), 18–21.

Hoyle, J. R. (1993). *Professional standards for the superintendency.* Arlington, VA: American Association of School Administrators.

Hoyle, J. R., Björk, L. G., Collier, V., & Glass, T. E. (2004). *The superintendent as CEO: Standards-based performance.* Thousand Oaks, CA: Corwin.

Johnson, B. C., & Fusarelli, L. D. (2003, April). *Superintendent as social scientist.* Paper presented at the annual meeting of the American Educational Research Association, Chicago.

Johnson, S. M. (1996). *Leading to change: The challenge of the new supeintendency.* San Francisco: Jossey-Bass.

Joyce, B. R. (1987). *Staff development awareness.* Columbia, SC: Unpublished paper.

Joyce, B. R., & Showers, B. (1980). Improving in-service training: The message of research. *Educational Leadership, 37,* 379–385.

Joyce, B. R., & Showers, B. (1983). *Power in staff development through research on training.* Washington, DC: Association for Supervision and Curriculum Development.

Kochan, F. K., Jackson, B. L., & Duke, D. L. (1999). *A thousand voices from the firing line: A study of educational leaders, their jobs, their preparation and the problems they face.* Columbia, MO: University Council for Educational Administration.

Kowalski, T. J. (1995). *Keepers of the flame: Contemporary urban superintendents.* Thousand Oaks, CA: Corwin.

Kowalski, T. J. (1998). The role of communication in providing leadership for school reform. *Mid-Western Educational Researcher, 11*(1), 32–40.

Kowalski, T. J. (1999). *The school superintendent: Theory, practice, and cases.* Upper Saddle River, NJ: Merrill, Prentice Hall.

Kowalski, T. J. (2000). Cultural change paradigms and administrator communication. *Contemporary Education, 71*(2), 5–10.

Kowalski, T. J. (2001). The future of local school governance: Implications for board members and superintendents. In C. C. Brunner & L. G. Björk (Eds.), *The new superintendency* (pp. 183–201). Oxford, England: JAI, Elsevier Science.

Kowalski, T. J. (2003, April). *The superintendent as communicator.* Paper presented at the annual meeting of the American Educational Research Association, Chicago.

Kowalski, T. J. (2005). Evolution of the school district superintendent position. In L. G. Björk & T. J. Kowalski (Eds.), *The contemporary superintendent: Preparation, practice, and development.* Thousand Oaks, CA: Corwin.

Kowalski, T. J., & Björk, L. G. (2005). Role expectations of the district superintendent: Implications for deregulating preparation and licensing. *Journal of Thought 40*(2), 73–96.

Kowalski, T. J., & Glass, T. E. (2002). Preparing superintendents in the 21st century. In B. Cooper & L. D. Fusarelli (Eds.), *The promises and perils facing today's school superintendent* (pp. 41–60). Lanham, MD. Scarecrow Education.

Kowalski, T. J. & Keedy, J. L. (2005). Preparing superintendents to be effective communicators. In L. G. Björk & T. J. Kowalski (Eds.), *The contemporary superintendent: Preparation, practice, and development.* Thousand Oaks, CA: Corwin.

Lave, J., & Wenger, E. (1991). *Situated learning: Legitimate peripheral participation.* New York: Cambridge University Press.

Leithwood, K. A. (1995a, March). Cognitive perspectives on school leadership. *Journal of School Leadership, 5,* 115–135.

Leithwood, K. A. (Ed.). (1995b). *Effective school district leadership: Transforming politics into education.* Albany: State University of New York Press.

Leithwood, K. A., & Stager, M. (1989). Expertise in principals' problem solving. *Educational Administration Quarterly, 25,* 126–161.

Leithwood, K. A., & Steinbach, R. (1992). Improving the problem solving expertise of school administrators: Theory and practice. *Education and Urban Society, 24*(3), 317–345.

Leithwood, K. A., & Steinbach, R. (1995). *Expert problem solving: Evidence from school and district leaders.* Albany: State University of New York Press.

Lewin, K. (1951). *Field theory in social science.* New York: Harper & Row.

March, J. G. (1974). Analytical skills and the university training of educational administrators. *Journal of Educational Administration, 12*(1), 17–44.

March, J. G. (1978). American public school administration: A short analysis. *School Review, 86*(2), 217–250.

Marchant, G., & Robinson, J. (1999). Is knowing the tax code all it takes to be a tax expert? On the development of legal expertise. In R. J. Sternberg & J. A. Horvath (Eds.), *Tacit knowledge in professional practice* (pp. 155–182). Mahwah, NJ: Erlbaum.

McCarthy, M. (1999). The evolution of educational leadership preparation programs. In J. Murphy & K. S. Louis (Eds.), *Handbook of research on educational administration* (2nd ed.) (pp. 119–139). San Francisco: Jossey-Bass.

McCarthy, M., Kuh, G., & Beckman, J. (1997). Characteristics and attitudes of educational administration doctoral students. *Phi Delta Kappan, 61*(3), 200–203.

Melby, E. O. (1955). *Administering community education.* Englewood Cliffs, NJ: Prentice Hall.

Milstein, M. M., Bobroff, B. M., & Restine, L. N. (1991). *Internship programs in educational administration: A guide to preparing educational leaders.* New York: Teachers College Press.

Milstein, M. M., & Krueger, J. A. (1997). Improving educational administration preparation programs: What we have learned over the past decade. *Peabody Journal of Education, 72*(2), 100–106.

Murphy, J. (1990a). Preparing school administrators for the twenty-first century: The reform agenda. In B. Mitchell & L. L. Cunningham (Eds.), *Educational leadership and changing contexts of families, communities, and schools.* (1990 NSSE Yearbook). Chicago: University of Chicago Press.

Murphy, J. (1990b). The reform of school administration: Pressures and calls for change. In J. Murphy (Ed.), *The reform of American public education in the 1980's: Perspectives and cases.* Berkeley: McCutchan.

Murphy, J. (1991). *Restructuring schools.* New York: Teachers College Press.

Murphy, J. (1992). *The landscape of leadership preparation: Reframing the education of school administrators.* Nashville, TN: National Center for Educational Leadership.

Murphy, J. (1993). Alternative designs: New directions. In J. Murphy (Ed.), *Preparing tomorrow's school leaders: Alternative designs* (pp. 225–253). University Park, PA: University Council for Educational Administration.

Murphy, J. (1994). The changing role of the superintendency in restructuring districts in Kentucky. *School Effectiveness and School Improvement, 5*(4), 349–375.

Murphy, J. (1999a). *The quest for a century: Notes on the state of the profession of educational leadership.* Columbus, MO: University Council for Educational Administration.

Murphy, J. (1999b). The reform of the profession: A self-portrait. In J. Murphy & P. Forsyth (Eds.), *Educational administration: A decade of reform.* Thousand Oaks, CA: Corwin.

Murphy, J., & Datnow, A. (2002). Leadership lessons from comprehensive school reform designs. In J. Murphy & A. Datnow (Eds.), *Leadership for school reform: Lessons from comprehensive school reform designs* (pp. 263–278). Thousand Oaks, CA: Corwin.

Murphy, J., & Hallinger, P. (1986). The superintendent as instructional leader: Findings from effective school districts. *Journal of Educational Administration, 24*(2), 213–236.

Murphy, J., & Hallinger, P. (1988). The characteristics of instructionally effective school districts. *Journal of Educational Research, 81*(3), 175–181.

Muth, R., & Barnett, B. G. (2001). Making the case for professional preparation: Using research for program improvement and political support. *Educational Leadership and Administration: Teaching and Program Development, 13,* 109–120.

National Commission of Excellence in Education. (1983). *A nation at risk: The imperative for educational reform.* Washington, DC: Government Printing Office.

National Policy Board for Educational Administration. (1989). *Improving the preparation of school administrators: An agenda for reform.* Charlottesville, VA: Author.

Neisser, U. (1976). General, academic, and artificial intelligence. In L. Resnick (Ed.), *The nature of intelligence* (pp. 135–144). Hillsdale, NJ: Erlbaum.

Nestor-Baker, N., & Hoy, W. (2001). Tacit knowledge of school superintendents: Its nature, meaning, and content. *Educational Administration Quarterly, 37*(1), 86–129.

Newel, C. (1952). *Handbook for the development of internship programs in educational administration.* New York: CPEA-MAR, Bureau of Publications, Teachers College, Columbia University.

Norton, M. (1999). *The status of student cohorts in educational administration preparation programs.* Tempe: Arizona State University, Division of Educational Leadership and Policy Studies.

Patel, V., Arocha, J., & Kaufman, D. (1999). Expertise and tacit knowledge in medicine. In R. J. Sternberg & J. Horvath (Eds.), *Tacit knowledge in professional practice: Researcher and practitioner perspectives* (pp. 75–100). Mahwah, NJ: Erlbaum.

Petersen, G. J., & Barnett, B. G. (2003, April). *The superintendent as instructional leader: History, evolution and future of the role.* Paper presented at the annual meeting of the American Educational Research Association, Chicago.

Peterson, K. D., Murphy, J., & Hallinger, P. (1987). Superintendents'perspective of the control and coordination of the technical core operations in effective school districts. *Educational Administration Quarterly, 23*(1), 79–95.

Polyani, M. (1967). *The tacit dimension.* Garden City, NY: Doubleday.

Reber, A. (1989). Implicit learning and tacit knowledge. *Journal of Experimental Psychology: General, 118,* 219–235.

Resnick, L. (1986). Constructing knowledge in schools. In L. Liben & D. Feldman (Eds.), *Development and learning: Conflict and congruence* (pp. 19–50). Hillsdale, NJ: Erlbaum.

Schlechty, P. C. (1997). *Inventing better schools.* San Francisco: Jossey-Bass.

Schön, D. A. (1987). Educating the reflective practitioner: Toward a new design for teaching and learning in the professions. San Francisco: Jossey-Bass.

Schön, D. A. (1992). The crisis of professional knowledge and pursuit of an epistomology of practice. *Journal of Interprofessional Care, 6*(1), 8–19.

Schwab, J. J. (1964). The professorship in educational administration: Theory—art—practice. In D. J. Willower & J. A. Culbertson (Eds.), *The professorship in educational administration* (pp. 47–70). Columbus, OH: University Council for Educational Administration.

Sergiovanni, T. (1989). Mystics, neats, and scruffies: Informing professional practice in educational administration. *Phi Delta Kappan, 72,* 521–526.

Sergiovanni, T. (1991). Constructing and changing theories of practice: The key to preparing school administrators. *Urban Review, 23,* 39–49.

Short, P., & Rinehart, J. (1993). Reflection as a means of developing expertise. *Educational Administration Quarterly, 29*(4), 501–521.

Singley, M., & Anderson, J. (1989). *The transfer of cognitive skill.* Cambridge, MA: Harvard University Press.

Sirotnik, K., & Goodlad, J. (Eds.). (1988). *School-university partnerships in action.* New York: Teachers College Press.

Spring, J. H. (1994). *The American school, 1642–1993* (3rd ed.). New York: McGraw-Hill.

Starratt, R. K. (1991). Building an ethical school: A theory for practice in educational leadership. *Educational Administration Quarterly, 27*(2), 185–202.

Sternberg, R. J. (1990). *Metaphors of mind: Conceptions of the nature of intelligence.* New York: Cambridge University Press.

Sternberg, R. J. (1996). *Successful intelligence: How practical and creative intelligence determine success in life.* New York: Simon & Schuster.

Sternberg, R. J., Forsyth, G., Hedlund, J., Horvath, J. A., Wagoner, R., Williams, W. M., Snook, S., & Grigorenko, E. (2000). *Practical intelligence in everyday life.* Cambridge, England: Cambridge University Press.

Sternberg, R. J., Wagoner, R., & Okagaki, L. (1993). Practical intelligence: The nature and role of knowledge in work and school. In H. W. Reese & J. M. Puckett (Eds.), *Mechanisms of everyday cognition* (pp. 205–227). Hillsdale, NJ: Erlbaum.

Sternberg, R. J., Wagoner, R., Williams, W. M., & Horvath, J. A. (1995). Testing common sense. *American Psychologist, 50,* 912–927.

Stout, R. T. (1973). *New approaches to recruitment and selection of educational administrators.* Columbus, OH: University Council for Educational Administration.

Tan, H. (1989). *Private sector training in the United States.* New York: Institute on Education and the Economy, Teachers College, Columbia University.

Thomas, W. B., & Moran, K. J. (1992). Reconsidering the power of the superintendent in the progressive period. *American Educational Research Journal, 29*(1), 22–50.

Tyack, D., & Hansot, E. (1982). *Managers of virtue: Public school leadership in America, 1820–1980.* New York: Basic Books.

Usdan, M. D. (2002). Reactions to articles commissioned by the National Commission for the Advancement of Education Leadership Preparation. *Educational Administration Quarterly, 38*(2), 300–307.

Wagoner, R. (1987). Tacit knowledge in everyday intelligent behavior. *Journal of Personality and Social Psychology, 52*(6), 1236–1247.

Wagoner, R., & Carter, R. (1996). Research outside the field of education. In K. Leithwood, J. Chapman, D. Corson, P. Hallinger, & A. Hart (Eds.), *International handbook of educational leadership and administration* (pp. 447–476). Boston: Kluwer.

Wagoner, R., & Sternberg, R. J. (1985). Practical intelligence in real-world pursuits: The role of tacit knowledge. *Journal of Personality and Social Psychology, 49*(2), 436–458.

Wagoner, R., Sujan, H., Sujan, M., Rashotte, C., & Sternberg, R. J. (1999). Tacit knowledge in sales. In R. Sternberg & J. Horvath (Eds.), *Tacit knowledge in professional practice* (pp. 155–182). Mahwah, NJ: Erlbaum.

Wenger, E. (1998). *Communities of practice: Learning, meaning, and identity.* New York: Cambridge University Press.

Wert-Gray, S., Center, C., Brashers, D. E., & Meyers, R. A. (1991). Research topics and methodological orientations in organizational communication: A decade of review. *Communication Studies, 42*(2), 141–154.

Wise, A. (1992). The case for restructuring teacher preparation. In L. Darling-Hammond (Ed.), *Excellence in teacher education: Helping teachers develop learning centered schools* (pp. 179–201). Washington, DC: National Education Association.

Young, K., Chambers, C., Kells, H., & Associates. (1983). *Understanding accreditation.* San Francisco: Jossey-Bass.

Young, M. D., Petersen, G. J., & Short, P. (2002). The complexity of substantive reform: A call for interdependence among key stakeholders. *Educational Administration Quarterly, 38*(2), 137–175.

5

The Superintendent as Instructional Leader

Current Practice, Future Conceptualizations, and Implications for Preparation

George J. Petersen and Bruce G. Barnett

Since the inception of the role, the demands on and expectations of the district superintendent have changed as a result of numerous social, political, and economic trends in our society. As Callahan (1964a) reminds us, "Sometimes the major thrust for change [of the superintendent's role] has come from outside the profession and sometimes within. Actually, the changes have always been a result of both forces—it is simply a matter of which is strongest in a particular period" (p. 3). Although most historical analyses imply that a specific role of the superintendent may have dominated in a particular time period, other scholars suggest that superintendents have always been expected to blend multiple roles, each of which might have dominated the scene in earlier years. For instance, Cuban (1976) contends that during the 1960s and 1970s, superintendents needed to be (a) a teacher-scholar (with expertise in educational and instructional leadership), (b) an administrative chief (with expertise in scientific management), and (c) a negotiator-statesman (with expertise in statesmanship, conflict resolution, and community support). Kowalski (1999), in summarizing Cuban's work, maintains the following:

> Superintendents were expected to assume each of these roles at varying times with different publics. Superintendents' success, and even survival, often depended on their ability to make successful transitions among these three distinct roles. To achieve this goal, they not only required an understanding of these roles, they also had to possess the personal flexibility to make appropriate adjustments. (p. 10)

The publication of *A Nation at Risk* in 1983, which condemned the state of American public education, further eroded confidence in schools and their leaders (Brunner et al., 2002; Carter & Cunningham, 1997). In addition, much of the educational literature of this era blamed the ills of education on superintendents, who were seen as thwarting change, rather than being innovators for improvement (Brunner et al., 2002). Serious questions about the nation's ability to compete at the international level were raised, often criticizing schools for the dismal comparisons with the achievement of students from other countries. To stimulate educational renewal, many state and national organizations began to develop standards and performance goals for students (Carter & Cunningham, 1997). Capping the decade, during President George H. Bush's education summit in Charlottesville, Virginia, with the nation's governors, national performance goals for education were established. As a result of the growing national and local pressures for school reform and performance standards, superintendents' power was further eroded, forcing them to build political coalitions, gain the support of a variety of external stakeholders, and develop strategic plans for school improvement.

This chapter examines and details various forces that have helped shape the work of the district superintendent. More specifically, this chapter centers on the role of superintendent as a "teacher of teachers." Using conceptual and empirical evidence along with current discourse, the authors discuss the relevance and context of the role of instructional leader in contemporary practice. In this chapter, we examine the influence of internal and external pressures along with extant work that challenges as well as supports the concept of superintendents as instructional leaders. This chapter also spends time presenting what we believe will be the future roles, conceptualizations, and implications for preparation and practice. We also consider how these new responsibilities will affect the preparation and daily practice of school leaders.

INSTRUCTIONAL LEADERSHIP
IN AN ERA OF REFORM

Since the early 1990s, individuals and organizations intent on educational reform have focused on a number of issues, but none more vigorously than the issue of public school governance and leadership. Federal and state legislation, litigation, changing social and economic conditions, alternative schooling, and increased calls for accountability have resulted in an uneasy tension between public school leaders and their communities. With growing importance on academic achievement, technology, diversity, equity, and the rapidly changing demographics of school districts in the United States, superintendents are required to make decisions about numerous and sometimes conflicting issues (Fusarelli, Cooper, & Carella, 2002). For school superintendents, responding to educational needs arising from social and economic problems is only a small part of their responsibilities. More fundamental is their involvement in promoting, facilitating, and maintaining organizational relationships and policies that advance the technical core of curriculum and instruction (Elmore, 1999; Morgan & Petersen, 2002).

In 1993, John Hoyle was the chairman of the American School Board Association Commission on Standards for the Superintendency. This commission published professional standards for the district superintendent. They ranged from leadership and district culture to organizational management to values and ethics of school leadership. Yet one standard is particularly germane for the focus of this manuscript: the standard of Instructional Management. This standard required superintendents to implement a system that would incorporate research findings on learning and instruction, instructional time, and resources to maximize student outcomes and to apply best practices in the integration of curriculum and resources for multicultural sensitivity as well as assessment strategies to help all students achieve high levels.

Although these standards were published nearly a decade ago, many within and outside the profession continue to believe the work of superintendents is so fragmented and consumed with politics and conflict that their ability to be instructional leaders is, at best, an elusive goal. Yet given the relentless scrutiny schools are receiving due to increased expectations of national standards and assessments (as well as privatization, choice, and special education), superintendents must expand their professional knowledge base and devote more time to the core issue of schooling: curriculum and instruction (Kowalski, 1999). In discussing the superintendent of the future, Doyle (1998) states, "The true superintendent will be the CAO: Chief Academic Officer. That is what schools should be about, that is what school leadership should be about . . . academics first, academics last. Everything else should contribute to the school's academic mission"

(p. 16). In an effort to understand the evolution of the role of instructional leader, we explore the current political mêlée that includes an examination of many of the external influences, internal pressures, and changes in the governance structure of many districts. Through an exploration of the extant literature, we also address the current discourse and debate surrounding the notion of the superintendent as instructional leader.

THE CURRENT POLITICAL MÊLÉE

Much of the work and controversy that a modern superintendent faces does not originate from their local board of education; they come from outside the school. Information and demands—requests from parents, teachers, principals, members of the board, federal and state departments, external advocates and programs, community groups, and so on—constantly bombard superintendents. In most school districts, the superintendent's work is subject to continual interruption as both internal and external groups thrust new information upon them (O'Day, 2002).

External Influences

As educational reform shifts in form and texture (Murphy, 1990), strongly voiced arguments for issues such as site-based management, teacher empowerment, parental choice coupled with reforms aimed at school curriculum, graduation requirements, the testing of teachers and students, and a growing disenchantment with bureaucratic forms of school management have brought significant challenges to the superintendent's authority and leadership (Grogan, 1996; Norton, Webb, Dlugosh, & Sybouts, 1996). Responding to calls for greater involvement of building administrators, teachers, and the community, superintendents often find themselves in a position in which they must support and facilitate school-based decisions, shared leadership, and other site-based approaches to school leadership (Carter & Cunningham, 1997; Crowson, 1987). A recent example is the Goals 2000 legislation, which requires school leaders to build broad-based panels and develop programs that will enable community members to participate in leadership decision making (Riley, 1994).

The external pressure for change and accountability has also affected the governance structure of many school districts. Ideas such as charter schools, choice, and decentralization provoke questions about the need for boards of education and the role and relationship they should assume with the district superintendent (Kowalski, 1999). In fact, a significant downturn in student achievement and K–12 education's ever-increasing demand on state budgets have motivated 23 states to pass laws authorizing state or city takeovers of schools perceived to be "in crisis" (Chaddock, 2002). In cities such as Boston (1991), Chicago (1995), Cleveland (1998), and

Philadelphia (2001), the state engineered takeovers because boards were not exhibiting leadership, and students were failing academically. Although the dysfunctionality and limitations of school boards and their reputations for pursuing single issues, personal power, fractionalism, and undermining the authority of the district superintendent have been noted (Blumberg & Blumberg, 1985; Danzberger, Kirst, & Usdan, 1992; Glass, Björk, & Brunner, 2000; Iannacone & Lutz, 1994; Trump, 1986), drastic changes in the governance structure severely impede the superintendent's ability to effectively implement the numerous reform initiatives faced by schools (Konnert & Augenstein, 1995). One could argue that boards should be maintained because potentially they represent the community and the purposes of education in a democracy (Schlechty, 1992). But in this rapidly changing environment, the notion of local control and local decision making becomes less and less a daily reality for districts throughout the nation (Petersen & Short, 2001).

Recent legislator enthusiasm for high-stakes testing seems to have reached a fever pitch (Cunningham & Sperry, 2001). Federal and state policymakers have concluded that schools are in crisis and that one option is reliance on mandates oriented at increasing educational outputs, especially as measured by standardized tests (Kowalski, 1999). This current climate with its emphasis on accountability has placed an enormous amount of political pressure on schools to demonstrate effective leadership at the district level (Ashbaugh, 2000; No Child Left Behind, 2002; Petersen & Young, 2004). O'Day (2002) points out that many of the current accountability policies, such as reporting of test scores, assume that after schools possess current and accurate data about the achievement of their students, they will take whatever action is necessary to improve the learning outcomes. Given that assumption, district leaders will now be held accountable to provide powerful, authentic, and rigorous learning for all students (Carter & Cunningham, 1997; No Child Left Behind, 2002).

> New accountability approaches, by their very nature, seek to influence from the outside what goes on inside schools. Moreover, such policies assume that external forces can play a determining role in changing the internal workings of schools. The limitations of such assumptions, however, have provided grist for the vast literature on policy implementation in education. (O'Day, 2002, p. 3)

Although there continues to be debate regarding the potential effects these accountability approaches will have on the achievement of students, it is important to keep in mind that these policy streams are very influential in the work of school superintendents and their attempts to be instructional leaders. "The nature of the community, prevailing laws, policies, and regulations, the people and groups who constitute the school district, and specific tasks influence administrator behavior" (Kowalski, 1999,

p. 36). The heart of the issue is the problematic relationship between external and internal sources of control and the implications of this relationship for organizational learning and improvement (O'Day, 2002). But rules dictated from outside the organization seem to have little impact, especially when it comes to the core technology of teaching and learning (Elmore, 1996).

Internal Pressures

Not only are superintendents required to be attentive to external issues that affect their districts, they are expected to be knowledgeable about all facets of education within the district as well (Grogan & Andrews, 2002). Superintendents understand the importance, complexity, and conflict of their role as instructional leaders (Blumberg & Blumberg, 1985; Carter & Cunningham, 1997), and few of them, regardless of district size, openly reject the argument that they should be focused on matters of curriculum and instruction (Kowalski, 1999; Petersen, 2002). Yet they frequently perceive this ideal role to be virtually unattainable because of numerous internal issues such as collective bargaining, school and community politics, and board relations (Trump, 1986). Anyone who has studied organizations understands that large formal systems such as public education tend toward bureaucracy and reliance on formal rules (O'Day 2002), and these systems have internal mechanisms that control the behavior of individuals and subunits (March, 1994).

> Superintendents lack effective tools with which to promote change. People the superintendent did not hire and cannot fire staff district organizations. Superintendents have little discretion over salaries, have few sanctions at their disposal, and are constrained by union contract . . . Furthermore the physical structure of most schools places the superintendent a long way from the classroom. (Hess, 1999, p. 188)

Perhaps one of the most time-consuming internal pressures faced by district superintendents is establishing and maintaining an effective and positive relationship with their boards of education. Research has repeatedly articulated that the relationship between the superintendent and board of education has far-reaching leadership and policy implications that greatly affect the quality of a district's educational program (McCurdy, 1992; Nygren, 1992; Odden, 1995). Blumberg and Blumberg (1985) suggest that the most critical association in running a school system is the interplay between the superintendent and board of education. Poor relations between these groups hinder the district's capability to serve the educational needs of the community (Feuerstein & Opfer, 1998). Yet in the long struggle for improvement of public schools, local boards of education have often been depicted as obstacles to reform (Hill, 2003). Local superintendents are expected to create school improvement strategies and work with the board of education to accomplish these goals. However, as most superintendents discover, the complex agency structure of school boards often channels and constrains their efforts (Smith & O'Day, 1991). With numerous investigations that point to the importance of the board of education-superintendent relationship in improving the academic achievement of the district, Kowalski (1995) found that there remains a general question regarding the importance school boards actually place on the superintendent's role as an instructional leader.

TODAY'S DISCOURSE: THE SUPERINTENDENT AS A TEACHER IN THE CONTEXT OF INSTRUCTIONAL LEADERSHIP

Although conventional wisdom would have us view district superintendents as "harried managers of complex bureaucracies" (Crane, 1989; Duignan, 1980; Pitner, 1979) rather than instructional leaders, the move toward instructional accountability of district leaders is not without merit or empirical evidence. Few would argue with the fact that district superintendents have a legal as well as a moral responsibility to see that schools achieve a high standard of excellence, and the position of the superintendent within the district hierarchy strongly suggests their ability to influence the focus and direction of the district organization (Peterson, 1984; Thomas, 1988). Fullan (1992) found that successful innovations and school improvements often have central office support. Other research has also demonstrated that superintendents are in the most expedient position to support instructional improvement within the district (Hord, 1993). Yet the notion of superintendent as "teacher of teachers" or instructional leader is not without some controversy.

Challenges to the Notion of the Superintendent as Instructional Leader

Because of the contextual and professional responsibilities of district superintendents, several authors have questioned the concept of *"superintendent as instructional leader."* These authors beg the question of whether or not historical expectations and current dynamics permit superintendents to actually aspire to the role of leader of curriculum and instruction. Some of this work has pointed to the highly political and conflict-ridden world in which they operate (Carter & Cunningham, 1997; Thomas, 2001); the organizational structure of districts, be they urban or rural (Eaton & Sharp, 1996; Hess, 1999; Kowalski, 1995; Ramirez & Guzman, 1999); the instability and turnover of the office of the superintendent (Carter & Cunningham, 1997; Glass, Björk, & Brunner, 2000; Jackson & Cibulka, 1991; Kowalski, 1999; Norton et al., 1996); superintendent and school board relations (Blumberg & Blumberg, 1985; Danzberger, Kirst, & Usdan, 1992; Glass, Björk, & Brunner, 2000; Iannacone & Lutz, 1994; Trump, 1986); and the ambiguity of educational outcomes (Hess, 1999; Thomas, 2001).

Some of this work implies that these issues in isolation or in concert impede superintendents from focusing on the technical core of curriculum and instruction. Others have argued that the work of top-level administrators has no direct impact on student achievement. In a study using data extracted from the National Education Longitude Study for the years 1988, 1990, and 1992, Zigarelli (1996) concluded that there was no evidence to support the claim that the relationship between central administration and schools improved student performance.

Yet before reviewing empirical work that has been conducted in this area, in most instances the investigations of the district superintendent as an instructional leader have been conducted in suburban and rural settings. Research findings by Coleman & LaRocque (1990), Petersen (1999), Peterson (1984), and Wissler & Ortiz (1988) have consistently noted that district size differentially influences the application of the ability of the superintendent's ability to focus on technical core issues of curriculum and instruction. Focusing on smaller districts is supported by current research on school size. This research suggests that smaller schools can provide a more effective learning environment as well as a more manageable organizational milieu for school personnel. These smaller settings provide opportunities to establish collaborative relationships and to work toward specified instructional goals (Kelley & Finnigan, 2003).

The Empirical Evidence

Thoroughly understanding the multifaceted roles and responsibilities of the district superintendent as an instructional leader has proved to be a long-standing and elusive endeavor. In spite of the consistency of research findings, instructional leadership continues to be one of the more controversial characteristics associated with the examination of the district superintendent (Lezotte, 1994). Although a growing body of literature has clearly articulated that building principals could and should be instructional leaders (Andrews & Soder, 1987; Bamberg & Andrews, 1990; Barnett, 1987; Bossert et al., 1982; Bullard & Taylor, 1993; Duke, 1982; Dwyer, 1984; Heck, Larsen, & Marcoulides, 1990; Levine & Lezotte, 1990; Murphy, 1988; Ogawa & Hart, 1985; Peterson, 1984; Short & Spencer, 1990; Smith and Andrews, 1989), there are only a handful of empirical investigations that have explored the role of the district superintendent as instructional leader and its effects on the academic achievement of the districts they lead (Björk, 1993; Bredeson, 1996; Bredeson & Johansson,

1997; Coleman & LaRocque, 1990; Herman, 1990; Hord, 1993; Morgan & Petersen, 2002; Murphy & Hallinger, 1986; Petersen, 1999, 2002; Peterson, 1984; Peterson, Murphy, & Hallinger, 1987; Wirt, 1990).

Peterson (1984) utilized extensive in-depth interviews that focused on the principal's relationship with the district office. He identified six mechanisms of control, which were utilized by superintendents to manage the work of principals. He classified four as hierarchical, including (1) supervision, (2) input control (personnel and monetary), (3) behavior control (rules procedures, directives, and required activities), and (4) output control (student achievement testing). Selection/socialization (patterns of principal hiring and socialization) and environmental control (community perceptions of the school) were noted as nonhierarchical. Peterson also noted that the size of the district differentially influenced the application of these controls.

Murphy & Hallinger (1986), on the other hand, employed concepts taken from school effectiveness studies and organizational literature to study how superintendents organize and manage instruction in effective school districts. They described superintendent instructional leadership practices (e.g., establishment of district goals, selection, supervision and evaluation of staff, establishment of an instructional and curricular focus, and monitoring curriculum and instruction) in school districts with high overall levels of student achievement. Their study found that superintendents of instructionally effective school districts were actively involved in three areas: establishing district direction in the area of curriculum and instruction, ensuring consistency and coordination among technical core operations, and monitoring internal processes and inspecting outcomes.

Peterson, in collaboration with Murphy and Hallinger (1986), reexamined the types of mechanisms used by superintendents to control, coordinate, and assess technical core activities. One essential component for superintendent control was the use of particular instructional practices and models. Use of a particular model permitted the superintendent to control the behavior of their principals, coordinate pedagogy, and increase the focus and specificity of teacher selection.

Contemporary Investigations

A synthesis of six contemporary investigations that examined the instructionally oriented skills, professional and personal behaviors, and organizational relationships and structures established by superintendents in leading curriculum and instruction within their districts are presented here. Coleman & LaRocque (1990) examined the link between district ethos and high levels of student achievement. They found that the leadership role of the district superintendent in high-performing districts involved a considerable amount of team building and collaboration with building principals and teachers. In their findings, they articulated that the most fundamental difference between high- and low-performing districts was the difference in the superintendent's personal judgment about the value of consensus and collaborative work of members in the organization toward the academic achievement of students. Herman's 1990 exploration of 48 district leaders found 5 instructional leadership-associated skills and competencies for district superintendents. These skills include allocation of instructional personnel, organization of the instructional program, support of the instructional program, development of instructional personnel, and planning for the instructional program. In a study that investigated superintendents' descriptions of their involvement in curriculum development and instructional leadership, Bredeson (1996) identified four major roles for district leaders: instructional visionary, instructional collaborator, instructional supporter, and instructional delegator. Petersen (1999) studied school districts of five instructionally recognized California superintendents. In this investigation of district leaders, four essential leadership attributes of the superintendent were identified: articulation of an instructional vision, creation of an organizational structure that supports that vision, assessment and evaluation of personnel and instructional programs, and organizational adaptation. In 2002, Petersen conducted a follow-up investigation with the principals, school board members, and community members in these districts. This investigation yielded a significant statistical relationship between the articulated vision of the superintendent and the mission and goals of the district, instructional planning, and community involvement in the academic success of the district. Finally, Morgan & Petersen (2002) conducted an investigation that examined five school districts of purposefully selected superintendents who had been identified as instructional leaders and five randomly chosen districts who were of a similar size, possessed similar student demographics, and superintendent tenure. The results of their investigation clearly demonstrated that superintendents in academically successful school districts possessed an instructional vision but were also closely involved in the evaluation and monitoring of instruction, as well as collaboratively planning and developing instructional goals with district personnel and members of the community. An overview summary and comparison of the findings of these investigations is offered in Table 5.1.

Although these inquiries do not conclusively identify a direct relationship between what superintendents do and student achievement, they clearly point to the fact that superintendents are "savvy social actors" (Bredeson, 1996) who can influence the views of school board members and others by articulating and demonstrating active involvement, a sincere interest in the technical core of curriculum and instruction, and viewing it as their primary responsibility. The findings from each of these investigations emphasize the importance of an instructional vision, coordination, and socialization of the individuals and groups responsible for teaching and learning, the importance of maintaining a high level of visibility, clear communication, and monitoring and evaluating instructional

Table 5.1   Similarity in the Research Findings of the District Superintendent as Instructional Leader

Similarities in the Findings of the District Superintendent as Instructional Leader	Murphy & Hallinger (1986)	Peterson, Murphy, & Hallinger (1987)	Coleman & LaRocque (1990)	Herman (1990)	Bredeson (1996)	Morgan & Petersen (2002)	Petersen (2002)
1. Collaboratively developing goals with administrators/board	++	++	++	++	++	++	++
2. Evaluating instructional effectiveness	++	++	++	–	+	++	++
3. Facilitating instruction through budget	–	++	–	++	+	+	–
4. Planning for instruction	+	+	+	+	++	++	++
5. Supervising instruction	++	++	–	–	+	–	–
6. Monitoring instructional programs	++	+	–	–	+	++	–
7. Developing principals as instructional leaders	+	++	+	+	+	++	++
8. Developing instructional policies	–	–	–	–	–	–	+
9. Reviewing research	–	–	–	–	–	+	+
10. Selecting personnel	++	++	+	+	+	+	++
11. Facilitating staff development	++	++	+	+	+	+	+
12. Communicating district expectations	–	–	+	–	+	++	++
13. Having a vision for instruction	–	–	++	+	+	++	++
14. Evaluating and monitoring	++	++	+	+	+	++	++
15. Involving the community in setting goals	–	–	++	–	–	+	++

NOTE: ++ Similar Findings; + Partially Found; – Not Found.

and curricular program implementation. More importantly, these studies provide evidence contrary to historical and current *conventional wisdom,* which implies that superintendents are too consumed with administrative and managerial issues to focus on the core technologies of curriculum and instruction.

FUTURE ROLES, CONCEPTUALIZATIONS, AND IMPLICATIONS FOR PREPARATION

What does the future hold for the roles, responsibilities, and expectations of superintendents? We attempt to answer this question by offering several observations of how the job is likely to change. As a backdrop to the future, we begin by exploring who typically has gained access to the role as well as their personal and professional qualities and how these features may change in the coming years. We then explore future implications for the role, including the social conditions likely to shape the expectations for superintendents' job performance and the importance of being "teachers of teachers," which will require educational leaders to be adroit in the language and practice of teaching and learning.

Superintendents' Characteristics and Career Paths

For the first 100 years of the superintendency, there was remarkable similarity in the personal characteristics of these school leaders. The profession has been dominated by married, middle-aged, white males, who have a strong religious (usually Protestant) background (Kowalski, 1999; Tyack & Hansot, 1982). The importance of a being an active church member was particularly important in the 1930s because superintendents were expected to be "guardians of decorum and morality" (Tyack & Hansot, 1982, p. 177). These gender and personal qualities of superintendents mirrored the characteristics of school boards (Tyack & Hansot, 1982), suggesting that boards were inclined to hire people who looked like, thought like, and acted like them. Few women and minorities were employed as superintendents until the 1960s; however, even today, these groups tend to be underrepresented in the ranks (Kowalski, 1999). Although in recent years large urban school systems have a better track record of employing minorities, the lack of mentoring opportunities and informal professional networks continues to disadvantage women, African Americans, Hispanic Americans, and other underrepresented racial and ethnic groups from gaining access to the superintendency (Kowalski, 1999). Given the growing number of minorities in urban and suburban areas of the country, the likelihood of women and people of color becoming superintendents is likely to increase.

Other factors have influenced job placement. For instance, age and salary have risen over time. In the early 1920s, the average age of superintendents was 43, compared with 50 in 1992 (Carter & Cunningham, 1997). Not surprisingly, salaries have increased over time as well, especially in large districts. The average salary in the 1920s was about $3,400, whereas superintendents earned nearly $60,000 in the early 1990s (Carter & Cunningham, 1997). The career path for becoming a superintendent has remained fairly constant. Until the 1940s, many successful candidates were high school teachers who had contact with the community (Tyack & Hansot, 1982). As school systems grew, so too did the professional administrative experience needed to become a superintendent. In recent times, many superintendents tend to come from outside their current district (Kowalski, 1999); have experience as teachers, principals, and central office administrators; and possess a doctoral degree, especially for positions in large urban school systems (Tyack & Hansot, 1982). Although there have been recent trends to hire business and military leaders to lead public school systems because of their political acumen (Usdan, 2002), the demand for instructional leadership may underscore the importance of selecting superintendents from within the educational system, particularly those with expertise in instruction, curriculum development, staff development, and/or assessment.

SOCIAL CONDITIONS SHAPING THE ROLE

Trends in the social and political conditions evident in the early twenty-first century will continue to shape the educational landscape in the ensuing years. The increasing rate of families living in poverty, single-parent families, and violence, substance abuse, and child abuse will demand that school systems work collaboratively with community agencies to provide needed social and educational services for children (Carter & Cunningham, 1997). Governing bodies, particularly federal and state legislators, likely will continue to enact laws intended to raise standards for student performance and hold schools accountable for student learning (Brunner et al., 2002; Carter & Cunningham, 1997). For example, the No Child Left Behind Act (NCLB) of 2002 will dramatically change the role of district leaders and how they are prepared. The superintendent's role has moved from that of a comprehensive manager to an instructional leader focused on the individual classroom (McEwan, 1998). The law focuses on increasing school accountability by demonstrating adequate student achievement regardless of race or ethnicity, limited English proficiency, or economic status. This new accountability in local schools has several implications that directly apply to school superintendents as instructional leaders. Four critical aspects of No Child Left Behind—accountability, parental choice, resource flexibility, and quality teachers—affect the instructional leadership of the superintendent, each of which will be touched on in the following sections.

Assessments for Accountability

NCLB makes schools more accountable for the results of all students by requiring states to test students annually in Grades 3 through 8 in reading and math knowledge. The superintendent's role as the instructional leader is more important now than ever (Gulek, 2003). The new assessment provisions have made student assessment high stakes for all districts. District administrators must have an increased philosophical and technical expertise in curriculum scope, sequence, and alignment. Research-based decision making in curricular decisions to ensure student success will change the landscape of district leadership preparation. Proven results, extensive evaluations, and data-driven decision making have moved the role of the superintendent from the sidelines to the front of the class.

Parental Choice

District leaders must provide more choices for parents of students in low-performance schools. Superintendents of school districts with failing schools could lose significant amounts of funding and could also lose active parents, thus making school improvement very difficult. Additionally, district administrators of high-performing schools could see a significant influx of students from failing schools (creating overcrowding in classrooms and numerous strains on district, school, and classroom resources), thus eroding the educational experience and performance of all students (Education Commission of the States, 2002). School administrators must successfully involve parents by creating various and creative formal and informal avenues for parent, business, and community participation. Superintendents must continually convey the vision and mission of the district to both existing and new families created by NCLB opportunities and challenges for parent choice.

Resource Flexibility

No Child Left Behind significantly changes how the district administrators receive, allocate, and maintain funding for programs focused on instruction and learning. Districts must now use district and building data to inform decisions regarding funding (Education Commission of the States, 2002). One of the most cost-effective areas that affects student achievement is the focus on the classroom-teaching environment (Cicchinelli et al., 2003). Superintendents must become entrepreneurial in practice, seeking external funding to increase the capacity for classroom data collection and program development.

Teacher Quality

Finally, school districts must recruit and retain highly qualified teachers in all classrooms. To be considered highly qualified, all teachers must have full state certification, pass a state licensing exam, or meet the requirements of the state's public charter school laws. District administrators must also ensure that current teachers strengthen and improve pedagogy by using researched-based instructional strategies in their teacher development and continuing education programs. Although districts may be in compliance with NCLB's teacher quality provision, this does not ensure increases in student achievement. Superintendents must focus on the tasks associated with long-term, sustained success that begin from improving the quality of the novice teacher, ensuring that teachers already in the classroom have the resources and learning opportunities they need to be most effective (Cicchinelli et al., 2003).

THE LANGUAGE OF SPINNING IS NOT THE LANGUAGE OF TEACHING AND LEARNING

In the past decade, the concept and emphasis of superintendent leadership has shifted from behaviors associated with management, control, power, and authority to those that emphasize collaboration, community, and relationship building (Brunner et al., 2002; Elmore, 1999; Morgan & Petersen, 2002). The notion of institutionalized leaders *"creating an organizational vision"* and then *"spinning that vision to the masses"* is quickly eroding to the language and behaviors of shared leadership.

The Discourse of Spinning

Spinning or the *"political advertising of ideas"* surrounding organizational issues has been commonplace in the leadership, organizational, and practitioner-oriented literature for some time. Some of what we know and have reinforced with students in leadership-preparation and professional development settings placed a heavy emphasis on management functions and the need for keen political skills and acumen. This emphasis often resulted in school leaders believing that they alone were responsible for the quality of the school and its success (Hackman & Wageman, 1995). Management competencies based on the work of organizational theorists such as Henry Mintzberg were offered as reasonable and expected roles and behaviors for burgeoning organizational leaders. They were informed from the outset that in order to be effective, they had to create an *image of greatness* through an *espoused vision;* then *build support for their vision,* "making dreams apparent to others and aligning people with them" (Bennis, 1997, p. 19). School leaders must have the ability to articulate a clear understanding of what and how they expect schools to deliver and to commission the support of people (Norton et al., 1996). To persuade multiple stakeholders, leaders were encouraged to use political skills focused on agenda setting, forming coalitions, bargaining, and negotiating (Bolman & Deal, 1997; Cuban, 1998). As a result, outstanding superintendents were often characterized by personal power and their ability to exert considerable influence over other school district employees (Kowalski, 1999).

The Discourse of Teaching and Learning

"Despite the presumption of order, a superintendent cannot rely simply on managerial authority to produce good teaching and learning, for school districts and schools are also decentralized organizations that defy close control" (Johnson, 1996, p. 220). The importance of management language and descriptions in defining the responsibilities of district leaders is substantially different from expectations for superintendents today. One of the main reasons for these new expectations lies in the renewed focus on the superintendent as instructional leader. "Superintendents are expected to cultivate an ethos that enables teaching and leadership. Exemplary leaders encourage and enlist the support of everyone needed to make the system work. All who have a stake in the vision of a successful school district must be involved in some way" (Carter & Cunningham, 1997, p. 239). Although the key to effectively leading school districts toward improvement might be constructing the "capacity for change" through political and managerial leadership (Johnson, 1996), Elmore (1999) points out that instructional improvement resides in those who deliver instruction rather than the individuals who mange them. Owens & Ovando (2000) underscore the importance of the superintendent involving the community in meaningful ways. They refer to this as leading through the community, not in spite or in absence of it. Kowalski (1999) points out that today's superintendents are expected to increase their contact and work with teachers and building leaders and to assist them in their decision-making efforts.

We advocate that superintendents create and sustain school systems in which the actions and conversations of teachers and principals continually focus on teaching and learning. Superintendents not only must be able to engage in this type of discourse themselves but also must provide the necessary human and financial capital to make these interactions thrive throughout the school system. At the classroom level, this will require teachers to have a strong command of their subject matter, to be knowledgeable about learning and assessing performance for different purposes and for different types of learners, and to be capable of refining their teaching practices through analysis and reflection (Darling-Hammond, 1998). Schools would become places in which continuous learning, collegiality, and experimentation become the norm. Darling-Hammond (1998) and Little (1982) report that these norms emerge as teachers are afforded opportunities to do the following:

- Observe and critique one another's teaching practices
- Jointly plan, deliver, and evaluate teaching materials
- Conduct demonstration lessons
- Discuss actual teaching and learning activities, such as lesson plans, student evaluations, and curricular materials
- Explore and critique actual cases of instructional and student assessment practices

These actions stimulate reflection and analysis, resulting in more "frequent, continuous and increasingly concrete and precise talk about teaching practice" (Little, 1982, p. 331).

At the school level, principals can encourage these collegial interactions by modeling the instructional leadership behaviors observed by Smith and Andrews (1989). In particular, principals can (a) become *resource providers* by locating human, material, and financial resources; (b) be *instructional resources* by becoming aware of new instructional and assessment strategies, sharing their knowledge about teaching and learning, and setting expectations for continuous improvement; (c) become effective *communicators* by articulating the school's vision, building relationships with teachers and parents, and focusing attention on academic goals; and (d) be a *visible presence* by consistently visiting classrooms, attending meetings, and conversing informally with teachers about teaching and learning.

PREPARING SUPERINTENDENTS TO DEVELOP AND FACILITATE INSTRUCTIONAL CAPACITY

The four key pillars of NCLB create a new and more complex playing field for school administrator preparation. To prepare district leaders for the challenges and opportunities embedded in NCLB, leadership-preparation programs must develop standards for school leaders that will integrate the tenants of instructional leadership (McEwan, 1998). Superintendents will be required to have specialized training in closing the achievement gap, improving and enhancing teachers, and building level administrative leadership by rewarding success and applying consequences to nonachieving students, teachers, and administrators (Lipsky, 2003).

Leadership-preparation programs are now responsible for preparing candidates who are financially savvy and expert purveyors of state-, district-, and school-level data. An increased emphasis on communication and partnership development with local businesses, parents, and local community leaders also adds another dimension. Preparation programs must construct and align themselves to best practices to develop candidates with the necessary background and expertise to substantively address the numerous reforms, call for realignment of the curriculum, and the recruitment and retention of high-quality teachers (Young, 2003; Young & Petersen, 2002). These conditions will also demand successful superintendents of the future to have a level of expertise in dealing with issues of social justice, school improvement, and teaching and learning (Brunner et al., 2002).

All these factors demand that superintendents must become "teachers of teachers" and have the ability to manage change in their school organizations. Recent research by Johnson (1996) highlights the importance of these two roles. First, effective superintendents become actively involved in the daily affairs of principals and teachers, demonstrating an ongoing commitment to the teaching mission of the district. Johnson (1996) discovered that successful superintendents enacted their teaching role in the educational, managerial, and political domains in the following ways:

- *Educational leadership.* Teaching others about the budget process; leading the district in a strategic planning process; regularly visiting schools and classrooms
- *Managerial leadership.* Conducting forums on critical issues; closely supervising new policies and practices
- *Political leadership.* Being visible in the community to learn about local issues; helping the board to work productively; helping educators, community members, and policymakers to consider new perspectives

Although these three leadership roles mirror what Cuban (1976) identified as important roles for superintendents almost three decades ago, Johnson (1996) maintains that these expectations are critical for the future success of public schools:

> [T]hrough their roles as teachers . . . these superintendents convinced others to lead them—to participate in shaping a vision for change, to take principled stands about important issues, and to engage colleagues in finding better approaches to schooling. (p. 278)

Second, superintendents must possess the ability to help others within and outside the school system cope with change and innovation (Johnson, 1996). Not only will superintendents need to assist individuals in dealing with various stages of change (Hall & Hord, 2001), but they will also have to redistribute power and influence to other bodies (e.g., school-based councils) and to reeducate themselves and others about current and future instructional and curricular practices (Johnson, 1996). By leading the change effort in this manner, superintendents would be viewed as the "lead learner," who teaches and also is willing to be taught. As Johnson (1996) advocates, such a vision means that a "superintendent can best prepare a district for change not by providing answers as the educational expert but by participating as an *educator among educators*" (p. 280, emphasis added).

As we have articulated throughout this book, superintendents are being required to become involved in directing district efforts to ensure that *all* children learn (No Child Left Behind, 2002). The bottom line for any school improvement effort is increased student learning. What students learn and eventually take away from their experience in schools is dependent on their opportunities to learn. Therefore, what gets taught is a strong predictor of student academic achievement (Spillane & Seashore Louis, 2002). Teaching and instruction are functions of what teachers know and can do with particular students around specific material (both physical and intellectual) (Cohen & Ball, 1998). With respect to instructional improvement, Cohen and Ball argue that "*instructional capacity*—the capacity to produce worthwhile and substantial learning—is a function of the interaction among elements of the instructional unit, not the sole province of any single element" (Cohen & Ball, 1998, p. 5). Instructional capacity involves the relationship among several important elements and the school organization. For example, Spillane & Seashore Louis (2002) indicated that there are several interrelated components necessary for the presence and maintenance of instructional capacity: the classroom as a site for teacher learning, the development of teachers' professional community, and organizational learning. These elements of instructional capacity are highly interactive and have important implications for school districts' efforts to improve the learning of students (Spillane & Seashore Louis, 2002). "Without an understanding of the knowledge necessary for teachers to teach well . . . school leaders will be unable to perform essential school improvement functions such as monitoring instruction and supporting teacher development" (p. 97).

Despite the remoteness of their central office from the classrooms in which decisions must ultimately be made, the empirical evidence strongly suggests that given their position within the district organization, superintendents are in the best position to foster the necessary organizational relationships and resources to support and facilitate this type of organizational shift (Grogan & Sherman, 2005; Petersen, 2002). Broadly speaking, building instructional capacity means that superintendents and other district leaders must frame a districtwide vision with measurable goals, implement tangible support systems to support the vision and goals, and monitor progress on these goals (Elmore, 2000; Morgan & Petersen, 2002; Petersen, 1999, 2002). If the concept of instructional capacity is to shape the future instructional leadership role of the superintendency, what are promising ways to prepare aspirants for these demands? Outlined in the following text are our suggestions for what the curricular content might include as well as how best to recruit, deliver, and assess the performance of educational leaders who are committed to building instructional capacity within their school systems.

CONTENT

To become proactive instructional leaders, future superintendents must develop the knowledge and skills necessary to build and maintain instructional capacity in their systems. In particular, superintendents would need to understand (a) how instructional capacity is practiced by principals and teachers at the school level and (b) the types of support systems that ensure that instructional capacity spreads throughout the organization, especially to the school level.

Instructional Capacity at the School Level

Over the past three decades, a mounting body of research paints an increasingly clearer picture of what principals and teachers can do to influence teaching and learning. These findings can serve as a framework for the types of actions, knowledge, and skills that should be nurtured at the school level. Because schools are where learning takes place, knowing how instructional capacity occurs at this level is essential. Our contention is that if future superintendents are able to understand and operationalize what instructional capacity looks like at the school level, they are more likely to communicate and support these expectations once they are on the job.

Our review of the literature suggests that instructional capacity is built and maintained when teachers and principals do the following:

- Understand the core technology of teaching and learning, particularly effective models of teaching (e.g., Joyce, Weil, & Calhoun, 2003; King, 2002).
- Engage in frequent conversations about teaching and learning (e.g., Blase & Blase, 2000; Darling-Hammond, 1998; Little, 1982; Pajak & Glickman, 1989).
- Create coherence by aligning curriculum, instruction, and standards (e.g., Knapp et al., 2003; NAESP, 2001).
- Use multiple sources of student assessment data (e.g., King, 2002; NAESP, 2001).
- Make adult learning a priority by providing relevant professional development (e.g., Blase & Blase, 2000; King, 2002; NAESP, 2001).

Effective Support System to
Ensure That Capacity Building Occurs

Besides knowing how instructional capacity is operationalized within schools, future superintendents need to be able to support principals' and teachers' efforts to improve teaching and learning. As King (2002) notes:

Today's instructional leaders devote significant time to developing instructional leadership capacity in others in their schools or districts. . . . Distributing leadership in this way goes beyond merely delegating responsibilities for tasks; it provides regular opportunities for everyone in the school community to share what they are learning about their own practice. School or district staff members gradually take on a variety of roles, including coach, facilitator, or participant, to reflect the purpose and content of the work. (p. 62)

In enacting this capacity-building role, superintendents can employ a two-pronged approach: (1) designing support structures and (2) funding instructionally focused positions, which should shape the curricular content of programs. On the one hand, superintendents can incorporate structures that intentionally facilitate school-based improvements. Examples of actual practices used by superintendents and school districts should be introduced, such as forming and participating in study groups, conducting school visitations and informal classroom walkthroughs, establishing clear guidelines for teacher and principal evaluations, examining student work, developing support groups for new principals or those dealing with high-risk populations, devising record-keeping systems and lesson plans, convening committees for curriculum and textbook decisions, explaining objectives for tests, and providing staff development to support new initiatives (e.g., Fink & Resnick, 2001; Gordon, 1997; Henry, 1997; King, 2002; Pajak & Glickman, 1989). On the other hand, superintendents can secure funds to hire instructional specialists at a variety of levels. For instance, these positions can include building-level teacher and administrative positions (e.g., instructional supervisors, lead teachers), as well as central office supervisors and curriculum coordinators devoted to providing instructional support directly to schools (Pajak & Glickman, 1989). To assist these teaching and learning experts, funds also can be obtained through external grants for professional development, such as helping teachers to incorporate instructional technology (Henry, 1997) or supporting principals in their efforts to improve their instructional supervision skills (Gordon, 1997).

PROGRAM RECRUITMENT, DELIVERY, AND ASSESSMENT

Although most literature on leadership preparation is devoted to the principalship (Grogan & Andrews, 2002), suggestions are emerging about how best to prepare superintendents for their role. Just as important as framing the content around instructional capacity is how candidates are recruited and selected, instruction is delivered, and learning is assessed. We will briefly describe our views on these aspects of preparation, keeping in mind the need to focus on developing candidates' instructional capacity.

Recruitment and Selection

Because superintendent preparation or certification often is embedded in a doctoral degree, many of the students attending these programs have little or no interest in the superintendency (Grogan & Andrews, 2002). However, a growing number of higher-education institutions and/or professional associations are designing preparation programs exclusively for superintendents. Examples include the Harvard Urban Superintendents Program; the University of Virginia's School Superintendent's Licensure Program; and Superintendents Prepared, a joint venture of the Institute for Educational Leadership, Joint Center for Political and Economic Studies, and the McKenzie Group (Grogan & Andrews, 2002).

To actively seek candidates for these programs, we might follow the lead that a number of universities are taking in recruiting candidates for their principal-preparation programs. In particular, university faculty can solicit nominations of educators who already have demonstrated instructional leadership in their systems from local school districts. Besides using some of the typical application criteria (e.g., grade point average, Graduate Record Examination scores), interviews and assessment center exercises can be used to determine educators' knowledge, skills, and commitment to building instructional capacity (Creighton & Jones, 2001; Lashway, 2002). If universities are serious about building the instructional leadership capacity of aspiring superintendents, they would be making a public statement that educators with the demonstrated potential to be effective instructional leaders would be the most highly sought-after candidates for program selection.

Program Delivery

In recent years, extensive criticisms of university-based school leadership preparation have been leveled from a variety of sources, including professors, practitioners, and professional associations (e.g., Haller, Brent, & McNamara, 1997; Schneider, 1998; Van Berkum, Richardson, & Lane, 1994). Although perceptions on the effectiveness of superintendent preparation are mixed (Grogan & Andrews, 2002), a common complaint is that "university and non-university based professional preparation programs share similar weaknesses that emerge from similar constraints on the nature of delivery. They tend to be *instructor-centered* and *classroom based*" (Glass et al., 2002, p. 161, emphasis added).

In attempting to build the instructional capacity of future superintendents, what are some promising ways to counteract these two major criticisms posed by Glass and his colleagues? First, constructivist, student-centered approaches should become the dominant paradigm for superintendent preparation (Boone, 2001; Murphy & Forsyth, 1999). Because most, if not all, candidates engaged in superintendent preparation have extensive experience in school systems, we should attempt to build on their knowledge and expertise, a basic tenet of adult learning theory (e.g., Merriam & Caffarella, 1998). Examples of how to move away from instructor-centered instruction would include problem-based learning using case studies (Bridges, 1992; Hart & Pounder, 1999), collaborative research (Milstein & Associates, 1993), and reflective seminars (Osterman & Kottkamp, 1993).

Second, classroom-dominated instruction can be reduced by infusing distance learning (McCarthy & Kuh, 1997) and having students work in selective clinical internships (Hart & Pounder, 1999; Milstein & Associates, 1993). Wherever feasible, careful selection of clinical sites should occur. If our goal is to develop the knowledge base and skills needed to be instructional capacity builders, then faculty should work closely with local school districts to identify people, programs, and practices that model the salient features of instructional capacity building. Careful attention should be given to identify (a) schools in which teaching and learning are at the forefront of discussions and actions, (b) district initiatives aimed at supporting school-based improvements, and (c) staffing patterns supporting instruction and student learning. In this way, the curricular of instructional capacity building is intentionally aligned with field-based learning experiences.

Assessment

If preparation programs are serious about implementing a student-centered, field-based approach to learning, they can incorporate some of the performance-based measures being advocated by professional associations and accrediting agencies (e.g., NCATE, 1995; NPBEA, 2002). As university-based preparation programs continue the trend of aligning their program content with national and state standards, assessment strategies can provide performance-based evidence that these standards have been achieved. For instance, many universities are embracing the Interstate School Leaders Licensure Consortium (ISLLC) standards (CCSSO, 1996). Early evidence suggests that when preparation programs align their content and field-based learning experiences with these standards, graduates score higher on the ISSLC performance assessments and receive higher performance evaluations from prospective employers (Valentine, 2000). In addition, students can prepare portfolios that document the activities they completed in their field-based experiences that address particular state standards providing tangible evidence of how prospective superintendents have demonstrated instructional capacity-building activities. Not only do portfolios provide evidence of learning within the program, but they also demonstrate to future employers graduates' instructional leadership capabilities (Barnett & Lee, 1994).

CONCLUSION

The roles and responsibilities of the superintendent have evolved over time, and although the expectations of the education and larger community can change, what is most evident is the underlying responsibility of school district leaders to improve the lives of students. As the empirical and historical evidence attests, before superintendents can provide the leadership needed for schools today, they must fully grasp the conditions within which they find themselves and the directions they will need to take their organizations (Carter & Cunningham, 1997). It is clear that focusing on the peripheral organizational concerns, with minimal time devoted to the technical core of curriculum and instruction, establishes a set of organizational values and commitment that our public schools and their leaders can no longer afford to ignore. A superintendent's failure to establish this consensus of the organization's mission and an environment of commitment to the academic performance of students because of a focus on managerial or administrative issues not related to the core technology will inhibit the establishment of collective responsibility and an environment of collaborative professional cultures (Leithwood, 1994). In this era of accountability, superintendents who do not have a primary focus on the academic success of students will not last long in their role of district leader. Superintendents must be dedicated to the continuous improvement of their schools, their administrators and teachers, and the diverse populations of students in their districts (Grogan & Sherman, 2005). They must use their influence to facilitate and support continuous improvement and achievement for all students as well as members of the school organization.

REFERENCES

Andrews, R. L., & Soder, R. (1987, March). Principal leadership and student achievement. *Educational Leadership, 44*(6), 9–11.

Ashbaugh, C. R. (2000). The superintendent's role as instructional leader. In P. M. Short & J. P. Scribner (Eds.), *Case studies of the superintendency* (pp. 9–21). Lanham, MD: Scarecrow Press.

Bamberg, J. D., & Andrews, R. L. (1990). *Instructional leadership, school goals, and student achievement.* Paper presented at the meeting of the American Educational Research Association, Boston.

Barnett, B. G. (1987). Using reflection as a professional growth activity. In W. Greenfield (Ed.), *Instructional leadership: Concepts, issues, and controversies* (pp. 271–286). Boston: Allyn & Bacon.

Barnett, B. G., & Lee, P. (1994). Assessment processes and outcomes: Building a folio. In L. Jackson & R. S. Caffarella (Eds.), *Experiential learning: A new approach. New directions in adult and continuing education, 62* (pp. 55–62). San Francisco: Jossey-Bass.

Bennis, W. (1997). *Why leaders can't lead: The unconscious conspiracy continues.* San Francisco. Jossey-Bass.

Bennis, W., & Nanus, B. (1985). *Leaders: The strategies for taking charge.* New York: Harper & Row.

Björk, L. G. (1993). Effective schools—effective superintendents: The emerging instructional leadership role. *Journal of School Leadership, 3,* 246–259.

Blase, J., & Blase, J. (2000). Effective instructional leadership: Teachers' perspectives on how principals promote teaching and learning in schools. *Journal of Educational Administration, 38*(2), 130–141.

Blumberg, A., & Blumberg, P. (1985). *The school superintendent: Living with conflict.* New York: Teachers College Press.

Bolman, L. G., & Deal, T. E. (1997). *Reframing organizations: Artistry, choice and leadership* (2nd ed.). San Francisco: Jossey-Bass.

Boone, M. (2001). *Preparing superintendents through standards-based instruction.* (ERIC Document Reproduction Service No. ED 461 165)

Bossert, S. T., Dwyer, D. C., Rowan, B., & Lee, G. V. (1982). The instructional management role of the principal. *Educational Administration Quarterly, 18*(3), 32–64.

Boyd, W. L. (1976, May). The public, the professionals, and educational policy: Who governs? *Teachers College Record, 77*(4), 539–578.

Bredeson, P. V. (1996). Superintendents' roles in curriculum development and instructional leadership: Instructional visionaries, collaborators, supporters, and delegators. *Journal of School Leadership, 6*(3), 243–264.

Bredeson, P. V., & Johansson, O. (1997). *Leadership for learning: A study of the instructional leadership roles of superintendents in Sweden and Wisconsin.* Paper presented at the annual conference of the American Educational Research Association, Chicago.

Bridges, E. M. (1992). *Problem-based learning for administrators.* Eugene, OR: ERIC Clearinghouse on Educational Management.

Brunner, C. C., Grogan, M., & Björk, L. G. (2002). Shifts in the discourse defining the superintendency: Historical and current foundations of the position. In J. Murphy (Ed.), *The educational leadership challenge: Redefining leadership for the 21st century* (pp. 211–238). Chicago: University of Chicago Press.

Bullard, P., & Taylor, B. O. (1993). *Making school reform happen.* New York: Simon & Schuster.

Callahan, R. E. (1964a). *Changing conceptions of the superintendency in public education 1865–1964.* Alfred D. Simpson Lecture on Administration. Cambridge, MA: New England School Development Council.

Callahan, R. E. (1964b). *The superintendent of schools: An historical analysis. Final report of Project S–212.* Washington, DC: U.S. Office of Education, Department of Health, Education, and Welfare.

Carter, G. R., & Cunningham, W. G. (1997). *The American school superintendent: Leading in an age of pressures.* San Francisco: Jossey-Bass.

Chaddock, G. R. (2002, February 26). Mayors, states push school boards aside. *The Christian Science Monitor.* Retrieved February 17, 2003, from http://www.csmonitor.com/2002/0226/p01s01-ussc.html

Cicchinelli, L., Lefkowits, L., Gaddy, B., & Miller, K. (2003). *No Child Left Behind: Realizing the vision.* Policy brief. Aurora, CO: Mid-continent Research for Education and Learning.

Cohen, D. K., & Ball, D. L. (1998). *Instruction, capacity and improvement (RR-42).* Philadelphia: Consortium for Policy Research in Education, University of Pennsylvania.

Coleman, P., & LaRocque, L. (1990). *Struggling to be good enough: Administrative practices and school district ethos.* London: Falmer Press.

Council of Chief State School Officers. (1996). *ISLLC standards.* Retrieved September 10, 2003, from http://www.ccsso.org/standards.html

Crane, D. C. (1989). *The leadership of an insider superintendent with a cosmopolitan orientation in an expanding and changing orientation.* Unpublished doctoral dissertation, University of California, Santa Barbara.

Creighton, T., & Jones, G. (2001). *Selection or self-selection? How rigorous are our selection criteria for education administration preparation programs?* Paper presented at the annual conference of the National Council of Professors of Educational Administration, Houston.

Crow, G., & Southworth, G. (2005). Preparing leaders for tomorrow's schools: An internship project. *Journal of School Leadership.*

Crowson, R. (1987). The local school district superintendency: A puzzling administrative role. *Educational Administration Quarterly, 23*(3), 49–69.

Cuban, L. (1976). *Urban school chiefs under fire.* Chicago: University of Chicago Press.

Cuban, L. (1998). The superintendent contradiction. *Education Week, 18*(7), 56.

Cunningham, W., & Sperry, J. (2001, April). The underpaid educator. *American School Board Journal,* 38–42.

Danzberger, J. P., Kirst, M. W., & Usdan, M. D. (1992). *Governing public schools: New times, new requirements.* Washington, DC: Institute for Educational Leadership.

Darling-Hammond, L. (1998). Teacher learning that supports student learning. *Educational Leadership, 55*(5), 6–11.

Doyle, D. P. (1998). The main thing—academic learning. In R. R. Spillane & R. Regnier (Eds.), *The superintendent of the future: Strategy and action for achieving academic excellence* (pp. 15–30). Gaithersburg, MD: Aspen Publishers.

Duignan, P. (1980, July). Administrative behavior of school superintendents: A descriptive study. *Journal of Educational Administration, 28*(1), 5–26.

Duke, D. (1982). What can principals do? Leadership functions and instructional effectiveness. *National Association of Secondary School Principals Bulletin, 66*(456), 1–12.

Dwyer, D. C. (1984). The search for instructional leadership: Routines and subtleties in the principal's role. *Educational Leadership, 41*(5), 32–37.

Eaton, W. E., & Sharp, W. L. (1996). Involuntary turnover among small-town superintendents. *Peabody Journal of Education, 71*(2), 78–85.

Education Commission of the States. (2002, April). *No Child Left Behind policy brief: Literacy.* Denver, CO: Kaverz.

Elmore, R. F. (1996). Getting to scale with successful educational practices. In S. Fuhrman & J. A. O'Day (Eds.), *Rewards and reform: Creating educational incentives that work* (pp. 294–329). San Francisco: Jossey-Bass.

Elmore, R. F. (1999, September). *Leadership of large-scale improvement in American education.* Washington, DC: Paper prepared for the Albert Shanker Institute.

Elmore, R. F. (2000). *Building a new structure for school leadership.* Washington, DC: Albert Shanker Institute.

Feuerstein, A., & Opfer, V. D. (1998, July). School board chairmen and school superintendents: An analysis of perceptions concerning special interest groups and educational governance. *Journal of School Leadership, 8,* 373–398.

Fink, E., & Resnick, L. B. (2001). Developing principals as instructional leaders. *Phi Delta Kappan, 82,* 598–606.

Firestone, W. A., & Corbett, H. D. (1988). Organizational change. In N. Boyan (Ed.), *Handbook of research on educational administration* (1st ed.). White Plains, NY: Longman.

Fullan, M. G. (1992). *Successful school improvement: The implementation perspective and beyond.* Modern Educational Thought. Bristol, PA: Open University Press.

Fusarelli, L. D., Cooper, B. S., & Carella, V. A. (2002). Dilemmas of the modern superintendency. In B. S. Cooper & L. D. Fusarelli (Eds.), *The promises and perils facing today's school superintendent* (pp. 5–20). Lanham, MD: Scarecrow Press.

Gilland, T. M. (1935). *The origins and development of the powers and duties of the city-school superintendent.* Chicago: University of Chicago Press.

Glass, T. E., Björk, L. G, & Brunner, C. C. (2000). *The 2000 study of the American school superintendency: A look at the superintendent of education in the new millennium.* Arlington, VA: American Association of School Administrators.

Gordon, W. M. (1997). Philbert: Battling bond barriers. In C. H. Chapman (Ed.), *Becoming a superintendent: Challenges of school district leadership* (pp. 187–195). Upper Saddle River, NJ: Prentice Hall.

Grogan, M. (1996). *Voices of women aspiring to the superintendency.* Albany: SUNY Press.

Grogan, M. (2000). Laying the groundwork for a reconception of the superintendency from feminist postmodern perspectives. *Educational Administration Quarterly, 36*(1), 117–142.

Grogan, M., & Andrews, R. (2002). Defining preparation and professional development for the future. *Educational Administration Quarterly, 38*(2), 233–256.

Grogan, M., & Sherman, W. (2005). Superintendents in Virginia dealing with issues surrounding the black-white test-score gap. In D. Duke, M. Grogan, P. Tucker, & W. Heinecke (Eds.), *Educational leadership in an age of accountability*. Albany: SUNY Press.

Gulek, C. (2003). Preparing for high-stakes testing. *Theory into Practice, 42*(1), 42–50.

Hackman, J. R., & Wageman, R. (1995). Total quality management: Empirical, conceptual, and practical issues. *Administrative Science Quarterly, 40*, 309–342.

Hall, G. E., & Hord, S. M. (2001). *Implementing change: Patterns, principles, and potholes*. Boston: Allyn & Bacon.

Haller, E. J., Brent, B. O., & McNamara, J. H. (1997). Does graduate training in school administration improve America's schools? *Phi Delta Kappan, 79*(3), 222–227.

Hart, A. W., & Pounder, D. G. (1999). Reinventing preparation programs: A decade of activity. In J. Murphy & P. Forsyth (Eds.), *Educational administration: A decade of reform* (pp. 115–151). Thousand Oaks, CA: Corwin.

Heck, R. H., Larsen, T. J., & Marcoulides, G. A. (1990). Instructional leadership and school achievement: Validation of a causal model. *Educational Administration Quarterly, 26*(2), 94–125.

Henry, D. A. (1997). Jackie: Big time challenges in a rural district. In C. H. Chapman (Ed.), *Becoming a superintendent: Challenges of school district leadership* (pp. 41–54). Upper Saddle River, NJ: Prentice Hall.

Herman, J. L. (1990). *Instructional leadership skills and competencies of public school superintendents: Implications for preparation programs in a climate of shared governance*. (ERIC Document Reproduction Service No. ED 328 980)

Hess, F. M. (1999). *Spinning wheels: The politics of urban school reform*. Washington, DC: Brookings Institution Press.

Hill, P. T. (2003, January). *School boards: Focus on school performance not money and patronage*. Washington, DC: Progressive Policy Institute. Retrieved March 17, 2003, from http://www.ppionline.org/ppi_ka.cfm?knlgAreaID=110

Hitt, W. D. (1990). *Ethics and leadership: Putting theory into practice*. Columbus, OH: Battle Press.

Hord, S. M. (1993). Smoke, mirrors or reality: Another instructional leader. In D. S. G. Carter, T. E. Glass, and S. M. Hord (Eds.), *Selecting, preparing, and developing the school district superintendent* (pp. 1–19). Washington, DC: Falmer Press.

Hoyle, R. J. (1993). *Professional standards for the superintendency*. Arlington, VA: American Association of School Administrators.

Iannacone, L., & Lutz, F. W. (1994). The crucible of democracy: The local arena. *Journal of Education Policy, 9*(5–6), 39–52.

Jackson, B. L., & Cibulka, J. G. (1991). Leadership turnover and business mobilization: The changing political ecology of urban systems. In J. G. Cibulka, R. Reed, & K. Wong (Eds.), *The politics of urban education in the United States* (pp. 71–86). London: Falmer Press.

Johnson, S. M. (1996). *Leading to change: The challenge of the new superintendency*. San Francisco: Jossey-Bass.

Joyce, B. R., Weil, M., & Calhoun, E. (2003). *Models of teaching*. Boston: Allyn & Bacon.

Kelleher, P. (2001, March 28). Implementing high standards. *Education Week on the Web*. Retrieved on March 18, 2003, from http://www.edweek.org/ew/ewstory.cfm?slug=28kelleher.h20

Kelley, C. J., & Finnigan, K. (2003, December). The effects of organizational context on teacher expectancy. *Educational Administration Quarterly, 39*(5), 603–634.

King, D. (2002). The changing shape of leadership. *Educational Leadership, 59*(8), 61–63.

Knapp, M. S., Copland, M. A., & Talbert, J. E. (2003). *Leading for learning: Reflective tools for school and district leaders*. Seattle: Center for the Study of Teaching and Policy, University of Washington.

Konnert, W. M., & Augenstein, J. J. (1995). *The school superintendency: Leading education into the 21st century.* Lancaster, PA: Technomic.

Kowalski, T. J. (1995). *Keepers of the flame: Contemporary urban superintendents.* Thousand Oaks, CA: Corwin.

Kowalski, T. J. (1999). *The school superintendent: Theory, practice, and cases.* Upper Saddle River, NJ: Prentice-Hall.

Lashway, L. (2002). *Developing instructional leaders.* Eugene, OR: ERIC Clearinghouse on Educational Management.

Leithwood, K. A. (1994). Leadership for school restructuring. *Educational Administration Quarterly, 30*(4), 498–518.

Leithwood, K. A., & Riehl, C. (2003). *What we know about successful school leadership.* Philadelphia: Laboratory for Student Success, Temple University.

Levine, D. U., & Lezotte, L. W. (1990). *Unusually effective schools: A review and analysis of research and practice.* Madison, WI: National Center for Effective Schools Research.

Lezotte, L. W. (1994). The nexus of instructional leadership and effective schools. *The School Administrator, 51*(6), 20–23.

Lipsky, D. K. (2003). The coexistence of high standards and inclusion, whole-school approaches can satisfy requirements of IDEA and NCLB Act. *The School Administrator, 3*(60), 32–35.

Little, J. W. (1982). Norms of collegiality and experimentation: Workplace conditions of school success. *American Educational Research Journal, 19*(3), 325–340.

March, J. G. (1994). *A primer on decision making: How decisions happen.* New York: Free Press.

Mathis, W. J. (2003). No Child Left Behind: Cost and benefits. *Phi Delta Kappan, 84*(9), 679–687.

McCarthy, M., & Kuh, G. (1997). *Continuity and change: The educational leadership professorate.* Columbia, MO: University Council for Educational Administration.

McCarty, D. J., & Ramsey, C. E. (1971). *The school managers.* Westport, CT: Greenwood.

McCurdy, J. M. (1992). *Building better board-administrator relations.* Arlington, VA: American Association of School Administrators.

McEwan, E. K. (1998). *Seven steps to effective instructional leadership.* Thousand Oaks, CA: Sage.

Merriam, S. B., & Caffarella, R. S. (1998). *Learning in adulthood: A comprehensive guide* (2nd ed.). San Francisco: Jossey-Bass.

Milstein, M. M., & Associates. (1993). *Changing the way we prepare educational leaders: The Danforth experience.* Thousand Oaks, CA: Corwin.

Morgan, C., & Petersen, G. J. (2002). The superintendent's role in leading academically effective school districts. In B. S. Cooper & L. D. Fusarelli (Eds.), *The promise and perils of the modern superintendency* (pp. 175–196). Lanham, MD: Scarecrow Press.

Murphy, J. (1988). The instructional leadership role of the school principal: An analysis. *Educational Evaluation and Policy Analysis, 10*(2), 71–79.

Murphy, J. (1990). The educational reform movement of the 1980s: A comprehensive analysis. In J. Murphy (Ed.), *The reform of American public education in the 1980s: Perspectives and cases* (pp. 277–303). Berkeley, CA: McCutchan.

Murphy, J., & Forsyth, P. (Eds.). (1999). *Educational administration: A decade of reform.* Thousand Oaks, CA: Corwin.

Murphy, J., & Hallinger, P. (1986). The superintendent as instructional leader: Findings from effective school districts. *Journal of Educational Administration, 24*(2), 213–236.

National Association of Elementary School Principals. (2001). *Leading learning communities: Standards for what principals should know and be able to do.* Alexandria, VA: Author.

National Council for the Accreditation of Teacher Education. (1995). *NCATE program standards: Advanced programs in educational leadership for principals, superintendents, curriculum directors, and supervisors.* Retrieved September 10, 2003, from http://www.ncate.org/standard/elccmatrix.doc

National Policy Board for Educational Administration. (2002). *Standards for advanced programs in educational leadership.* Arlington, VA: Author.

No Child Left Behind—Public Law 107-100. (2002, January 8). Washington, DC: 107th U.S. Congress. Retrieved October 3, 2003, from http://www.ed.gov/legislation/ESEA02/107-110.pdf

Norton, M. S., Webb, L. D., Dlugosh, L. L., & Sybouts, W. (1996). *The school superintendency: New responsibilities, new leadership.* Boston: Allyn & Bacon.

Nygren, B. (1992, July). Two-party tune up. *American School Board Journal, 178*(7), 35.

O'Day, J. A. (2002, Fall). Complexity, accountability, and school improvement. *Harvard Educational Review, 72*(3). Retrieved March 1, 2003, from http://gseweb.harvard.edu/~hepg/oday.html

Odden, A. R. (1995). *Educational leadership for America's schools.* New York: McGraw-Hill.

Ogawa, R. T., & Hart, A. W. (1985). The effect of principals on the instructional performance of schools. *Journal of Educational Administration, 23*(1), 59–72.

Osterman, K. F., & Kottkamp, R. B. (1993). *Reflective practice for educators: Improving schooling through professional development.* Thousand Oaks, CA: Corwin.

Owens, J., & Ovando, M. (2000). *Superintendent's guide to creating community.* Lanham, MD: Scarecrow Press.

Pajak, E. F., & Glickman, C. D. (1989). Dimensions of school district improvement. *Educational Leadership, 46*(8), 61–64.

Petersen, G. J. (1999, May). Demonstrated actions of instructional leaders: A case study of five superintendents. *Education Policy Analysis Archives, 7*(18). Retrieved July 22, 2003, from http://epaa.asu.edu/epaa/v7n18.html

Petersen, G. J. (2002). Singing the same tune: Principals' and school board members' perceptions of the superintendent's role in curricular and instructional leadership. *Journal of Educational Administration, 40*(2), 158–171.

Petersen, G. J., & Short, P. M. (2001, October). The school board president's perception of the district superintendent: Applying the lens of social influence and social style. *Educational Administration Quarterly, 37*(4), 533–570.

Petersen, G. J., & Young, M. D. (2004). The No Child Left Behind Act and its influence on current and future district leaders. *Journal of Law and Education, 33*(3), 327–347.

Peterson, K. D. (1984, December). Mechanisms of administrative control over managers in educational organizations. *Administrative Science Quarterly, 29*(4), 573–597.

Peterson, K. D., Murphy, J., & Hallinger, P. (1987). Superintendents' perceptions of the control and coordination of the technical core in effective school districts. *Educational Administration Quarterly, 23*(1), 79–95.

Pitner, N. J. (1979). *So go the days of our lives: A descriptive study of the superintendency.* Eugene, OR: University of Oregon, Oregon School Study Council. (ERIC Document Reproduction Service No. ED 165 299)

Ramirez, A., & Guzman, N. (1999, October). *The rural school district superintendency: A Colorado perspective.* Paper presented at the annual conference of the National Rural Education Association, Colorado Springs, CO. (ERIC Document Reproduction Service No. ED 437 235)

Riley, R. (1994, February). *Education and goals 2000.* Keynote address at the annual conference of the American Association of School Administrators, San Francisco.

Robbins, S. P. (1997). *Managing today.* Upper Saddle River, NJ: Prentice Hall.

Schlechty, P. C. (1992). Deciding the fate of local control. *American School Board Journal, 178*(11), 27–29.

Schneider, J. (1998). University training of school leaders isn't the only option. *The AASA Professor, 22*(1), 7–8.

Sergiovanni, T. J. (1990). Adding value to leadership gets extraordinary results. *Education Leadership, 47*(8), 23–27.

Short, P. M., & Spencer, W. A. (1990). Principal instructional leadership. *Journal of Research and Development in Education, 23*(2), 117–122.

Smith, M. S., & O'Day, J. (1991 September). A national curriculum in the United States? *Educational Leadership, 49*(1), 74–81.

Smith, W. F., & Andrews, R. L. (1989). *Instructional leadership: How principals make a difference.* Alexandria, VA: Association for Supervision and Curriculum.

Spillane, J. P., & Seashore Louis, K. (2002). School improvement processes and practices: Professional learning for building instructional capacity. In J. Murphy (Ed.), *The educational leadership challenge: Redefining leadership for the 21st century* (pp. 83–104). Chicago: University of Chicago Press.

Spillane, R. R., & Regnier, P. (1998). This is now; this is then. In R. R. Spillane & R. Regnier (Eds.), *The superintendent of the future: Strategy and action for achieving academic excellence* (pp. 1–12). Gaithersburg, MD: Aspen.

Spring, J. H. (1994). *The American school, 1642–1993* (3rd ed.). New York: McGraw-Hill.

Starratt, R. J. (2003). *Centering educational administration: Cultivating meaning, community, responsibility.* Hillsdale, NJ: Lawrence Erlbaum.

Teddlie, C., & Reynolds, D. (2000). *The international handbook of school effectiveness research.* New York: Falmer Press.

Thomas, A. B. (1988). Does leadership make a difference to organizational performance? *Administrative Science Quarterly, 33*(3), 388–400.

Thomas, J. Y. (2001). *The public school superintendency in the twenty-first century: The quest to define effective leadership.* Washington, DC: Department of Education, Center for Research on the Education of Student Placed At Risk (CRESPAR). (ERIC Document Reproduction Service No. ED 460 219)

Trump, J. M. (1986). *What hinders or prevents superintendents from working on instructional improvement?* (ERIC Document Reproduction Service No. ED 284 366)

Tyack, D., & Hansot, E. (1982). *Managers of virtue: Public school leadership in America, 1820–1980.* New York: Basic Books.

Usdan, M. D. (1975). The future viability of the school board. In P. J. Cistone (Ed.), *Understanding school boards: Problems and prospects* (pp. 265–276). Toronto: Lexington Books.

Usdan, M. D. (2002). Reactions to articles commissioned by the National Commission for the Advancement of Education Leadership Preparation. *Educational Administration Quarterly, 38*(2), 300–307.

Valentine, J. (2000). *Goals 2000 principal leadership development project: Final report.* Final report of Goals 2000 grant. Columbia: University of Missouri.

Van Berkum, D. W., Richardson, M. D., & Lane, K. E. (1994). *Professional development in educational administration programs: Where does it exist?* Paper presented at the annual meeting of the National Council of Professors of Educational Administration, Indian Wells, CA.

Wirt, F. M. (1990). *The missing link in instructional leadership: The superintendent, conflict, and maintenance.* (ERIC Document Reproduction Service, No. ED 327 945)

Wissler, D. F., & Ortiz, F. L. (1988). *The superintendent's leadership in school reform.* New York: Falmer Press.

Young, M. D. (2003, Spring). Let's practice what we teach. *UCEA Review, XLV*(2), 6–7.

Young, M. D., & Petersen, G. J. (2002). Enabling substantive reform in the preparation of school leaders. *Educational Leadership Review, 3*(1), 1–15.

Zigarelli, M. A. (1996). An empirical test of conclusions from effective schools research. *The Journal of Educational Research, 90,* 103–100.

6

Superintendent as Organizational Manager

Tricia Browne-Ferrigno and Thomas E. Glass

Contemporary superintendents have multiple responsibilities as administrators of complex educational systems. They must possess skills in vision setting, policy implementation and priority establishment, public relations and collaboration, communication and participatory decision making, student learning accountability and program evaluation, to mention only a few (Hoyle, Björk, Collier, & Glass, 2005; Kowalski, 1999, 2003; Lunenburg & Ornstein, 2004). Superintendents must ensure that leadership capacity is expanded throughout district schools to implement and sustain successful reform innovations (Johnson, 1996) while at the same time appropriately distribute fiscal, material, and human resources to ensure continuous student learning (Fullan, 2003, 2004). These tasks alone require a staggering knowledge base and range of skills (Konnert & Augenstein, 1990; Kowalski, 2003; Norton, Webb, Dlugosh, & Sybouts, 1996).

This chapter focuses on the work of a superintendent as an *organizational manager,* one of the five major roles identified by Callahan (1966) and Kowalski (2005). Although the superintendency was first conceived in the mid-1800s as a teacher-scholar who supervised teachers and ensured that state curriculum was implemented, the need for school-district management emerged with the consolidation of school districts and expansion of education laws and programs. The transformation of the superintendency during the nineteenth and twentieth centuries mirrors the social, political, and economic evolution of America from a rural agrarian to an urban industrial society, as well as waves of capable and assimilating successive immigration (Kowalski & Björk, n.d.; Razik & Swanson, 2001). Additionally, management principles espoused by business and industry during this era significantly influenced the superintendency (Brunner, Grogan, & Björk, 2002). As local boards of education became fiscally independent enterprises with taxing and policy-making authority, they needed executive officers to oversee the day-to-day administration of their school districts (Cunningham & Cordeiro, 2003; Konnert & Augenstein, 1990; Lunenburg & Ornstein, 2004). Although several distinctive role expectations for the American superintendency emerged over time, management emerged and was inextricably embedded as one of the most important role expectations.

In the following discussion, italics highlight superintendent managerial tasks. For example, Griffiths (1966) suggests that a superintendent's work falls into four major categories: *finance, personnel, instruction,* and *public relations.* Although Cuban (1976) perceived that the superintendency is a highly situational position based upon expectations by school boards and configured by unique local circumstances, he asserts that all superintendents manifest behavioral elements within four roles he identified as educator, *business executive,* politician, and social scientist. Taking a slightly different perspective, Blumberg (1985) believes that the superintendency has less to do with the education of children and more with *"maintaining the viability of the school system as a human organization,* in its several dimensions—political, *economic,* social, and psychological" (p. 2).

Nearly a decade after suggesting that the superintendency can be described as four different roles, Cuban (1988) condensed them into "three dominant images of what a superintendent should be: instructional supervisor, *administrative chief* [emphasis added], and negotiator-statesman" (p. 113). He observed that "how these roles are enacted" (p. 142) is quite diverse among school system executives. Johnson (1996) affirmed Cuban's framework through findings from her cross-case study of 12 superintendents—veteran and novice, male and female—through their first two years of administration in a district. Because her research focused on the superintendents' leadership as observed and assessed by others, she did not use Cuban's framework. Nonetheless, she found the same three dimensions in their practices—educational, political, and *managerial*—that Cuban suggested were the three dominant images for the superintendency. Johnson notes that

> superintendents were expected by their constituents to exercise *managerial* leadership. School districts are fundamentally bureaucratic organizations, some more formal and elaborate than others, but all requiring thoughtful and thorough management. These

superintendents had to be creative in using the structures of their organization to encourage communication and participation, allocate resources efficiently, provide supervision and support, make plans for moving forward, and ensure accountability and consistent understanding of standards. (p. 24)

Although during the closing decades of the twentieth century the role of the superintendent shifted to emphasize greater leadership-for-change responsibilities, management remains critically important in the successful operation of local education agencies (Callahan, 1962; Glass, 2003; Hoyle et al., 2005; Johnson, 1996; Konnert & Augenstein, 1990; Kowalski, 2003, 2005).

BUSINESS INFLUENCES ON THE SUPERINTENDENCY

Although the superintendency has a long history of transformation based on changing economic, political, and societal influences (Kowalski, 2005), the last two decades of the twentieth century introduced demands on the superintendency created by calls for educational reform and greater student-learning accountability (Björk, Kowalski, & Young, 2005; Glass, 2004b). Long-term ambiguity about the work of superintendents provoked the American Association of School Administrators (AASA) to issue resolutions in 1994 to clarify "the roles and responsibilities between superintendents and boards of education" (p. 19). New preparation and practice standards for district and school leaders during the 1990s (Council of Chief State School Officers [CCSSO], 1996; Hoyle, 1993; Hoyle, English, & Steffy, 1998) in many ways mirror the changed expectations during that same period for the chief executive officer (CEO) of large corporations.

Today's superintendent, like the contemporary corporate CEO, must achieve high standards of productivity through less-hierarchically structured organizations (Naisbitt, 1985; Peters & Waterman, 1982; Toffler, 1980) in which individuals are empowered and decision making is distributed among those most closely engaged in the work (Bennis & Mische, 1995; Pasternack & Viscio, 1998). Although leadership has been reconceptualized from authority residing in a position to actions by individuals (Bennis & Townsend, 1995; Collins, 2001), management of the enterprise remains important and necessary and usually vested in CEOs (Collins & Porras, 1997; Graham, 1995).

New directives and standards for both district and school leaders reflect changed perceptions about educational administration (AASA, 1994; CCSSO, 1996; Hoyle, 1993; Hoyle et al., 1998). These changes clearly shifted the superintendency to a combination of leadership and management (Hoyle et al., 2005; Kowalski, 1998, 2005; Murphy, 2005). As a result, the following questions need to be answered: What is leadership? What is management? How do they differ? How can they be blended together in a superintendent's practice?

Leadership Versus Management

In 1978, Burns stunned the world by claiming that the "crisis of leadership today is the mediocrity or irresponsibility of so many of the men and women in power . . . [who] know far too little about *leadership*" (p. 1). He then proceeded to explore the power, purpose, structure, and origins of leadership before offering his definition.

> Leadership is the reciprocal process of mobilizing, by persons with certain motives and values, various economic, political, and other resources, in a context of competition and conflict, in order to realize goals independently or mutually held by both leaders and followers. (p. 425)

He asserted that the purposes of leadership goals require two important distinctions. Transactional leadership occurs when an individual contacts another for the purpose of exchanging something or bargaining for a personal interest. In these circumstances, the interaction between supervisor and employee is based solely upon an exchange, and the parties go their separate ways. Conversely, transformational leadership engages individuals in an influence relationship for the purpose of achieving mutual goals emerging from pooled or collective interests. In these situations, leaders and followers share a common purpose.

The publication of Burns's seminal work about leadership launched "a bifurcation in leadership thinking around two broad polarities" (Gronn, 2000), one based upon transformational leadership (Bass, 1985) and the other upon management (Jaques, 1989). In his comprehensive analysis of leadership studies, Rost (1991) discussed the differences between leadership and management, something that he contends Burns (1978) failed to do explicitly when he presented his definitions for transactional and transformational leadership. Rost asserts that he and other leadership scholars

> reinterpreted Burns's model of leadership to be, in reality, a model of management and leadership. This reinterpretation states quite simply that Burns's transactional leadership is management, and his transformational leadership is leadership, and the difference between the two is the distinction between leadership and management. (p. 132)

However, Rost stipulates that Burns does not agree with the many interpretations of his conceptual framework in which leadership and management are compared to transactional and transformational leadership (Avolio & Bass, 1988; Enochs, 1981; Graham, 1988).

Rost also cites evidence of widespread backlash against management through the popularly held distinction between leadership and management suggested by Bennis and Nanus (1985) who claim that managers "are people who do things right and leaders are people who do the right thing" (p. 21). According to Johnson (1996), the contrasts in the literature are quite distinctive: "Managers, though competent and dependable, are nevertheless pedestrian, inhibited by the rules and procedures of their organization. Leaders, by contrast, are imaginative, passionate, and freewheeling, if sometimes unpredictable and unreliable" (p. 219). Another example of the distinction made between leadership and management, offered by Zaleznik (1992), is that whereas "managers act to limit choices, leaders develop fresh approaches to long-standing problems and open issues to new options" (p. 129).

To eliminate the confusion, Rost (1991) believes that carefully developed definitions for both leadership and management are needed. Thus, he sought to define leadership in a way that reflects a paradigm shift away from industrial assumptions and values in order to be more suitable for the twenty-first century. He offers his definition as a beginning point for this new era: *Leadership is an influence relationship among leaders and followers who intend real changes that reflect their mutual purposes* (p. 102).

Rost (1991) then crated a definition for management, not based on opposition to or absence of leadership, but instead framed by four essential elements that correspond to the definition of leadership. Rost also offers his definition for management as a starting point for further discussion: *Management is an authority relationship between at least one manager and one subordinate who coordinate their activities to produce and sell particular goods and/or services* (p. 145). He then explained what each element in the definition means.

Although management is based upon a relationship between at least two individuals, only the manager has the authority to manage. At times, management contains coercive behaviors that are clearly understood between the manager and subordinates because the one who manages has been contracted specifically for this function. Thus, management "is a two-way relationship that is primarily top-down as to the directives given and bottom-up as to the responses given" (p. 147). Rost (1991) believes that management exists in all types of organizational models (e.g., hierarchical, democratic, flat). Coordination of activities by the manager and subordinates is required for the accomplishment of goals because "the raison d'être of management" (p. 147) is a specified outcome: producing goods, selling products, providing services, and responding to client or customer needs.

With leadership and management both defined using four elements, Rost (1991) believes that it is now possible to differentiate more easily between the two. Although both are based on relationships, leadership uses influence, whereas management requires authority. Leadership influence is multidirectional, but never coercive; management is top-down directional and coercive when or if necessary. Those engaged in the two relationships are defined differently: Leadership involves leaders and followers, whereas management requires managers and subordinates to be identified in a power relationship based upon clearly identified and understood positions of authority. Unlike leadership that can be initiated by anyone, management is distinctly the task of a manager. Hence, according to Rost, "the words *leader* and *manager, follower* and *subordinate . . .* cannot be used interchangeably" (p. 151).

Two additional distinctions emerge from the two definitions. The underlying purpose for leadership is initiating change—a task accomplished through the intentions of leaders and followers. Alternatively, the outcome of management is the production or selling of goods or services through the joined forces of managers and subordinates. When managers and subordinates attempt to change the processes used in producing or selling, then their relationship can transform into leadership provided that the other three elements in the leadership definition are also present (i.e., relationship is based upon influence; interactions are multidirectional; purpose is mutual). Finally, leadership and management differ in the fourth element: the fundamental reason for the relationship. Leaders and followers share a mutual purpose for coming together; the common purposes of intending change may alter through noncoercive interactions among leadership and followers. Leadership is thus a dynamic relationship. However, management requires coordinated, yet often independent and varied, activities completed by managers and subordinates acting to achieve predetermined objectives. Although leadership might or might not include the coordination of activities, management cannot exist without coordinated activities toward the specific goal of producing or selling goods and/or services. Rost (1991) cautions that both leadership and management are relationships that are basically neutral; only when either relationship is evaluated can labels such as effective or ineffective, good or bad, excellent or mediocre be added.

Leadership and Management

The expectation that superintendents be leaders is clearly evident in the standards-based performances for educational administration that proliferated during the closing decade of the twentieth century (CCSSO, 1996; Hoyle, 1993; Hoyle et al., 2005; Hoyle et al., 1998). The words *leader* and *leadership* appear often throughout various documents that serve as blueprints or guidelines for improving the practice of educational administrators. Embedded within the statements, however, are references to managerial topics, dispositions, and skills required by educational leaders. To function successfully as the CEO of a contemporary school system, a superintendent must be both a leader and a manager.

Local school boards are comprised of elected or appointed officials who delegate authority to superintendents to ensure the delivery of educational and support services to children, youth, and parents in their communities by the district's employees. Most school districts are bureaucratic-like organizations, and thus, much of the work of superintendents and other educational administrators "involves the mundane work of making a bureaucracy work . . . [and] activities quite distant from those implied by a conception of administration as heroic leadership" (March, 1978, p. 233). Unlike businesses and industries that are not dependent on taxes as their sources of revenue, school districts are accountable to taxpayers who support them and policymakers who regulate them. Thus, businesses are less constrained and open to innovation (Collins & Porras, 1997), whereas school districts are regulated and bureaucratic. To ensure order, uniformity, and accountability in public schooling, management must be dispersed throughout school districts. Without effective management (e.g., buses run on schedule, bills paid on time, personnel hired and trained appropriately, student reports delivered regularly, students accounted for, work performance evaluated), school systems collapse into chaos (Johnson, 1996). Without excellent management, leadership is not possible (Fullan & Stiegelbauer, 1991; Gardner, 1990).

Management accomplishes the tasks that leadership envisions and empowers (Bennis & Nanus, 1985; Hersey & Blanchard, 1988). For example, a school district does not need good leadership to survive because poor leadership might not affect the overall operation for years; however, poor management quickly impairs the effectiveness of an organization (Lunenburg & Ornstein, 2004). Effective superintendents understand that they must adopt a balanced blend of leadership and management to function successfully (Johnson, 1996; Leithwood, 1995a). They lead and manage what Leithwood considers to be "the flattest public or private organizations [that] one can imagine, organizations that defy close supervision, even if close supervision seemed like a good idea" (p. 319). They must rely on their principals, teachers, and other administrators to use leadership to achieve district goals and management to complete their assigned work. Although leadership and management are defined as distinctly different relationships to achieve distinctly different purposes (Rost, 1991), both are critically essential dispositions and skills for educational administrators. Moreover, districts need "strong leaders who are also strong managers" (Hanson, 2003, p. 156).

MANAGEMENT TASKS OF THE CONTEMPORARY SUPERINTENDENT

Superintendent as organizational manager is a conceptualization found throughout educational literature (Callahan, 1966; Cuban, 1988; Glass, 2003; Kowalski, 2001, 2003, 2005) and contemporary textbooks used in preparing educational administrators (Cunningham & Cordeiro, 2003;

Davies & Ellison, 1998; Glass, 2004b; Hoyle et al., 2005; Lunenburg & Ornstein, 2004; Norton et al., 1996; Ray, Hack, & Candoli, 2001). Managerial tasks required by superintendents are evident in the knowledge, disposition, and performance expectations found in the AASA standards for superintendents (Hoyle, 1993) and the Interstate School Leadership Licensure Consortium (ISLLC) standards for all educational administrators (CCSSO, 1996). Further, assessment of management performance by superintendents and principals is included in the Educational Leadership Constituent Council (ELCC) standards used in accrediting preparation programs (National Policy Board for Educational Administration [NPBEA], 2002). Although calls for sweeping educational reform have reconfigured much of the work of contemporary superintendents (Björk, Kowalski, & Young, 2005), the need for effective management has remained a primary expectation.

A comparison of the AASA standards for superintendents and the ISLLC standards for educational administrators (Björk, Kowalski, & Browne-Ferrigno, 2005) suggests that six managerial responsibilities exist within both documents: (1) school law, (2) personnel administration, (3) finance and budgeting, (4) facilities administration, (5) collective bargaining and contract maintenance, and (6) public relations. Management is also required for several multirole responsibilities spanning all standards (e.g., motivation, organizational change and development, ethical practice, diversity and multicultural administration, conflict resolution).

In the following discussion, the six functions required of superintendents are based on the definition suggested by Rost (1991). That is, management authority resides with the superintendent or those to whom authority is delegated; work done by subordinates is coordinated and intended to produce something or deliver services. How closely a superintendent works with district employees or others to coordinate the activities depends upon the size of the school system. The influence of district size on a superintendent's managerial behavior will be discussed later in this chapter.

The six major management tasks—governmental regulations, district personnel, finances and budgets, facilities, contractual negotiations, public relations—for a superintendent are discussed in the following sections. It is important to emphasize that whether delegating managerial tasks or doing them personally, a successful superintendent understands that management is an essential component of leading a school district (Kowalski, 1999; Sergiovanni, Burlingame, Coombs, & Thurston, 1999).

Managing Governmental Regulations

American public schools are institutions regulated by federal and state statutes and local policies (Pulliam & Van Patten, 1999; Tyack & Cuban, 1995). School districts are governed by state boards of education that give authority to chief state school officers and staffs in state departments of education to lead and administer public education. Authority to monitor schools is delegated to local boards by states that in turn delegate powers to superintendents to ensure that policies are interpreted and implemented appropriately and that all children have opportunities to learn (Hoyle et al., 2005; Leithwood, 1995a). Hence, a superintendent must stay abreast of changes in school laws to ensure that all district employees comply with, adhere to, and uphold school laws and regulations. Superintendents might delegate compliance reporting to others, but they usually seek assistance personally from attorneys about interpretations of new statutes or regulations, guidance in avoiding or solving a legal matter, or advice about contracts or negotiations (Hoyle et al., 2005; Kowalski, 1999; Lunenburg & Ornstein, 2004). A superintendent must review and recommend policy options to the board about solving problems and planning for the future. Failure by a superintendent or those directed to manage this regulatory function associated with school laws and policies can lead to costly litigation and removal from office (Glass, 2004a).

Special education and most pupil personnel issues are regulated by federal or state statutes and board policies and thus must be supervised by the superintendent to ensure that appropriate programs, accommodations, and services are provided (Kowalski, 1999; Norton et al., 1996). Pupil personnel services include health and counseling, student attendance and accounting, school safety and student discipline, school security, family support, extracurricular activities, and such (Cunningham & Cordeiro, 2003; Lunenburg & Ornstein, 2004). Although many of these management tasks related to students are delegated to principals in district schools, the superintendent is accountable for providing the services.

Managing District Personnel

School districts—whether large or small—are defined by the individuals who work in them, the human resources framework that organizes the work, and the administrators who oversee work performance (Alvesson, 2002; Bolman & Deal, 1997, 2002; Castetter, 2001; Rebore, 2000). A superintendent of a large district usually manages the human resources function by delegating authority to subordinate administrators to ensure that educational and support services are provided to students and ancillary services are delivered to support the enterprise (Lunenburg & Ornstein, 2004). A superintendent of a small district will personally perform most or all of the personnel management tasks (Kowalski, 1999). According to Webb and Norton (2002), this management process comprises six distinct human resource programs: (1) human resource planning, (2) recruitment, (3) selection, (4) professional development, (5) performance appraisal, and (6) compensation. A superintendent must use discretion in hiring those who manage human resources activities (Castetter, 2001; Rebore, 2000) because success in managing the human resources enterprise "is dependent upon the effectiveness of district personnel" (Hoyle et al., 2005, p. 161).

Additionally, as CEO of a learning organization, the superintendent also serves as culture manager (Kotter, 1992; Schein, 1992), a role closely linked to leadership. Organizational structures and administrative processes affect organizational culture and external perceptions about the organization (Lunenburg & Ornstein, 2004). Thus, when attempting to implement initiatives toward improving district functions, student learning opportunities, or employee morale, a superintendent must ensure that communication, rules and procedures, resource allocations, organizational structures, and use of time are aligned to achieve the leadership goals (Deal & Kennedy, 1984, 1999; Kowalski, 1999; Norton et al., 1996).

Managing Finances and Budgets

A school district is a trustee of a community's children and youth and its tax dollars; thus, efficient and appropriate management of public tax dollars is a key responsibility for every superintendent (Glass, 2004a). The development and administration of the district budget is often how a superintendent's performance is assessed (Norton et al., 1996), making fiscal management the most visible management function performed by a superintendent (Kowalski, 1999). Like personnel management, the degree to which a superintendent is involved in the process depends on district size. Fiscal management includes several key responsibilities: (a) program and financial planning; (b) financial data management and budget creating; (c) accounting and auditing; (d) cash flow and debt management; (e) purchasing, inventory management, and materials distribution; (f) risk management; and (g) salary and wage management (Hoyle et al., 2005; Hoyle et al., 1998; Kowalski, 1999).

A major challenge in fiscal management for contemporary superintendents is distributing limited resources in a manner that ensures equitable learning opportunities for all students in an efficiently run district (King, Swanson, & Sweetland, 2003). High-quality financial management is a characteristic of academically high-performing districts; lack of competent fiscal and operational management skills is associated with low student performance and is a leading reason for board dismissal of superintendents (Glass, Björk, & Brunner, 2000).

Managing Facilities

The value of the land upon which schools are built, the buildings themselves, and the equipment in them constitute the single largest investment of public funds in most communities (Glass, 2004a; Hoyle et al., 1998). Public schools serve as custodians of children and youth because of compulsory school attendance laws (Goodlad, 1997), and school districts are often the largest employer in communities (Cunningham & Cordeiro, 2003). Hence, a superintendent is obligated to ensure that district and school buildings are healthful, safe, and adequately maintained (Kowalski, 1999). Although maintenance, construction, and renovation of buildings may seem like "housekeeping aspects of school administration" (Griffiths, 1966, p. 71), facility management has become a major task and challenge for multiple reasons.

Many school districts have experienced burgeoning population growth that has exceeded their capacity to build enough schools; other communities have diminished tax bases because industries have closed, and unemployment makes it difficult for citizens to fund education adequately (King et al., 2003; Kowalski, 1999; Lunenburg & Ornstein, 2004). The expansion of information technology and the demand for updated personal computers, telephones in classrooms for safety reasons, voice mail, and video communication have further expanded the facility maintenance responsibilities of superintendents (Cunningham & Cordeiro, 2003; Sergiovanni et al., 1999). Additionally, environmental hazards (e.g., asbestos, radon gas, lead, toxic indoor air) must be removed, and school infrastructures (e.g., carpentry and masonry, heating and air conditioning, plumbing and sewer) must be repaired and updated, which further requires facilities management (Lunenburg & Ornstein, 2004; Ornstein & Cienkus, 1990).

Managing Contractual Negotiations

Depending on school board policies and procedures, state constitution provisions and statutory laws, district size, and degree of collaboration between parties, collective bargaining and other contractual agreements related to the district are managed personally by the superintendent or an appointed representative (Hoyle et al., 2005; Kowalski, 1999). Contractual agreements between a school board and the professional staff that the district employs must be carefully conducted to ensure that principals, curriculum specialists, business managers, counselors, teachers, and the like have the requisite professional licensure or certification (Lunenburg & Ornstein, 2004). Among the most difficult legal problems a superintendent must handle are those that involve personnel issues (e.g., salary and benefits, tenure, nonrenewal of contract, dismissal); hence, avoidance through careful attention to contracts is the best course of action (Hoyle et al., 2005).

Management of nonpersonnel contractual agreements for purchasing supplies and materials, maintaining and operating facilities, transporting students, supplying and operating food and custodial services, maintaining information databases, and acquiring insurance and employee benefits are also a superintendent's responsibilities (Konnert & Augenstein, 1990). Negotiating contracts for facility construction and renovation is another (Hoyle et al., 1998).

Managing Public Relations

As chief executive of the school system, a superintendent represents the district, and thus must communicate regularly with the broader community and the media (Hoyle et al., 2005). Maintaining good relations with the public is important on a day-to-day basis because perceived performance of the district is often linked directly to approval of the superintendent's performance (Leithwood, 1995b). Public satisfaction with the superintendent and district becomes critically important when additional revenues for capital improvements are needed. Local school boards in most states have taxing authority, but the taxpayers make ultimate decisions about funding school construction or renovation (Norton et al., 1996). The superintendent usually coordinates levy and bond issue campaigns, and although other administrators might be involved, the success or failure of the fundraising efforts rests with the superintendent (Konnert & Augenstein, 1990).

School board meetings are open to the public, and this forum provides transparency for viewing the relationship the superintendent has with the board in its entirety and with various individual members. A superintendent's leadership and management styles are easily visible and thus open to public scrutiny and critique (Johnson, 1996; Kowalski, 1999). Because the superintendent sets the agenda with input from the board, makes executive recommendations, and implements and evaluates policy, he or she cannot be neutral about educational issues (Zeigler, Kehoe, & Reisman, 1985). How conflict is resolved and how advocacy is conducted are linked to how a superintendent manages public relations.

SCHOOL-DISTRICT SIZE AND SUPERINTENDENT MANAGEMENT STYLE

The level of day-to-day management assumed by a superintendent depends primarily upon board expectations of work performance, available dollars from taxing revenues, and district size based upon student enrollment (Konnert & Augenstein, 1990; Lunenburg & Ornstein, 2004). Districts with large student enrollments and sufficient revenues often have large central office staffs that allow the superintendent to delegate managerial responsibilities to others. In the majority of American school districts that serve approximately 2,400 students (Glass et al., 2000), however, superintendents perform managerial tasks themselves, or share the work with one or two other administrators or staff members (Kowalski, 1999). Although superintendents might delegate managerial tasks to others, they retain supervisory responsibility to ensure that the work is completed promptly and correctly because they are ultimately accountable to the local board of education, the community, and the state for effective and legal district management (Glass, 2004a).

The nearly 15,000 school districts in America (Lunenburg & Ornstein, 2004) have been categorized into four groupings based upon student enrollment for the last 50 years that AASA has conducted 10-year studies of the superintendency (Glass, 1992; Glass et al., 2000). The following discussion about ways that superintendents perform managerial tasks is based upon those district-size categories.

Very Large Districts

This grouping of 238 districts includes school systems that serve more than 25,000 students and are usually situated in metropolitan areas in California, Florida, Texas, and Maryland (Lunenburg & Ornstein, 2004). Superintendents in very large districts usually work as general supervisors who delegate managerial authority to deputy or assistant superintendents assigned oversight responsibilities for major divisions such as business, instruction, and administration (Kowalski, 1999). Tasks within divisions are then distributed to directors who assume responsibility for specific functions (e.g., financial management, personnel and pupil services management, community relations, curriculum and instruction, special education, testing and evaluation, facilities maintenance, transportation and safety, food services). Hence, the superintendent typically manages district systems from a distance, relying on information delivered during periodic staff meetings, need-to-know sessions, and regular communication. Because management in large urban districts is a very complex undertaking, these superintendents need skill in recruiting and hiring competent senior managers, working collaboratively with multiple stakeholder groups, managing billion-dollar budgets, and communicating with the media (Glass, 2004a).

Large Districts

Superintendents of the 3,680 districts that serve from 3,000 to 25,000 students (Lunenburg & Ornstein, 2004) have differentiated management responsibilities based on the number of students served. In districts with more than 10,000 students, superintendents usually have the opportunity to hire a number of central office administrators to whom they delegate managerial responsibilities, but their management style is similar to a coordinator, rather than a general supervisor. Superintendents in districts enrolling between 3,000 and 10,000 students assume greater hands-on responsibilities for management tasks, depending upon availability of funds to hire additional district administrators. As central office staffs grow smaller, superintendents and principals work more closely together (Glass, 2004a).

Medium-Sized Districts

Approximately 7,400 school districts have student enrollments that range from 300 to 3,000 students. Smaller districts in this grouping may not have the financial capability to hire a complement of central office staff, so superintendents complete many managerial functions with occasional assistance from one or two central office administrators. A typical central office staff of the average American school district serving 2,400 students usually has an assistant superintendent, business manager, facilities director, transportation director, and food service director. The superintendent of this district size usually supervises directly the work completed by the central office staff and building principals (Glass, 2004a).

Small Districts

Nearly 3,300 districts fall into the category of districts enrolling fewer than 300 students, in which a superintendent works closely with a business manager and principal to perform the myriad management tasks common to districts of all sizes. Glass (2004a) suggests that the superintendent in a small district is actually a management worker simply because no one else is available to do the work. Fortunately, county, regional, and intermediate cooperatives often assist these small districts (Glass et al., 2000).

SUPERINTENDENT SELECTION BASED ON DISTRICT NEEDS

Differentiated expectations about who can best serve as superintendent should be addressed in the employment process, and a district's organizational contexts should determine which skills are needed most. Management expertise is more essential in centralized systems that require a superintendent to distribute authority in hierarchical organizations, whereas leadership expertise is more essential in decentralized systems in which more work is distributed to unit schools and a superintendent works collaboratively with principals (Johnson, 1996; Kowalski, 1999; Lunenburg & Ornstein, 2004).

Determining whether the same or different leadership style is needed is another important selection consideration (Kowalski, 1999). Replacement needs tend to fall into one of three categories: (1) a superintendent who can stabilize a system that has experienced turmoil and bring it back under control, (2) one who can provide continuity by refining initiatives already in place to ensure continuing progress, or (3) one who can introduce changes to remove stagnant or outdated programs or procedures and improve overall district performance (Glass et al., 2000; Johnson, 1996; Lutz & Merz, 1992). Because these three alternatives are situation-based and influenced by the desired goals set by board members, they each require different management and leadership skills.

A district might have passed through an intense series of reforms that proved to be counterproductive or contradictory, and board members might feel that it is imperative to hire a new superintendent who can steady the district, resolve problems and conflicts, and achieve equilibrium. Another task in stabilizing a district might be to evaluate the reform efforts and transform the parts into a cohesive whole, bringing coherence from chaos (Johnson, 1996). In such instances, a superintendent would need strong management skills and the ability to develop trust. The preference for a *stabilizer* superintendent tends to be most prevalent in districts in which tenures of previous superintendents are short (Glass, 2004a).

A school board satisfied with its district's performance might purposefully select a superintendent who is more adept at management than leadership because the objective is to maintain the status quo. These boards tend to be proud of their district's accomplishments and want a superintendent who will refine what already works well. In these communities, citizens might recognize the need for continuous improvement but they are not enthusiastic about employing a change agent. These situations often create a *developer* perspective, that is, the image of a superintendent who refines ideas or programs already in place (Glass, 2004a; Johnson, 1996).

Finally, a superintendent who is conversant about school reform and has previous experience leading change initiatives might be hired by a district to be a *change agent*. To achieve desired changes, a school board tends to seek candidates with strong leadership and management skills and who are career-oriented administrators from outside the community (Johnson, 1996). When school board members seek a stabilizing performance, however, they tend to select place-bound superintendents who are already employed by the district (Carlson, 1972; Miklos, 1988). Only 8% of the superintendents responding to the 2000 AASA-sponsored survey reported that their boards hired them to be reform leaders. Conversely, a vast majority of superintendents perceive that their school boards sought administrators with abilities to develop programs and effectively manage district resources (Glass et al., 2000).

PREPARING SUPERINTENDENTS FOR MANAGEMENT

Chapter 4 presents a framework for superintendent preparation and development based on an extensive review of research and literature about what works and does not work in preparing new generations of district administrators. The proposed framework requires carefully coordinated and maintained university-district partnerships that organize selected superintendent candidates into cohorts with their peers and that provide work-embedded learning opportunities to support theory-to-practice connections (Björk, Kowalski, & Browne-Ferrigno, 2005). Because the role of superintendent as organizational manager is influenced by multiple contextual factors, preparing superintendents for management must be essentially job-embedded.

Most aspiring superintendents tend to be veteran educational administrators who have served as deputy or assistant superintendents, district administrators, and principals (Björk, Glass, & Brunner, 2005). Occasionally, former business executives, elected officials, and retired military officers seek superintendent positions, even if they do not have firsthand experience in the field of education (Fuller et al., 2003; Usdan, 2002). Regardless of their career patterns, aspiring superintendents typically have developed craft knowledge about managerial practices before they begin their professional preparation for district administration. Their craft knowledge, based on learning situated in previous professional experiences (Brown, Collins, & Duguid, 1989; Hansman, 2001; Schön, 1983), needs to be oriented to the management responsibilities of the superintendency (Björk, 2001). Thus, superintendent preparation requires the inclusion of "an enhanced 'multiple-perspective' orientation to the study of organizational and leadership issues" (Jackson & Kelley, 2002, p. 204).

Work-Embedded Learning Opportunities

Although the literature provides descriptions about the superintendency and its roles and expectations, little information about the actual practice of this position is available (Kowalski, 1999). Hence, aspiring superintendents need opportunities to explore district management through carefully planned and monitored field-based practica, in which they observe superintendents' managerial behaviors in practice and assume managerial responsibilities under the guidance of mentors (Björk, Kowalski, & Browne-Ferrigno, 2005; Fuller et al., 2003; Lave & Wenger, 1991). Because field-based learning is contextual, aspiring superintendents engaged in mentored apprenticeships have opportunities for informal and incidental learning that address their self-identified specific needs (Glickman, Gordon, & Ross-Gordon, 2004; Kerka, 1998; Marsick & Watkins, 1990, 2001; Wilson, 1993). To help aspiring superintendents make connections between practice and theory, they also need concurrent opportunities to meet regularly with cohort peers, university professors, and management practitioners. During cohort sessions away from their work sites, aspiring superintendents can discuss openly what they are observing, doing, and learning in the field and reflect about those experiences (Björk, 2001; Browne-Ferrigno & Muth, 2004; Merriam & Clark, 1993; Schön, 1987).

Because management requirements and practices vary significantly among districts (Glass et al., 2000; Johnson, 1996), superintendent candidates need opportunities to work in several different-sized districts throughout a formal yearlong internship—or, more ideally, through a practicum series concurrent with formal preparation coursework, followed by a formal yearlong apprenticeship. A goal of preparation programs should be to have a cadre of trained mentors representing various work conditions (e.g., different-sized districts located in different settings) to allow prospective superintendents to rotate through two or three districts during their program-sponsored clinical practice. Rotation of job-embedded experiences enhances an aspirant's opportunities for being hired after program completion (Browne-Ferrigno & Muth, 2004; Muth & Browne-Ferrigno, 2004).

Management Socialization

Socialization into a role requires reflection on and about practice with those who can help aspiring administrators work through the ambiguities and uncertainties of role-identity transformation (Browne-Ferrigno, 2003; Schön, 1987). Opportunities to study administrative theories and discuss how leadership and management are essential to superintendents should be a core element of professional preparation. Socialization to a new role requires transformative and self-directed learning, networking with members of the aspired community of practice, and informal coaching and mentoring with veteran practitioners (Brookfield, 1986; Cranton, 1994; Glickman et al., 2004; Mezirow, 1981; Mezirow & Associates, 1990; Wenger, 1998).

During the closing decades of the twentieth century, the field of educational administration, perhaps influenced by postindustrial thinking but most certainly by demands for educational reform, made leadership appear to be the panacea for solving public education's problems. Strategies for reforming schools are linked to flattening bureaucratic organizational structures, distributing leadership throughout schools and districts, and collaborating with stakeholder groups, to name a few. This same idea about the importance of leadership over management appears in calls for changing the way principals and superintendents are prepared (Björk, Kowalski, & Browne-Ferrigno, 2005; Murphy, 1992; Young & Petersen, 2002), in new standards for the preparation and practice of educational administrators (AASA, 1994; CCSSO, 1996; Hoyle, 1993; Hoyle et al., 1998), and recently published books for use during superintendent preparation (Cambron-McCabe, Cunningham, Harvey, & Koff, 2004; Lowery & Harris, 2003).

Leadership is a critically important element of educational administration because leadership is required to make changes (Burns, 1978; Rost, 1991). However, as this chapter has characterized, superintendents must also use management to complete critically important tasks delegated to them by school boards or stipulated by state policies. As Fullan and Stiegelbauer (1991) and Gardner (1990) assert, leadership is not possible without management. Hence, preparation programs for aspiring superintendents must provide times when candidates explore the critical differences between leadership and management. They need opportunities to practice relating with others using influence and authority skills through simulations, case studies, and role-playing activities within the risk-safe environments of closed-cohort sessions. Working independently or with cohort peers, they need to conduct disciplined inquiries within districts to explore how leadership and management are used by superintendents and evaluated by others.

Stages of Superintendent Development

Adult learning is influenced by a variety of factors, including learner's age and gender, life experiences, career aspirations, and experiences, to name just a few (Clark & Caffarella, 1999; Cross, 1991; Merriam & Caffarella, 1999; Merriam & Clark, 1993). Hence, the notion that an aspiring superintendent is fully prepared to assume leadership of a district immediately after program completion is not always true. Previous professional experiences (e.g., high school principal versus elementary school principal, work in a large central office complex versus a small district office), board expectations of work performance (e.g., change agent versus stabilizer or developer), and type of district (e.g., urban, exurban, suburban, rural) also affect an aspirant's readiness for a specific superintendent position.

Findings from the last two AASA 10-year studies of the superintendency (Glass, 1992; Glass et al., 2000) indicate that an increasing number of new superintendents had already worked as central office administrators before assuming the superintendency. District-level administration provided them greater opportunities to gain a variety of management experiences than earlier career patterns did. This trend prompted Glass (2004a) to propose an identification system—based upon three levels of management certificates—to indicate an aspiring superintendent's professional development, experience, and readiness to assume the role as organizational manager.

The three-tiered mastery of management preparation would accommodate differences in district sizes, types, and budgets and an aspirant's professional expertise (Glass, 2004a). The highest tier in the certification sequence, called *executive management*, would indicate that an aspiring superintendent has received training and has proven through satisfactory performance assessments to be ready to serve a large district (enrollment between 3,000 and 25,000 students). The second certification level, *registered management*, applies to a candidate's readiness to assume leadership of a medium-sized district (enrollment between 300 and 3,000 students), whereas *qualified management* certification would indicate readiness for a small district (enrollment fewer than 300 students). Although Glass perceives that separate performance requirements would need to be developed for each certification level, he does not envision that every aspiring superintendent would need to begin at the bottom tier.

The superintendency of districts situated in large urban and exurban settings, however, appears to require something quite different. Based on findings from their study of the superintendency in the 100 largest districts in America, Fuller et al. (2003) assert that "the big-city superintendency should be considered a public management position, one that should encourage people to get their basic preparation . . . [through careers] providing experience in complex organizations, surrounded by difficult political and governance issues" (p. 62). These 100 superintendents included those who were trained traditionally (through university-based educational administration preparation programs and experience as school principal and occasionally as central office administrator) and those trained nontraditionally (through careers in social services administration, city management, law, and business). Nontraditional superintendents reported feeling more prepared in "managing conflict, creating coalitions, [and] dealing with community relations" and had more "management skills in finance, personnel, and real estate" (p. 60) than the traditional superintendents.

Like the multiple stages of adult development, superintendent development depends on many different factors. Management skills learned in other settings can be adaptable for the superintendency, so flexibility is needed to provide individualized preparation when appropriate.

Multiple Stakeholder Partnerships

Preparing superintendents to be effective organizational managers requires all stakeholders—universities, school districts, professional associations, state agencies—to work together as partners in providing a variety of work-embedded learning experiences, socialization opportunities, and reflective seminars (Björk, Kowalski, & Browne-Ferrigno, 2005; Glass, 2004a). Although the AASA and ISLLC standards provide blueprints concerning knowledge, disposition, and performance expectations for all educational administrators, many district-level management requirements are not stipulated in those standards. Collaboration across institutional boundaries is needed to develop an approved superintendent-preparation curriculum that includes management tasks specific to the dimensions of the job (e.g., working with the public and media, negotiating contracts related to personnel and real estate issues, operating complex systems, and handling financial responsibilities). Delivering the curriculum requires the coordinated efforts by university professors and administrative practitioners, with support from members of professional organizations. Developing a tiered certification system requires collaboration with state agencies to gain support for its adoption and then its oversight after it is implemented. Clearly, the responsibility for preparing superintendents requires boundary- crossing collaboration among state education agencies, professional organizations, universities, and districts.

The responsibility and accountability of successful preparation of superintendents as organizational managers must be shared and can no longer remain the sole responsibility of universities. Kowalski and Glass

(2002) recommend that partners in the process align their efforts to ensure that effective management preparation for both aspiring and veteran superintendents is provided. Initial licensure in any profession, including school administration, ensures basic competence; it does not constitute a warranty that practitioners know everything they will need during an entire career (Kowalski, 2004). Therefore, Kowalski and Glass (2002) propose that state education agencies support superintendent development further by (a) requiring districts to provide release time for training, internships, and apprenticeships; (b) providing incentives for principals and central office administrators to enter superintendent training programs, and (c) establishing systems to update and monitor continually the skills of central office administrators already recognized.

CONCLUSION

Organizational management is a critical role assigned to superintendents, whether authority is stipulated in state educational policy or delegated by local school boards. Performance as successful CEOs depends on understanding differences between leadership and management and knowing when to use the appropriate role. Depending on the size and structure of the district in which they work, superintendents must either supervise others or complete the work themselves to ensure that governmental regulations, district personnel, finances and budgets, facilities, contractual negotiations, and public relations are managed appropriately.

Preparing superintendents to be organizational managers must be a coherent integration of knowledge development through professional seminars and formal courses, skill development through guided and independent field-based learning experiences, and competency development through personal self-assessment and performance evaluation by mentors and others. The experiences must align with state requirements for licensure and prepare practitioners for successful placement as superintendents. The responsibility for preparing superintendents requires boundary-crossing collaboration among state education agencies, professional associations, universities, and districts.

REFERENCES

Alvesson, M. (2002). *Understanding organizational culture.* Thousand Oaks, CA: Sage.

American Association of School Administrators. (1994). *Roles and responsibilities: School boards and superintendents.* Arlington, VA: Author.

Avolio, B. J., & Bass, B. M. (1988). Transformational leadership, charisma, and beyond. In J. G. Hunt, B. R. Baliga, H. P. Dachler, & C. A. Schriescheim (Eds.), *Emerging leadership vistas* (pp. 29–49). Lexington, MA: Lexington Books.

Bass, B. M. (1985). *Leadership and performance beyond expectations.* New York: Free Press.

Bennis, W., & Mische, M. (1995). *The 21st century organization: Reinventing through reengineering*. San Francisco: Jossey-Bass.

Bennis, W., & Nanus, B. (1985). *Leaders: The strategies for taking charge*. New York: Harper & Row.

Bennis, W., & Townsend, R. (1995). *Reinventing leadership: Strategies to empower the organization*. New York: Quill.

Björk, L. G. (2001). Preparing the next generation of superintendents: Integrating formal and experiential knowledge. In C. C. Brunner & L. G. Björk (Eds.), *The new superintendency: Advances in research theories of school management and educational policy* (pp. 19–54). Oxford, UK: JAI Elsevier Press.

Björk, L. G., Glass, T. E., & Brunner, C. C. (2005). Characteristics of American school superintendents. In L. G. Björk & T. J. Kowalski (Eds.), *The contemporary superintendent: Preparation, practice, and development*. Thousand Oaks, CA: Corwin.

Björk, L. G., Kowalski, T. J., & Browne-Ferrigno, T. (2005). Learning theory and research: A framework for changing superintendent preparation and development. In L. G. Björk & T. J. Kowalski (Eds.), *The contemporary superintendent: Preparation, practice, and development*. Thousand Oaks, CA: Corwin.

Björk, L. G., Kowalski, T. J., & Young, M. D. (2005). National education reform reports: Implications for professional preparation and development. In L. G. Björk & T. J. Kowalski (Eds.), *The contemporary superintendent: Preparation, practice, and development*. Thousand Oaks, CA: Corwin.

Blumberg, A. (1985). *The school superintendent: Living with conflict*. New York: Teachers College Press.

Bolman, L. G., & Deal, T. (1997). *Re-framing organizations: Artistry, choice, and leadership* (2nd ed.). Thousand Oaks, CA: Corwin.

Bolman, L. G., & Deal, T. (2002). *Re-framing the path to school leadership: A guide for teachers and principals*. Thousand Oaks, CA: Corwin.

Brookfield, S. (1986). *Understanding and facilitating adult learning*. San Francisco: Jossey-Bass.

Brown, J. S., Collins, A., & Duguid, P. (1989). Situated cognition and the culture of learning. *Educational Researcher, 18*(1), 32–42.

Browne-Ferrigno, T. (2003). Becoming a principal: Role conception, initial socialization, role-identity transformation, purposeful engagement. *Educational Administration Quarterly, 39*(4), 468–503.

Browne-Ferrigno, T., & Muth, R. (2004). Leadership mentoring in clinical practice: Role socialization, professional development, and capacity building. *Educational Administration Quarterly, 40*(4), 468–494.

Brunner, C. C., Grogan, M., & Björk, L. G. (2002). Shifts in the discourse defining the superintendency: Historical and current foundations of the position. In J. Murphy (Ed.), *The educational leadership challenge: Redefining leadership for the 21st century* (pp. 211–238). One Hundred-first Yearbook of the National Society for the Study of Education, Part 1. Chicago: University of Chicago Press.

Burns, J. M. (1978). *Leadership*. New York: Harper Torchbooks.

Callahan, R.E. (1962). *The education and the cult of efficiency: A study of the social forces that have shaped the administration of public schools*. Chicago: University of Chicago Press.

Callahan, R. E. (1966). *The superintendent of schools: A historical analysis*. (ERIC Document Reproduction Service No. ED 0104 410)

Cambron-McCabe, N., Cunningham, L. L., Harvey, J., & Koff, R. H. (2004). *The superintendent's fieldbook: A guide for leaders of learning*. Thousand Oaks, CA: Corwin.

Carlson, R. E. (1972). *School superintendents: Careers and performance*. Columbus, OH: Merrill.

Castetter, W. B. (2001). *The personnel function in educational administration* (7th ed.). Columbus, OH: Merrill.

Clark, M. C., & Caffarella, R. S. (1999). *An update on adult development theory: New ways of thinking about the life course. New Directions for Adult and Continuing Education* (No. 84). San Francisco: Jossey-Bass.

Collins, J. C. (2001). *Good to great: Why some companies make the leap . . . and others don't.* New York: HarperBusiness.

Collins, J. C., & Porras, J. I. (1997). *Built to last: Successful habits of visionary companies.* New York: HarperBusiness.

Council of Chief State School Officers. (1996). *Interstate School Leaders Licensure Consortium: Standards for school leaders.* Washington, DC: Author.

Cranton, P. (1994). *Understanding and promoting transformative learning.* San Francisco: Jossey-Bass.

Cross, K. P. (1991). *Adults as learners.* San Francisco: Jossey-Bass.

Cuban, L. (1976). *Urban school chiefs under fire.* Chicago: University of Chicago Press.

Cuban, L. (1988). *The managerial imperatives and the practice of leadership in schools.* Albany: State University of New York Press.

Cunningham, W. G., & Cordeiro, P. A. (2003). *Educational leadership: A problem-based approach* (2nd ed.). Boston: Allyn & Bacon.

Davies, B., & Ellison, L. (1998). *School leadership for the 21st century: A competency and knowledge approach.* New York: Routledge.

Deal, T. E., & Kennedy, A. A. (1984). *Corporate cultures: The rites and rituals of corporate life.* Reading, MA: Addison-Wesley.

Deal, T. E., & Kennedy, A. A. (1999). *The new corporate cultures: Revitalizing the workplace after downsizing, mergers, and reengineering.* Reading, MA: Perseus Books.

Enochs, J. C. (1981, November). Up from management. *Phi Delta Kappan, 63*(3), 175–178.

Fullan, M. (2003). *The moral imperative of school leadership.* Thousand Oaks, CA: Corwin.

Fullan, M. (2004). *Leadership and sustainability.* Thousand Oaks, CA: Corwin.

Fullan, M., & Stiegelbauer, S. (1991). *The new meaning of educational change.* New York: Teachers College Press.

Fuller, H. L., Campbell, C., Celio, M. B., Harvey, J., Immerwahr, J., & Winger, A. (2003, July). *An impossible job? The view from the urban superintendent's chair.* A report prepared under a grant from The Wallace Foundation. Seattle: University of Washington.

Gardner, J. W. (1990). *On leadership.* New York: Free Press.

Glass, T. E. (1992). *The study of the American school superintendency.* Arlington, VA: American Association of School Administrators.

Glass, T. E. (2003). *The superintendency: A managerial imperative?* Paper presented at the annual meeting of the American Educational Research Association, Chicago.

Glass, T. E. (2004a, April). *Preparing and training superintendents for the mission of executive management.* Paper presented at the annual meeting of the American Educational Research Association, San Diego, CA.

Glass, T. E. (2004b). *The history of educational administration viewed through its textbooks.* Lanham, MD: Scarecrow.

Glass, T. E., Björk, L. G., & Brunner, C. C. (2000). *The study of the American school superintendency: A look at the superintendent in the new millennium.* Arlington, VA: American Association of School Administrators.

Glickman, C. D., Gordon, S. P., & Ross-Gordon, J. M. (2004). *SuperVision and instructional leadership: A developmental approach* (6th ed.). Boston: Pearson.

Goodlad, J. I. (1997). *In praise of education.* New York: Teachers College Press.

Graham, J. W. (1988). Transformation leadership: Fostering follower autonomy, not automatic followership. In J. G. Hunt, B. R. Baliga, H. P. Dachler, & C. A. Schriescheim (Eds.), *Emerging leadership vistas* (pp. 73–79). Lexington, MA: Lexington Books.

Graham, P. (Ed.). (1995). Mary Parker Follett—Prophet of management: A celebration of writings from the 1920s. Boston: Harvard Business School Press.

Griffiths, D. (1966). *The school superintendent.* New York: Center for Applied Research in Education.

Gronn, P. (2000). Distributed properties: A new architecture for leadership. *Educational Management & Administration, 28*(3), 317–338.

Hansman, C. A. (2001). Context-based adult learning. In S. Mirriam (Ed.), *The new update on adult learning theory. New Directions of Adult and Continuing Education* (No. 89). San Francisco: Jossey-Bass.

Hanson, E. M. (2003). *Educational administration and organizational behavior* (5th ed.). Boston: Allyn & Bacon.

Hersey, P., & Blanchard, K. (1988). *Management and organizational behavior.* Englewood, NJ: Prentice Hall.

Hoyle, J. R. (1993). *Professional standards for the superintendency.* Arlington, VA: American Association of School Administrators.

Hoyle, J. R., Björk, L. G., Collier, V., & Glass, T. E. (2005). *The superintendent as CEO: Standards-based performance.* Thousand Oaks, CA: Corwin.

Hoyle, J. R., English, F., & Steffy, B. (1998). *Skills for successful 21st century school leaders: Standards for peak performers.* Arlington, VA: American Association of School Administrators.

Jaques, E. (1989). *Requisite organization: The CEO's guide to creative structure and leadership.* Arlington, VA: Cason Hall.

Jackson, B. L, & Kelley, C. (2002). Exceptional and innovative programs in educational leadership. *Educational Administration Quarterly, 38*(2), 192–212.

Johnson, S. M. (1996). *Leading to change: The challenge of the new superintendency.* San Francisco: Jossey-Bass.

Kerka, S. (1998). *New perspectives on mentoring.* ERIC Digest No. 194. (ERIC Document Reproduction Service No. ED 418 249)

King, R., Swanson, A. D., & Sweetland, S. R. (2003). *School finance: Achieving high standards with equity and efficiency* (3rd ed.). Boston: Allyn & Bacon.

Konnert, M. W., & Augenstein, J. J. (1990). *The superintendency in the nineties: What superintendents and board members need to know.* Lancaster, PA: Technomic.

Kotter, J. P. (1992). *Corporate culture and performance.* New York: Free Press.

Kowalski, T. J. (1998). Critiquing the CEO. *American School Board Journal, 185,* 43–44.

Kowalski, T. J. (1999). *The school superintendent: Theory, practice, and cases.* Upper Saddle River, NJ: Merrill.

Kowalski, T. J. (2001). The future of local school governance: Implications for board members and superintendents. In C. C. Brunner & L. G. Björk (Eds.), *The new superintendency* (pp. 183–201). Oxford, UK: JAI Elsevier Press.

Kowalski, T. J. (2003). *Contemporary school administration* (2nd ed.). Boston: Allyn & Bacon.

Kowalski, T. J. (2004). The ongoing war for the soul of school administration. In T. J. Lasley (Ed.), *Better leaders for America's schools: Perspectives on the Manifesto* (pp. 92–114). Columbia, MO: University Council for Educational Administration.

Kowalski, T. J. (2005). Evolution of the school district superintendent position. In L. G. Björk & T. J. Kowalski (Eds.), *The contemporary superintendent: Preparation, practice, and development.* Thousand Oaks, CA: Corwin.

Kowalski, T. J., & Björk, L. G. (n.d.). *Role expectations of the district superintendent: Implications for deregulating preparation and licensing.* Unpublished manuscript.

Kowalski, T. J., & Glass, T. E. (2002). Preparing superintendents in the 21st century. In B. Cooper & L. Fusarelli (Eds.), *The promises and perils facing today's school superintendent* (pp. 41–60). Lanham, MD: Scarecrow Education.

Lave, J., & Wenger, E. (1991). *Situated learning: Legitimate peripheral participation.* New York: Cambridge University Press.

Leithwood, K. (1995a). Toward a more comprehensive appreciation of effective school district leadership. In K. Leithwood (Ed.), *Effective school district leadership: Transforming politics into education* (pp. 315–340). Albany: State University of New York Press.

Leithwood, K. (1995b). *Effective school district leadership: Transforming politics into education.* Albany: State University of New York Press.

Lowery, S., & Harris, S. (2003). *Standards-based leadership: A case study book for the superintendency.* Lanham, MD: Scarecrow Education.

Lunenburg, F. C., & Ornstein, A. C. (2004). *Educational administration: Concepts and practices* (4th ed.). Belmont, CA: Wadsworth.

Lutz, F. W., & Merz, C. (1992). *The politics of school/community relations.* New York: Teachers College Press.

March, J. G. (1978). American public school administration: A short analysis. *School Review, 86,* 217–250.

Marsick, V. J., & Watkins, K. (1990). *Informal and incidental learning in the workplace.* New York: Routledge.

Marsick, V. J., & Watkins, K. E. (2001). Informal and incidental learning. In S. Merriam (Ed.), *The new update on adult learning theory. New Directions for Adult and Continuing Education* (No. 89). San Francisco: Jossey-Bass.

Merriam, S., & Caffarella, R. (1999). *Learning in adulthood* (2nd ed.). San Francisco: Jossey-Bass.

Merriam, S. B., & Clark, M. C. (1993). Learning from experience: What makes it significant? *International Journal of Lifelong Education, 12*(2), 129–138.

Mezirow, J. D. (1981). A critical theory of adult learning and education. *Adult Education, 32*(1), 3–24.

Mezirow, J. D., & Associates. (1990). *Fostering critical reflection in adulthood: A guide to transformative and emancipatory learning.* San Francisco: Jossey-Bass.

Miklos, E. (1988). Administrator selection, career patterns, succession, and socialization. In N. J. Boyan (Ed.), *Handbook of research on educational administration* (pp. 53–76). New York: Longman.

Murphy, J. (1992). *The landscape of leadership preparation: Reframing the education of school administrators.* Thousand Oaks, CA: Corwin.

Murphy, J. (2005). Uncovering the foundations of *ISLLC Standards* and addressing concerns in the academic community. *Educational Administration Quarterly.*

Muth, R., & Browne-Ferrigno, T. (2004). Why don't our graduates take administrative positions, and what's the cost? In C. S. Carr & C. L. Fulmer (Eds.), *Educational leadership: Knowing the way, showing the way, going the way* (pp. 294–306). Twelfth Annual Yearbook of the National Council of Professors of Educational Administration. Lanham, MD: Scarecrow Education.

Naisbitt, J. (1985). *Re-inventing the corporation.* New York: Warner Books.

National Policy Board for Educational Administration. (2002). *Standards for advanced programs in educational leadership for principals, superintendents, curriculum directors, and supervisors.* Retrieved April 12, 2002, from http://www.npbea.org/ELCC

Norton, M. S., Webb, L. D., Dlugosh, L. L., & Sybouts, W. (1996). *The school superintendency: New responsibilities, new leadership.* Boston: Allyn & Bacon.

Ornstein, A. C., & Cienkus, R. C. (1990). The nation's school repair bill. *American School Board Journal, 177,* 4A.

Pasternack, B. A., & Viscio, A. J. (1998). *The centerless corporation: A new model for transforming your organization for growth and prosperity.* New York: Simon & Schuster.

Peters, T., & Waterman, R. (1982). *In search of excellence.* New York: Warner Books.

Pulliam, J. D., & Van Patten, J. J. (1999). *History of education in America* (7th ed.). Upper Saddle River, NJ: Merrill.

Ray, J. R., Hack, W. G., & Candoli, C. (2001). *School business administration: A planning approach* (7th ed.). Boston: Allyn & Bacon.

Razik, T. A., & Swanson, A. D. (2001). *Fundamental concepts of educational leadership* (2nd ed.). Upper Saddle River, NJ: Merrill.

Rebore, R. W. (2000). *Human resources administration: A management approach* (6th ed.). Boston: Allyn & Bacon.

Rost, J. C. (1991). *Leadership for the twenty-first century.* Westport, CT: Praeger.

Schein, E. H. (1992). *Organizational culture and leadership* (2nd ed.). San Francisco: Jossey-Bass.

Schön, D. A. (1983). *The reflective practitioner: How professionals think in action.* New York: Basic Books.

Schön, D. A. (1987). *Educating the reflective practitioner: Toward a new design for teaching and learning in the professions.* San Francisco: Jossey-Bass.

Sergiovanni, T. J., Burlingame, M., Coombs, F. S., & Thurston, P. W. (1999). *Educational governance and administration.* Boston: Allyn & Bacon.

Toffler, A. (1980). *The third wave.* New York: Bantam Books.

Tyack, D., & Cuban, L. (1995). *Tinkering toward utopia: A century of public school reform.* Cambridge, MA: Harvard University Press.

Usdan, M. D. (2002). Reactions to articles commissioned by the National Commission for the Advancement of Education Leadership Preparation. *Educational Administration Quarterly, 38*(2), 300–307.

Webb, L. D., & Norton, M. S. (2002). *Human resources administration: Personnel issues and needs in education* (4th ed.). Upper Saddle River, NJ: Prentice Hall.

Wenger, E. (1998). *Communities of practice: Learning, meaning, and identity.* New York: Cambridge University Press.

Wilson, A. L. (1993). The promise of situated cognition. In S. Merriam (Ed.), *An update on adult learning theory. New Directions for Adult and Continuing Education* (No. 57). San Francisco: Jossey-Bass.

Young, M. D., & Petersen, G. J. (Eds.). (2002). Ensuring the capacity of university-based educational leadership preparation: The collected works of the National Commission for the Advancement of Educational Leadership Preparation [Special issue]. *Educational Administration Quarterly, 38*(2).

Zaleznik, A. (1992, March–April). Managers and leaders: Are they different? *Harvard Business Review,* 126–135.

Zeigler, H., Kehoe, E., & Reisman, J. (1985). *City managers and school superintendents: Response to community conflict.* New York: Praeger.

7

Superintendent as Educational Statesman and Political Strategist

Lars G. Björk and D. Keith Gurley

For many, the term "statesman" conjures images of stately Founding Fathers wisely and benevolently guiding their country through democratic processes and striving to preserve the commonwealth. The role of *educational statesman* is conceptualized as one of the most important roles that superintendents must play to effectively function in their jobs (Callahan, 1967). The term does not evoke an image of today's school superintendents, however, especially considering the harsh political realities they face when performing their duties (Björk & Lindle, 2001; Boyd, 1974). Pressures stemming from unrelenting calls for school reform, heightened levels of instructional accountability, demands for providing a broader range of support services to more students, increased interest group activity, and the politicization of educational policy in contexts characterized by declining resources depict the harsh reality of superintendents' present circumstances that can limit opportunities for reasoned discourse (Björk & Keedy, 2001; Cibulka, 1995; Rowan & Miskel, 1999). However, responding to demands from multiple and diverse groups and graciously enduring criticism require more than street-level political savvy. They require understanding the purpose of public education and acuity for achieving balance through democratic processes. These qualities suggest the role of statesman. A discussion of the history and evolution of the superintendent's role as statesman examines the original use of the term, explores the implications, and assesses the appropriateness of the term in understanding the function of American school superintendents throughout their history and into the twenty-first century.

BACKGROUND

Callahan (1967) identified four stages in the evolution of the American superintendency (1865–1966) and describes them as distinct role conceptualizations: *scholarly leaders* (1850–1900), *business managers* (1900–1930), *educational statesmen* (1930–1950), and *social scientists* (1950–1967). Kowalski (2003) argues persuasively that a fifth role conceptualization, *communicator*, is needed to describe how they enacted their role over the course of history (1850–2003). After the stock market crash at the end of the 1920s, the aura of business efficiency faded and the American populace embraced the populist idea that schools should prepare America's youth for work and life in a democratic society (Kowalski, 1999). As a consequence, between 1930 and the mid-1950s, the role of the superintendent again shifted to meet expectations held by communities and local boards of education to serve as *educational statesman* Callahan (1967). This new role of superintendent as statesman resulted from a growing belief that "public schools should practice and model democracy and develop symbiotic relationships with the communities in which they functioned" (Kowalski, 1999, p. 191). To better understand Callahan's (1967) role conceptualization of the superintendent as educational statesman, we need to briefly explore the philosophical roots of the term and the construct of political statesman as presented by Plato and the American statesman Alexander Hamilton.

Plato's Politicus

The notion of the statesman has its roots in the writings of Plato. When, in 400 B.C.E., Plato wrote the dialogue *Politicus* (Latin for "statesman"), he asserted that the ideal form of government would be based upon "the supremacy not of law, but of the wise and kingly man"[1] (Plato, trans. 1961). Although the notion of a sovereign statesman-king may on its face seem antithetical to the role of leadership in a democratic state, a brief examination of some of the key characteristics of Plato's statesman may prove enlightening when considering the application of this role conceptualization to the American superintendency and to the evaluation of its relevance for school leadership today and in the future.

In the dialogue, Plato distinguished between the knowledge that an individual possesses and the application of that knowledge to the practice of government. Plato characterized the statesman as acting from the basis of a reservoir of expert and tacit knowledge as well as applying that knowledge, as a craftsman, to the benefit of all governed. Plato's (trans. 1961) statesman was the "one who really understands what is for the good of the commonwealth, and is right, and consequently makes the commonwealth better, whether by gentle measures or by sharp 'social surgery'" (p. 229). This skillful, benevolent application of knowledge Plato called the "art of politics" (Plato, trans. 1961).

In fulfilling his role as political statesman, a leader acts unilaterally and paternalistically to control and direct every major function of society, including, most notably, matters of military, rhetoric (i.e., diplomacy), and education. Specifically, in the educational arena, Plato's statesman is the sole determiner not only of who in the society—based upon merit—is to be educated but also of what curriculum is best suited to meet the needs of the society. Near the end of his dialogue, Plato elaborates on the function of the statesman task through the use of a weaving metaphor, wherein the master weaver is careful to sort out the bad material from the good, choosing only the best to be used in building the social fabric. It should be noted that in ancient Greece, a small percentage of the population were citizens and accorded privileges as a matter of course associated with a democratic society. In this regard, Plato's notions of democracy with respect to who rules and who benefits are about the few rather than the many.

Given the autocratic nature, then, of Plato's original conception of statesman, one might wonder just how appropriately it can be applied to school leadership in a democracy. Alexander Hamilton's interpretation of the statesman, on the other hand, is very different from that of Plato's. A brief look at this variation helps to illuminate the role from a different angle.

Hamilton's Early American Statesmanship

Alexander Hamilton's view of statesmanship, although still quite centralized in the leadership of one man, was considerably different from that of Plato's original conception. Hamilton believed that the statesman had to be the "true politician," conscious of and responsive to at least two constituencies: the common people and the economic elite (Miroff, 1993, p. 27). During the years surrounding the forging of the new American nation, Hamilton agreed with Plato that the statesman must operate from a position of knowledge and strength. Hamilton also believed, however, that the statesman had to be practical and pragmatic in his approach to navigate the political landscape and to fulfill his role as architect for the common good (Miroff, 1993).

Nevertheless, Hamilton's statesman remained aloof and above the people, maintaining his position as an aristocrat. Miroff (1993) concluded that Hamilton's vision of the statesman was "rooted in disenchantment with and distrust of the American people . . . [who were] incapable of making good use of political freedom" (p. 30). His views of a democratic society with respect to who rules and who benefits is not unlike Plato's in that they are decidedly paternalistic rather than egalitarian and about the few rather than the many.

Callahan's Educational Statesman

Exactly how, then, did Callahan (1967) conceive of the role of the superintendent as educational statesman? Was it, indeed, Callahan's intent to characterize the superintendent as a sovereign autocrat, working benevolently for the good of all children as Plato's statesman suggests? Was his idea more akin to that of Hamilton's statesman: the superintendent as expert leader, clearly positioned as superior to the "common people" of schools, yet acting as a political strategist (Boyd, 1974; Brunner, Grogan, & Björk, 2001), aptly influencing the "elite" powerbrokers and decision makers of the community? Or is it possible that Callahan's use of the metaphor of statesman is a misnomer given what we will suggest is the long-standing highly political nature of the history of the American superintendency and its record (Carter & Cunningham, 1997; Kowalski, 1995, 1999; Ortiz & Marshall, 1988)?

Superintendent as Negotiator-Statesman

In his original presentation of the four-role conceptualizations of the superintendent, including the educational statesman role, Callahan (1967) suggested that the roles represented roughly distinct and consecutive eras of leadership. His presentation implied that the roles evolved and developed in a normative fashion, wherein superintendents, though not entirely abandoning a previous role, focused primarily on the role best suited to meet the contextual demands of the day. For example, although the principles of scientific management were by no means laid aside during the era of the statesman, superintendents were expected to act differently, more as statesmen and democratic leaders than as bureaucratic managers. In addition, district size and community contexts influenced the way superintendents enacted their roles. For example, superintendents serving in large urban, suburban, and rural districts would adopt a leadership style best suited to their respective circumstances.

Cuban (1976) offered a more blended, holistic interpretation in his analysis of interviews with key urban superintendents and of the proceedings and public addresses of the National Education Association's Department of Superintendence and the professional dialogue published in the *American School Board Journal*, 1870 to 1950. Across these eight decades, Cuban noted three basic types of role conceptualizations—*teacher-scholar, chief administrator,* and *negotiator-statesman*—which closely corresponded to Callahan's (1967) first three conceptualizations. Cuban's analysis differs from that of Callahan, however, in that he explicitly states, "each [role] waxed and waned as time passed, yet none disappeared. They competed; they were durable" (p. 21). Cuban pointed out that the multiple roles of the American superintendent existed simultaneously and that superintendents donned each role as the individual contexts dictated. The specific role of the negotiator-statesman, according to Cuban, was never a distinct, time-bound conceptualization; it was an abiding, if steadily increasing, reality of the position. Such an assertion, that the role of the superintendent had always been (Cuban, 1976) or at least was emerging (Callahan, 1967) as a decidedly political enterprise, was clearly a challenging one in a profession that had traditionally regarded political involvement as inappropriate and even unprofessional (Björk & Lindle, 2001; Cibulka, 1995; Kowalski, 1995, 1999; Sykes, 1999).

Superintendent as Political Strategist

Nearly three decades ago, Boyd (1974) raised the question of whether the role of superintendent is more appropriately conceptualized as statesman or as political strategist. Through his analysis of elementary school districts in the urban Chicago area, Boyd concluded that superintendents who tried to ignore or suppress conflict in a school district or community (i.e., attempted to emulate Plato's model of the statesman and retain an apolitical approach) were actually successful only in intensifying the conflict, whereas superintendents who were both politically sensitive and proactive in their management approaches met with greater success in addressing multiple and often conflicting interests within a community.

There is broad agreement among policymakers, professors, and practitioners that the nature of schooling is becoming increasingly complex and decidedly political. Although superintendents require sound managerial skills to ensure operational stability, analysts concur that dynamic contexts also require higher levels of political acuity to succeed than their predecessors. Johnson (1996) notes that superintendents work in political contexts characterized by demands for greater participation, patronage, and partisan power struggles. Participatory politics occur during periods in which group membership is fluid and alliances are ad hoc with the ebb and flow of interactions among community interest groups on varying issues. On the other hand, partisan politics are depicted as circumstances in which "distinct political groups or parties compete over education issues." Johnson (1996) describes patronage politics as occurring in contexts in which "programs, jobs, or funds are allocated or withheld on the basis of personal affiliations" (p. 156).

The assertion that the superintendency is a political position depends on the definition of the term *political*. School district operations not only garner considerable public attention but also are viewed as conflict-ridden arenas in which competing interest groups influence the distribution of scarce resources. Laswell (1958) referred to the political process as "who gets, what, where, when and how" (p. 187). Thus, superintendents faced with negotiating demands from multiple and diverse community interest groups are engaged in politics viewed as practicing the art of the possible. Cuban (1988) crystallizes the concept of superintendents' political leadership in discussing the need to build coalitions, to negotiate the distribution of resources among multiple and diverse interest groups to gain their support for district initiatives.

Blumberg (1985) notes that community conflict is inevitable. As our nation increasingly becomes ethnically and racially diverse, expectations for schools will differ, and individuals and groups will become more contentious as they press policymakers and school officials to satisfy their needs. In these contexts, politics is an enduring characteristic of public schooling, and contrary to prevailing professional norms, it is not inherently corrupt. Quite the contrary, politics ultimately is a process through which individuals and groups openly express real needs and interests and reconcile their differences. The notion that individuals and interest groups can reconcile their differences through consultation and negotiation (Morgan, 1997) suggests that politics is central to organizational well-being in a democratic society (Keedy & Björk, 2002).

Conflicts arise when the values and interests of individuals and groups diverge and generate heightened levels of political activism within communities that contest the purposes and goals of public education and influence changes in local community power structures and administrators. The level of conflict experienced by superintendents has increased exponentially because of at least three reasons during the last half of the twentieth century: (1) American society has changed dramatically in becoming more ethnically and racially diverse, (2) expectations for schooling have become more disparate, and (3) demands of participation in policy and decision-making processes increased as interest groups pressed for acceptance of their respective agendas (Carter & Cunningham, 1997; Keedy & Björk, 2002).

Schools are subject to the consequences of the weakening of shared values and beliefs that ground the meaning of citizenship. The cultural divide described by Hunter (1991) is often expressed through discordant perspectives of orthodox conservative groups and progressives regarding their moral views of America and its place in the world order. The third reason is related to an unrelenting partisan political struggle for power and the capacity to support their respective ideological positions through public policies that often eclipse the pursuit of the common good.

Given all these sources for community conflict, there is increasing uncertainty about who will actually control public education (Kowalski, 1999). However, there are few who would dispute that the superintendency has become more politicized when viewed within a context of competing social and ideological forces bent on defining the nature of public schooling in the twenty-first century. As a consequence, they are at the vortex of interest group politics that demand greater political acuity and a different way of enacting this role than during previous decades.

Superintendent as Democratic Statesman

In a comprehensive analysis of the discourse regarding the evolution of the role conceptualization of the American superintendent, Brunner, Grogan, and Björk (2001) did not use the term "statesmanship" when describing the various stages and characteristics of the role as it evolved from 1820 to the present. Brunner et al. presented seven stages of the role, describing superintendents as performing roles as clerks (1820–1850), master educators (1850–1900), expert managers (1900–1954), communicators (1954–1970), managers of conflict (1970–1980), political strategists (1980–1990), and collaborators (1990 to present). It is our opinion that historical definitions of the term *statesman* are not (and may never have been) appropriate role conceptions for the American superintendency, inasmuch as the role has never been about a stately patriarch ubiquitously and benevolently guiding school systems single-handedly toward a goal of success for all, as Plato's statesman suggests. Although perhaps closer to the actual experience of the American superintendency, Hamilton's conception of the political statesman is not appropriate, either, because the role has never explicitly been characterized as an elite and aloof expert, adeptly manipulating various constituencies toward accomplishing the common good. Instead, we propose that the American superintendency has always been about respecting the public's lawful claim to its schools, managing them efficiently to ensure that students became literate and numerate, and leading them wisely to make certain that the commonwealth is served. The social and political context in which they labor is daunting and promises to become no less challenging in the coming decades. For whether functioning as a clerk for a local board during the nineteenth century to possessing expert knowledge, serving as a professional advisor, working collaboratively to orchestrate district responses to multiple and diverse interest group demands in the twenty-first century, it is evident that a superintendent's role is neither like Plato's patriarch nor like Hamilton's elite statesman. Rather, it is one uniquely defined by America's political experience. As we enter the twenty-first century, changing demographics and community contexts might require viewing superintendents as democratic leaders.

Several separate yet related implications emerge out of the discussion about superintendents as statesmen and politicians. The first is that educators as a group should be aware that the enduring myths that the education enterprise is apolitical is unrealistic and inhibits viewing the close relationship between districts and communities and engaging in inclusive discourse about the purpose and performance of schooling characteristic of democratic societies. Second, the notion that schools are apolitical has created professional norms, beliefs, and attitudes that are dysfunctional and can inhibit or limit effective engagement of the public in reforming education. Third, viewing superintendents as Machiavellian politicians who manipulate the public is also without merit and creates an equally misleading line of thinking and action. Thus, representing superintendents as statesman or politicians depicts the opposite ends of a conceptual continuum, neither of which represents reality. Rather, superintendents must have a high level of political acuity tempered by moral principles and the capacity to communicate effectively with a broad range of community-based constituents and work collaboratively for the common good. These observations however, must be tested against the reality of superintendents' practice in emerging contexts.

MACRO- AND MICROPOLITICS

Over the past 30 years, scholars periodically attempted to define, synthesize, interpret, and chart the evolution of the politics of education as an area of study (Johnson, 2003). These sense-making activities intermittently renewed interest in the field and recently stimulated investigations of the role of superintendents as political actors (Björk & Lindle, 2001). The nature and scope of investigations, however, were dominated by political science traditions and theoretical orientations including "behaviorism, pluralism, and elitism" (Johnson, 2003, p. 4). For example, during the 1950s, Eliot (1959) examined the structure, behavioral dynamics, and voting patterns in federal, state, and local education agencies. During the 1970s and 1980s, limitations of these process-oriented frameworks in explaining complex decision-making processes in public sector organizations were acknowledged, and investigators looked for a broader range of conceptual frameworks. Perspectives drawn from the social science disciplines enriched the political science knowledge base. As a consequence, the study of education politics moved from a field of study influenced by political science that focused on electoral patterns, organizational processes, and local governance issues to a multidisciplined area that examined educational policy making and implementation at the state and federal levels of government (Berman & McLaughlin, 1978; Iannacone & Lutz, 1970; Jennings & Ziegler, 1970).

Johnson (2003) observes that the release of *A Nation at Risk* by the National Commission on Excellence in Education (1983) heightened concern for public education issues and sustained attention to reform-oriented initiatives in state and federal policy arenas for the next two decades. For example, attention to education reform initiatives reinforced the value of a policy orientation among politics of education scholars at state and federal levels (Kirst, 1984; Marshall, Mitchell & Wirt, 1989), the devolution of governance to the school level (Malen & Ogawa, 1990); micropolitics (Blase, 1993; Blase & Blase, 2002), and the dynamics of educational reform (Fuhrman, 1993). Advocates for strengthening the policy focus of research on education persuasively argue that politics and policy making are closely linked in that the objective of the former is to accomplish the latter (Johnson, 2003). In this regard, superintendents' work requires understanding large-scale (macro) as well as internal organizational politics (micro) to effectively negotiate the landscape of influence, policy, and decision making, as well as implementation.

Macropolitics

Educational politics involve the study of power, authority, and influence in the allocation of scarce resources at different education levels. Although at an abstract level they appear to be conceptually distinct, according to Johnson (2003), macro- and microeducational politics are qualitatively different. For example, political scientists have traditionally studied macro levels of state and federal levels of government with prevailing interests in the well-being of society and "good" government. Their work focuses on policy, power, and the allocation of resources particularly with regard to the well-being of a democratic society when they are not equitably distributed. Macro politics focuses on the external environment at the national, state, and local levels of government—as well as interactions, relationships, and political maneuvering of interest groups as they attempt to influence which goals are pursued and how resources are allocated to accomplish them. For example, macro analysis can be focused on the society level (suprasystem); the national level (Congress, the Department of Education, the American Association of School Administrators, political and religious interest groups); the state level (state education agencies, the legislature, state boards of education, chief state school officers, state professional associations, organized interest groups); and the local level (school boards, school superintendents, interest groups) (Björk & Keedy, 2001; Blase & Blase, 2000; Wirt & Kirst, 2001).

Interest Groups

The term *politics* conveys the notion of a set of activities that surrounds decision making and involves the mobilization of individuals and groups to achieve partisan interests in decision outcomes (Gamson, 1968; Johnson, 2003; Laswell, 1958). Although Petracca (1992) argues that "American politics is the politics of interests" (p. 3), democratic processes tend to move in the direction of achieving a workable consensus. Activities used to influence decisions at different stages of the policy cycle include normative persuasion, debate, negotiation, pressure, and coalescing and mobilizing groups (Lindbloom, 1993). On the whole, they are viewed as normative political activities that reflect and ultimately serve the commonwealth. Thus, interest groups holding dissimilar values and beliefs that are actively engaged in advancing their interests, yet are willing to reconcile differences (Rowan & Miskel, 1999), reflect the reality of how democratic societies function.

Thomas and Hrebenar (1999) note that an interest group is "any association of individuals, whether formally organized or not, that attempts to influence public policy" (p. 153) to gain support for their position. Thus, there is a wide spectrum of interest groups that might be active in the educational policy domain, including parent and citizen groups, professional associations, foundations, ideologically oriented policy institutes, partisan political parties, corporations, and the media. The fusion of interest group values and desires with public action (Salisbury, 1991) characterizes the natural direction of influence patterns and are often revealed in public policy debates. For example, during recent years, contentious debates over school decentralization, choice, prayer, and vouchers have heightened awareness of conservative and progressive ideologies. Hunter (1991) contends that the polarization of the citizenry into these ideological camps is contributing to a cultural war that is weakening efforts to build a national consensus on school reform. These groups fundamentally disagree on the role of government in public education, and ideological differences have manifested in divergent views about how to accomplish educational reform over the past several decades. The powerful association between parents, policymakers, and activist lawyers that helped to pass PL 94-142 (to ensure that handicapped and challenged students are educated in the "least restrictive environment") is a classic example of the efficacy of a parent-centered interest group coalition influencing public policy (Cooper, Fusarelli, & Randall, 2004; Kowalski, 1999; St. John & Clements, 2004). Professional associations have defended the rights of educators and supported licensure and professional standards (Wirt & Kirst, 2001). A civil rights group has advanced the interests of all citizens by insisting on equal treatment under the law (McKinney, 2004). When corporate leaders were convinced that the nation was on the verge of forfeiting its preeminent position in science, technology and industrial productivity also played an important role in shaping the nature and direction of education reform during the 1980s and 1990s (Björk, 1996; Kearns, 1988; Koppich & Guthrie, 1993). Linking education and the economy legitimized their participation, and once involved, they championed notions that included traditional values, accountability standards for schools, deregulating licensure, and market competition strategies (e.g., vouchers, tuition tax credits, and charter schools) (Chubb & Moe, 1990; Finn, 1990; McCarthy, 2000). Although educators view "schooling as a sacred trust that should not be tainted by partisan politics, manipulated by community interest groups, or demeaned by power struggles" (Björk &

Keedy, 2001, p. 276), district leadership, management, and policy making is rooted in politics (Johnson, 1996) at both the macro and micro levels of the education system.

Micropolitics

Scholars make a distinction between macro- and micropolitics. Whereas macropolitics is externally focused on federal, state, and local district levels of government as well as private and interest group activities, micropolitics is focused on the internal actions of individuals within district offices and at the school level, and on groups attempting to influence decision and policy making (Blase & Blase, 2002; Johnson, 2003). Blase and Blase (2000) note that for the most part, the study of micropolitics in education acknowledges the importance of external factors (i.e., macropolitics) that influence internal (micropolitical) processes and structures. Although there is a lack of consensus in the field as to the conceptual parameters of micropolitics (Blase & Blase, 2002; Malen, 1994), many scholars viewed it as occurring at the school level (Blase, 1991; Iannacone, 1975). However, others contend that it can occur at any level in the education system as well as in society (Bachrach & Mundell, 1995; Bolman & Deal, 1997; Morgan, 1986; Pfeffer, 1981). In the sense that micropolitics can occur at numerous levels (including department, school, district, state, federal, and society levels), it "is not defined by its context but, rather by its nature. That is, micropolitics (all levels) involves strategic contests among interest groups over different logics of action" (Bachrach & Mundell, 1995, p. 432). Blase (1991) defines micropolitics as "the use of formal and informal power by individuals to achieve their goals in organizations. In large part, political action results from perceived differences between individuals and groups, coupled with the motivation to use power to influence and/or protect" (p. 11). As a consequence, micropolitics influences key aspects of formal organizations, including structures, policies, programs, curricula, and informal dimensions such as culture and social relations (Pfeffer, 1981). Blase (1998) views micropolitics as the central mechanism that drives the organization because it shapes the characteristics of the formal organization (structure, patterns of hierarchical authority), culture (ideologies, decision making, power distribution), social relations (individual and group behavior), and how work is done.

SUPERINTENDENT AND SCHOOL BOARD RELATIONS

The nature of school district politics and the relationship between superintendents and local school board members have interested scholars throughout the nineteenth and twentieth centuries (Björk & Lindle, 2001; Burlingame, 1988; Cistone, 1975; Iannacone, 1991; Tyack & Hansot, 1982). During the first two decades of the twentieth century, reformers believed that partisan politics was corrupting school districts and worked to change the way board members were elected. They pressed policymakers to separate board elections from general partisan elections, create nonpartisan electoral processes, or move toward appointed board members (Björk & Lindle, 2001; Tyack & Hansot, 1982). By the 1950s, political scientists recognized local board elections as an essential part of representative democracies and viewed them as a legitimate political arena worthy of study (Burlingame, 1988). Since the early 1970s, researchers have focused their attention on how relationships between communities, local boards of education, and superintendents define their roles (Boyd, 1976; Iannacone & Lutz, 1995; McCarty & Ramsey, 1971).

McCarty and Ramsey (1971) analyzed linkages between community influence patterns and political configurations of local boards of education to understand superintendents' role behavior. Recent investigations by Glass, Björk, and Brunner (2000), Björk and Lindle (2001), and Björk and Keedy (2001) underscore the importance of this line of inquiry. They found that the influence patterns identified by McCarty & Ramsey (1971) persisted over a 30-year period (1971–2000), affirming that superintendents are influenced by local community power structures and board political configurations. They concluded that superintendents must have political acuity to navigate complex political landscapes. McCarty and Ramsey's typology of Community-School Board-Superintendent relations (see Table 7.1) shows how community, school board, and superintendent role characteristics are aligned.

McCarty and Ramsey (1971) describe "dominated communities" as being an elite power model in which a small number of citizens exerted an extraordinary amount of political influence in local affairs and who are intolerant of opposition. They note that elite status is achieved through economic dominance or historical status of ethnic, religious, or racial groups in the community. A dominated community power structure tends to influence who is elected or appointed to the local school board. In other words, an elite community power structure will produce a dominated school board that in turn will require superintendents to serve in a functionary role. A superintendent serving in this capacity identifies with and takes cues from community elites and board members. Glass et al. (2000) found that only 2.6% of superintendents view their school boards as dominated by a community elite and enact their role as a functionary (1.2%). (See Table 7.2.)

According to McCarty & Ramsey (1971), "factional communities" are characterized as having interest groups that coalesce around economic, religious, racial, or ethnic issues; openly challenge school board policy; and support the election of board members who endorse their positions.

Table 7.1 Types of Community and Board Power Structures and Superintendent Roles

Community Power Structure	School Board	Role of the Superintendent
Dominated. The community power structure is controlled by a few individuals at the apex of the hierarchy and is "top-down" (an "elite" power model). The decision-making group is likely to be the "economic elite" in the community, but also may be derived from religious, ethnic, racial, or political power structures. Opposition to their position is rarely successful.	*Dominated.* School board members are chosen because their views are congruent with the views and ideology of the dominant group (power elite), and they take advice from community leaders. Any organized opposition in the community is strong enough to displace the elite.	*Functionary.* The superintendent identifies with the dominant group, takes cues from it, and perceives the superintendent role to be an administrator who carries out board policies rather than as a policymaker. The board selects a superintendent who reflects a willingness to work within this context.
Factional. Several groups that hold relatively equal power compete for control over important policy decisions and can coalesce around economic, religious, ethnic, racial, or political power philosophies.	*Factional.* School board members represent the viewpoint of factions and act in accordance with their views. Voting is more important than discussing issues. If the issue is important, the majority faction always wins. Board elections tend to be hotly contested.	*Political Strategist.* The superintendent must work with the majority and must realign with the new majority when it changes. The superintendent behaves in a manner that does not alienate other factions because the majority may shift again in the future. The superintendent takes a middle course on controversial issues.
Pluralistic. Power is contested by interest groups and is dispersed, pluralistic, and diffused. High levels of concern for important issues and active involvement of interest groups in decisions is evident.	*Status Congruent.* School board members are active, but not rigidly bound to one group or position. Members are viewed as equals, and discussion of issues is conducted in an objective fashion.	*Professional Advisor.* The superintendent acts as a statesman, giving professional advice based on research and experience. The superintendent expresses professional opinions and might propose alternative courses of action in an open and objective fashion.
Inert. Power in communities is latent or dominated by the status quo. Radical experimentation might not be acceptable.	*Sanctioning.* Board members hold views congruent with pervasive values and views of the community and do not receive overt reinforcement. They follow the lead of the superintendent on proposals and approve them without question.	*Decision Maker.* The superintendent initiates action and provides leadership to ensure district effectiveness. The school board "rubber-stamps" superintendent proposals. The superintendent provides leadership, but is constrained by latent community values that emphasize the status quo.

SOURCE: Björk, L. G. (2001, April); adapted from Glass, T. E., Björk, L. G., & Brunner, C. C. (2000); McCarty & Ramsey (1971). From paper presented by author at the Annual Meeting of the American Educational Research Association (Session 35.50), Seattle, Washington.

Table 7.2   Comparison of Community Power Structure, School Board
Characteristics, and Superintendent Roles, 1971 to 2000

Community Power Structure Power Type			School Board Characteristics Power Type			Role of Superintendent Role Type		
	1971	2000		1971	2000		1971	2000
Dominated	16%	—	Dominated	13%	2.6%	Functionary	2%	1.2%
Factional	14%	—	Factional	32%	19%	Political Strategist	1%	1.6%
Pluralistic	45%	—	Status Congruent	63%	65.9%	Professional Advisor	33%	47.7%
Inert	25%	—	Sanctioning	3%	12.5%	Decision Maker	64%	49.5%

SOURCE: Björk, L. (2001, April); adapted from Glass, T., Björk, L., & Brunner, C. (2000); McCarty & Ramsey (1971). From paper presented by author at the Annual Meeting of the American Educational Research Association (Session 35.50), Seattle, Washington.

When power in communities is distributed among interest groups, conflict is inevitable. As a consequence, superintendents must be aware of their respective positions on issues and their connection with board members. In these circumstances, superintendents might adopt a political strategist role and work with the board majority without alienating others. Glass et al. (2000) found that 19% of superintendents viewed their boards as factional; however, only 1.6% adopted a political strategist role. Although they recognize that they are immersed in micropolitical contexts, they are reluctant to define their role as a political strategist.

Although *pluralistic communities* are composed of multiple and diverse interest groups, they are different in terms of how they work. Pluralistic communities tend to focus on the nature of the issue and respond without rigid adherence to interest group positions. Members of "status-congruent" boards work as colleagues to objectively evaluate problems and a range of solutions. In these circumstances, superintendents act as professional advisors that offer boards their professional opinions and advice regarding alternative solutions. Although Glass et al. (2000) found that nearly 66% of superintendents characterized their school boards as status congruent, only 48% indicated that they served as a professional advisor role (refer to Table 7.2).

Although *inert communities* tend to be relatively disengaged from politics, they are highly proscriptive with regard to board policy making and superintendent action. In these community contexts, perspectives and actions of board members and superintendents must be congruent with the latent community culture, values, and beliefs. In sum, superintendents in inert communities are allowed considerable independence in managing district affairs, and boards tend to accept superintendents' advice and recommendations. Glass et al. (2000) found that although only 12.5% of superintendents characterized their boards as sanctioning, almost 49.5% indicated that their boards served as decision makers. This might reflect superintendents' predisposition for managerial action.

McCarty and Ramsey (1971) believe that there is a general alignment between community power structures, political configurations of local school boards, and superintendents' role expectations. A comparison of findings of the McCarty and Ramsey (1971) and Glass et al. (2000) studies indicates that although superintendents' two dominant roles (as professional advisor and decision maker) have persisted for nearly 30 years (1971–2000), some important changes have occurred. First, superintendents in 2000 characterized fewer school boards as being dominated or factional (Glass et al., 2000) than were reported by McCarty & Ramsey (1971) (refer to Table 7.2), indicating that elite and political power structures in communities are declining. Second, data indicate that a significant percentage of communities are pluralistic and consequently elect status-congruent boards (66%). This may indicate an increase in community tolerance for different perspectives that require superintendents to work democratically to ensure that all voices are heard in decision- and policy-making processes. For example, in 1971, 33% said they served as a professional advisor; however, in 2000, 48% said they served in this capacity. Björk, Bell, and Gurley (2002) observe that the role of "professional advisor" is congruent with professional norms and values of superintendents and necessitates their working more inclusively with multiple and diverse community groups—a quality that reflects democratic statesmanship. Third, the propensity of superintendents to view their role as decision maker remains significant (49.5%) despite incongruence with community power structures and political board characteristics of boards. Björk, Bell, and Gurley (2002) also suggest that professional and organizational socialization might explain persistence of this role over time. They note that throughout the twentieth century, administrators have been educated, selected, and promoted to serve as managers and decision makers. Organizational and professional socialization processes have ensured the continuation of these norms of professional behavior and consequently surface as a major role expectation. Although McCarty and Ramsey's (1971) typology provides a framework for understanding the dynamics of community and board politics and superintendents' role configurations, general principles can be influenced by professional norms of behavior.

SUPERINTENDENT AS DEMOCRATIC STATESMAN: IMPLICATIONS FOR PRACTICE

Demands for greater levels of involvement in decision and policy making increased in the post-World War II period and accelerated during the era of education reform (1983–2003) (Cunningham & Hentges, 1982; Glass, 1992;

Glass et al., 2000). Demands for increased participation in school and district decision and policy making by parents, teachers, community citizens, and interest groups during the past several decades is a prominent theme that cuts across national commission and task force reports (Björk, Kowalski, & Young, 2005), as well as analyses of community political dynamics released during the past decade (Björk, 1996; Björk & Lindle, 2001; Cooper, Fusarelli, & Randall, 2004; Tyack, 1993). As a consequence, improving student learning was coupled with strengthening linkages with communities and parents, which became prominent features of school improvement initiatives (Björk & Keedy, 2001; Chance & Björk, 2003; Driscoll, 1992; Leithwood & Jantzi, 1999). As demographic changes alter the social, economic, and political landscape of communities and demands for higher levels of participation increase, accomplishing these tasks is becoming increasingly difficult and complex. For example, superintendents are brought into frequent contact with elected officials, community interest groups, school board members, and parents. Superintendents must understand the differing views of each group (Blumberg, 1985) as they work with boards in framing district policies. In addition, they must understand school organizations and cultures, as well as the wide-ranging issues of school staff to successfully enlist their support in changing the nature of educational practice. As a consequence, superintendents must have acuity for understanding and working in macro- and micropolitical contexts that define the landscape of their role as democratic statesmen. These emerging characteristics of superintendents' work suggest that changes in conventional preparation and development programs are crucial for enhancing their effectiveness.

SUPERINTENDENT AS DEMOCRATIC STATESMEN: IMPLICATIONS FOR PREPARATION AND DEVELOPMENT

The landscape of community and district politics is a pervasive, complex, and challenging aspect of superintendents' work. "The issue for new superintendents is not whether to engage in politics but 'what kind of politics prevail here'" (Johnson, 1996, p. 155). Although superintendents would find it difficult to remain above the political fray, they do have a moral obligation to serve as democratic statesmen in an ethical fashion and work on behalf of all children. When reflecting on how the next generation of superintendents should be prepared or how to sharpen the acuity of veterans to serve as democratic statesmen, knowledge and context are inextricably entwined.

Several key elements of the professional knowledge base are central to democratic statesmanship. First, aspiring and veteran superintendents must have a deeply rooted understanding of the history, purpose, and current issues facing public schooling, including emerging demands for more inclusive policy and decision-making processes. Without this essential grounding, few chief executive officers (CEOs) can provide credible leadership. Second, they must have a sound understanding of the politics of public education and the dynamics of policy decision making about how resources are distributed at the federal and state (macro) levels of government, as well as at local and school (micro) levels within districts. Without a sound understanding of the politics of education, effectively leading district improvement efforts could be jeopardized. Third, superintendents must be well versed in how to successfully work with school boards, negotiate and mediate issues among competing community interest groups, communicate with constituents and professionals within the district organization, and effectively diagnose and collaboratively develop plans to resolve problems.

Although knowledge is the foundation for effective action, how it is acquired can influence the depth of understanding as well as whether it is successfully applied in policy- and decision-making venues. In politics, context matters. In professional preparation, it matters even more. Although knowledge provides a sound foundation for professionals working in the field, empirical findings indicate that integrating its acquisition with hands-on, work-embedded experiences is indispensable to improving relevance of learning and transference to new situations, developing tacit understanding of how organizations work, gaining insight into the dynamics of local politics, and understanding the complexity of interpersonal relations (Björk, Kowalski, & Browne-Ferrigno, 2005). Combining the acquisition of professional knowledge and practical skills can thus enhance superintendent performance.

Several interrelated elements can enhance professional preparation and development programs for superintendents.

- *Sharing responsibility for preparation.* Viewing administrator preparation as a shared university-district responsibility provides an essential building block for reconfiguring and enhancing superintendent preparation. On the one hand, universities are adept at transmitting professional knowledge and developing analytical skills of aspiring district leaders. However, they lack organizational contexts in which to apply knowledge to improving practice and are accused of neglecting practical intelligence (Sergiovanni, 1989). School districts, on the other hand, control access to educational settings in which aspiring leaders can gain hands-on, work-embedded experience. Thus, collaboration between the academic and practice arms of the profession is fundamental for preparing individuals who have the intellect and capacity to serve as democratic statesmen to work.

- *Recruiting aspiring district leaders.* Superintendents play critical roles in the success of school districts. Universities and school districts should therefore collaborate in identifying and recruiting capable individuals and forming learning cohorts. This strategy is fundamental for attracting and developing highly committed and talented administrators. In addition, efforts to increase admission requirements and performance standards are essential to ensure that aspiring district leaders possess and demonstrate qualities needed to succeed in complex community and organizational settings. Additionally, using a variety of means for identifying and recruiting aspiring district leaders will enable cohorts to reflect diverse ethnic, racial, and gender differences in society (NPBEA, 1989).

• *Forming closed cohorts.* Improving the quality of instruction and student performance, cultivating a sense of community among students and faculty, and enhancing persistence and commitment to learning can be accomplished through the use of "closed cohorts" (Basom, Yerkes, Norris, & Barnett, 1995). Closed cohorts provide opportunities for aspiring superintendents to learn and practice collective goal setting, community building, conflict resolution, and culture-management skills (McCarthy, 1999). These skills are essential for superintendent success.

• *Instituting work-embedded learning.* A fundamental assumption of university-based educational administration programs is that knowledge, concepts, skills, and strategies learned in university classrooms are readily transferred to work settings and problems (Hoberman & Mailick, 1994). As Björk, Kowalski, and Browne-Ferrigno (2005) point out, this may not be correct. Evidence suggests that knowledge, skills, and strategies learned in either classroom or field settings are not readily transferred (Calabrese & Straut, 1999). Studies on situated learning, however, found that professional knowledge acquired while performing related work enhances meaning, retrieval, and transference to new situations (Bridges & Hallinger, 1992). Thus, a cornerstone of rebuilding professional preparation programs is to situate the acquisition of professional knowledge in work settings (Björk, Kowalski, & Browne-Ferrigno, 2005; Tan, 1989). That can be accomplished either by embedding practicum experiences within each superintendent course throughout the program or by placing students in well-designed and implemented internships with authentic work responsibilities while attending university programs. Although the latter is preferable, both provide opportunities to enact democratic statesmen roles in district settings.

• *Using peer mentoring.* Peer mentoring is a common practice in the profession (Glass et al., 2000) and is a powerful way to enhance learning and skill transference into practice (Björk, Kowalski, & Browne-Ferrigno, 2005; Browne-Ferrigno & Muth, 2003). Mentoring experiences for aspiring administrators need to have clearly defined purposes and goals for both aspirants and veteran practitioners. Mentors need to be well-respected by their colleagues and highly effective in their own practice; they also must be innovative leaders who are skilled at providing overseeing experiences of aspiring and veteran superintendents (Browne-Ferrigno & Muth, 2003;

Lave & Wenger, 1991; Wenger, 1998). Working with highly successful superintendents provides those aspiring to the position with an opportunity to acquire tacit knowledge, not only of how organizations work, but also how superintendents work in political contexts and serve as democratic statesmen.

• *Adopting continuous professional development.* The nature and context of superintendents' work is constantly changing. In these circumstances, aspiring and veteran superintendents confronted with complex problems and turbulent environments must develop the capacity to make sense of ambiguous, complex problems in key work areas and develop the capacity to solve them expertly (Leithwood & Stager, 1989). As a consequence, a central challenge facing the field is to view professional learning and skill building as a continuous relational process. Thus, learning strategies enumerated previously (Björk, Kowalski, & Browne-Ferrigno, 2005) are relevant both to aspiring and veteran superintendents. This perspective can be particularly relevant to a field that is attempting to reconfigure how the next generation of superintendents is prepared (as well as how those presently in the profession practice). The notion of continuous learning over time is also relevant to reculturing the profession and building the capacity of superintendents to serve as democratic statesmen.

These precepts are based on an assumption that universities and school districts share a common interest in developing a high-performing cadre of leaders who are capable of working with and through others to improve schooling for all children.

CONCLUSION

As we enter the twenty-first century, it is evident that prevailing circumstances preclude the superintendent's political role being defined as either Plato's patriarch or Hamilton's elite statesman. Rather, America's socioeconomic and political circumstances are uniquely defining it as being a democratic leader. This definition requires that superintendents be well-grounded in democratic values and processes and have a sound understanding of the politics of education, school board relations, and the dynamics of human political behavior at macro and micro levels of government and organizations. The way that aspiring (as well as veteran) superintendents acquire professional knowledge and skills related to serving as democratic statesmen is central both for reconfiguring professional preparation and development programs and for improving practice. The nature of their work and learning suggests that school districts and universities must collaborate to ensure that work-embedded learning is at the center rather than on the periphery of learning.

REFERENCES

Bachrach, S., & Mundell, B. (1995). Organizational politics in schools: Micro, macro, and logics of action. *Educational Administration Quarterly, 29,* 423–452.

Basom, M., Yerkes, D., Norris, C., & Barnett, B. (1995). *Exploring cohorts: Effects on principal and leadership practice.* Evaluative report supported through a mini-grant from the Danforth Foundation, St. Louis, MO.

Bennett, W. (1993). *The index of leading cultural indicators.* Washington, DC: Heritage Foundation.

Berman, P., & McLaughlin, M. (1978). *Federal programs supporting educational change, Vol. III: Implementing and sustaining innovations.* Santa Monica, CA: Rand Corporation.

Björk, L. G. (1996). The revisionists' critique of the education reform reports. *Journal of school Leadership, 6(3),* 290–315.

Björk, L. G. (2001, April). *The politics of board-superintendent relations: Perceptions and predispositions.* Paper presented at the annual meeting of the American Educational Research Association (Session 35.50), Seattle, WA.

Björk, L. G., Bell, R., & Gurley, D. (2002). Politics and the socialization of superintendents. In Perreault, G. (Ed.), *The changing world of educational administration* (pp. 294–31). Lanham, MD: Scarecrow Press.

Björk, L. G., & Keedy, J. L. (2001). Changing social context of education in the United States: Social justice and the superintendency. *Journal of In-Service Education, 27(3),* 409–431.

Björk, L. G., Kowalski, T. J., & Browne-Ferrigno, T. (2005). Learning theory and research: A framework for changing superintendent preparation and development. In L. G. Björk & T. J. Kowalski (Eds.), *The contemporary superintendent: Preparation, practice, and development.* Thousand Oaks, CA: Corwin.

Björk, L. G., Kowalski, T. J., & Young, M. (2005). National education reform reports: Implications for professional preparation and development. In L. G. Björk & T. J. Kowalski (Eds.), *The contemporary superintendent: Preparation, practice, and development.* Thousand Oaks, CA: Corwin.

Björk, L. G., & Lindle, J. C. (2001). Superintendents and interest groups. *Educational Policy, 15(1),* 76–91.

Blase, J. (Ed.). (1991). *The politics of life in schools: Power, conflict, and cooperation.* Newbury Park, CA: Sage.

Blase, J. (1993). The micropolitics of effective school-based leadership: Teachers' perspectives. *Educational Administration Quarterly, 29,* 142–163.

Blase, J. (1998). The micropolitics of educational change. In A. Hargreaves (Ed.), *The international handbook of educational change* (pp. 544–557). London: Kluwer.

Blase, J., & Blase J. (2000). *Empowering teachers: What successful principals do* (2nd ed.). Thousand Oaks, CA: Corwin.

Blase, J., & Blase, J. (2002). The micropolitics of instructional supervision: A call for research. *Educational Administration Quarterly, 38(1),* 6–44.

Blumberg, A. (1985). *The school superintendent: Living with conflict.* New York: Teachers College Press.

Bolman, L., & Deal, T. (1997). *Reframing organizations: Artistry, choice and leadership* (2nd ed.). San Francisco: Jossey-Bass.

Boyd, W. L. (1974). The school superintendent: Educational statesman or political strategist. *Administrator's Notebook, 22(9).*

Boyd, W. L. (1976). The public, the professionals, and educational policy making: Who governs? *Teachers College Record, 77(4),* 539–577.

Bridges, E. M., & Hallinger, P. H. (1992). *Problem-based learning for administrators.* Eugene, OR: ERIC/CEM.

Browne-Ferrigno, T., & Muth, R. (2003). Effects of cohorts on learners. *Journal of School Leadership, 13(6),* 621–643.

Brunner, C. C., Grogan, M., & Björk, L. G. (2001). Shifts in the discourse defining the super-intendency: Historical and current foundations of the position. In J. Murphy (Ed.), *The educational leadership challenge: Redefining leadership for the 21st century* (pp. 211–238). Chicago: University of Chicago Press.

Burlingame, M. (1988). The politics of education and educational policy: The local level. In N. Boyan (Ed.), *The handbook of research on educational administration* (pp. 439–451). New York: Longman.

Calabrese, R. L., & Straut, D. (1999). Reconstructing the internship. *Journal of School Leadership, 9,* 400–421.

Callahan, R. E. (1967). *The superintendent of schools: An historical analysis.* (ERIC Document Reproduction Service No. ED 010 410)

Carter, G., & Cunningham, W. (1997). *The American school superintendent: Leading in the age of pressure.* San Francisco: Jossey-Bass.

Chance, P., & Björk, L. G. (2003). Social dimensions of public relations. In T. J. Kowalski, *Public relations in schools* (3rd ed.) (pp. 125–150). Upper Saddle River, NJ: Merrill, Prentice Hall.

Chubb, J., & Moe, T. (1990). Politics, markets and America's schools. Washington, DC: Brookings Institution for the Advancement of Teaching.

Cibulka, J. G. (1995). The institutionalization of public schools: The decline of legitimizing myths and the politics of organizational instability. In R. T. Ogawa (Ed.), *Advances in research and theories of school management and educational policy: Vol. 3* (pp. 123–158). Greenwich, CT: JAI Press.

Cistone, P. (Ed.). (1975). *Understanding school boards.* Lexington, MA: Lexington.

Cooper, B., Fusarelli, L. D., & Randall, V. (2004). *Better policies, better schools: Theories and applications.* Boston: Allyn & Bacon.

Cuban, L. (1976). *The urban school superintendent: A century and a half of change.* Bloomington, IN: Phi Delta Kappa Educational Foundation.

Cuban, L. (1988). How schools change reforms: Redefining reform success and failure. *Teachers College Record, 99*(3), 453–477.

Cuban, L. (1990, December). Four stories about national goals for American education. *Phi Delta Kappan, 72*(4), 264–271.

Cunningham, L. L., & Hentges, J. T. (1982). *The American school superintendency, 1982: A summary report.* Arlington, VA: American Association of School Administrators.

Driscoll, E. (1992). School-community relations and school effectiveness. In R. Crowson, *School-community relations under reform* (pp. 19–42). Berkeley, CA: McCutchan.

Eliot, T. (1959). Toward an understanding of public schools politics. *American Political Science Review, 53*(4), 1032–1051.

Finn, C. E., Jr. (1990). The biggest reform of all. *Phi Delta Kappan, 71,* 584–592.

Fuhrman, S. (Ed.). (1993). *Designing coherent educational policy.* San Francisco: Jossey-Bass.

Gamson, W. A. (1968). *Power and discontent.* Homewood, NJ: Dorsey.

Glass, T. E. (1992). *The study of the American school superintendency 1992: America's education leaders in a time of reform.* Arlington, VA: American Association of School Administrators.

Glass, T. E., Björk, L. G., & Brunner, C. C. (2000). *The study of the American superintendency: 2000.* Arlington, VA: American Association of School Administrators.

Hoberman, S., & Mailick, S. (1994). Some learning theory. In S. Hoberman & S. Mailick (Eds.), *Professional education in the United States: Experiential learning, issues and prospects* (pp. 19–26). Westport: CT: Praeger.

Hunter, J. D. (1991). *Culture wars: The struggle to redefine America.* New York: HarperCollins.

Iannacone, L. (1975). *Educational policy systems: A study guide for educational administrators.* Fort Lauderdale, FL: Nova University Press.

Iannacone, L. (1991). Micropolitics of education: What and why. *Education and Urban Society, 23*(4), 465–471.

Iannacone, L., & Lutz, F. W. (1970). *Politics, power and policy: The governing of local school districts.* Columbus, OH: Merrill.

Iannacone, L., & Lutz, F. W. (1995). The crucible of democracy: The local arena. In J. D. Scribner & D. H. Layton (Eds.), *The study of educational politics, the 1994 commemorative yearbook of the Politics of Education Association (1969–1994)* (pp. 39–52). Philadelphia: Falmer Press.

Jennings, M., & Ziegler, H. (1970). *Interest representation in local school governance.* Paper presented at the annual meeting of the American Political Science Association Los Angeles.

Johnson, R. (2003). Those nagging headaches: Perennial issues and tensions in the politics of education field. *Educational Administration Quarterly, 39*(1), 41–67.

Johnson, S. M. (1996). *Leading to change: The challenge of the new supeintendency.* San Francisco: Jossey-Bass.

Kearns, D. L. (1988). An education recovery plan for America. *Phi Delta Kappan, 69,* 565–570.

Keedy, J. L., & Björk, L. G. (2002). Superintendents and local boards in an era of cultural and political polarization and decentralization: The call for use of political strategist skills. In B. S. Cooper & L. D. Fusarelli (Eds.), *Reconceptualizing leadership: The superintendency in transition.* Lanham, MD: Scarecrow Press.

Kirst, M. (1984). State policy in an era of transition. *Education and Urban Society, 16*(2), 225–238.

Koppich, J. E., & Guthrie, J. W. (1993). Examining contemporary education-reform efforts in the United States. In H. Beare & W. Boyd, *Restructuring schools: An international perspective on the movement to transform control and performance of schools* (pp. 12–29). Washington, DC: Falmer Press.

Kowalski, T. J. (1995). *Keeper of the flame: Contemporary urban superintendents.* Thousand Oaks, CA: Corwin.

Kowalski, T. J. (1999). *The school superintendent: Theory, practice, and cases.* Upper Saddle River, NJ: Prentice Hall.

Kowalski, T. J. (2003, April). *The superintendent as communicator.* Paper presented at the annual meeting of the American Educational Research Association, Chicago.

Laswell, H. (1958). *Politics: Who gets what, when and how.* Cleveland, OH: Meridian Books.

Lave, J., & Wenger, E. (1991). *Situated learning: Legitimate peripheral participation.* New York: Cambridge University Press.

Leithwood, K. A., & Jantzi, D. (1999). The relative effects of principal and teacher sources of leadership on student engagement with school. *Educational Administration Quarterly, 35,* 679–706.

Leithwood, K. A., & Stager, M. (1989). Expertise in principals' problem solving. *Educational Administration Quarterly, 25,* 126–161.

Lindbloom, C. E. (1993). *The policy making process* (3rd ed.). Englewood Cliffs, NJ: Prentice Hall.

Malen, B. (1994). The micropolitics of education: Mapping the multiple dimensions of power relations in school politics. *Journal of Educational Policy, 9,* 147–167.

Malen, B., & Ogawa, R. (1990). Community involvement: Parents, teachers and administration working together. In S. B. Bachrach (Ed.), *Education reform: Making sense of it all* (pp. 103–120). Boston: Allyn & Bacon.

Marshall, C., Mitchell, D., & Wirt, F. (1989). *Culture and educational policy in American states.* London: Falmer Press.

McCarthy, M. (1999). The evolution of educational leadership preparation programs. In J. Murphy & K. S. Louis, *Handbook of research on educational administration* (2nd ed.) (pp. 119–139). San Francisco: Jossey-Bass.

McCarthy, M. (2000, January). What is the verdict on school vouchers? *Phi Delta Kappan, 81*(1), 371–377.

McCarty, D., & Ramsey, C. (1971). *The school managers.* Westport, CT: Greenwood.

McKinney, J. (2004). Legal and ethical aspects of public education. In T. J. Kowalski (Ed.), *Public relations in schools* (pp. 68–95). Upper Saddle River, NJ: Pearson.

McNeil, L. J. (1988). Contradictions of control, Part 2: Teachers, students, and curriculum. *Phi Delta Kappan, 69*, 432–438.

Miroff, B. (1993). *Icons of democracy: American leaders as heroes, aristocrats, dissenters, & democrats.* New York: Basic Books.

Morgan, G. (1986). *Images of organizations.* Beverly Hills, CA: Sage.

Morgan, G. (1997). *Images of organizations* (2nd ed.). Thousand Oaks, CA: Sage.

National Commission on Excellence in Education. (1983). *A nation at risk: The imperative for educational reform.* Washington, DC: U.S. Government Printing Office.

National Policy Board for Educational Administration. (1989). *Improving the preparation of school administrators: An agenda for reform.* Charlottesville, VA: Author.

Ortiz, F. I., & Marshall, C. (1988). Women in educational administration. In N. Boyan (Ed.), *The handbook of research on educational administration* (pp. 123–141). New York: Longman.

Petracca, M. P. (1992). The rediscovery of interest group politics. In M. P. Petracca (Ed.), *Politics of interests: Interest groups transformed* (pp. 3–31). Boulder, CO: Westview.

Pfeffer, J. (1981). *Power in organizations.* Marshfield, MA: Pitman.

Plato. (1961). *Politicus* (A. E. Taylor, Trans.). London: Thomas Nelson (Original work published circa. 400 B.C.E.)

Rowan, B., & Miskel, C. G. (1999). Institutional theory and the study of educational organizations. In J. Murphy & K. S. Louis (Eds.), *The handbook of research on educational administration* (2nd ed.) (pp. 359–383). San Francisco: Jossey-Bass.

Salisbury, R. (1991). Putting interests back into interest groups. In A. J. Ciglar & A. B. Loomis (Eds.), *Interest group politics* (3rd ed.) (pp. 371–384). Washington, DC: CQ Press.

Sergiovanni, T. (1989). Mystics, neats, and scruffies: Informing professional practice in educational administration. *Phi Delta Kappan, 72*, 521–526.

St. John, E., & Clements, M. (2004). Public opinions and political contexts. In T. J. Kowalski (Ed.), *Public relations in schools* (pp. 47–67). Upper Saddle River, NJ: Pearson.

Sykes, G. (1999). The new professionalism in education: An appraisal. In J. Murphy & K. S. Louis (Eds.), *The handbook of research on educational administration* (2nd ed.) (pp. 227–249). San Francisco: Jossey-Bass.

Tan, H. (1989). *Private sector training in the United States.* New York: Institute on Education and the Economy, Teachers College, Columbia University.

Thomas, O., & Hrebenar, R. (1999). Interest groups in states. In V. Gray et al. (Eds.), *Politics in the American states* (pp. 113–43). Washington, DC: CQ Press.

Tyack, D. B. (1993). School governance in the United States: Historical puzzles and anomalies. In J. Hannaway & M. Carnoy (Eds.), *Decentralization and school improvement* (pp. 1–32). San Francisco: Jossey-Bass.

Tyack, D. B., & Hansot, E. (1982). *Managers of virtue: Public school leadership in America.* New York: Basic Books.

Wenger, E. (1998). *Communities of practice: Learning, meaning, and identity.* New York: Cambridge University Press.

Wirt, F., & Kirst, M. (2001). *The political dynamics of American education* (2nd ed.). Berkeley, CA: McCutchan.

8

Reconceptualizing the Superintendency

Superintendents as Applied Social Scientists and Social Activists

Bonnie C. Fusarelli and Lance D. Fusarelli

Within the past decade, particularly with the passage of the No Child Left Behind Act (NCLB), superintendents have been called to lead districtwide, systemic reform efforts and educate *all* children to proficiency, regardless of ethnicity, income, or family background. No more excuses, no more explanations—just a firm mandate to eliminate the achievement gap and bring all students to academic proficiency. This shift in federal educational priorities, from equal opportunity to (near) equal outcomes, is dramatic and unprecedented. Unfortunately, while our expectations for educational excellence have risen, public support (particularly in the form of increased financing) has not similarly increased, forcing superintendents and other central office administrators to do more with less.

The solution, according to federal officials, is for superintendents to allocate their limited resources more effectively, building upon what works and junking educational fads and follies that, although politically correct, have little or no demonstrated connection to improved student achievement for all children. This requires superintendents to assume the role of applied social scientist—to use scientifically based research to determine what works and what does not. As leaders of school systems with limited resources and elevated expectations, superintendents and other central office personnel (including associate superintendents for curriculum and instruction) must be well-grounded in the research on effective schools. They must be able to discern quality studies from those that are poorly designed and/or advocacy-driven from those with limited empirical basis or those utilizing substandard research designs and methods (U.S.D.O.E., 2003). The demands on superintendents to become outcomes-based, data-driven decision makers require superintendents to assume a new role (on top of all the others): that of superintendent as applied social scientist.

Accompanying this new role, contemporary superintendents are expected to tap more effectively into local resources to meet the needs of their districts. Because more money is not forthcoming while expectations have increased, superintendents are also required to assume the role of social activists—engaging the entire community in school reform initiatives. This role is very public and requires superintendents to become actively involved with business and community organizations—in effect, to assume the role of public advocate and activist. An increasingly skeptical public, which is beset with concerns both at home and abroad, is no longer willing to unquestioningly fund public education. As a result, superintendents must more effectively market and sell their product (public schools) to an unprecedented degree and in ways that they never before imagined. Long gone are the days when superintendents simply asked the community (and state and federal officials) for more resources; today, superintendents must also justify, often in great detail, why those additional resources are needed and exactly how they will be used to benefit all children. This shift also represents a significant shift in public attitudes and educational practice. What has been called the "toughest job in America" has become even more difficult now that superintendents are expected to also assume the role of social activist to garner the community resources and support necessary to initiate and sustain systemic reform initiatives.

In this chapter, we explore the emerging role of superintendents as applied social scientists and social activists. We begin by examining the evolution of the superintendency in theory (administrative preparation) and in practice. We explore how the superintendency has changed over time, and how these changes affect the emergent role of superintendents as applied social scientists and social activists. In light of recent educational reforms, including NCLB, and changes in administrator preparation, we conclude that effective superintendents perform a holistic role as applied social scientists, broadly defined—encompassing knowledge of research, effective administrative practice, collaborator, and activist.

CHANGING METAPHORS OF THE SUPERINTENDENCY

We begin by examining historical conceptualizations of the superintendency—how the roles and responsibilities of superintendents have changed over time. In their historical analysis of the shifting discourse surrounding the superintendency, Brunner, Grogan, and Björk (2002) identified several distinct discursive stages. From approximately 1900–1954, superintendents acted as expert managers and adopted the values and practices of business and industry. The predominant view of administration emphasized the principles of scientific management—Callahan's cult of efficiency—and adopted a thoroughly business ethos (Cooper & Boyd, 1987; Taylor, 1911). This corporate ideology continued to permeate the superintendency, even as superintendents themselves transitioned into other roles such as communicator, accountability expert, political strategist, and collaborator (Brunner, Grogan, & Björk, 2002). This rational-technical "system of production" ideology remains "firmly embedded in the psyche of policy makers and pervade[s] most educational reforms promulgated since the early 1980s" (Goldring & Greenfield, 2002, p. 2).

Shortly after World War II, educational administration emerged as an established academic discipline (Culbertson, 1981). The creation of an annual gathering of professors of educational administration—the National Conference of Professors of Educational Administration (NCPEA) in 1947—coupled with the founding of the University Council for Educational Administration (UCEA) in 1956 (led by Daniel Griffiths, Jack Culbertson, and Paula Silver), spurred the emergence of the theory movement in educational administration.[1] Scholars believed that effective administration of educational systems consisted of more than a loose collection of individual anecdotal experiences; more than a mere collection of "war stories." Superintendents needed skills to enable them to "generalize effectively beyond the immediate data" (Culbertson, 1981, p. 26). It was during this period that superintendents first assumed roles as applied social scientists. Beck and Murphy (1993) identified the 1950s as the decade of the theory-guided administrator. Beginning in the late 1950s and 1960s, superintendents and other school leaders "were being trained to be applied social scientists" (Cooper & Boyd, 1987, p. 11). Would-be superintendents were exposed to an emergent knowledge base rooted in principles borrowed from the social and behavioral sciences (Murphy, 1992).

The model of superintendent as applied social scientist that emerged and became dominant in the 1950s "rests on an intellectual paradigm borrowed from social psychology, management, and the behavioral sciences" and emphasized "empiricism, predictability, and 'scientific' certainty" (Cooper & Boyd, 1987, p. 4). The movement reflected "a determined effort to bring the social science disciplines (particularly psychology, sociology, and social psychology) to bear upon administrator preparation in education" (Crowson & McPherson, 1987, p. 47). As the social sciences developed and matured, financial support provided by the Kellogg Foundation facilitated the integration of the social sciences into superintendent preparation (Kowalski, 2003). With additional insights drawn from the fields of political science and economics, educational leaders were schooled in the principles of motivation, individual and group interaction, resource allocation, and the nature and functioning of public bureaucracies. Furthermore, argued Campbell (1981), because "educational administration also deals with ends, hence the humanities—particularly literature, philosophy, and religion—are also relevant" (p. 12). The professionalization of the superintendency marked a dramatic shift in the preparation of superintendents—a shift away from the traditional practice of elevating the best teacher in the system up through the ranks to the superintendency (Wilson, 1960).

During this period, the focus of educational administration moved from "how to do it" to an orientation based on inquiry (Getzels, 1977). Administration became not only an arena for action but also an area of study (Getzels, 1977). This shift is readily identifiable in texts on educational administration. Noted Getzels (1977), "None of the texts before 1950 referred to theory; virtually none of those after 1960 did not refer to it" (p. 10). The study of theory was necessary to deal effectively with the new barrage of social issues that school administrators were increasingly called on to address.

It is no accident that during this same period, the field of educational administration emerged as a legitimate academic discipline, on a par with business management and public administration. Superintendents were trained and well-grounded in the latest advances in social science theories and practices. However, as will be shown later in this chapter, the role conceptualization of superintendent as applied social scientist did not sustain itself in subsequent decades, as a series of crosscurrents buffeted superintendents, forcing them into other roles and responsibilities.

After *Brown v. Topeka Board of Education* (1954), schools became the primary institution for resolving discrimination and other societal ills in America. As a result, various groups became militantly involved in school politics and internal school affairs (Goldhammer, 1977). Further, Goldhammer (1977) contends:

Heretofore voiceless segments of the community now became vocal and demanded that now school officials give attention to the issues that concern them. The great problem of the school administrator was that he [*sic*] could not remain neutral. Policy that would appease one group would antagonize another. Even failure to act was viewed as a commitment to one point of view and an instrument to be used by one group against another. The effective school administrator had to learn how to contain conflict, how to manage conflict, and how to negotiate and win compromises among contending forces. (p. 155)

The study and practice of administration, which had historically faced inward upon relations within the school system, necessarily turned its focus outward to relations of the school system to other systems with which it was inextricably bound—political, legal, and economic systems, among others (Getzels, 1977). An increasingly pluralistic society necessitated a different emphasis on the social role of the school than the one with which administrators were accustomed to dealing (Goldhammer, 1977).

By the 1970s, coursework in educational administration was thoroughly infused with behavioral science concepts and content, reflecting the belief that the practice of administration was "more than the execution of technical tasks" (Miklos, 1983, p. 159). Accordingly, would-be superintendents were encouraged to adopt a holistic approach and to see how education fit within the larger social system—how education was related to the larger political, social, economic, and legal order—and, conversely, how other institutions and organizations affected the educational system (Getzels, 1977; Miklos, 1983). Consistent with the intellectual ferment of the period, superintendents were encouraged to view public education as an instrument of social policy, rather than as isolated enclaves within the broader society (Goldhammer, 1977). This paradigm became firmly entrenched in administrator-preparation programs across the country and laid the foundation for the later emergence of superintendents as social activists.

Unfortunately, the social sciences were unable to provide answers to the myriad problems confronting the United States in the 1960s and 1970s: war, inflation and stagflation, rising unemployment, chronic poverty and homelessness, welfare dependency, drug and alcohol abuse, increased rates of crime and domestic violence, and perceived moral decay. In education, significant disparities in educational opportunities and outcomes became apparent, and the inability of superintendents as applied social scientists to solve these problems led to a series of attacks against education schools and, by extension, the preparation of school leaders (Hess, 2004; Kramer, 1991; Tucker, 2003). University-based administrator-preparation programs were criticized as being too theoretical and divorced from the actual practice of educational administration. The knowledge base in educational administration was questioned, and sharp disagreements arose over whether education schools were the best place to train and prepare superintendents, a controversy that continues to this day, despite the decidedly mixed performance of nontraditionally trained (nontraditional route) superintendents across the United States (Cooper, Fusarelli, Jackson, & Poster, 2002).

Andrews and Grogan (2002) observed that "Few universities have programs tailored specifically for the position [of superintendent] although most Ph.D. and Ed. D. programs in educational administration are considered to be preparation programs for superintendents" (p. 8). Preparation programs for superintendents tend "to be extensions of principal-oriented programs" (Björk, Kowalski, & Browne-Ferrigno, 2005, p. 18). The lack of substantive differentiation in the preparation of building-level administrators (principals) and district-level administrators (superintendents) is a significant issue because "the work of superintendents is qualitatively different than principals" (Björk, Kowalski, & Browne-Ferrigno, 2005, pp. 17–18). In addition to these problems, educational leaders were criticized as all too often adopting the *reform du jour* method of decision making and program adoption, rather than carefully evaluating alternatives. In his analysis of the politics of urban school reform, Hess (1999) found that superintendents work in an environment in which constant reform is expected, and almost every reform is enacted, regardless of merit.

To compound these difficulties, critics charged that schools of education had become little more than diploma mills, the cash cows of universities (Tucker, 2003). Critics questioned the comparatively low admissions standards and quality of graduate students enrolling in advanced administrator-preparation programs. They also questioned the content and academic rigor of coursework, particularly (and interestingly) the movement away from traditional social science methods (read: quantitative methods) toward an embrace of critical theory and postmodernism (dominated by qualitative approaches) that, to conservative critics, smacked of educational relativism, in which every approach has merit and no one approach is better than another. Particularly insofar as these approaches had their roots in neo-Marxism, critics attacked schools of education for indoctrinating practitioners with political correctness at the expense of academic rigor. Although they border on hyperbole, these criticisms will be addressed later in this chapter in our recommendations for improving the preparation of superintendents.

SUPERINTENDENTS AS APPLIED SOCIAL SCIENTISTS AND SOCIAL ACTIVISTS: SHIFTING THE METAPHOR

Three significant, distinct, yet interrelated policy and ideational currents have come together to shape the reemergent view of superintendents as applied social scientists and social activists. The three currents include (1) powerful demographic and societal changes that challenge efforts at school improvement; (2) recent systemic reform initiatives such as the No Child Left Behind Act (NCLB) that emphasize "the well being and learning of all children" so that no children are left behind (Björk, 2003, p. 2); and

(3) changes in administrator preparation, focusing on issues of equity and social justice. Although distinct, each ideational current draws from and is affected by the other two currents. We shall examine each current and highlight how it contributes to the reemergent metaphor of superintendent as applied social scientist and social activist.

Demographic Change and the Persistence of Educational Failure

Unfortunately, the wide array of urban school reform initiatives implemented across the nation in the past three decades has not produced significant and sustained results. Notes Hess (1999), "A cacophony of reform efforts marketed as solutions to unsatisfactory school performance has produced little substantive change in urban schooling" (p. 10). Despite wave after wave of school reform, the condition of education—particularly in urban areas populated by the nation's most impoverished, disadvantaged children—remains perilous. Reading and math scores in many large cities remain abysmally low. One-fifth of the public schools in Chicago and New York City are either on probation or in need of immediate intervention ("Saving Public Education," 1997). Performance data show wide and persistent gaps in student achievement, and some indicators suggest that the performance gap among minority groups is widening (Fusarelli, 2000). For example, although the performance gap in reading among 17-year-olds narrowed from 1975 to 1990, it has widened since then (Center for Education Reform, 2002; Reyes, Wagstaff, & Fusarelli, 1999).[2] On nearly every index of student achievement, student performance still lags terribly, despite wave after wave of school reform (Henig, Hula, Orr, & Pedescleaux, 1999; Viteritti, 2002).

Poor student performance has been blamed on teachers' unions, the micropolitics of local school boards, high faculty and administrator turnover, overbureaucratization and red tape, the monopolistic nature of public education, and a lack of competition (Hess, 1999). However, we argue that the failure of past reforms was because the reforms produced only superficial changes in schools but did not affect the nature (the deep structure) of schooling or of society itself. Reforms such as schedule changes (block scheduling, year-round schools), evaluation (authentic assessment, portfolios, standardized testing), professional development (teacher teams, collaborative planning), and school-based management neither affected instruction in the classroom nor addressed the fundamental problems that schools, and the children within them, face. To a great extent, such superficial changes in schooling amount to little more than rearranging the deck chairs on the *Titanic*—the action is earnest but does not address the underlying problem. What is needed is substantive change in the structure and design of schooling, and educational leaders committed to equity and excellence must lead this effort.

Given the perceived crisis in American education today, superintendents "not only are expected to know and articulate why reforms are needed but also must be willing to use their position to change school structures, practices, and relations with the broad community. These circumstances accentuated the political and moral dimensions of their leadership role in changing the nature of schooling and schools" (Brunner, Grogan, & Björk, 2002, p. 225). Consequently, "closer relations with local and state agencies are necessary" (Goldhammer, 1977, p. 161). With the expanded social significance of school functions, coordination with other agencies and the preservice training necessary to coordinate effectively became imperative (Johnson, 2003). As Lunenberg (2003) observes, "Sustained districtwide school improvement is not possible without a strong connection across levels of organization (school, district, community and state)" (p. 41). To initiate such reform successfully, the roles of applied social scientist and social activist must be joined together in the form of social science as praxis.

Social Science as Praxis

Educational reform cannot be debated outside the space of politics and social power because when educators do not engage in social/cultural analysis, there exists a conspiracy of silence, a tacit recognition, about the relationships between moral/social concerns and formal education (Freire, 1989; Giroux & Simon, 1989; Purpel, 1989). Many educators deny that schools are political entities, that schools reflect more than they shape policy/beliefs, or that they exist to protect the status quo. However, as "sociopolitical and highly normative systems," schools and school districts are "nested within larger social, cultural, economic, and political environments containing other dynamic institutions" (Goldring & Greenfield, 2002, p. 2). For school reform (especially urban school reform) to produce lasting, improved outcomes for all children, educators and policymakers must accept that "education is politics" (Counts, 1969; Freire, 1970). In their study of efforts to build civic capacity in 11 cities, Stone, Henig, Jones, and Pierannunzi (2001) found that "Successful educational reform ultimately requires a broad and sustainable coalition of support, and the route to this goes directly through, and not around, politics" (p. 1). A first step in this process is the recognition that although schools in the United States have historically served labor market interests and cultural uniformity, schools and those who lead them must become agents of social justice—and, therefore, superintendents must become social activists. The process of becoming social activists and agents of social justice must begin during leadership preparation.

Unfortunately, assuming the role of social activist runs contrary to much of the training and socialization of superintendents.[3] In fact, Murphy and Hawley (2003) identified the role of school leader as social architect (what we term social activist) as one of the new emergent roles for which preparation programs should prepare school leaders. The phrase itself, *social architect,* suggests an active, interventionist role for superintendents—a role consistent with the idea of social science as praxis. Because most superintendents are former principals, the dominant paradigm and administrative practice is to remain out of politics and as far removed from politics as possible. The "science" of administration teaches principals to stay out of politics, and the occupational socialization of principals reinforces such behavior ("don't rock the boat"). However, as principals assume district-level leadership positions in school systems, they must become adept at moving the entire system toward school improvement. Systemic reform is difficult and requires the active involvement of school leaders with a variety of community-based players and leaders who inhabit the political world. Effective leadership at this level requires "playing politics"—getting multiple partners with diverse interests to buy into your vision and provide you with the resources necessary to achieve that vision. Particularly in large urban systems, systemic reform is not possible without broad-based community support and commitment led by superintendents committed to equity and social justice.

Goldring and Hausman (2000) point out that preparation programs need to go beyond skill development. Preparation programs need to reshape how school leaders view their roles. In their survey of 38 elementary principals in Cincinnati and St. Louis, Goldring and Hausman (2000) asked principals how they would spend time if they could magically find an additional 10 hours per week. They found that principals placed relatively little importance on interacting with the school's external environment to build support and garner resources. The researchers conclude: "Building civic capacity is not incongruent with instructional leadership. In fact, a strong case can be made that civic capacity enables principals to serve as effective instructional leaders" (p. 24). Preparation programs should help would-be superintendents embrace this expanded role and build the civic, social supports necessary to meet the nonacademic needs of students that are often prerequisites to academic achievement—including active involvement in building civic capacity to initiate and implement comprehensive social policies to reinvigorate local communities. Specifically, superintendents need to possess "an exquisite understanding of how to draw together disparate groups by proving clear and direct benefits to cooperation, defining an inclusive vision, and pragmatically zeroing in on doable tasks and realizable goals" (Stone, Henig, Jones, & Pierannunzi, 2001, p. 1).

Systemic Reform and the No Child Left Behind Act

More than ever before, superintendents are required to use data to drive decision making and be proactive in identifying obstacles to achieving equity in schools (Scheurich & Skrla, 2003). Gone are the days when superintendents were the benevolent, symbolic leaders of school systems or distant managers far removed from the daily realities and inner workings of schools. In today's increasingly competitive environment, in which school leaders are beset with all manner of accountability and calls for educating all children to proficiency, superintendents must become active interventionists in leading school improvement. They "need to be focused on measurable outcomes . . . be constantly looking at their performance data and feeding it back into a process of continuous improvement" (Stanton, 2004, p. 1). As Björk, Kowalski, and Browne-Ferrigno (2005) assert, "the reality of educational accountability requires considerable knowledge of testing, data analysis, and interpretation to successfully sustain enduring efforts to improve schooling" (p. 16). Therefore, superintendents must work with teams of "principals, curriculum specialists/ instructional coaches, and researchers to observe current practices, discuss student performance data with the staff, and assist in the development and implementation" of school improvement plans (Lunenberg, 2003, p. 40). Outcomes-based accountability systems, such as those mandated under the NCLB, enable superintendents to direct more effectively "the flow of fiscal, human, and material resources" in schools (Fuller & Johnson, 2001, p. 280).

NCLB mandates the use of "scientifically based research to guide their decisions about which interventions to implement" (U.S.D.O.E., 2003, p. iii). Shavelson and Towne (2002) explain that "recent enthusiasm for 'evidence-based' policy and practice in education—now codified in the federal law . . . [has] brought a new sense of urgency to understanding the ways in which the basic tenets of science manifest in the study of teaching, learning, and schooling" (paragraph 1). In October 2002, Congress approved the Education Sciences Reform Act, legislation that further emphasizes and expands the role of educational research and development in federal education policy (Fleischman, Kohlmoos, & Rotherham, 2003). Consequently, demands increased for a strong education-knowledge infrastructure that includes research, development, dissemination, technical assistance, professional development, evaluation, and other research-based applications (Fleischman et al., 2003).

Scientific research "can yield reliable and replicable findings that build confidence in the effectiveness (or failure) of the many alternatives advocated or practiced in education. These findings should increase the willingness of policymakers and educators to make required changes or stick with proven—albeit often difficult—reforms" (Fleischman et al., 2003, paragraph 13). To flourish in this new era, superintendents will need to create an environment that values evidence-based educational practices and work to better prepare school district employees to participate in research and evaluation and apply research-based school improvement techniques.

Superintendent Preparation and Social Justice

As state and federal policymakers undertake reforms to ensure that no children are left behind, a host of academic and professional associations are placing renewed emphasis on narrowing the achievement gap and enhancing equity for all students. Björk (2003) observes that the "AASA, ISLLC, and NCATE standards-based licensure and reform initiatives . . . provide a template for shifting the focus and nature of instruction from management to leadership for learning" with an emphasis on concern for effective education for children of color (p. 17).

There is some evidence to suggest that the external pressures of the National Council for the Accreditation of Colleges of Teacher Education (NCATE) and the Interstate School Leadership Licensure Consortium (ISLLC) have helped to increase preparation programs' attention to diversity and social justice issues. Both NCATE and ISLLC include a diversity component. On the ISLLC Web page, the organization notes the changing nature of society:

> Looking to the larger society that envelopes schooling, the Consortium identified a handful of powerful dynamics that will likely shape the future of education and, perforce, the types of leadership required for tomorrow's schools. To begin with, our vision of education is influenced by the knowledge that the social fabric of society is changing . . . we are becoming a more diverse society—racially, linguistically and culturally. . . . Poverty is increasing. Indexes of physical, mental, and moral well-being are declining. The stock of social capital is decreasing as well. . . . We believe that these challenges will require new types of leadership in schools.

Educational research has found that the underlying source of many of the most vexing problems school leaders face are societal problems (Berg, Gaynor, Grogan, & McGrevin, 1999; Kochan, Jackson, & Duke, 1999; Prestine, 1997). Complex societal issues such as poverty, racism, unemployment and underemployment, drugs, and violence affect both the nature of schools and schooling and the expectations the public has placed upon those who lead educational institutions (Kochan et al., 1999). Björk, Kowalski, and Browne-Ferrigno (2005) noted that "As [these] social factors became entwined with improving student learning a profoundly different reality of work emerged" for superintendents—work for which many were unprepared (p. 11). Many school superintendents feel ill prepared to address social justice issues. To make matters worse, many educators have come to believe that injustice in society, as well as in public institutions such as schools, is natural, inevitable, and entirely unalterable (Larson & Ovando, 2001).

Changing demographics, especially when coupled with the push for high-stakes standardized tests and the resulting racial and socioeconomic status (SES) achievement gap, necessitate a rethinking of the way universities prepare school leaders. Rusch (1999) found that superintendents, like principals, are sharply aware of the increased complexity of the "sociology of schools," noting the increased violence, gang activity, the changing values of students and parents, and the increased diversity in the populations they serve. Accordingly, superintendents must be well-grounded in the "what is" of administration, as well as provide a vision of "what ought to be" (Miklos, 1983, p. 161). Björk, Kowalski, and Browne-Ferrigno (2005) argue that "superintendents must draw upon the social sciences to understand differing needs and values, expertly disaggregate student test data, are proficient in analyzing the causes of social and learning problems, and are proactive in building political coalitions in support of socially just organizational policies and practices" (p. 11).

To effectively address diversity issues, educational leaders need to be skilled in relating to people who have different needs and different values. Questions arise about the degree to which administrator-preparation programs develop proficiencies that support the development of shared and enacted visions, build coalitions of community leaders, or support the growth of political expertise (Rusch, 1999). As Macedo (1998) sees it, scholars should abandon many current approaches to studying inequity. He argues that researchers must not be satisfied with simply identifying inequity again and again. A social justice perspective, with the superintendent acting in their role as applied social scientist and social activist, would enable superintendents to go beyond noting differences and discrimination, and provide them with the skills to take action and to proactively implement socially just policies and practices—to be leaders for social justice.

Reflecting this change, in the past two decades, the field of educational leadership has shifted its focus toward "what leadership is *for*" as opposed to what leadership is or does (Furman, 2003, p. 1). Noting the dramatic differences between the first *Handbook of Research on Educational Administration,* published in 1988, and the second *Handbook,* published in 1999, Björk (2003) asserted that "the shift in emphasis from school management to transformational leadership" is "an unambiguous attempt to re-center the field of educational administration" (p. 23). A key component of this re-centering is the emergence of the moral purposes of educational leadership as the central focus of reform efforts (Furman, 2003). Reviewing criticisms of administrator-preparation programs, Murphy and Hawley (2003) assert that the profession had drifted from concerns over the ethical and moral dimensions of schooling and had lost its heart and soul in the process. In response, several administrator-preparation programs have incorporated or integrated ethics and servant leadership (through both formal coursework and practical applications of case studies) into their master's and doctoral coursework. This shift in emphasis is consistent with the goals and objectives of NCLB and with states' efforts to implement systemic educational reform initiatives designed to reduce the achievement gap. Furman (2003) attributes the re-centering of educational administration on the moral purposes of leadership to the convergence of at least three theoretical strands—critical-humanist leadership, constructivist leadership, and distributive leadership—which draw attention to societal inequities. At its core, school leadership is a profoundly moral enterprise, and superintendents, as the most visible leaders of school systems, play a key role as moral agents (Sergiovanni, 1992; Starratt, 1991).

In their review of the evolution of leadership in education, Goldring and Greenfield (2002) note that "Much of the work of school administration involves making value judgments about the right thing to do in the face of more than one desirable choice. At other times the challenge may be choosing the least harmful from among several undesirable alternatives" (p. 3). Ethics and social justice, therefore, form the *core* of superintendents' work in their role as applied social scientists and in their efforts to develop better policies to improve educational outcomes for all children (Cooper, Fusarelli, & Randall, 2004). As leaders in creating collaborative work environments, superintendents play a key role in helping teachers, parents, and the community understand the needs of all children (Pounder, Reitzug, & Young, 2002).

In their role as stewards of public education, superintendents are responsible for guiding and developing "the public's understanding of and support for what public schools need to be doing, the goals they should be achieving, and the critical role of public education in developing a more socially just and democratic society" (Goldring & Greenfield, 2002, p. 4). As moral steward, superintendents "must use their personal platform to 'engage participants in the organization and the community in reinterpreting and placing new priorities on guiding values for education'" (Moorman, cited in Murphy, 2002, p. 76). Such stewardship requires superintendents to address four key challenges: (1) to combat the anti-intellectual sentiment so prevalent in American society (Hofstadter, 1963); (2) to encourage politicians and business leaders to adopt more comprehensive, holistic social policies, including a "livable wage for working parents, affordable housing, day care for infants and young children, and health care" (Goldring & Greenfield, 2002, p. 4); (3) to educate the community about the importance of and challenge of educating all children well; and (4) to "cultivate support for the development of intercultural competence among children" (Goldring & Greenfield, 2002, p. 5). These four challenges require superintendents to expand their current role if they are to function as effective social activists. Pounder, Reitzug, and Young (2002) observe that "Part of leading for social justice . . . is understanding that one is not just a leader but an activist for children, an activist who is committed to supporting educational equity and excellence for all children" (p. 272). In their role as applied social scientists, superintendents must become social activists.

SUPERINTENDENTS AS APPLIED SOCIAL SCIENTISTS AND SOCIAL ACTIVISTS: IMPLICATIONS FOR PREPARATION AND PRACTICE

Freire and Shor's (1998) work on oppression and liberation suggests the beginning of a solution: Preparing future leaders from a social justice framework could help to bridge the divide between exposure to ideas and demands for action—between what is taught in preparation programs and what is needed to be an effective school leader. A change in preparation programs might be particularly necessary as schools attempt to reduce barriers to academic achievement and increasingly play a greater role in meeting students' nonacademic needs—in part as a response to legislation such as NCLB. Educators will be expected to be more flexible and take on additional responsibilities for the welfare of students.

As the position of superintendent has grown in complexity, so too have the skills and capabilities of superintendents. Over the past three decades, the percentage of superintendents earning doctoral degrees has increased from 29% in 1971 to 45% in 2000 (Glass, Björk, & Brunner, 2000). The intensive nature of doctoral study, with its emphasis on holistic, "big-picture" conceptualization and critical thinking skills, provides superintendents with the tools to become applied social scientists, even social activists. We argue that as applied social scientists, superintendents must develop "theories and strategies for redressing enduring norms of injustice in education" (Larson & Murtadha, 2002, p. 135). Because superintendents are ultimately charged with the responsibility for educating *all* children, this advocacy responsibility falls squarely on their shoulders. If not them, whom? Counts (1969) argued that school leaders must play an active role in creating a more just society. He stated, "To refuse to face the task of creating a vision of a future America immeasurably more just and noble and beautiful than the America of today is to evade the most crucial, difficult, and important educational task" (p. 55). To Counts, whether superintendents should function as social activists (or architects) is not a question at all, but rather a moral imperative.

Therefore, preparation programs must train superintendents to see the big picture—as applied social scientists, as social activists, and as social advocates for all children. University-based preparation programs have the resources to expose students to a broader, more holistic view of educational systems than do professional administrator organizations. As Pounder, Reitzug, and Young (2002) observe, "administrative work requires administrators to synthesize and apply the understandings from these multiple disciplines to complex problems of practice" (p. 281).

The importance of inculcating a broad-based, social-scientific framework into superintendent training can be demonstrated in the following analogy. At the Aspen Institute, top corporate executives attend retreats, focusing not on learning the latest developments in the worlds of finance, banking, advertising, or law, but rather on studying literature, drama, and philosophy—all in an effort to stretch their minds, opening these executives up to the world of ideas offering fresh perspectives—helping them see the "big picture" (Cooper & Boyd, 1987, p. 20). As leaders responsible for the "whole system," superintendents must be educated through a broad-based, holistic social science paradigm. The value of such an approach is exemplified by comments made by practitioners schooled in such methods. Reflecting back on how this paradigm influenced his practice as a school principal, Hills (1975) commented that although "I almost never found myself making direct applications of program content in considering specific problems . . . my behavior was governed to a considerable degree by a rather generalized, closely interrelated mixture of empirical beliefs and values" (p. 2). Hills (1975) stated emphatically that "I am firmly committed to the view that the school administrator needs to be reasonably well-grounded in developmental psychology, learning studies, socialization, cultural variation, instructional methods and materials, and curricular developments" (p. 13).

After his stint as a principal, Donmoyer (1995) agreed and noted the value of insights drawn from anthropology, political science, and sociology to the practice of educational administration. While important to principals, such skills are critical to superintendents. With these analytical skills at hand, superintendents can engage in "taking apart issues, situations, and problems; dividing complex questions, operations, and situations into manageable parts; [and] looking across cases for similarities and differences, i.e., skill in classification" (Hills, 1975, p. 13). Such skills lead to a "disinclination to accept things as given, or at face value . . . to 'look beneath' the surface confusion for orderly relations, to make conceptual sense of what one observes and does" (p. 14). Accordingly, advanced administrator preparation must go beyond narrowly prescribed skill sets and devote more attention to insights derived from cognitive and social psychology, brain research, learning theory, political science, history, economics, philosophy, sociology, and anthropology.

The roles and responsibilities of the superintendent have expanded, and the need to look beyond the schoolhouse door for answers to lingering educational dilemmas is imperative for real, sustainable educational improvement to occur. Kotter (1996) notes that leadership defines what the future should look like, aligns people with that vision, and inspires them to make it happen despite the obstacles—in sum, leadership produces change. As Goldhammer (1977) explained more than 25 years ago, "designed as a position of educational leadership, [the superintendency] is now more significantly marked as a position of coordination and orchestration rather than one of independent leadership. . . . The opportunities for statesmanship, leadership, and direction, although more complex and exacting, are possibly even greater today than ever before" (p. 164).

To inculcate the skills necessary to produce such leadership for change, preparation programs should adopt models of strategic planning and organizational change from business and the military. Often, individuals from outside the traditional educational establishment who become superintendents are amazed at how seldom strategic planning models are used in education. Former Seattle superintendent John Stanford, a former military general and county executive, was shocked that the School Improvement Plans (SIPs) developed by each school seldom contained measurable objectives, nor were they used for strategic management or program planning. SIPs were created and then put on shelves, not to be looked at until the next year when the plans were re-created. Stanford spent much of his tenure as superintendent emphasizing the development, use, and constant updating of SIPs as an essential tool for school improvement. Few university-based preparation programs give more than lip service to such training, yet detailed models of strategic planning and organizational change are essential in the preparation of superintendents for their role as applied social scientists and activists.

Finally, we view the shift in federal education policy, exemplified by the No Child Left Behind Act, with its emphasis on scientifically based research, data-based decision making and evaluation, and priority of eliminating the achievement gap and improving educational outcomes for all children as consistent with the reemergent role of superintendent as applied social scientist and social activist. Consistent with this emphasis, university-based preparation programs for superintendents should train students more effectively in applied research methods, including data-based decision making, strategic planning and management, and evaluation techniques. Federal officials assert that "many practitioners have not been given the tools to distinguish interventions supported by scientifically rigorous evidence from those which are not" (U.S.D.O.E., 2003, p. iii). We agree and suspect that a surprising number of would-be superintendents are not equipped with the necessary methodological skills to initiate, or even understand and critique, relatively simple evaluation studies. As evidenced by much research and scholarship in educational leadership and administration over the past decade, university-based preparation programs have strayed from their social science roots and de-emphasized these skills (Murphy & Louis, 1999). This must be addressed and corrected if preparation programs are to equip future superintendents with the knowledge and skills as applied social scientists and social activists that are required for leadership in the twenty-first century.

NOTES

1. Culbertson was UCEA's first executive director and led the organization for 22 years.

2. Based on average student proficiency in reading from the National Assessment of Educational Progress (NAEP); see National Center for Education Statistics, *Digest*

of Education Statistics 2001 (Washington, DC: U.S. Department of Education, 2002), Table 112, p. 133.

3. The authors are indebted to John Keedy for this insight and for his thoughtful critique of an earlier version of this chapter.

REFERENCES

Andrews, R., & Grogan, M. (2002). *Defining preparation and professional development for the future.* Paper commissioned for the First Meeting of the National Commission for the Advancement of Educational Leadership Preparation. Wingspread Conference Center, Racine, WI.

Beck, L. G., & Murphy, J. (1993). *Understanding the principalship: Metaphorical themes, 1920s–1990s.* New York: Teachers College Press.

Berg, J. H., Gaynor, A. K., Grogan, M., & McGrevin, C. (1999). Treacherous waters: Vexing problems in the superintendency. In F. K. Kochan, B. L. Jackson, & D. L. Duke (Eds.), *A thousand voices from the firing line: A study of educational leaders, their jobs, their preparation and the problems they face.* Columbia, MO: University Council for Educational Administration.

Björk, L. G. (2003). *National commissions and new directions for superintendent preparation programs.* Unpublished monograph.

Björk, L. G., Kowalski, T. J., & Browne-Ferrigno, T. (2005). Learning theory and research: A framework for changing superintendent preparation and development. In L. G. Björk & T. J. Kowalski (Eds.), *Brown v. Board of Education of Topeka,* 347 U.S. 483 (1954) (*Brown I*).

Brunner, C. C., Grogan, M., & Björk, L. G. (2002). Shifts in the discourse defining the superintendency: Historical and current foundations of the position. In J. Murphy (Ed.), *The educational leadership challenge: Redefining leadership for the 21st century* (pp. 211–238). Chicago: University of Chicago Press.

Campbell, R. F. (1981). The professorship in educational administration—a personal view. *Educational Administration Quarterly, 17*(1), 1–24.

Center for Education Reform. (2002, June 11). *CER Newswire, 4*(22). Downloaded from http://www.edreform.com

Cooper, B. S., & Boyd, W. L. (1987). The evolution of training for school administrators. In J. Murphy and P. Hallinger (Eds.), *Approaches to administrative training in education* (pp. 3–27). Albany: State University of New York Press.

Cooper, B. S., Fusarelli, L. D., Jackson, B. L., & Poster, J. (2002). Is "superintendent preparation" an oxymoron? Analyzing changes in programs, certification, and control. *Leadership and Policy in Schools, 1*(3), 242–255.

Cooper, B. S., Fusarelli, L. D., & Randall, E. V. (2004). *Better policies, better schools: Theories and applications.* Boston: Pearson Education.

Counts, G. S. (1969). *Dare the school build a new social order?* New York: Arno Press.

Crowson, R. L., & McPherson, R. B. (1987). The legacy of the theory movement: Learning from the new tradition. In J. Murphy & P. Hallinger (Eds.), *Approaches to administrative training in education* (pp. 45–64). Albany: State University of New York Press.

Culbertson, J. A. (1981). Antecedents of the theory movement. *Educational Administration Quarterly, 17*(1), 25–47.

Donmoyer, R. (1995). A knowledge base for educational administration: Notes from the field. In R. Donmoyer, M. Imber, & J. J. Scheurich (Eds.), *The knowledge base in educational administration: Multiple perspectives* (pp. 74–95). Albany: State University of New York Press.

Fleischman, S., Kohlmoos, J. W., & Rotherham, A. J. (2003, March 12). From research to practice. *Education Week, 22*(26), 48, 34.

Freire, P. (1970). *Pedagogy of the oppressed.* New York: Seabury Press.

Freire, P. (1989). Foreword. In H. A. Giroux & R. I. Simon, *Popular culture, schooling, and everyday life.* Granby, MA: Bergin & Garvey.

Freire, P., & Shor, I. (1998). *A pedagogy for liberation.* Westport, CT: Bergin & Garvey.

Fuller, E. J., & Johnson, J. F., Jr. (2001). Can state accountability systems drive improvements in school performance for children of color and children from low-income homes? *Education and Urban Society, 33*(3), 260–283.

Furman, G. (2003). The 2002 UCEA presidential address. *UCEA Review, 65*(1), 1–6.

Fusarelli, L. D. (2000). Leadership in Latino schools: Challenges for the new millennium. In P. M. Jenlink (Ed.), *Marching into a new millennium: Challenges to educational leadership* (pp. 228–238). Lanham, MD: Scarecrow Press.

Getzels, J. W. (1977). Educational administration twenty years later, 1954–1974. In L. L. Cunningham, W. G. Hack, & R. O. Nystrand (Eds.), *Educational administration: The developing decades* (pp. 3–24). Berkeley, CA: McCutchan.

Giroux, H. A., & Simon, R. I. (1989). *Popular culture, schooling, and everyday life.* Granby, MA: Bergin & Garvey.

Glass, T. E., Björk, L. G., & Brunner, C. C. (2000). *The study of the American school superintendency: 2000.* Arlington, VA: American Association of School Administrators.

Goldhammer, K. (1977). The role of the American school superintendent, 1954–1974. In L. L. Cunningham, W. G. Hack, & R. O. Nystrand (Eds.), *Educational administration: The developing decades* (pp. 147–164). Berkeley, CA: McCutchan.

Goldring, E. B., & Greenfield, W. (2002). Understanding the evolving concept of leadership in education: Roles, expectations, and dilemmas. In J. Murphy (Ed.), *The educational leadership challenge: Redefining leadership for the 21st century* (pp. 1–19). Chicago: University of Chicago Press.

Goldring, E. B., & Hausman, C. (2000, April). *Civic capacity and school principals: The missing links for community development.* Paper presented at the annual meeting of the American Educational Research Association, Seattle, WA.

Henig, J. R., Hula, R. C., Orr, M., & Pedescleaux, D. S. (1999). *The color of school reform.* Princeton, NJ: Princeton University Press.

Hess, F. M. (1999). *Spinning wheels: The politics of urban school reform.* Washington, DC: Brookings Institution Press.

Hess, F. M. (2004). *Common sense school reform.* New York: Palgrave Macmillan.

Hills, J. (1975). The preparation of administrators: Some observations from the "firing line." *Educational Administration Quarterly, 11*(3), 1–20.

Hofstadter, R. (1963). *Anti-intellectualism in American life.* New York: Knopf.

Johnson, B. C. (2003). Coordinated, school-linked services and principal preparation. In F. C. Lunenberg & C. S. Carr (Eds.), *Shaping the future: Policy, partnerships, and emerging perspectives* (pp. 329–339). Lanham, MD: Scarecrow Education.

Kochan, F. K., Jackson, B. L., & Duke, D. L. (1999). *A thousand voices from the firing line: A study of educational leaders, their jobs, their preparation and the problems they face.* Columbia, MO: University Council for Educational Administration.

Kotter, J. P. (1996). *Leading change.* Boston: Harvard Business School Press.

Kowalski, T. J. (2003, April 21). *Superintendent as communicator: The fifth role conceptualization.* Paper presented at the annual meeting of the American Educational Research Association, Chicago.

Kramer, R. (1991). *Ed school follies.* New York: Free Press.

Larson, C. L., & Murtadha, K. (2002). Leadership for social justice. In J. Murphy (Ed.), *The educational leadership challenge: Redefining leadership for the 21st century* (pp. 134–161). Chicago: University of Chicago Press.

Larson, C. L., & Ovando, C. J. (2001). *The color of bureaucracy: The politics of equity in multicultural school communities.* Wadsworth Press.

Lunenberg, F. C. (2003). The post-behavioral science era: Excellence, community, and justice. In F. C. Lunenberg & C. S. Carr (Eds.), *Shaping the future: Policy, partnerships, and emerging perspectives* (pp. 36–55). Lanham, MD: Scarecrow Education.

Macedo, D. (1998). Foreword. In P. Freire, *Pedagogy of freedom*. New York: Rowman & Littlefield.

Miklos, E. (1983). Evolution in administrator preparation programs. *Educational Administration Quarterly, 19*(3), 153–177.

Moorman, H. (1990). *Reinventing school leadership* (pp. 98–103). Working memo prepared for the Reinventing School Leadership Conference. Cambridge, MA: National Center for Educational Leadership.

Murphy, J. (1992). *The landscape of leadership preparation: Reframing the education of school administrators.* Newbury Park, CA: Sage.

Murphy, J. (2002). Reculturing the profession of educational leadership: New blueprints. In J. Murphy (Ed.), *The educational leadership challenge: Redefining leadership for the 21st century* (pp. 65–82). Chicago: University of Chicago Press.

Murphy, J., & Hawley, W. (2003). The AASA "leadership for learning" master's program. *Teaching in Educational Administration Newsletter, 10*(2), 1–5.

Murphy, J., & Louis, K. S. (Eds.). (1999). *The handbook of research on educational administration* (2nd ed.). San Francisco: Jossey-Bass.

National Center for Education Statistics. (2002). *Digest of education statistics 2001.* Washington, DC: U.S. Department of Education.

Pounder, D., Reitzug, U., & Young, M. D. (2002). Preparing school leaders for school improvement, social justice, and community. In J. Murphy (Ed.), *The educational leadership challenge: Redefining leadership for the 21st century* (pp. 261–288). Chicago: University of Chicago Press.

Prestine, N. (1997). *Principals interviews: Vexing problems—Thousand voices from the firing line.* Paper presented at the Annual Conference of the University Council for Educational Administration, Orlando, FL.

Purpel, D. (1989). *The moral and spiritual crisis in education.* Granby, MA: Bergin & Garvey.

Reyes, P., Wagstaff, L. H., & Fusarelli, L. D. (1999). Delta forces: The changing fabric of American society and education. In J. Murphy & K. Seashore Louis (Eds.), *Handbook of research on educational administration* (2nd ed.) (pp. 183–201). San Francisco: Jossey-Bass.

Rusch, E. A. (1999). The experience of the piñata: Vexing problems. In F. K. Kochan, B. L. Jackson, & D. L. Duke (Eds.), *A thousand voices from the firing line: A study of educational leaders, their jobs, their preparation and the problems they face.* Columbia, MO: University Council for Educational Administration.

"Saving Public Education." (1997, February 17). *The Nation, 17,* 18, 20–25.

Scheurich, J. J., & Skrla, L. (2003). *Leadership for equity and excellence.* Thousand Oaks, CA: Corwin.

Sergiovanni, T. J. (1992). *Moral leadership: Getting to the heart of school improvement.* San Francisco: Jossey-Bass.

Shapiro, J. P., & Stefkovich, J. A. (2001). *Ethical leadership and decision making in education: Applying theoretical perspectives to complex dilemmas.* Mahwah, NJ: Lawrence Erlbaum.

Shavelson, R. L., & Towne, L. (2002). *Committee on scientific principles for education research.* National Research Council. Retrieved April 12, 2003 from http://www.nap.edu/catalog/10236.html.

Stanford, J. (1999). *Victory in our schools.* New York: Bantam Books.

Stanton, P. (2004). *Preparing a new breed of principals: Leadership from the university president's office.* Atlanta: Southern Regional Education Board.

Starratt, R. K. (1991). Building an ethical school: A theory for practice in educational leadership. *Educational Administration Quarterly, 27*(2), 185–202.

Stone, C. N., Henig, J. R., Jones, B. D., & Pierannunzi, C. (2001). *Building civic capacity: The politics of reforming urban schools.* Lawrence: University Press of Kansas.

Taylor, F. W. (1911). *Shop management.* New York: Harper & Row.

Tucker, M. (2003). Out with the old. *Education Next, 3*(4), 20–24.

U.S. Department of Education. (2003). *Identifying and implementing educational practices supported by rigorous evidence: A user friendly guide.* Washington, DC: Coalition for Evidence-Based Policy.

Viteritti, J. P. (2002). Coming around on school choice. *Educational Leadership,* 44–47.

Wilson, R. E. (1960). *School superintendent: Its principals and practices.* New York: Harper & Brothers.

9

Preparing Superintendents to Be Effective Communicators

Theodore J. Kowalski and John L. Keedy

S ince 1980 there has been mounting evidence that communication has become a "core" competency for all school administrators (e.g., Carter & Cunningham, 1997; Gousha & Mannan, 1991) and that communication practices used by them have influenced both school culture and productivity (e.g., Friedkin & Slater, 1994; Petersen & Short, 2002). Such findings certainly are not novel to education; many authors (e.g., Toth, 2000; Vihera & Nurmela, 2001) have discussed linkages between the development and deployment of appropriate communication processes and organizational effectiveness. Despite its saliency to organization productivity, communication has received relatively little attention in relation to normative standards, professional preparation, and state licensing in school administration (Kowalski & Keedy, 2003).

The purpose of this chapter is to address preparation and licensing issues pertaining to the characterization of superintendent as communicator.

First, four traditional conceptualizations described in the first chapter of this book are discussed in relation to communication to demonstrate that communication was viewed as a role-based skill. Next, communication is examined in the context of modern school reform, especially in relation to reshaping institutional culture. The debilities of classical communication models and the advantages of relational communication as they pertain to superintendent responsibilities in learning organizations are identified. The argument is made that appropriate communication is no longer contingent on role-based skills, but rather on the pervasive application of relational communication—a transition that justifies the reclassification of communication as a separate role. The construct of relational communication is described and communication competence is defined within the framework of a three-dimensional learning model. Implications for applying this model to superintendent preparation and licensing are then summarized.

TRADITIONAL ROLES AND COMMUNICATION

Historical analyses of the school superintendent authored by Raymond Callahan (1962, 1964) have shaped much of the literature on this important position. Callahan began his intense studies in 1956. His intellectual curiosity centered on a hypothesis that preparation for and practice in the superintendency were shaped circa 1910 to 1930 when many leading figures in this position abandoned their identity as teachers and reinvented themselves as managers. Using a discursive analysis that relied heavily on rhetoric and writings from 1865 to 1966 (Brunner, Grogan, & Björk, 2002), he concluded that four separate role conceptualizations had emerged prior to 1970. Although he did not address communication separately, normative communicative behavior was implicit in each role.

During the period in which the conceptualization of scholarly educational leader developed (1865–1910), little mention was made of communication. The character of a superintendent's work inside the organization (i.e., within the school district) entailed two primary functions: suggesting ways teachers could improve instruction and conducting evaluations of curricular compliance and teaching effectiveness. Principals also had the same charge and they typically had even less contact with the public. When communication occurred with individuals and groups outside the organization, the context was primarily professional, most notably through written journal articles and presentations at professional meetings (Callahan, 1964). By its very nature, the role of professional expert apparently did not encourage administrators to develop broad or open communication channels; virtually all their communication entailed giving directives and suggestions to teachers and principals and responding to information requests from school board members.

Professor Callahan, in the scholarly book *Education and Cult of Efficiency* (1962), described why and how superintendents in the most visible school districts were transformed from scholar-teachers to managers during and immediately following the Industrial Revolution. He concluded that these role models were in reality "dupes"—powerless and vulnerable individuals unwilling to defend their profession and organizations. Not all scholars agreed with this harsh conclusion. Burroughs (1974) and Tyack (1972), for instance, saw these same superintendents in a different light, describing them as cunning, intelligent, political pragmatists who skillfully responded to social realities. Thomas and Moran (1992) offered yet another and less flattering perspective; they claimed that the superintendents embraced industrial management principles to expand and protect legitimate power.

Motives aside, the fact is that the most prominent superintendents between 1910 and 1930 embraced a new role conceptualization defined by the tenets of classical theory and scientific management. As part of their conversion, they emulated the normative behaviors of business and industrial managers. In so doing, they erected what Schneider (1994) describes as a *control core culture* (i.e., an authoritative, impersonal, and task-oriented set of values and beliefs). The classic communication paradigm—a model that casts bottom-up and lateral information transmissions as counterproductive (Miller, 2003)—became institutionalized in this organizational climate. Within districts and schools, it is likely that communication became increasingly restrictive and complementary; the concept of complementary communication describes information exchanges in which the parties maximize their differences, especially in relation to one interactant being dominant and the other interactant(s) being submissive (Burgoon & Hale, 1984).

The third role conceptualization, superintendent as democratic leader, emerged circa 1930 and remained in vogue until the early 1950s. The leading spokesperson for this conceptualization was Ernest Melby, a former dean of education at Northwestern University and New York University (Callahan, 1964). Melby (1955) believed that the community was public education's greater resource, and he urged administrators to "release the creative capacities of individuals" and to "mobilize the educational resources of communities" (p. 250). Even if he did not address normative communication specifically, differences between the internal, authoritative dispositions of traditional management and the external, political dispositions of democratic administration were quite apparent. Democratic leaders were expected to galvanize policymakers, employees, and other taxpayers to support the district's initiatives (Howlett, 1993); managers were expected to control information and issue directives and advice as needed (Luthans, 1981). The push for democratic leadership, however, did not eradicate managerial responsibilities; it simply made management a less prominent role (Callahan, 1964). Consequently, superintendents during the period in question faced the competing demands of protecting information and sharing authority. Effective communication depended on the role that a superintendent was assuming at any given time (Kowalski, 2004a).

The last conceptualization identified by Callahan (1964), superintendent as applied social scientist, was prominent in the 1950s and 1960s. The application of concepts, theories, and methods from the social sciences accorded administrators rank and status that justified their treating teachers as subordinates (Fusarelli & Fusarelli, 2003). Preparation curricula for superintendents became less practice-based, more theoretical, and increasingly dissimilar from graduate study completed by teachers. As a result, these administrators were thought to possess an ability to engage in decision making and problem solving at a higher level than other school employees. In all likelihood, this perception encouraged superintendents to communicate as experts, not as colleagues. In this regard, the applied social scientist conceptualization was more aligned with the classical communication model than it was with the expectations of democratic leadership.

PURSUIT OF SCHOOL REFORM IN AN INFORMATION-BASED SOCIETY

Current communicative expectations reflect a confluence of reform initiatives and the social environment in which they are being pursued. Since the early 1990s, the dominant reform strategies have been state deregulation and district decentralization, concepts requiring superintendents to work collaboratively with internal and external groups to build visions and strategic plans (Kowalski, 2003). These strategies are fueled by a perception that school bureaucracies are inefficient and unresponsive, and are therefore "mired in rules and cut off from their clients—students, parents, and community members" (Elmore, 1995, p. 34). The tactics also are based on a belief that substantive involvement, autonomy, and resource control by those closest to students contribute to improved educational outcomes (Weiss, 1993). Accordingly, power should be shifted to teachers and principals—educators who historically have been excluded from district-level governance (Clune & White, 1988)—and organizational norms should be revamped (Keedy, 1991).

In truth, however, many school districts retain counterproductive organizational cultures, that is, shared belief systems that sustain employee isolation (teachers and administrators working individually and in seclusion) (Gideon, 2002) and closed organizational climates (administrators attempting to avoid community interventions) (Blase & Anderson, 1995). Policy analysts who have examined resistance to change have concluded appropriately that meaningful school reform will remain elusive unless present school cultures are reconstructed (Bauman, 1996). Although contemporary reforms affect the roles of all involved in the education enterprise

(Keedy, MacPhail-Wilcox, Mullin, & Campbell Wooten, 1998), the implications for administrators are especially noteworthy because the importance of administrative communication to culture change strategies is well established in the literature (e.g., Goodman, Willis, & Holihan, 1998; Kowalski, 1998b; Quirke, 1996).

Current reform efforts are rooted in the conviction that reforming complex institutions necessitates a social systems perspective (Chance & Björk, 2004; Murphy, 1991b; Schein, 1996). "Systemic thinking requires us to accept that the way social systems are put together has independent effects on the way people behave, what they learn, and how they learn what they learn" (Schlechty, 1997, p. 134). In public schools, these interactions, which occur both inside and outside the formal organization, focus largely on philosophical differences. Restructuring efforts that ignore the ubiquitous nature of political disagreements almost always fail, either because key implementers and stakeholders are excluded from visioning and planning or because the values and beliefs expressed in the reforms are incongruous with prevailing institutional culture (Schlechty, 1997).

Many scholars (e.g., Henkin, 1993; Murphy, 1994) believe that school improvement needs to be pursued locally and that superintendents must be key facilitators. This responsibility threatens many superintendents for at least three reasons:

• Facilitating school restructuring requires superintendents to engage stakeholders in what many see as intractable and deeply troubling problems involving governance, the distribution of power, and organizational design (Carlson, 1996). The potential for such discussions to produce serious conflict is substantial.

• Unlike intensification mandates promoted during much of the 1980s (i.e., forcing schools to do more of what they were already doing), state deregulation and district decentralization require local school boards to fashion reform programs that reflect real needs in their districts. Predictably, school board members expect superintendents to provide leadership in crafting a vision and plan that is effective and politically acceptable (Kowalski, 2003).

• A century of failed reforms has incrementally reinforced a belief shared by most educators that substantial change is neither necessary nor politically advantageous (Sarason, 1996). After being socialized to their workplace, even new teachers and administrators come to accept things as they are (Streitmatter, 1994). Institutional culture is central to school restructuring because it determines what individuals and groups truly believe and value about education (Trimble, 1996) and how they promote and accept change (Leithwood, Jantzi, & Fernandez, 1994). Yet cultural change is exceedingly difficult.

Anthropologist Edward Hall (1997) concluded that communication and culture are inextricably linked. This nexus undoubtedly extends to organizational cultures. In this vein, Conrad (1994) wrote, "Cultures are communicative creations. They emerge and are sustained by the communicative acts of all employees, not just the conscious persuasive strategies of upper management. Cultures do not exist separately from people communicating with one another" (p. 27). Despite the fact that most organizational research has categorized culture as a causal variable and communication as an intervening variable (Wert-Gray, Center, Brashers, & Meyers, 1991), many scholars prefer to describe the relationship between organizational culture and communication as reciprocal. Axley (1996), for instance, characterized this interdependence: "Communication gives rise to culture, which gives rise to communication, which perpetuates culture" (p. 153). In this vein, communication is a process through which organizational members express their collective inclination to coordinate beliefs, behaviors, and attitudes—in schools, communication gives meaning to work and forges perceptions of reality. As such, culture influences communicative behavior and communicative behavior is instrumental to building, maintaining, and changing culture (Björk, 2001; Kowalski, 1998b). In the case of schools and districts, normative communicative behavior for administrators is shaped largely by two realities: the need for them to assume leadership in the process of school restructuring (Björk, 2001; Murphy, 1994) and the need for them to change school culture as part of the restructuring process (Heckman, 1993; Kowalski, 2000).

The role of the superintendent as communicator in part might require the "setting" of behavioral expectations (or norms) that can be communicated to teachers and principals through daily interactions as the proactive superintendent helps change school culture (see Griffiths, Stout, & Forsyth, 1988, p. 288, for superintendent as culture builder). The essence of this culture change implies replacing the norms of bureaucratic, regulated organizations to risk-taking, entrepreneurial organizations designed for the Information Age and the highly competitive global marketplace. Superintendents need to reconfigure their working relationships around the team model so that they, other central office personnel, principals, and teachers collaborate across a wide array of administrative tasks. Decentralization and shared governance imply a different orientation to practice: one that requires a reconfiguration of organization structures, rules, regulations, and behaviors (Björk, 2001).

A case study of a North Carolina superintendent of the year (Keedy, 1997) is instructive with respect to demonstrating a superintendent's role as culture builder. A former deputy superintendent in one of the state's largest districts, he became superintendent in a rural coastal district serving 6,100 students. Convinced that the district's traditional workplace culture was not conducive to necessary changes, he advised the school board members that necessary improvements were unlikely without external pressures.

Building on the momentum established by an outcomes-based education grant awarded in the mid-1990s, the new superintendent held town forums in which teachers, parents, and business leaders developed student exit outcomes in the context of a community-school partnership. The partnership proved to be invaluable in at least three ways. First, it produced a subtle form of pressure that prompted school employees to be more open to change. Second, it provided a forum to discuss *why* change was necessary. Third, it generated communicative products, such as videotapes, that explained both a need for change and the nature of desired changes.

In addition to the partnership, the superintendent recognized that he had a pivotal role as a communicator. More specifically, he needed to articulate the importance of organizational culture, the reasons why school reform had become essential, and the critical nexus between culture and change. In this vein, he established a reading group that consisted of representatives across the district and community. He provided the members with books and articles, facilitated discussions, and modeled the behavior he was seeking in the revamped district culture. His ability to communicate effectively with multiple publics was essential to his role as a change agent.

Experiences with failed reform efforts over the past 25 years demonstrate that coercive change strategies (e.g., imposed legislative change), rational change strategies (e.g., providing employees evidence that change is necessary), and reeducation change strategies (e.g., staff development) have failed to produce the desired level of school reform. The explanation for this inertia centers largely on an imposed, intractable institutional culture found in most public schools (Fullan, 2001; Sarason, 1996). Schein (1992) argues that highly effective organizations overcome this problem by developing a *learning culture*—one that is built "on the assumption that communication and information are central to organizational well-being and must therefore create a multi-channel communication system that allows everyone to connect to everyone else" (p. 370). In the case of public schools, such cultures are unlikely if administrators, and especially superintendents, are incapable of applying relevant communicative behaviors. The nexus between effective leader communication and organizational effectiveness, however, is not restricted to public education; recent studies of embattled business executives reveal that most of them were ineffective communicators (Perina, 2002).

COMMUNICATOR SKILLS
VERSUS COMMUNICATOR ROLES

An *organizational role* is commonly defined as a set of expected behaviors associated with a particular position (Hanson, 2003). These expectations are seldom absolute or comprehensive (Yukl, 2002), but in the case of the school superintendent, they certainly have been discernible as demonstrated by the four role conceptualizations previously described here. A skill, by comparison, refers "to the ability to do something in an effective manner" (Yukl, 2002, p. 176). McCroskey (1982) defined a communication skill as "the ability of an individual to perform appropriate communicative behavior in a given situation" (p. 3). In the case of superintendents, effective communication is broadly interpreted as the ability to know when to communicate as a manager and when to communicate as a leader. Because school administrators rarely study communication science formally, normative behavior was most likely learned through a combination of socialization, on-the-job experience, and emulation (Kowalski, 1999). Even some relatively recent articles (e.g., Wentz, 1998) suggest that administrators hone their communication skills by observing the behavior of effective practitioners. Perhaps the strongest of these forces has been socialization, long known to be a major determinant of communicative behavior in organizations (Jablin, 1987).

The treatment of communication as a role-based skill has not been unique to education. Literature on generic management research and theory typically examined interpersonal communication contextually (Henderson, 1987). The most frequently cited contextual variables have been administrative function and the nature of the organization. Zaleznik (1989), for example, described how management and leadership functions differed with respect to normative standards for transferring information across all organizations. Mintzberg (1973) described how organizational types (e.g., mechanical bureaucracy versus professional bureaucracy) required varying communicative behaviors. Treating communication as a role-based skill appears to have contributed to a dismissive attitude about the necessity of studying communication as a discipline. In the business world, for instance, communication has commonly been treated as something everyone could do appropriately if he or she understood role expectations (Walker, 1997).

FROM CLASSICAL TO RELATIONAL COMMUNICATION

For much of the past century, management science has advocated a classical communication model in which instructions and commands are transmitted down the chain of command, and only from one person to the person or persons below (Luthans, 1981). This narrow perspective of exchanging information reflected only organizational and managerial interests. In the early 1960s, for example, a leading textbook on organizational communication (Thayer, 1961) identified only four functions of administrative communication: informing, instructing (or directing), evaluating, and influencing. Within this normative context, managers frequently believed that their communication effectiveness depended solely on the quality of the messages they composed and transmitted (Clampitt, 1991). Not unexpectedly, school administrators, focused on efficiency and managerial effectiveness, often emulated this behavior by interacting with subordinates in an impersonal manner (Achilles & Lintz, 1983). Much of their communication was unilateral—information exchanges initiated by them and terminated by the receiver(s) in some manner other than face-to-face (Schmuck & Runkel, 1994). Subordinates, such as teachers and staff members, were encouraged neither to generate messages nor to respond to those they received from administrators. This pattern of restricted communication was sustained despite evidence showing that manager communication behavior often affected employee commitment to the organization and job satisfaction negatively (e.g., Guzley, 1992; Trombetta & Rogers, 1988).

Beginning in the 1980s, however, the classical communication model, long deemed the ideal for managers (Luthans, 1981), came under attack. In the case of education, discontent centered on three major issues:

- *Emerging needs.* The pursuit of reform in the context of an information society created needs for administrators to (a) work with others to develop shared understandings (Hoy & Miskel, 1996), (b) implement modern reform strategies (Kowalski, 1998b), (c) respond appropriately with respect to identifying and solving problems in an information-based society (Hanson, 2003), and (d) engage in moral and ethical practice (Sergiovanni, 2001).

- *Changing perceptions of effectiveness.* Studies of administrator communication (e.g., Richmond, McCroskey, Davis, & Koontz, 1980; Snavely & Walters, 1983) produced empirical evidence revealing that administrators who used traditional, one-way communication were often perceived negatively by others.

- *Philosophical dispositions.* Recognizing the incongruity between the detached nature of management and the moral dimension of dealing with people while pursuing school reform, a growing number of authors (e.g., Fullan, 2001; Sergiovanni, 2001) encouraged administrators to adopt uniform behaviors that would be appropriate for these dissimilar functions.

In light of these circumstances, interest in symmetrical communication models, such as relational communication, increased markedly (Kowalski, 2004a).

Relational communication pertains to both the manner in which information is exchanged and interpersonal perceptions of the exchange (Littlejohn, 1992). As used here, this model is more restrictive than interpersonal communication, which at times has been defined very broadly to include any information exchange involving two or more parties (e.g., Ehling, White, & Grunig, 1992). Relational communication is defined here as a more exclusive and definitive process in which information is exchanged in multiple directions and persons influence one another's behavior over and above their organizational role, rank, and status (Cappella, 1987). It is a symmetrical process intended to benefit all participating parties (Grunig, 1989), and the interactants behave similarly and minimize differences, including those involving legitimate (position-based) power in the organization (Burgoon & Hale, 1984). By contrast, the classical communication model promotes one-way, directive, coercive exchanges designed to reduce opportunities for mutual influence and information sharing (McGregor, 1967). This form of communication is commonly referred to as *complementary*; that is, the parties maximize differences, especially in relation to dominance and submission (Burgoon & Hale, 1984).

In summary, the pursuit of reform in an information-based society has produced new communicative expectations for superintendents. The idea that behavior should be contingent on role expectations is no longer acceptable. Instead, superintendents are encouraged to employ a consistent form of symmetrical communication focused on engaging others in identifying and solving problems associated with organizational development (Conrad, 1994). The process involves mutual understandings, mutual influence, negotiation, openness, credibility, and trust (Toth, 2000). As such, communication should no longer be viewed as a role-based skill but rather as a distinctive role conceptualization.

DEFINING COMMUNICATION COMPETENCE

When relational communication is presented as a conceptualization, an obvious question emerges: What constitutes competency? Wiemann (1977) described communication competence as "the ability of an interactant to choose among available communicative behaviors in order that one may successfully accomplish one's own interpersonal goals during an encounter while maintaining the face and line of one's fellow interactants within the constraints of the situation" (p. 198). This definition has a distinctive behavioral tone indicating that competence and performance are inextricably intertwined; that is, to be found competent, one must not only know what behavior is appropriate, one also must demonstrate competency in performing the behavior. McCroskey (1982) cautioned, however, that performance alone is insufficient to determine competence because competent communicators do not always succeed and incompetent communicators do not always fail when pursuing interpersonal goals. That is, outcomes of communication can be affected, positively or negatively, by extraneous variables.

McCroskey (1982) described communication competence across three domains of learning: cognitive, psychomotor, and affective. Each is cogent to preparing superintendents to be interpersonal communicators:

- *Cognitive domain.* To apply interpersonal communication, individuals must demonstrate that they know and understand the basic field of communication (Larson, Backlund, Redmond, & Barbour, 1978). Superintendents, for example, should have conceptual knowledge about the relationship between communication and culture and the difference between symmetrical and complementary information exchanges.

- *Psychomotor domain.* To apply interpersonal communication, individuals must demonstrate their abilities to apply their knowledge and understanding (Wiemann, Takai, Ota, & Weimann, 1997). The application component of competence focuses on specific skills. Superintendents cannot meet role expectations if they are unable to encode and decode messages, to use correct grammar, to listen effectively, to apply principles of nonverbal communication, to communicate in context, to work effectively with print and broadcast media, to build credibility and trust, to resolve conflict, and to use appropriate technology.

- *Affective domain.* To apply interpersonal communication, individuals must possess supportive attitudes and feelings about the process (McCroskey, 1982). This philosophical component of competence is clearly the most ignored and possibly the most damaging component of communication competence. Prospective superintendents can learn communication concepts and acquire application skills, but unless they view interpersonal communication as beneficial and accept the moral-ethical aspects of this process, they are unlikely to implement it when they enter practice.

This model is nearly identical to the one that was offered several years later by Spitzberg and Cupach (1984). The three components of their paradigm are *knowledge* (recognizing the appropriateness of a communication practice), *skill* (ability to perform the selected practice), and *motivation* (desire to communicate in an appropriate and effective manner). Such models provide a relevant framework for academic preparation and they demonstrate why skills alone are an insufficient measure of competence (McCroskey, 1982).

CRITIQUE OF CURRENT REQUIREMENTS IN COMMUNICATION

Historically, states have required both the completion of a program of academic study and a license[1] to serve as a school district superintendent. In the absence of a national curriculum to prepare superintendents, criteria for both professional preparation and licensing have varied considerably from state to state. To this day, there are strong disagreements over the status of superintendents and the required qualifications for the position. Kowalski (2004b) identifies three groups holding distinctively different positions on this matter:

- *Anti-professionists.* These individuals, primarily individuals not directly affiliated with educational administration, seek to deregulate practice in school administration by having current licensing laws rescinded. Their underlying philosophy is found in two recent documents: *Better Leaders for America's Schools: A Manifesto,* published by the Broad Foundation and Thomas B. Fordham Institute (2003), and *A License to Lead? A New Leadership Agenda for America's Schools* (Hess, 2003).

- *Status-quo professionists.* These individuals, largely educational administration professors and practitioners, resist both deregulation and massive reforms. They seek recognition as a full profession without having stringent national standards (e.g., a national curriculum) that would eliminate 50% to 70% of the current programs.

- *Reform professionists.* These individuals, largely educational administration professors, believe that current requirements are inadequate. They argue that deregulation is harmful to society and propose massive reforms to ensure that both preparation and licensing are practice-based.[2]

The different positions held by these groups reflect an unstable policy environment in which states are moving in different directions with respect to the superintendency. Although 41 states still require preparation and licensing for this position, more than half of them (54%) have provisions allowing waivers or emergency certificates to be issued. In addition, 15 of these 41 states (37%) allow or sanction alternative routes to licensure (i.e., other than university-based study) (Feistritzer, 2003). Consequently, requirements to study communication have to be evaluated in light of current uncertainty about the future of preparation of licensing.

Traditionally, the inattention given to communication in professional preparation and licensing appears to be part of what Murphy (1991a) described as an unfortunate gap between professors and the realities of practice. In the eyes of many, the recent attention given to communication competence has resolved this problem. The study of communication, for instance, has been widely advocated for both teachers (e.g., Hunt, Simonds, & Cooper, 2002) and administrators (e.g., Lester, 1993; Osterman, 1994). Closer scrutiny, however, reveals that much of the recent attention has centered on intensifying an outmoded perspective of communication.

In an effort to define competency based on practice, two notable standards documents were developed during the past decade. The first, sponsored by the American Association of School Administrators (AASA) (Hoyle, 1994), applies exclusively to superintendents. The second, sponsored by the Interstate School Leaders Licensure Consortium (ISLLC)

(Shipman, Topps, & Murphy, 1998), is focused on licensing criteria and applies to both principals and superintendents. Both the AASA and ISLLC standards identify communication as a core competency. And although approximately 80% of the states have now embraced the ISLLC standards to some extent, no state has adopted a policy requiring administrators to complete a course in communication science.

Communication also has been addressed by assessment centers. For example, the National Association of Secondary School Principals (NASSP) Assessment Center evaluates candidates and practicing principals on 12 dimensions, including oral and written communication (NASSP, 1995). The communication focus, however, is on performance skills; knowledge and dispositions, especially with respect to alternative communication models, have not been assessed.

The subject of communication received some attention in the late 1980s as a result of mounting criticism of administrator preparation; school administration professors voiced much of the discontent (e.g., Achilles, 1984; Griffiths, Stout, & Forsyth, 1988; Pitner, 1988). Such dissatisfaction prompted several reform reports (e.g., National Commission on Excellence in Educational Administration, 1988). It contained the following reference to superintendents and communication: "They [superintendents] must symbolize education in the community. Through their public statements they must express, project, and embody the purpose and character of public education" (p. 7). The same report advocated that candidates for licensure should be assessed with respect to their knowledge in pedagogy, leadership, management, and communication. Griffiths et al. (1988) specified nine skills for administrators, including effective speaking, writing (e.g., memos, press releases, announcements), and conducting meetings.

Identifying communication as being important to practice, although laudable, does not ensure that aspiring superintendents will be prepared adequately. To this point, recommendations from reform reports and standards documents fail to provide specificity with respect to the qualitative aspects of administrator communication. Hence, states embracing the ISLLC standards and universities preparing superintendents in those states might be interpreting communication narrowly as a basic skill and not as a pervasive and critical role. As such, graduate students and practitioners might be expected to hone skills individually without having studied communication science. Consider the following examples obtained from two professors in 2004:

- A professor at an urban research university in the South indicated that superintendents as principal candidates at his institution had to be "exposed to communication" because of the ISLLC standards. The professor provided syllabi for two of the four courses required for a superintendent license in that state. The first course, School System Administration, identified "effective communication" as an indicator for ISLLC Standard 1; yet "effective communication" was not defined, and no communication-specific content was listed. The second syllabus, for the School Super-intendency, listed no course objectives related to communication.

- A professor from a regional university in the Midwest indicated that communication was addressed in a course on superintendent-board rela-tions. When asked how this was accomplished, he indicated that students were required to make presentations justifying an annual budget to the other class members who assumed the role of board members during the simulation.

Responses such as these support the suspicion that communication is still being treated as a role-based skill. Consequently, professors might or might not integrate relevant content into their courses. And where com-munication is identified as a course objective or component, the instruc-tion is likely to be uneven and not focused on either knowledge or dispositions. Consequently, the added attention given to communication over the past two decades appears to have had only a limited effect on preparation curricula, licensing standards, and actual administrative behav-iors (Kowalski & Keedy, 2003). A study of school principals, for example, found that academic preparation in communication varied considerably, including differences in undergraduate study and exposure to communi-cation in educational administration courses and staff development (Kowalski, 1998a).

BUILDING COMMUNICATION COMPETENCE

Historically, superintendents have been expected to be scholars, managers, political activists, and applied social scientists. Since the 1980s, they also have been expected to be effective communicators who use information and interactions to resolve conflict and change behavior in a manner con-ducive to school improvement. Unfortunately, many professors and prac-titioners have equated improved communication with the intensification of classical organizational communication (Kowalski, 2004a).

Preparing superintendents to be competent communicators is most likely to be accomplished if the process is guided by a comprehensive model, such as the one developed by McCroskey (1982). That is, learn-ing must be addressed in the knowledge, skill, and disposition domains. Mastery of the cognitive domain appears unlikely unless educators are required to study communication in general and relational communica-tion specifically. Ideally, students preparing to be teachers should be required to complete a basic undergraduate course in communication so that they have a fundamental understanding of communication as a disci-pline and relational communication as an alternative process. Educators who then enter the study of school administration should be exposed to communication at a more advanced level through a discipline-centered curriculum (i.e., an approach that infuses the study of communication and development of communication skills into practice-based functions assumed by administrators) (Kowalski, in press).

This curriculum can be delivered by deploying case studies and simulations in administration courses and communication assignments in out-of-class group activities, work-based assignments, and internships. Communicative behavior should be documented through assessment and evaluation and evidence of competence should be compiled in a portfolio or similar document.

Dispositions are clearly the most difficult component of communication competence. Students must have opportunities to analyze and challenge the traditional communication processes typically found in their workplaces. They need to be exposed to positive role models who demonstrate the power of interpersonal communication to change people, especially with respect to getting teachers and other administrators to behave in a manner conducive to school improvement. Dispositions toward interpersonal communication should be assessed and evaluated in the classroom and in practice (e.g., internships, practica, and problem-based learning).

FINAL COMMENTS

Historically, communication has been treated as a role-related skill that superintendents acquired naturally as they gained professional experience. The disadvantages of this view in an information-based and reform-minded society were discussed in this chapter. Accepting the superintendent as communicator, however, requires both a new mind-set that characterizes relational communication as a pervasive expectation and revised preparation programs that groom practitioners to be effective communicators.

At least three issues need to be addressed if superintendents are to develop communication competence during prepractice preparation. First, the value placed on communication in professional preparation should be elevated. This is unlikely unless the professors delivering graduate education abandon the myopic conclusion that everyone can learn to communicate effectively once immersed in the realities of practice (Dilenschneider, 1996; Walker, 1997). Next, communication competence in school administration generally and in the superintendency specifically needs to be defined. Wilson and Sabee (2003), communication scholars, argue that competence is most meaningful when defined in the context of a student's discipline or profession. Third, school administration professors and communication professors should collaborate to identify instructional strategies for ensuring competence (Dannels, 2001). This interdisciplinary approach focuses on having prospective superintendents studying communication within school administration rather than studying it by simply completing one or two graduate courses in communication departments (Kowalski, in press).

NOTES

1. Many states historically have elected to use the term *certificate* instead of *license*. From a legal perspective, certificates issued by these states have been the equivalent of a license. In professions, certificates are issued to license holders to certify competence in a given area of practice; a license is required to practice in a profession (Kowalski, 2003).

2. As an example, six professors (Lars Björk, Cyrss Bruner, Margaret Grogan, Theodore Kowalski, Joseph Murphy, and George Petersen) are currently working with several states to develop new standards for superintendent preparation and licensing. The intent is to build a national curriculum similar to those found in other professions.

REFERENCES

Achilles, C. M. (1984). Forecast: Stormy weather ahead in educational administration. *Issues in Education, 2*(2), 127–135.

Achilles, C. M., & Lintz, M. N. (1983, November). *Public confidence in public education: A growing concern in the 80's.* Paper presented at the annual meeting of the Mid-South Educational Research Association, Nashville, TN.

Axley, S. R. (1996). *Communication at work: Management and the communication-intensive organization.* Westport, CT: Quorum Books.

Bauman, P. C. (1996). *Governing education: Public sector reform or privatization.* Boston: Allyn & Bacon.

Björk, L. G. (2001). Institutional barriers to educational reform: A superintendent's role in district decentralization. In C. C. Brunner & L. G. Björk (Eds.), *The new superintendency* (pp. 205–228). New York: JAI Press.

Blase, J., & Anderson, G. (1995). *The micropolitics of educational leadership: From control to empowerment.* New York: Teachers College Press.

Broad Foundation & Thomas B. Fordham Institute. (2003). *Better leaders for America's schools: A manifesto.* Los Angeles: Authors.

Brunner, C. C., Grogan, M., & Björk, L. G. (2002). Shifts in the discourse defining the superintendency: Historical and current foundations of the position. In J. Murphy (Ed.), *The challenge of school leadership: Redefining leadership for the 21st century. National Society for the Study of Education yearbook* (pp. 111–138). Chicago: University of Chicago Press.

Burgoon, J. K., & Hale, J. L. (1984). The fundamental topic of relational communication. *Communication Monographs, 51,* 193–214.

Burroughs, W. A. (1974). *Cities and schools in the gilded age.* Port Washington, NY. Kennikat.

Callahan, R. E. (1962). *Education and the cult of efficiency: A study of the social forces that have shaped the administration of public schools.* Chicago: University of Chicago Press.

Callahan, R. E. (1964). *The superintendent of schools: An historical analysis.* Final report of project S-212. Washington, DC: U.S. Office of Education, Department of Health, Education, and Welfare.

Cappella, J. N. (1987). Interpersonal communication: Definitions and fundamental questions. In C. R. Berger & S. H. Chaffee (Eds.), *Handbook of communication science* (pp. 184–238). Newbury Park, CA: Sage.

Carlson, R. V. (1996). *Reframing and reform: Perspectives on organization, leadership, and school change.* New York: Longman.

Carter, G. R., & Cunningham, W. G. (1997). *The American school superintendent.* San Francisco: Jossey-Bass.

Chance, P. L., & Björk, L. (2004). The social dimension of public relations. In T. J. Kowalski (Ed.), *Public relations in schools* (3rd ed.), (pp. 125–150). Upper Saddle River, NJ: Merrill, Prentice Hall.

Clampitt, P. G. (1991). *Communicating for managerial effectiveness.* Newbury Park, CA: Sage.

Clune, W., & White, P. (1988). *School-based management: Institutional variation, implementation, and issues for further research.* New Brunswick, NJ: Center for Policy Research in Education, Eagleton Institute of Politics, Rutgers University.

Conrad, C. (1994). *Strategic organizational communication: Toward the twenty-first century* (3rd ed.). Fort Worth, TX: Harcourt Brace College Publishers.

Dannels, D. P. (2001). Time to speak up: A theoretical framework of situated pedagogy and practice for communication across the curriculum. *Communication Education, 50*(2), 144–158.

Dilenschneider, R. L. (1996). Social IQ and MBAs: Recognizing the importance of communication. *Vital Speeches, 62*, 404–405.

Ehling, W. P., White, J., & Grunig, J. E. (1992). Public relations and marketing practice. In J. E. Grunig (Ed.), *Excellence in public relations and communication management* (pp. 357–393). Hillsdale, NJ: Lawrence Erlbaum.

Elmore, R. F. (1995). Structural capacity and high-performance standards. *Educational Researcher, 24*(9), 23–26.

Feistritzer, E. (2003). *Certification of public-school administrators.* Washington, DC: The National Center for Education Information.

Friedkin, N. E., & Slater, M. R. (1994). School leadership and performance: A social network approach. *Sociology of Education, 67*, 139–157.

Fullan, M. (2001). *Leading in a culture of change.* San Francisco: Jossey-Bass.

Fusarelli, B. C., & Fusarelli, L. D. (2003, November). *Preparing future superintendents to be applied social scientists.* Paper presented at the annual meeting of the University Council for Educational Administration, Portland, OR.

Gideon, B. H. (2002). Structuring schools for teacher collaboration. *Education Digest, 68*(2), 30–34.

Goodman, M. B., Willis, K. E., & Holihan, V. C. (1998). Communication and change: Effective change communication is personal, global, and continuous. In M. B. Goodman (Ed.), *Corporate communication for executives* (pp. 37–61). Albany: State University of New York Press.

Gousha, R. P., & Mannan, G. (1991). *Analysis of selected competencies: Components, acquisition and measurement perceptions of three groups of stakeholders in education.* (ERIC Document Reproduction Service No. ED 336 850)

Griffiths, D. E., Stout, R. T., & Forsyth, P. B. (1988). The preparation of educational administrators. In D. E. Griffiths, R. T. Stout, & P. B. Forsyth (Eds.), *Leaders for America's schools: The report and papers of the National Commission on Excellence in Educational Administration* (pp. 284–304). Tempe, AZ: University Council for Educational Administration.

Grunig, J. E. (1989). Symmetrical presuppositions as a framework for public relations theory. In C. H. Botan (Ed.), *Public relations theory* (pp. 17–44). Hillsdale, NJ: Lawrence Erlbaum.

Guzley, R. (1992). Organizational climate and communication climate: Predictors of commitment to the organization. *Management Communication Quarterly, 5*, 379–402.

Hall, E. T. (1997). *The silent language.* New York: Doubleday.

Hanson, E. M. (2003). *Educational administration and organizational behavior* (5th ed.). Boston: Allyn & Bacon.

Heckman, P. E. (1993). School restructuring in practice: Reckoning with the culture of school. *International Journal of Educational Reform, 2*(3), 263–272.

Henderson, L. S. (1987). The contextual nature of interpersonal communication in management theory and research. *Management Communication Quarterly, 1*(1), 7–31.

Henkin, A. B. (1993). Social skills of superintendents: A leadership requisite in restructured schools. *Educational Research Quarterly, 16*(4), 15–30.

Hess, F. M. (2003). *A license to lead? A new leadership agenda for America's schools.* Washington, DC: Progressive Policy Institute.

Howlett, P. (1993). The politics of school leaders, past and future. *Education Digest, 58*(9), 18–21.

Hoy, W. K., & Miskel, C. G. (1996). *Educational administration: Theory, research, and practice* (5th ed.). New York: McGraw-Hill.

Hoyle, J. R. (1994). What standards for the superintendency promise. *School Administrator, 51*(7), 22–23, 26.

Hunt, S. K., Simonds, C. J., & Cooper, P. J. (2002). Communication and teacher education: Exploring a communication course for all teachers. *Communication Education, 51*(1), 81–94.

Jablin, F. M. (1987). Organizational entry, assimilation, and exit. In F. Jablin, L. Putnam, K. Roberts, & L. Porter (Eds.), *Handbook of organizational communication: An interdisciplinary approach* (pp. 679–740). Newbury Park, CA: Sage.

Keedy, J. L. (1991). Traditional norms of schooling and the issues of organization change. *Planning & Changing, 21,* 140–145.

Keedy, J. L. (1997). Don Drake: Breaking the mold by reading at dawn. In C. H. Chapman (Ed.), *Becoming a superintendent* (pp. 147–160). Upper Saddle River, NJ: Prentice Hall.

Keedy, J. L., MacPhail-Wilcox, B., Mullin, A. G., & Campbell Wooten, W. (1998). *Principal transformational leadership for successful schools: Cases and strategies for teacher and student empowerment.* Tempe: Arizona Educational Information System, Arizona State University.

Kowalski, T. J. (1998a). Communication in the principalship: Preparation, work experience, and expectation. *Journal of Educational Relations, 19*(2), 4–12.

Kowalski, T. J. (1998b). The role of communication in providing leadership for school reform. *Mid-Western Educational Researcher, 11*(1), 32–40.

Kowalski, T. J. (1999). *The school superintendent: Theory, practice, and cases.* Upper Saddle River, NJ: Merrill, Prentice Hall.

Kowalski, T. J. (2000). Cultural change paradigms and administrator communication. *Contemporary Education, 71*(2), 4–12.

Kowalski, T. J. (2003). *Contemporary school administration: An introduction* (2nd ed.). Boston: Allyn & Bacon.

Kowalski, T. J. (2004a). School public relations: A new agenda. In T. J. Kowalski (Ed.), *Public relations in schools* (pp. 3–29). Upper Saddle River, NJ: Merrill, Prentice Hall.

Kowalski, T. J. (2004b). The ongoing war for the soul of school administration. In T. J. Lasley (Ed.), *Better leaders for America's schools: Perspectives on the Manifesto* (pp. 92–114). Columbia, MO: University Council for Educational Administration.

Kowalski, T. J. (in press). Evolution of the school superintendent as communicator. *Journal of Communication Education.*

Kowalski, T. J., & Keedy, J. (2003, November). *Superintendent as communicator: Implications for professional preparation and licensing.* Paper presented at the annual meeting of the University Council for Educational Administration, Portland, OR.

Larson, C. E., Backlund, P. M., Redmond, M. K., & Barbour, A. (1978). *Assessing communicative competence.* Falls Church, VA: Speech Communication Association and ERIC.

Leithwood, K., Jantzi, D., & Fernandez, A. (1994). Transformational leadership and teachers' commitment to change. In J. Murphy & K. S. Louis (Eds.), *Reshaping the principalship* (pp. 77–98). Thousand Oaks, CA: Corwin.

Lester, P. E. (1993). *Preparing administrators for the 21st century.* Paper presented at the annual meeting of the New England Educational Research Organization, Portsmouth, NH.

Littlejohn, S. W. (1992). *Theories of human communication* (4th ed.). Belmont, CA: Wadsworth.

Luthans, F. (1981). *Organizational behavior* (3rd ed.). New York: McGraw-Hill.

McCroskey, J. C. (1982). Communication competence and performance: A research and pedagogical perspective. *Communication Education, 31*(1), 1–7.

McGregor, D. (1967). *The professional manager.* New York: McGraw-Hill.

Melby, E. O. (1955). *Administering community education.* Englewood Cliffs, NJ: Prentice Hall.

Miller, K. (2003). *Organizational communication: Approaches and processes* (3rd ed.). New York: Wadsworth.

Mintzberg, H. (1973). *The nature of managerial work.* New York: Harper & Row.

Murphy, J. (1991a). Bridging the gap between professors and practitioners. *NASSP Bulletin, 75*(539), 22–30.

Murphy, J. (1991b). *Restructuring schools.* New York: Teachers College Press.

Murphy, J. (1994). The changing role of the superintendency in restructuring districts in Kentucky. *School Effectiveness and School Improvement, 5,* 349–375.

National Association of Secondary School Principals Assessment Center. (1995). *Assessor's manual* (Rev. ed.). Reston, VA: National Association of Secondary School Principals.

National Commission on Excellence in Educational Administration (1988). *Leaders for tomorrow's schools: The report and papers of the National Commission on Excellence in Educational Administration.* Berkeley, CA: McCutchan.

Osterman, K. F. (1994). Communication skills: A key to collaboration and change. *Journal of School Leadership, 4*(4), 382–398.

Perina, K. (2002). When CEOs self-destruct. *Psychology Today, 35*(5), 16.

Petersen, G. J., & Short, P. M. (2002). An examination of school board presidents' perceptions of their superintendent's interpersonal communication competence and board decision making. *Journal of School Leadership, 12,* 411–436.

Pitner, N. J. (1988). School administrator preparation: The state of the art. In D. E. Griffiths, R. T. Stout, & P. B. Forsyth (Eds.), *Leaders for America's schools: The report and papers of the National Commission on Excellence in Educational Administration* (pp. 367–402). Tempe, AZ: University Council for Educational Administration.

Quirke, B. (1996). *Communicating corporate change.* New York: McGraw-Hill.

Richmond, V. P., McCroskey, J. C., Davis, L. M., & Koontz, K. A. (1980). Perceived power as a mediator of management communication style and employee satisfaction: A preliminary investigation. *Communication Quarterly, 28*(41), 37–46.

Sarason, S. B. (1996). *Revisiting the culture of the school and the problem of change.* New York: Teachers College Press.

Schein, E. H. (1992). *Organizational culture and leadership* (2nd ed.). San Francisco: Jossey-Bass.

Schein, E. H. (1996). Culture: The missing concept in organization studies. *Administrative Science Quarterly, 41*(2), 229–240.

Schlechty, P. C. (1997). *Inventing better schools.* San Francisco: Jossey-Bass.

Schmuck, R. A., & Runkel, P. J. (1994). *The handbook of organization development in schools and colleges* (4th ed.). Prospect Heights, IL: Waveland.

Schneider, W. E. (1994). *The reengineering alternative: A plan for making your current culture work.* Burr Ridge, IL: Irwin.

Sergiovanni, T. J. (2001). *The principalship: A reflective practice perspective* (4th ed.). Boston: Allyn & Bacon.

Shipman, N. J., Topps, B. W., & Murphy, J. (1998, April). *Linking the ISLLC standards to professional development and relicensure.* Paper presented at the annual meeting of the American Educational Research Association, San Diego, CA.

Snavely, W. B., & Walters, E. V. (1983). Differences in communication competence among administrative social styles. *Journal of Applied Communication Research, 11*(2), 120–135.

Spitzberg, B. H., & Cupach, W. R. (1984). *Interpersonal communication competence*. Beverly Hills, CA: Sage.

Streitmatter, J. (1994). *Toward gender equity in the classroom: Everyday teachers' beliefs and practices*. Albany: SUNY Press.

Thayer, L. O. (1961). *Administrative communication*. Homewood, IL: Irwin.

Thomas, W. B., & Moran, K. J. (1992). Reconsidering the power of the superintendent in the progressive period. *American School Board Journal, 29*(1), 22–50.

Toth, E. L. (2000). From personal influence to interpersonal influence: A model for relationship management. In J. A. Ledingham & S. D. Bruning (Eds.), *Public relations as relationship management* (pp. 205–220). Mahwah, NJ: Lawrence Erlbaum.

Trimble, K. (1996). Building a learning community. *Equity and Excellence in Education, 29*(1), 37–40.

Trombetta, J. J., & Rogers, D. P. (1988). Communication climate, job satisfaction, and organizational commitment: The effects of information adequacy, communication openness, and decision participation. *Management Communication Quarterly, 1*(4), 494–514.

Tyack, D. (1972). The "One Best System": A historical analysis. In H. Walberg & A. Kopan (Eds.), *Rethinking urban education* (pp. 231–246). San Francisco: Jossey-Bass.

Vihera, M. L., & Nurmela, J. (2001). Communication capability as an intrinsic determinant for an information age. *Futures, 33*(3/4), 245–265.

Walker, G. (1997). Communication in leadership. *Communication Management, 1*(4), 22–27.

Weiss, C. (1993, February). *Interests and ideologies in educational reform: Changing the venue of decision making in the high school* (Occasional Paper #19). Cambridge, MA: National Center for Educational Leadership.

Wentz, P. J. (1998). Successful communications for school leaders. *NASSP Bulletin, 82*(601), 112–115.

Wert-Gray, S., Center, C., Brashers, D. E., & Meyers, R. A. (1991). Research topics and methodological orientations in organizational communication: A decade of review. *Communication Studies, 42*(2), 141–154.

Wiemann, J. M. (1977). Explication and test of a model of communication competence. *Human Communication Research, 3*, 195–213.

Wiemann, J. M., Takai, J., Ota, H., & Wiemann, M. O. (1997). A relational model of communication competence. In. B. Kovacic (Ed.), *Emerging theories of human communication* (pp. 25–44). Buffalo: State University of New York Press.

Wilson, S. R., & Sabee, C. M. (2003). Explicating communicative competence as a theoretical term. In J. O. Greene & B. R. Burleson (Eds.), *Handbook of communication and social interaction* (pp. 3–50). Hillsdale, NJ: Lawrence Erlbaum.

Yukl, G. (2002). *Leadership in organizations* (5th ed.). Upper Saddle River, NJ: Prentice Hall.

Zaleznik, A. (1989). *The managerial mystique: Restoring leadership in business*. New York: Harper & Row.

10

Women Superintendents and Role Conception

(Un)Troubling the Norms

Margaret Grogan and C. Cryss Brunner

Although studies of women superintendents have greatly increased over the past 15 years (see Alston, 1999; Beekley, 1996, 1999; Bell, 1995; Blount, 1998, 1999; Brunner, 1998a, 1998b, 1999, 2000a, 2000b, 2003; Chase, 1995; Chase & Bell, 1990; Grogan, 1996, 1999, 2000a, 2000b; Grogan & Blackmon, 2001; Grogan & Smith, 1998; Jackson, 1999; Kamler & Shakeshaft, 1999; Marietti & Stout, 1994; Méndez-Morse, 1999; Ortiz, 1999, 2000; Pavan, 1999; Scherr, 1995; Sherman & Repa, 1994; Skrla, Reyes, & Scheurich, 2000; Tallerico, 2000; Tallerico & Burstyn, 1996; Tyack & Hansot, 1982; Wesson & Grady, 1994; and others), relatively little national-level information has been available. Targeted studies have revealed information about women's leadership styles, career paths, personal sacrifices, networks of support, career aspirations, barriers that deter them from becoming superintendents, and other important information. However, we do not know how women across the nation conceptualize the role of the superintendent.

Because most studies have been qualitative ones focused on small samples of women, researchers can draw conclusions about individual conceptualizations of the role, but cannot, even cautiously, generalize the information to other women superintendents. Even the American Association of School Administrators' [AASA] national study, *The Study of the American School Superintendency* (Glass, Björk, & Brunner, 2000), with a representative sample, surveyed only 294 women superintendents, and for only a select number of the questions were the data reported disaggregated by gender or race.

The dearth of national-level research on women superintendents draws attention to the need for further study focused only on women. We hope that these findings, which give us an indication of how women conceive of the role of superintendent, will prompt others to focus on the question in further large studies. Our assertions in this chapter are grounded in our findings about superintendents from the AASA-funded Study of Women Superintendents and Central Office Administrators (Brunner & Grogan, 2003). This study is the first in history to include *all* women superintendents in the United States.

WOMEN SUPERINTENDENTS AND NORMATIVE ROLE CONCEPTUALIZATIONS

To be sure, women's conceptualizations of the role of superintendent fall within a range that can be referred to as "normative," or within the range of the norms that have been established by men. Even recent studies confirm the fact that the overwhelming majority of superintendents have always been men (Glass, Björk, & Brunner, 2000); thus, the norms or normative standards (standards of practice, philosophy, attitudes, rhetoric, language, values, goals) for the role have been established by men. Women's views of the superintendent as instructional leader, manager, political strategist, social scientist, and communicator can be said to be similar to the views of the established norms. However, there is more to the story. Although similar to those of men, women's conceptions of their role in the superintendency do include important nuances and noteworthy differences. In part, these differences are grounded in gender-specific socialization, a recognized and thoroughly researched phenomenon that has resulted in women's career paths and other experiential variations.

In this chapter, we first draw attention to brief examples of socially driven variations in the experiences of women superintendents. Second, we provide an overview of our 2003 study, from which our findings are drawn, and we examine the responses to some of the questions from the 2000 and 2003 studies that help illustrate how women conceive of the superintendency. Third, we discuss the implications of the findings for future preparation and development of women superintendents.

WOMEN SUPERINTENDENTS: BACKGROUND AND EDUCATIONAL EXPERIENCES AS INFLUENCE

In this section, we provide a few examples of how the background experiences and attitudes of women superintendents vary from those of men superintendents. We believe that these variations account for some of the ways that women superintendents actively and philosophically trouble the current male-defined norms of the superintendency.

We compared the teaching experiences of men superintendents (Glass, Björk, & Brunner, 2000) with those of women at two points in time (Glass, Björk, & Brunner, 2000; Brunner & Grogan, 2003). Table 10.1 shows that almost half of the women superintendents entered their teaching careers in elementary schools, whereas the largest portion of men superintendents were social studies teachers. Much could be said about the differing philosophies of elementary schools as compared with secondary schools, but this single difference in background training and experience could account for a differing conception of the superintendent as instructional leader. Women are not only more likely than men to teach at the elementary levels, but they also move into elementary administrative positions more often. Slightly more than 60% of women superintendents in the 2003 study had served as an elementary assistant principal or elementary principal.

Compared with men, women usually spend longer in teaching positions before they take an administrative position. Nearly 40% of male superintendents spent five years or fewer in the classroom, whereas 40% of women superintendents have had more than 10 years of experience in the classroom. This particular difference again highlights an element of

Table 10.1   Teaching Experiences of Men and Women Superintendents

Subject Taught	Men—2000 % (# of men) n = 1952		Women—2000 % (# of women) n = 297		Women—2003 % (# of women) n = 723	
Elementary	17.0	(332)	43.8	(130)	38.0	(275)
English	9.0	(175)	14.5	(43)	16.3	(118)
Math	11.5	(224)	3.4	(10)	5.9	(43)
Science	12.9	(252)	4.0	(12)	4.8	(35)
Social Studies	23.2	(453)	6.1	(18)	5.7	(41)
Special Education	3.0	(59)	11.1	(33)	8.7	(63)

background experience that could result in women attending more closely than men to matters of academic instruction and learning. Other researchers report that women on average teach 10 years longer than men before they enter administrative positions (Lunenberg & Ornstein, 1991; Riehl & Byrd, 1997; Shakeshaft, 1989). In addition, this study revealed that significantly more women superintendents (58%) than men (24%) majored in education in their undergraduate degrees.

Women superintendents are more up-to-date in their academic preparation for the position. In the past 10 years, 36% of men earned their highest degree, compared with 47% of women. Moreover, 42% of male superintendents earned their highest degree 15 or more years ago. Women superintendents also report more professional development activities in the field of curriculum and instruction. Seventy-three percent of women, compared with 39% of men, participated in ASCD-sponsored activities. Ten percent more women superintendents than men rate educational research as highly useful or usually useful. These gender-related variations in experience and preparation suggest the following. First, women's view of the role is likely to be somewhat different from men's view. Second, if the superintendency were dominated by women, the normative conceptions of the role would likely be somewhat different in intent and focus.

OVERVIEW OF THE 2003 AASA STUDY OF WOMEN SUPERINTENDENTS AND CENTRAL ADMINISTRATORS

In 2002, AASA provided funds to conduct a comprehensive national survey, based on the AASA survey that has been used for the 10-year studies of superintendency, targeted at all women in superintendent and central office positions. The resulting research is the largest study of this kind ever conducted. Surveys were mailed to every female superintendent, deputy superintendent, associate superintendent, and assistant superintendent in the United States. Twenty-five hundred of the survey recipients were superintendents, and 3,000 were central office administrators. Seven hundred and twenty-three superintendents and 472 central office personnel responded. Thus, nearly 30% of the total population of women superintendents is represented in this national sample. The population was compiled using the AASA and MDR (Market Data Retrieval) databases to ensure that the surveys reached both AASA members and nonmembers. MDR listed 13,728 districts in 2000 (Glass, Björk, & Brunner 2000). This study indicates that women lead 18% of districts—an all-time high.[1] The primary objectives of the study were to (a) maintain and update trend data on women from earlier studies (1992 & 2000) and (b) provide a more comprehensive overview of the perspectives of these district leaders.

RESULTS: INDICATIONS OF WOMEN SUPERINTENDENTS' UNDERSTANDING OF THE ROLE

To arrive at a better understanding of how women conceive of the super-intendent's role, this section explores pertinent responses of the women superintendents and central office personnel to the 2003 study. Where pos-sible and relevant, some comparison has been made with the responses of superintendents in the 2000 study (Glass, Björk, & Brunner, 2000).

A wide range of district sizes was represented in the data. The major-ity of respondents were Caucasian; however, there is a noteworthy sample of women of color (6.8% of the superintendents and 9.5% of the central office administrators). Of interest in determining role conceptualization from these data is that the women central office personnel held a variety of positions, but almost half of these respondents held an assistant super-intendent's position for curriculum and instruction. Thus, if and when these individuals reach the superintendency, it is likely that their world-view will be shaped by this prior experience. Close to 40% of the central office respondents report aspiring to the superintendency. It is also worth noting that the majority of respondents had not worked in a district headed by a female superintendent. Clearly, women's role conceptualiza-tions, as stated earlier, are still largely influenced by observing and working with male superintendents.

Two other broad areas on the 2003 survey reveal interesting data that give us an indication of how women superintendents view their role: (1) working with board and community and (2) superintendent training and development.

Working With Board and Community

Several questions asked respondents about policy and decision mak-ing that suggest ways in which superintendents work with the board and the community. Table 10.2 compares the 2003 study of women superinten-dents' perception of their board's primary expectations with the percep-tions of male and female superintendents reported in the 2000 study. Both groups chose educational leader as their top choice, but significantly more women in both studies felt it to be the primary expectation.

Significantly fewer of the current respondents chose managerial leader as a role that they perceive their boards want them to fill, which suggests that the notion of superintendent as managerial leader may be more strongly associated with male norms for the superintendency. However, with more than a quarter of women superintendents in both studies reporting high managerial expectations, the role conceptualization of superintendent as manager is certainly important for both men and

Table 10.2   Primary Expectations of Board for Superintendents

	2003 Women	2000 Men	2000 Women
Educational leader	46.3%	38.2%	51.4%
Political leader	11.4%	13.4%	8.8%
Managerial leader	24.4%	37.8%	27.7%
Leader of school reform initiative	9.9%	2.7%	3.4%
Community leader*	3.9%	*	*
Other	4.2%	7.9%	8.8%

*Data were either not collected or not reported in 2000.

women superintendents. It is interesting to note the increase in women reporting primary expectations of political leadership in the 2003 study. This could indicate that more women in 2003 served in diverse, pluralistic communities in which boards of education expected them to use their political skills to garner support for district initiatives.

Another figure worth noting in this table is that 9.9% of the women superintendents felt their board expected them to be leaders of reform initiatives. This is in contrast with only 2.8% of all superintendents in the earlier study. In the intervening three years since the earlier study was conducted, there has been a nationwide push for school reform spearheaded by the No Child Left Behind Act of 2001 (NCLB) (P.L. 107-110). Thus, on the one hand, the educational climate change in the country might account for this difference. On the other hand, it might reflect the responses of women of color who seem to be more associated with reform efforts than in the past. The 2003 study found that women of color were twice as likely to be hired as school reformers as white women and twice as likely to be brought in to lead reform efforts than the general population of minority superintendents in the 2000 study. In addition, 40% of the women superintendents of color in the 2003 study were hired in districts of 3,000 students or larger. Because size of district affects the likelihood of a more economically and demographically diverse community, these superintendents are highly likely to be drawing on their political skills to develop local policy options to influence change in the district. Development of policy is a shared task for the majority of women superintendents.

A comparison of responses to the question about who primarily develops policy and policy options in the district indicates that women superintendents have a slightly different role conceptualization. Male superintendents in 2000 saw themselves more often in this role than did the women in either of the studies (44% of men compared with 35% of women). At the same time, the current respondents reported depending more on the school board and board chair for policy direction than was reported by male superintendents in the 2000 study (13% of women, compared with 7.6% of men). However, more than one-third of both groups saw policy making as a shared responsibility between the board and superintendent. Overall, the differences point to a preference for sharing this task on the part of women superintendents. When all the responses are examined, the women were somewhat more likely to view others as sources of policy making than were the male superintendents.

The following discussion reports levels of community involvement in superintendent decision making from different angles as revealed through an examination of three different questions. First, the survey question that asked how frequently superintendents actively seek citizen participation in district decision making revealed a difference in women's and men's perceptions. Seventy-three percent of the women sought citizen participation very frequently, compared with 68% of the men. All superintendents valued participation in decision making; however, more women than men reported being more likely to solicit input regularly. It is also interesting to contrast those responses with the responses to another question, which asked superintendents how much weight they place on information from various sources for decision-making purposes.

All superintendents highly ranked information from district administrators, school board members, fellow superintendents, and teachers. However, 69% of women reported placing great or considerable weight on information from parents, compared with 59% of the general population of superintendents; 83% of women valued input from teachers, compared with 72% of the general population. Less than 40% of the general population of superintendents placed any weight on community groups, students, or others; whereas 50% of the women valued information from students, 42% from community groups, and 65% from others. This appears consistent with the idea that women superintendents are redefining the position as being centered more firmly around children and families, and as being more concerned with community building (Brunner, 2000; Grogan, 1999; Grogan & Sherman, 2003).

A related question asked superintendents to indicate in which planning areas they seek citizens' advice. The responses show that women superintendents have somewhat different perspectives about the kind of involvement they seek. More women in the 2003 study reported that they seek involvement in finance and budget issues than the general superintendent population in the 2000 study did, but more superintendents in general seek involvement in curriculum issues than the women in the 2003 study did. This seems consistent with the instructional focus of women superintendents, many of whom bring expertise in curriculum and instruction to the superintendency, according to this study, which makes them less likely to seek advice on such issues.

Superintendent Training and Development

Male and female superintendents both rate their preparation for the superintendency highly—true in both studies. In seeking information about preparation and training, however, a few questions help us gain an

Table 10.3   Areas to Be Included in Both Inservice and Preservice Training for
                  Superintendents

	2000	2003
High-stakes, state-mandated accountability testing	74.7%	83.7%
Effective public relations skills	73.3%	76.9%
Assessing educational outcomes	71.5%	82.2%
Administrator-board relations	71.4%	66.0%
Student discipline	70.7%	69.5%
Demands for new ways of teaching or operating the educational program	70.0%	78.4%
Changes in societal values and behavioral norms	69.5%	64.4%
Staff and administrator evaluation	69.3%	70.3%
Refinancing schools	69.0%	65.4%
Changing priorities in curriculum	67.9%	80.6%

understanding of how women view their role as superintendents. A question on both surveys asked women superintendents to indicate whether they wanted preservice training, inservice training, or both for a wide variety of skills or on a wide variety of topics. See Table 10.3.

Items that were marked as necessary in both preservice training and inservice training were selected for discussion here. It seems reasonable to assume that superintendents believed them to be the most important skills and knowledge that they should acquire and develop to enable them to serve as superintendent, giving us an indication of how respondents view their role.

There is quite a difference between the women's responses in the 2003 study and the general responses in the 2000 study. Respondents in 2003 likely felt the need for intensified training and development in several of these areas due to the recently increased pressure on high-stakes testing and accountability. The first item, high-stakes testing and accountability, and the last item, changing priorities in curriculum, seem closely related to this phenomenon. The items, demands for new ways of teaching or operating the educational program, and assessing educational outcomes might also be seen as indicative of the changed priorities in education. Nevertheless, if women superintendents do see themselves as more focused on curriculum and instruction, they might be placing more emphasis on training and development in these areas because they view their role differently from the way the general population of superintendents does. This might explain why a much greater proportion of the women in 2003 were in agreement that high-stakes, state-mandated accountability testing, assessing educational outcomes, and changing priorities in curriculum deserved attention both in preservice training and in ongoing professional development opportunities. Other areas with 60% or more of the women in strong agreement included changing demographics and their effects on race/ sociocultural issues, changes in societal values and behavioral norms, community involvement in district decision making, and students' rights. All these responses point to convincing indicators of interest in community issues, students, and their families. It is noteworthy that the responses to many questions like this one show a significant consensus of opinion among women superintendents. Compared with the high percentage of women in agreement about the need for training in top-ranked areas in Table 10.3, there was significantly less agreement among the general population of superintendents in the 2000 study for training at both levels.

Another question relating to training and development asked superintendents which knowledge or skills they believed were most helpful in advancing the career opportunities of those women who aspire to the superintendency. In Table 10.4, the responses from the two studies are compared, giving us insights into the strengths women believe they bring to the superintendency. The central office perspectives are also reported in this table to see whether they differ from the superintendents' perspectives, and whether the perspectives of the two groups—aspirants and nonaspirants—differ from each other.

These responses are consistent with the conception of the role of women superintendents as focused heavily on curriculum and instruction.

Table 10.4   Important Factors Advancing Career Opportunities for Women*

	Women Supts. 2003	Aspiring Women COs 2003	Nonaspiring Women COs 2003	Women Supts. 2000	Men Supts. 2000
Emphasis placed on improving instruction	63.8%	65.5%	61.5%	61%	44.8%
Knowledge of instructional process (teaching and learning)	61.5%	63.0%	59.3%	62.2%	46.0%
Knowledge of curriculum	58.5%	60.3%	57.1%	60.2%	44.4%
Ability to maintain organizational relationships	80.5%	82.4%	82.0%	76.1%	50.6%
Interpersonal skills	88.6%	85.5%	87.4%	83.3%	61.7%
Responsiveness to parents and community groups	79.3%	83.5%	82.2%	75.8%	51.6%

*Highest weighted response on a four-point scale.

In examining the first three items, there is significant agreement among all groups of women that improving curriculum and instruction, knowledge of teaching and learning, and knowledge of curriculum are considered to be strengths for women. In addition, they are viewed as factors helpful in advancing women's career opportunities. The male responses to the first three items suggest that men were not as convinced. This could be because men do not believe that women have such strengths or possibly that these strengths will not necessarily help advance women's careers. If the latter is true, this suggests that perhaps the majority of men do not conceive of the role of superintendent as being an instructional leader. Considering male responses to several related questions, men superintendents appear to differ more among each other than women superintendents do about their main responsibilities in the position. And although the reform efforts have prioritized instructional issues for all superintendents, it is not clear that male superintendents view themselves as needing expertise in the area.

Most interesting in this comparison is that women seemed to have gained confidence in the value of the last three items in the three intervening years between the surveys. This suggests that there is more general support for seeing these skills and knowledge as important in the superintendency. It seems reasonable to assume that interpersonal skills, the ability to maintain organizational relationships, and responsiveness to parents and community groups all contribute to the way women conceive of the role of superintendent. In addition to the desirability of being seen as competent in the curriculum- and instruction-related areas of improving instruction, the teaching and learning process, and building curriculum, Table 10.4 suggests that collaborative skills and community-building expertise are also highly valued. It is also interesting to note that with the exception of interpersonal skills, the aspirant group is slightly more confident that all these skills and knowledge will help advance their careers than the nonaspirant group. This may help to explain why some women central office administrators aspire to the superintendency and others do not.

A related question sought information on perceptions of what barriers limit women's opportunities to reach the superintendency. See Table 10.5.

Of the 12 possible limitations, there was strong agreement among women in all groups on the four areas listed in the table. More women in 2003 than in 2000 perceived these four items to be important barriers; however, the responses in 2000 and 2003 were similar. What is curious about these perceptions is that more women aspirants viewed three of them as barriers, compared with either the sitting superintendents or with those central office administrators who did not aspire to the superintendency. It is not surprising that women aspirants believed such items to be slightly more inhibiting than the incumbents (the mobility issue is a noteworthy exception here), but it would seem intuitive that more nonaspirants than aspirants would see these factors as barriers, and therefore would not aspire to

Table 10.5   Barriers Most Commonly Reported as an Important Factor
Inhibiting Women's Career Opportunities*

	Women Supts. 2003	Aspiring Women COs 2003	Nonaspiring Women COs 2003	Women Supts. 2000	Men Supts. 2000
Lack of mobility of family members	44.9%	34.8%	31.6%	41.0%	21.1%
Perception of school board members that women are not strong managers	39.9%	49.0%	37.4%	38.1%	6.7%
Perception of school board members that women are unqualified to handle budgeting and finances	38.0%	48.5%	35.5%	33.7%	3.6%
Perception that women will allow their emotions to influence administrative decisions	30.4%	46.0%	31.6%	25.0%	5.1%

*Highest weighted response on a four-point scale.

the position. One possible explanation is that aspirants acknowledge
the existence of barriers but are prepared to fight to overcome them. The
willingness to take steps to break down such barriers might accompany a
strong desire to reach the goal, no matter what obstacles exist. Another
way to explain it is to assume that nonaspirants have given the matter less
thought and are not concerned as much about possible limitations.

Another difficult-to-explain response is the fact that approximately
40% of the sitting women superintendents in both studies viewed one or
more of these factors as barriers—although they have obviously overcome
them. It is possible that these responses reflect what the superintendents
believe keeps other women out of the superintendency. It is also possible
that some women superintendents are sensitive to the prevailing gender
stereotypes, and that although *they* conceive of the role of superintendent
as one closely associated with curriculum and instruction, and community
building, and although they see themselves as having strengths in those
areas, they believe that others (most important of whom are board
members) do not see the role that way. The contrasting male perception that
only the lack of mobility might be a possible limiting factor is also interesting. It might suggest that men believe that there are no real limiting factors

Table 10.6   Issues and Challenges of Significance Facing Superintendents
Today*

	2000	2003
Financing schools	1 (96.7%)	1 (97.6%)
Assessing and testing for learner outcomes	2 (93.2%)	2 (96.0%)
Accountability/credibility	3 (87.5%)	3 (91.3%)
Demands for new ways of teaching or operating educational programs	4 (85.9%)	4 (90.6%)
Changing priorities in the curriculum	5 (85.5%)	7 (83.2%)
Administrator/board relations	6 (83.1%)	9 (77.0%)
Compliance with state and federal mandates	7 (82.2%)	5 (88.0%)
Teacher recruiting	8 (79.6%)	6 (83.9%)
Timely/accurate information for decision making	9 (76.9%)	8 (78.9%)
Change societal values/behavioral norms	10 (76.6%)	15 (63.8%)
Programs for children at risk	14 (70.9%)	10 (70.6%)

*A combination of the two highest weighted responses ("of great significance" and "significant") on a four-point scale.

for women (or men). It is also possible that few men have given women's career opportunities much thought.

Finally, there is one more question that sheds some light on how women superintendents see the role of superintendent. This is a question that seeks information on the issues and challenges that are significant today. See Table 10.6. Those items that are ranked highest indicate areas of concern, which helps define how superintendents see the role. The higher the rank means that more respondents rated the item either as of great significance or as significant.

It is assumed that the rating of an item as having great significance or significance gives us an indication of the value placed on it. Superintendents who see themselves as concerned with issues of instruction, for instance, would rate those issues as significant. Challenges can be seen as areas that superintendents want to strengthen on the one hand, and sources of conflict or vexing problems on the other. Either view means that superintendents must pay attention to them. It is too early to tell what effect these challenges may have on future conceptions of the role of superintendent, but with items such as assessing and testing for learner outcomes, accountability/credibility, demands for new ways of teaching or operating educational programs, and changing priorities in the curriculum ranked in the top 10 for both groups, we can infer that superintendents in general cannot ignore the instructional focus of their position today.

In comparing the responses, we find that the top nine concerns in 2000 remain the top nine concerns in 2003. Thus, women superintendents do not have a significantly different view of the most fundamental concerns of public education than the general population of superintendents. But the order in which concerns are ranked is a little different. The top four—financing schools, assessing and testing for learner outcomes, accountability/credibility, and new demands on teaching and programs—were the same for both groups. However, demands for new ways of teaching or operating educational programs were considered very significant by 90.6% of the women in 2003 and by 85.9% of the general population in 2000. One reason why more women in 2003 viewed this item as highly significant could be a result of the intensified pressure on high-stakes testing and accountability. Similarly, 88% of the women in 2003 rated compliance with state and federal mandates as providing a highly significant challenge, in comparison with 82.2% of the general population. Again, the explanation might be found in an increased number of such mandates demanding attention in 2003.

Consistent with the notion of community building and relationship development, only 77% of the women in 2003 rated administrator/board relations as highly challenging, compared with 83.1% of the general population in 2000—a rank of ninth compared with sixth most significant. This cannot be accounted for by a lapse in time because the importance of creating and maintaining good relationships with the board and district administrators remains equally as important today as it was in the years leading up to 2000. Therefore, it is likely that the item ranked in the top 10 because of its importance, but it ranked ninth on the list because, consistent with information reported in Table 10.4, women believe that they have strengths in this area, and it was not as pressing a concern as were some others.

The tenth most significant challenge was different for the two groups. Seventy-seven percent of the general population rated changes in societal values and behavioral norms as highly challenging, but only 63.8% of the women in 2003 thought similarly. Seventy-one percent of the women in 2003 rated programs for children at risk as a highly challenging area for superintendents (making it tenth in 2003), and 70.9% of the general population rated them the same way. However, because the distribution of items rated by the general population was more widely spread than the distribution of items rated by the women, the item is ranked differently among the two groups. It is the tenth-highest concern for the women and the fourteenth-highest concern for the general population. This seems consistent with women's continued focus on the needs of children and families.

DISCUSSION OF SUPERINTENDENT ROLE CONCEPTIONS

Although the AASA surveys were not focused primarily on determining how superintendents view their role, there are several indications of how they think about the job and what gets their attention. The 2003 Study of Women Superintendents and Women Central Office Administrators, in particular, gives us good insights into how we might generalize across the largest-ever national sample of women incumbents. The idea of role conception is closely associated with the historical study of the superintendency. Several authors in this volume have discussed the most common superintendent role conceptions: teacher-scholar, manager, democratic leader, applied social scientist (Callahan, 1966), and communicator (Kowalski, 2003). There is no doubt that women have embraced all these roles because they have participated in the same preparation and training programs as their male counterparts. Some of the survey questions, however, have provided interesting information on how women might prioritize their work as superintendents and which knowledge and skills they bring to the role.

Indicators for the women included the following: prior background and training; the length of time they devote to teaching before entering administration; their academic preparation; beliefs about what should be included in preservice and inservice training; factors that help to advance and to inhibit their careers; perceptions of the board's primary expectations of them as superintendent; views of who develops policy and policy options; levels of community involvement they seek in planning and decision making; and issues and challenges they see in the position. Women's responses to many of these questions have been compared with the general superintendent population's responses from the AASA 2000 study (Glass, Björk, & Brunner, 2000). Where possible, some of the disaggregated data from the earlier study were also used to highlight the comparison between women in the 2000 study and the 2003 study of women.

Instructional Leader

The results of the current study reveal a strong emphasis on women superintendents as instructional leaders with expertise in curriculum and instruction. Other studies have found that superintendents, men and women, conceive of themselves as instructional leaders (Petersen & Barnett, 2005), which is a modern version of the teacher-scholar role conception. The fact that on average, women superintendents teach longer than men, and the fact that women superintendents bring a more education-related academic preparation to the position reinforce the notion of an evolved teacher-scholar or instructional leader. When compared with other conceptions of the superintendency such as managerial or political leader, the majority of women reported that their school board's primary expectation of them was to be an educational leader. This clearly suggests prioritizing teaching and learning and providing adequate resources to teachers and administrators who are directly responsible for student achievement. In addition, three factors viewed as important in enhancing women's careers shown in Table 10.4 dealt with instructional issues: emphasis placed on improving instruction, knowledge of instructional process, and knowledge of curriculum. There was strong agreement among the majority of women respondents in both studies that women have strengths in these areas, and these areas would help to provide career opportunities for women. Whether women superintendents bring a background of curriculum and instruction supervision to the superintendency or not, women in the 2003 study expressed particular interest in staying current with curriculum issues. For instance, changing priorities in curriculum was third most important of the list of areas to be included in both inservice and preservice training for superintendents.

Democratic Leader

Moreover, women's focus on instruction is enhanced by an emphasis on children and families and on community building. The study reveals that more women superintendents than men superintendents actively seek citizen participation in district decision making. This work is associated with women's approach to the superintendency, according to data from the surveys. Women's responsiveness to parents and community groups (refer to Table 10.4) is seen as an advantage for women—helpful for their success in the superintendency. Community building includes working closely with teachers and administrators, the school board, and the various citizen groups that comprise the larger community. This work assumes both the political skills implied in the role of superintendent as democratic leader and the academic skills of the applied social scientist. Kowalski (2005) points out that when the concept was developed, an important responsibility of the democratic leader was to garner the resources to support district initiatives. He asserts that democratic administration of a school district is still necessitated by the intertwining of policy and politics in a democracy. Women superintendents' focus on community is a strong indication of their acceptance of such a role. An advantage in this endeavor is the particularly strong relational dimension to leadership that women superintendents bring to the position. Both men and women superintendents viewed interpersonal skills as a strength women share, and both believed that it is valued in the superintendency (refer to Table 10.4).

Applied Social Scientist

The data in this study revealed that women's academic preparation for the superintendency was more up-to-date than men's. As recent or relatively recent graduates from leadership preparation programs that emphasize the importance of research and the behavioral sciences (Fusarelli & Johnson, 2004), there is a strong likelihood that women superintendents are comfortable in the role of applied social scientist. In particular, because

Fusarelli and Fusarelli (2003) argue that this role has become associated with reform initiatives and social justice efforts to bring about more equity, equality, and diversity in districts, the role seems consistent with the data that show high levels of interest in improving teaching and learning, and a strong desire for both inservice and preservice opportunities to learn more about changing demographics and their effect on sociocultural issues such as race relations, integration, segregation, and immigration. This role suggests an emphasis on data gathering and analysis, strategies to eliminate the achievement gap, and other efforts to challenge the status quo. Women of color emerge in this study as particularly associated with reform efforts in mid-sized to large districts. This finding resonates with other research that talks of women administrators of color taking an activist role and leading with their lives (Ah Nee-Benham & Cooper, 1998; Dillard, 1995).

Manager

The role of superintendent as manager is also certainly familiar to women superintendents. As Glass (2003) asserts, superintendents of small districts manage the community's largest transportation and food service programs. With few or no support staff members, they also wear many more hats than their larger district counterparts, and they manage the fiscal affairs of the district even if there is a financial officer. Like the 2000 study, the profile of superintendents in this study revealed that 60% of the respondents served in districts with fewer than 3,000 students. Thirty-two percent of the women headed districts of 900 or fewer students. Therefore, a significant number of women must assume the kind of managerial role that Glass describes. However, it is interesting to note that more men serve as superintendents in small districts than women. Seventy-two percent of men in the 2000 study led districts of fewer than 3,000 students, and 38% of men superintendents served in districts of 900 students or fewer. District size notwithstanding, other factors make it imperative that women superintendents take on a managerial role. This study indicates emphases on such activities as shared policy making and community involvement in decision making, which require effective leadership and effective management (Kowalski, 2005). Indeed, managing community input so that effective, acceptable policy gets crafted requires sound management skills. Management can be seen to precede leadership. Linda Hill (2003) argues that "Not only do managers need to develop the personal capacity to manage, but they also must be able to create a context in which others are willing to learn and change . . ." (p. xii). This implies that simply providing opportunities for increased participation in decision making will not necessarily yield desired results. Communities of learning like the women in this study seem to be creating require good management as well as leadership skills.

Communicator

The conception of superintendent as communicator has been posited by Kowalski (2003, 2005). For Kowalski, the notion of communicator is built on the idea of a leader with good communication skills, but it also encompasses a broader view. He believes that these expectations of communication have been present since the 1980s, when district leadership began to be challenged by an increasingly critical and diverse public. According to this view, effective communicators "engag[e] others in open political dialogue, facilitat[e] the creation of shared visions, buil[d] a positive school district image, gai[n] community support for change, provid[e] an essential network for information management, marke[t] programs and kee[p] the public informed about education." The tasks of engaging diverse others in open political dialogue and facilitating the creation of shared visions resonate strongly with the priorities identified by the women superintendents in both studies and echo other literature on women in the superintendency (Grogan, 1996, 1999, 2000c). In seeking advice and information from the wide variety of groups indicated in the 2003 study, women create the opportunities for the necessary dialogues to occur. By prioritizing children and families in the improvement of teaching and learning, women superintendents suggest that they are not satisfied with the status quo. There are several indications in this study that women superintendents are engaged in change processes that allow for healthy dissensus among the community of administrators, teachers, parents, board members, and the wider public. Indeed, these activities seem to be the mark of a superintendent as communicator as it has been defined.

So in one sense, women superintendents are troubling the norms of the superintendent as managerial leader or as democratic/political strategist, but it is not clear from this study the extent to which women in the role are redefining the position. It is quite possible that the timing of the 2003 study, placed against the background of the NCLB (2001), and the many high-stakes testing responses that states have made to the NCLB's demands for accountability, shaped the women's answers more definitively than they might have been shaped had there not been such a highly publicized and politically charged reform under way. Only time will tell. One of the reasons we feel confident that we have identified a clear focus on the instructional leader and community builder in the women's responses to the survey is the large amount of agreement among them on many instruction- and community-related items.

Still, superintendent role conceptions are no doubt always developed in response to the prevailing social, economic, and political context of the period. Educational policy and practice emerge as a result of the forces at work. A question that remains is this: Because the current conditions appear to favor those aspiring to the superintendency who bring the skills and knowledge of instructional leaders, will more women gain access to the position?

RECOMMENDATIONS FOR SUPERINTENDENT PREPARATION AND DEVELOPMENT TO HELP RECRUIT AND RETAIN WOMEN

To provide the best possible opportunities for women to reach the superintendency and to develop as successful district leaders, the content of superintendent preparation and development efforts first needs to be updated to meet the current reform pressures. One of the questions on the survey asked respondents to decide whether 28 given issues should be included in preservice preparation programs only, included in inservice education only, included in both, included in neither, or don't know. Some of the responses to this question are listed in Table 10.3, which provides a comparison between women superintendents' top responses in the 2003 study and the general superintendent population's top responses in the 2000 study. For reasons already discussed, among the greatest concerns of both groups were issues of high-stakes testing and accountability, and assessing educational outcomes. Superintendents felt strongly about including these issues in both preservice and inservice experiences, most likely because traditional leadership programs have dealt neither with testing issues nor with data-driven decision making in the past. Not only was there high agreement between the two groups of superintendents on the need for knowledge in these areas, but the women central office administrators also responded similarly. A related issue on new ways of teaching or operating the educational program was also rated highly for inclusion in both arenas by all superintendents and by the women central office administrators in 2003. In addition, more than 70% of all groups of respondents from both studies rated effective public relations skills as important enough to be included in both preservice and inservice education. Clearly, women superintendents have the same preparation and development needs as their male counterparts, but the data reveal that they also have different needs.

In line with earlier research showing that women administrators have different experiences en route to the superintendency, this study also revealed that fewer women superintendents than men serve in central office positions associated with finance, facilities, or personnel. Fewer women serve as high school principals, who are more closely associated with the athletic program than other principals. Therefore, superintendent internships should be created for women to ensure that they get the necessary exposure to the nonacademic side of the position. Preparation programs must tailor internships to the needs of the individual aspirant in close collaboration with the appropriate district administrators. Current trends in administrator preparation and development suggest the kind of partnering between institutions of higher education, school districts, and professional organizations necessary to achieve this (Cambron-McCabe, 1999; Grogan & Andrews, 2002; Young, Petersen, & Short, 2002). Together with individualized internships, women in superintendent-preparation programs should also be provided with appropriate mentoring.

The majority of women superintendents in the 2003 study were mentored into the position. Seventy-two percent report having had mentors, most of whom were male because the majority of superintendents are still male. However, although 85% of women superintendents are now mentoring others, fewer women in central office positions report having been mentored (60%). The need for mentoring into leadership has been documented in much recent research (see 2004 special issue of *Educational Administration Quarterly*; Capasso & Daresh, 2001; Crow & Matthews, 1998; Gardiner, Enomoto, & Grogan, 2000). Not only is mentoring important for all aspirants to a position to gain insider information and to learn from the experiences of those who have gone before, but it is especially important for women, and women and men of color, who have been traditionally marginalized in the superintendent's role. Multiple mentors are needed to help these aspirants navigate the unchartered waters of traditional routes to the superintendency. It is clear from the AASA studies that mentors are available for superintendent aspirants, but not all who hold the necessary information and power (such as former superintendents and executives of superintendent and school board associations) are prepared to take risks with aspirants who appear to be outside the white, male, middle-class norm. Sylvia Méndez-Morse (2004) writes of the notion of constructed mentoring, which is particularly necessary for women of color to obtain the kinds of benefits that have been most often passed on to traditional aspirants (see also Enomoto, Gardiner, & Grogan, 2000). She describes the experiences of Latina educators who aspired to the principalship, but who had had no Latina role models and few opportunities to learn from others in the profession. Looking back on their path to leadership, these principals realized that they had constructed their own mentoring from various experiences of being with others—some professional and some personal. At the very least, then, although there might not be anyone designated in the mentor's role, the advantages of mentoring can be gained by seeking out and capturing others' wisdom and ideas.

The best course of action for those who want to collaborate in the preparation and development of the next generation of superintendents to be effective in reaching all of America's children is to actively *recruit* women and other aspirants of color, to provide the necessary *support* for them to succeed in the program, to *assist* them in networking to find a position, and then to continue to *mentor* them in the field. It should be a comprehensive process that is shared by professors in higher education and practitioners. If we do not change our current approaches to all four of those activities, it is unlikely that the numbers of women or women of color in the superintendency will increase significantly. Although the gains women have made in accessing the superintendency over the past 50 years are substantial, they are still not good enough for a field dominated by women. As Juanita Simmons (2005) argues, we must acknowledge race and gender stereotyping in program content and practices. Our textbooks must reflect the experiences of women superintendents and superintendents of color, and our instructors and mentors must include women and persons of color. Our deliberate efforts to change the face of educational leadership are crucial for the continued success of privileged children in our schools and for the much-hoped-for success of all our other children.

NOTE

1. This figure is the highest recorded percentage of women superintendents nationwide to hold superintendencies of all types. See Blount (1998) for a discussion of the historical facts about women holding up to 27% of intermediate superintendencies in the early to mid-twentieth century.

REFERENCES

Ah Nee-Benham, M., & Cooper, J. (1998). *Let my spirit soar! Narratives of diverse women in leadership*. Thousand Oaks, CA: Corwin.

Alston, J. A. (1999). Climbing hills and mountains: Black females making it to the superintendency. In C. C. Brunner (Ed.), *Sacred dreams: Women and the superintendency* (pp. 79–90). New York: SUNY Press.

Alston, J. A. (2000). Missing from action: Where are the Black female school superintendents? *Urban Education, 35*(5), 525–531.

Beekley, C. (1996). *Gender, expectations and job satisfaction: Why women exit the public school superintendency*. Paper presented at the annual meeting of the American Educational Research Association, New York.

Beekley, C. (1999). Dancing in red shoes: Why women leave the superintendency. In C. C. Brunner (Ed.), *Sacred dreams: Women and the superintendency* (pp. 161–176). Albany: SUNY Press.

Bell, C. S. (1995). "If I weren't involved in schools, I might be radical": Gender consciousness in context. In M. Dunlap & P. A. Schmuck (Eds.), *Women leading in education* (pp. 288–312). Albany: State University of New York Press.

Blount, J. (1998). *Destined to rule the world: Women and the superintendency, 1873–1995*. Albany: SUNY Press.

Blount, J. (1999). "Turning out the ladies": Elected women superintendents and the push for the appointive system, 1900–1935. In C. C. Brunner (Ed.), *Sacred dreams: Women and the superintendency* (pp. 9–28). Albany: SUNY Press.

Brunner, C. C. (1998a). Can power support an ethic of care? An examination of the professional practices of women superintendents. *Journal for a Just and Caring Education, 4*(2), 142–175.

Brunner, C. C. (1998b). Women superintendents: Strategies for success. *Journal of Educational Administration, 36*(2), 160–182.

Brunner, C. C. (1999). *Sacred dreams: Women and the superintendency*. New York: SUNY Press.

Brunner, C. C. (2000a). *Principles of power: Women superintendents and the riddle of the heart*. Albany: SUNY Press.

Brunner, C. C. (2000b). Unsettled moments in settled discourse: Women superintendents' experiences of inequality. *Educational Administration Quarterly, 36*(1), 76–116.

Brunner, C. C. (2003). Invisible, limited, and emerging discourse: Research practices that restrict and/or increase access for women and persons of color to the superintendency. *Journal of School Leadership, 13*(4), 428–450.

Brunner, C. C., & Grogan, M. (2003, April). *AASA national survey of women in the superintendency and central office: Preliminary results.* Paper presented at the annual conference of the American Educational Research Association, Chicago.

Callahan, R. E. (1966). *The superintendent of schools: A historical analysis.* (ERIC Document Reproduction Service No. ED 0104 410)

Cambron-McCabe, N. H. (1999). Confronting fundamental transformation of leadership preparation. In J. Murphy & P. B. Forsyth (Eds.), *Educational administration: A decade of reform* (pp. 217–227). Thousand Oaks, CA: Corwin.

Capasso, R. L., & Daresh, J. C. (2001). *The school administration handbook: Leading, mentoring, and participating in the internship program.* Thousand Oaks, CA: Corwin.

Chase, S. (1995). *Ambiguous empowerment: The work narratives of women school superintendents.* Amherst: University of Massachusetts Press.

Chase, S., & Bell, C. (1990). Ideology, discourse, and gender: How gatekeepers talk about women school superintendents. *Social Problems, 37*(2), 163–177.

Collins, P. (1991). *Black feminist thought.* New York: Routledge.

Crow, G. M., & Matthews, L. J. (1998). *Finding one's way: How mentoring can lead to dynamic leadership.* Thousand Oaks, CA: Corwin.

Dillard, C. (1995). Leading with her life: An African-American feminist for an urban high school principal. *Educational Administration Quarterly, 31*(4), 539–563.

Enomoto, E. K., Gardiner, M. E., & Grogan, M. (2000). Notes to Athene: Mentoring relationships for women of color. *Urban Education, 35*(5), 567–583.

Fusarelli, B. C., & Fusarelli, L. D. (2003). Systemic reform and organizational change. *Planning and Changing, 34*(3&4), 169–177.

Fusarelli, L. D., & Johnson, B. C. (2004). Educational governance and the New Public Management. *Public Administration and Management: An Interactive Journal, 9*(2), 118–127.

Gardiner, M., Enomoto, E., & Grogan, M. (2000). *Coloring outside the lines: Mentoring women into educational leadership.* Albany: SUNY Press.

Glass, T. E. (2003, April). *The superintendency: A managerial imperative?* Paper presented at the annual meeting of the American Educational Research Association, Chicago.

Glass, T. E., Björk, L. G., & Brunner, C. C. (2000). *The study of the American school superintendency, 2000.* Arlington, VA: American Association of School Administrators.

Grogan, M. (1996). *Voices of women aspiring to the superintendency.* New York: SUNY Press.

Grogan, M. (1999). A feminist poststructuralist account of collaboration: A model for the superintendency. In C. C. Brunner (Ed.), *Sacred dreams: Women and the superintendency* (pp. 199–216). New York: SUNY Press.

Grogan, M. (2000a). The short tenure of a woman superintendent: A clash of gender and politics. *Journal of School Leadership, 10*(2), 104–130.

Grogan, M. (2000b). A Black woman superintendent tells. *Urban Education, 35*(5), 597–602.

Grogan, M. (2000c). Laying the groundwork for a reconception of the superintendency from feminist/postmodern perspectives. *Educational Administration Quarterly, 36*(1), 117–142.

Grogan, M., & Andrews, R. (2002). Defining preparation and professional development for the future. *Educational Administration Quarterly, 38*(2), 233–256.

Grogan, M., & Blackmon, M. (2001). A superintendent's approach to coalition building: Working with diversity to garner support for educational initiatives. In C. C. Brunner & L. G. Björk (Eds.), *The new superintendency* (pp. 95–113). Amsterdam: JAI Press.

Grogan, M., & Sherman, W. (2003). Superintendents in Virginia dealing with issues surrounding the black-white test-score gap. In D. Duke, M. Grogan, P. Tucker, & W. Heinecke (Eds.), *Educational leadership in an age of accountability* (pp. 155–180). Albany: SUNY Press.

Grogan, M., & Smith, F. (1998). A feminist perspective of women superintendents' approaches to moral dilemmas. *Just and Caring Education, 4*(2), 176–192.

Hill, L. A. (2003). *Becoming a manager* (2nd ed.). Cambridge, MA: Harvard Business School Press.

Jackson, B. L. (1999). Getting inside history—against all odds: African American women school superintendents. In C. C. Brunner (Ed.), *Sacred dreams: Women and the superintendency* (pp. 141–160). New York: SUNY Press.

Kamler, E., & Shakeshaft, C. (1999). The role of the search consultant in the career paths of women superintendents. In C. C. Brunner (Ed.), *Sacred dreams: Women and the superintendency* (pp. 51–62). Albany: SUNY Press.

Kowalski, T. J. (2003, April). *The superintendent as communicator.* Paper presented at the annual meeting of the American Educational Research Association, Chicago.

Kowalski, T. J. (2005). Evolution of the school district superintendent position. In L. G. Björk & T. J. Kowalski (Eds.), *The contemporary superintendent: Preparation, practice, and development.* Thousand Oaks, CA: Corwin.

Lunenberg, F., & Ornstein, A. (1991). *Educational administration: Concepts and practices.* Belmont, CA: Wadsworth.

Marietti, M., & Stout, R. (1994). School boards that hire female superintendents. *Urban Education, 8*(4), 383–397.

Méndez-Morse, S. E. (1999). Re-definition of self: Mexican American women becoming superintendents. In C. C. Brunner (Ed.), *Sacred dreams: Women and the superintendency* (pp. 125–140). New York: SUNY Press.

Méndez-Morse, S. E. (2000). Claiming forgotten leadership. *Urban Education, 35*(5), 584–595.

Méndez-Morse, S. E. (2004). Constructing mentors: Latina educational leaders' role models and mentors. *Educational Administration Quarterly, 39.*

Murtadha-Watts, K. (2000). Cleaning up and maintenance in the wake of an urban school administration tempest. *Urban Education, 35*(5), 603–615.

No Child Left Behind Act of 2001. Washington, DC: U.S. Government Printing Office. Retrieved from www.ed.gov/policy/elsec/leg/esea02/107-110.pdf

Ortiz, F. I. (1982). *Career patterns in education: Women, men and minorities in public school administration.* New York: Prager.

Ortiz, F. I. (1999). Seeking and selecting Hispanic female superintendents. In C. C. Brunner (Ed.), *Sacred dreams: Women and the superintendency* (pp. 91–102). New York: SUNY Press.

Ortiz, F. I. (2000). Who controls succession in the superintendency: A minority perspective. *Urban Education, 35*(5), 557–566.

Pavan, B. N. (1999). The first years: What should a female superintendent know beforehand? In C. C. Brunner (Ed.), *Sacred dreams: Women and the superintendency* (pp. 105–124). Albany: SUNY Press.

Petersen, G. J., & Barnett, B. G. (2005). The superintendent as instructional leader: Evolution, future conceptualizations and implications for practice and preparation. In L. G. Björk & T. J. Kowalski (Eds.), *The contemporary superintendent: Preparation, practice, and development.* Thousand Oaks, CA: Corwin.

Riehl, C., & Byrd, M. (1997). Gender differences among new recruits to school administration: Cautionary footnotes to an optimistic tale. *Education Evaluation and Policy Analysis, 19*(2), 45–64.

Scherr, M. W. (1995). The glass ceiling reconsidered: Views from below. In M. Dunlap & P. A. Schmuck (Eds.), *Women leading in education* (pp. 313–323). Albany: SUNY Press.

Shakeshaft, C. (1989). *Women in educational administration.* Newbury Park, CA: Sage.

Shakeshaft, C. (1999). The struggle to create a more gender-inclusive profession. In J. Murphy & K. Seashore Louis (Eds.), *Handbook of research on educational administration* (2nd ed.) (pp. 99–118). San Francisco: Jossey-Bass.

Sherman, D., & Repa, T. (1994). Women at the top: The experiences of two superintendents. *Equity and Choice, 10*(2), 59–64.

Simmons, J. C. (2005). Superintendents of color: Perspectives on racial and ethnic diversity and implications for professional preparation and practice. In L. G. Björk & T. J. Kowalski (Eds.), *The contemporary superintendent: Preparation, practice, and development.* Thousand Oaks, CA: Corwin.

Skrla, L., Reyes, P., & Scheurich, J. J. (2000). Sexism, silence, and solutions: Women superintendents speak up and speak out. *Educational Administration Quarterly, 36*(1), 19–43.

Tallerico, M. (2000). Gaining access to the superintendency: Headhunting, gender, and color. *Educational Administration Quarterly, 36*(1), 18–43.

Tallerico, M., & Burstyn, J. N. (1996). Retaining women in the superintendency: The location matters. *Educational Administration Quarterly, 32*, 642–664.

Tallerico, M., Burstyn, J. N., & Poole, W. (1993). *Gender and politics at work: Why women exit the superintendency.* Fairfax, VA: National Policy Board for Educational Administration.

Tyack, D. B., & Hansot, E. (1982). *Managers of virtue: Public school leadership in America, 1820–1980.* New York: Basic Books.

Wesson, L., & Grady, M. (1994). An analysis of women urban superintendents: A national study. *Urban Education, 8*(4), 412–424.

Young, M. D., Petersen, G. J., & Short, P. M. (2002). The complexity of substantive reform: A call for interdependence among key stakeholders. *Educational Administration Quarterly, 38*(2), 137–175.

11

Superintendents of Color

Perspectives on Racial and Ethnic Diversity and Implications for Professional Preparation and Practice

Juanita Cleaver Simmons

This chapter addresses the five role conceptualizations of superintendents (communicator, political leader, manager, instructional leader, and researcher) as relevant to superintendents of color. These roles, discussed in this text by various authors, are thought to have evolved as focuses around which the public school district superintendency has developed over time. However, to provide the reader with a broader view of the role conceptualizations of superintendents from a minority and ethnic perspective, this chapter provides the reader with the historical backdrop that precipitated the development of superintendents of color, including the sociopolitical underpinnings that shaped the role of superintendents of color.

The history of the emergence of superintendents of color is a phenomenon that exists outside of the realm of traditional superintendent-preparation programs. Because early superintendents of color were excluded from the traditional preparation programs, they emerged in a separate and distinctly different context from that of their white counter-parts. Historical information on Asian American, Hispanic American, and Native American superintendents is very difficult to obtain due to the fact that their numbers have been very low or virtually nonexistent. Therefore, this chapter draws largely from the recorded experiences of African American superintendents. Yet it is because of the many social and political circumstances that affect today's American public schools that the five role conceptualizations (and the additional role in civic capacity building) are most needed in the preparation and socialization of superintendents, espe-cially those of color. Thus, this chapter, while chronicling the unique devel-opments in the evolution of superintendents of color, explores the combination of the five role conceptualizations and aligns them with cur-rent and past data that list the needs of superintendents of color. These needs and barriers are summarized to overlap with the five role conceptu-alizations and to point to the most pressing need of superintendents of color: an additional conceptualization, noted in this chapter as *civic capacity building,* defined by Henig, Hula, Orr, and Pedescleaux (1999) as

> . . . the ability to draw together and hold together a viable coalition of public and private stakeholders linked not necessarily by coinci-dent interests, shared visions, or altruistic motives, but by habits of collaboration, a requisite level of trust, and a pragmatic orientation toward making things work. (p. 27)

The final section of the chapter addresses recommended approaches that are appropriate for aspiring and veteran superintendents of color, the implications for preparation programs, and information for designers of administrator-preparation programs that describes the urgency of recruit-ing new candidates and retaining the decreasing numbers of superinten-dents of color.

It is important to understand that the chronicle of developments in the history of American superintendents of color begins with the struggles of African Americans to exercise the right to read. The genesis of this strug-gle begins with slavery, continues through America's post-slavery move-ment in America (Anderson, 1988; Baker, 1996), and continues to still exist with the challenges of today's national achievement gap (Education Trust, 2002; Harvard Civil Rights Project, 2003).

THE EVOLUTION OF SUPERINTENDENTS OF COLOR

Although little is known about the early appointments or elections of superintendents of color before 1930, it is known that ex-slaves, prior to receiving aid for developing universal schooling sought from Republican politicians, the Freedmen's Bureau, northern missionary societies, and the Union army (Anderson, 1988), had created "native schools" as early as 1862. Anderson further posits that upon the arrival of the northern missionaries who were assigned to establish schools for ex-slaves, the missionaries were "astonished, and later chagrined, to discover that many ex-slaves had established their own educational collectives and associations, staffed schools entirely with black teachers, and were unwilling to allow their educational movement to be controlled by the "civilized Yankees" (p. 6).

John W. Alvord, the national superintendent of schools for the Freedmen's Bureau, was first appointed as "inspector of schools" in September 1865 (Anderson, 1988), but this title was later changed to "general superintendent of schools" around July of 1865. In Goldsboro, North Carolina, Alvord discovered "[t]wo colored young men, who but a little time before commenced to learn themselves, had gathered 150 pupils, all quite orderly and hard at study . . . no white man, before me, had ever come near them" (p. 7). Long before 1862 when northern benevolent societies entered the South, and even before Abraham Lincoln issued the Emancipation Proclamation in 1863, African Americans had established and supervised their own schools and desired to have a voice in the decision-making process of these schools. Anderson (1988) quotes William Channing Gannett, a white American missionary association teacher, who spoke about his 1861 experiences with ex-slaves:

> They have a natural praiseworthy pride in keeping their educational institutions in their own hands. There is a jealousy of the superintendence of the white man in this matter. What they desire is assistance without control. (p. 5)

Much of the efforts of the slaves' educational developments were modeled from and guided by an African American female, Deveaux, who began her literacy campaign in Savannah, Georgia, during and following the Civil War and as early as 1833 (Anderson, 1988). Through the individual and collective efforts of ex-slaves, adds Anderson (1988), as many as 4,000 of their children attended schools that were established and secretly grouped into clusters of 22 schools. Some of these existed, for example, in northeastern South Carolina (p. 8). Gutman (1976) documents ex-slaves' contributions of money and labor and their idea to organize a responsible committee to supervise the schools.

Although Deveaux, the African American female school organizer and teacher who established a literacy campaign in 1833, was not a "superintendent" in title, her efforts were consistent with that of today's public school superintendent. Thus, her work (and the work of the ex-slaves who successfully designed a supervising school committee) demonstrates that contrary to historical omissions in the context of mainstream literature, there is an early history of African American supervision of schools. And this supervision included staffing, facility construction, fundraising, curriculum acquisition and design, and other managerial responsibilities. Moreover, the early supervision of African Americans in schools included females where a committee of interested individuals whose racial composition mirrored that of the students and their parents aided the supervisors' efforts. Unfortunately, this important segment of American history has yet to earn its way into such courses as the history of American public education. This must change.

THE REVOLUTION OF SUPERINTENDENTS OF COLOR: BEFORE AND DURING THE *BROWN VERSUS BOARD* ERA

According to Glass, Björk, and Brunner (2000), between the 1930s and 1950s, the sparse number of minority superintendents (mostly African Americans) was employed in southern and predominantly African American districts. Sizemore (1986) cites Jones (1985) in her explanation that "the first Black superintendents were selected in all Black districts primarily in the South, such as Boley, Clearview, Rentiesville, Redbird, and Taft, Oklahoma, between 1930 and 1958" (p. 2). Moody's (1971) study found superintendents of color in Inkster, Michigan; Lincoln Heights, Ohio; and Macon County, Alabama. Scott (1980) explains that the first black superintendent appointed to a prominent urban system was Ersel Watson, who in 1969 became superintendent of Trenton, New Jersey, schools. In July 1970, Marcus Foster was appointed superintendent of Oakland, California, schools, followed by Hugh Scott, who became superintendent of Washington, DC, schools in October of 1971. But managing the largest urban school system of that period, posits Scott (1980), was Roland Patterson, who was appointed to the Baltimore, Maryland, school superintendency in October of 1971 (p. 42).

Moody (1971), the first to study African American superintendents, asserts that "the emergence of the Black administrator was an outgrowth of the desegregation struggle" (p. 3). The desegregation struggle in American education surfaced on May 17, 1954. Citizens of 17 states and the District of Columbia, immediately faced with the realities and prospects of forced public school integration in their states, grappled with the future of American public education. That day marked the Supreme Court's decision that "separate schools are not equal" in the *Brown versus Board of Topeka, Kansas* case. Never in the history of American education had so many Americans voiced their opinions about public education. Prior to this day and the events leading to this landmark case, most citizens had left vital decisions about public education in the hands of politicians. These politicians, in turn, handed their mandates down to superintendents and their local educators (Anderson, 1988). The landmark case of *Brown versus Board* represented a new era in student and staff integration in American public schools, and it stimulated conversations about equitability in school finance and resources (Baker, 1996; Henig et al., 1999). These resources included personnel and staffing assignments in relationship to student racial and ethnic representation in school districts. Most controversial was the discussion about the congruence of student populations with appointed or elected school district leaders and governing boards (Stone, 1968). Because most of the leaders were white and their constituents were minorities, there was little understanding of the needs of their populations.

During the late 1950s to the mid-1960s, many grassroots African Americans and their representative community organizations raised their heads from the dizzying effects of the vitriolic resistance to the integration of their children into public education and met to discover that "forced integration" had given birth to new and different problems (Anderson, 1988; Stone, 1968). Some of these problems included African American students being disproportionately sorted into vocational and lower-level curricula tracks. African American students also began expressing feelings of poor self-esteem resulting from the lack of opportunities to explore leadership positions and acceptance into extracurricular activities in their integrated school settings. Moreover, many of the minority students began to perceive that their teachers and administrators held low expectations for their social and academic performance. Indeed, many African American parents and community stakeholders came to realize that their children were not benefactors of the nation's efforts to achieve integration by legal force (Baker, 1996). However, these parents were reminded of their opportunity to advocate for race representation in leadership and governance of their children's schools. Because many Whites had already opted out of the school integration dilemma by fleeing with their children to the suburbs, the African American community's demand for African American school superintendents and board members was a viable option. The African American community, according to the renowned African American teacher, Richard R. Wright, Sr., desired African American teachers and superintendents because "white teachers employed pedagogical methods ill-suited to the mental, moral and physical constitution of blacks" (Ryan, 1976, p. 344). Additionally, Fairclough (2000) cites John W. Cromwell, another pioneer African American teacher, who argued that white teachers were "too imbued with the false and wicked ideas bred by slavery safely to instruct black children" (p. 31). Therefore, the "white-flight movement" that had left African Americans a majority minority in such cities as Atlanta, D.C., Baltimore, and Detroit (Henig et al., 1999) had also precipitated a rapid change and political mobility for African Americans. Similarly, minority communities in rural southern areas were seeking leadership and governance that reflected the race and ethnicity of their students and constituents.

SUPERINTENTENDENTS OF COLOR AND THE POST-*BROWN* ERA

The 1960s and 1970s quest for racial and ethnic representation in the public school superintendency and governing boards heightened during and shortly after the Civil Rights Act of 1964. This era, sparked by the nationally televised civil rights movement, helped to affirm and legitimize the typically overlooked presence of African Americans, Hispanic Americans, Native Americans, and other minorities—particularly those who inhabited minority-populated cities and towns. Minority communities were demanding equal representation. These demands became priority items on the agendas of such organizations as the National Association for the Advancement of Colored People (NAACP), the Black Panther Party, the Southern Christian Leadership Conference (SCLC), ministerial alliances, and other grassroots organizations in minority communities. The demands, echoed in unison from these organizations and the Mexican American La Rasta groups, consisted of a well-constructed list of priority areas in which increased representation was considered important. This list included the racial and ethnic representation of superintendents, local school administrators, teachers, and school board trustees/representatives, and political representation. At that time, "white flight" had resulted in minorities becoming majorities in many cities (with the exception of a few predominantly African American and Mexican American southern rural towns). However, few superintendents of color were known or recognized, and the power players of most cities remained White.

Suddenly, African Americans began to rid themselves of such terms as "coloreds," "Negroes," and "Negresses," and began to replace them with the empowering title of African American. This self-empowered recognition helped to announce their alignment with (and to expose the long-suppressed—or socially silenced—connections to) Africa. This open acknowledgment refuted many myths and historically inaccurate narratives about slavery and Jim Crow laws, and began to acknowledge America's hand in legislating those inhumane events. Moreover, this increased level of empowerment transformed the role that the African American community played vis-à-vis the public schools.

Although White Americans were abandoning many urban cities and taking their coffers with them, they still controlled the power levers of these cities. White public officials, school superintendents, and school governing boards were left intact to rule their minority-populated school districts. Black activists, believing that equity in school administration would result in better education for minorities, openly protested against race and ethnic underrepresentation in the schools and municipal arenas, including school superintendents, school board trustees, mayors, city council members, and other strategic positions of power (Ryan, 1976). Carmichael and Hamilton (1976) argue, "White decision-makers have been running those schools with injustice, indifference and inadequacy for too long" (p. 59). Consequently, the demand for minority superintendents to lead these urban centers created the obvious awareness that few, if any, minority superintendents existed. Certainly minority superintendents existed during the pre-*Brown* era as the separate school systems (de facto and de jure) necessitated a cadre of African American superintendents who served their own "racially reflective" populations. However, the institutionalization of desegregation in the post-*Brown* era manipulated the protection of White teachers and administrators "while blacks lost their jobs" (Ryan, 1976, p. 28).

Although a nascent body of research on minority superintendents has recently evolved, very few mainstream publications include the early history of minority superintendents that would aid in elaborating on the number of qualified minorities who were available to fill this demand of the mid-1960s. However, the history of African Americans' struggle to gain educational access does include school leaders who, in spite of sociopolitical restraints, led thousands of ex-slaves to literacy long before their emancipation. (See Appendix A, "Chronology of the Evolution of the Superintendent of Color: What the History of American Education/Foundations Never Taught You.")

SUPERINTENDENTS OF COLOR BEYOND THE TURBULENT 1960S

During the turbulent mid-1960s period, many minority grassroots leaders believed that minority students would receive better educational opportunities from minority superintendents and elected political officials, believing that these representatives would best reflect and support their interests. With the fading White majority and increasing Black and Brown city dwellers, this seemingly easy process proved to be more difficult than perceived. Although the mid-1960s population transitions showed marked changes in the public school demographics, and in spite of African Americans' accusations that White teachers and White administrators were crippling inner-city schools (Ryan, 1976; Meier, England, & Stewart, 1989), it would be another 10 years before an African American superintendent or African American mayor would take charge of America's largest urban cities and school districts. As Scott (1980) blatantly asserts:

> Black superintendents will inherit the effects of increased societal deterioration, unabated decline in academic achievement, deficient financial resources, higher percentages of black students and

students from low-income families, a black majority or activist blacks on the school board, large numbers of blacks in the community, and demands from vocal blacks in the community. (p. 188)

By 1970, predominantly African American inner-city dwellers of the large municipalities experienced new African American governing elites that included general electoral offices, city council seats, mayoral positions, school superintendencies, and school board positions. Henig et al.'s (1999) study reveals that Atlanta, Georgia (somewhat of an anomaly from most predominantly African American cities), experienced tremendous transitions in 1973. That year, the citizens of Atlanta elected an African American mayor and school superintendent, and their city council and school boards also became a majority of African Americans. Although the city had been an African American majority since 1970, Atlanta's "white flight" had left the school enrollment a majority African American population since 1963. Baltimore, Maryland, is often compared with Atlanta in its major "white flight" transitions, yet Baltimore's school enrollment became predominantly African American in 1960—11 years before the election of an African American superintendent in 1971. Interestingly, Baltimore's school board did not become majority African American until 1973, and residents did not elect an African American mayor until 1987. Similarly, Detroit's school enrollment became majority African American in 1962—12 years before voters appointed/elected an African American superintendent in 1974. Although Detroit's school board and city councils did not become majority African American until 1977, their citizens elected an African American mayor in 1973. Although these superintendent and political appointments were largely due to the high percentage of minority students in urban cities and schools (Moody, 1971; Jones, 1985; Scott, 1980), with these appointments came the inheritance of "critical financial conditions and educational problems accrued from years of neglect and deprivation" (Sizemore, 1986, p. 189). Moreover, as Scott (1980) accurately predicted:

Even though the number of black superintendents will never be as large as the number of white superintendents, there will be an increase. However, this increase will not be linked to any assertive affirmative action program in the education establishment. The expansion in the ranks of black superintendents will be related to whites not wanting to deal with the engrossing problems of the cities. (pp. 187–188)

Scott's prediction became a reality literally days after he spoke these words. Although urban financial bankruptcies or near-empty coffers became a major challenge for superintendents of color, they had finally received their appointments made by predominantly minority constituents.

In some cases, however, the price of their superintendent appointments proved to be somewhat of a Cadmean victory, in which the victor, in spite of the fact of winning the position of superintendent, becomes involved in even greater danger than previously. This price, unfortunately, continues to be paid by many superintendents of color today.

TODAY'S SUPERINTENDENTS OF COLOR IN THE MIDST OF URBAN CRISES

Superintendents of color, as most superintendents of today, are challenged by a plethora of what often seems to be insurmountable responsibilities, including the management and implementation of such federally mandated policies as No Child Left Behind (NCLB). However, superintendents of color are confronted with at least three additional barriers: (1) problems precipitated by race (including access into the superintendency), (2) the economic and social deterioration of the districts that they inherit, and (3) difficulty in accessing the necessary political and social power relationships needed to reform their districts. As Scott (1980) states, "The black superintendents' efforts are affected by multifaceted impositions and barriers that are uniquely linked to society's treatment of blacks and black leadership" (p. 48). Given that the largest percentage of superintendents of color are appointed to urban, high-poverty, minority districts and/or predominantly minority small towns, superintendents of color are placed at the helm of being or becoming America's most challenged leaders of our time.

As recently as November 2001, the National Alliance of Black School Educators (NABSE) reported 292 African American superintendents in its *Directory of African-American Superintendents* (NABSE, 2001). This number represents 1.8% of the more than 14,000 superintendents throughout the United States and the Caribbean. Together, African American superintendents are responsible for more than 14,500,000 public school students and have control of more than $21 billion (p. 1). During that same reporting period, NABSE noted that there were 18 states without African American superintendents (See Appendix B, "States Without Any African American Superintendents."). As of January 2004, NABSE reported a total of 271 African American superintendents—an indication of a decline in the number of African American superintendents during the past three years. Although current data on African American superintendents and their districts are pending NABSE's 2004 publication, data from the Council of the Great City Schools (CGCS) (CGCS, 2003) also indicated a decline in the number of African American superintendents who lead urban districts (p. 2). Interestingly, there is an increase in the numbers for White and Hispanic American superintendents who have taken recent leadership in urban districts (see Appendix C, "GCS Superintendents by Race/Ethnicity and Gender: July 1997, July 1999, July 2001, and July 2003"). Yet the same needs posited by Moody (1983), Sizemore (1986), Scott (1980), and Jones (1985) are congruent with recent studies done by the Council of the Great City Schools (2003).

SIGNIFICANT NEEDS OF SUPERINTENDENTS OF COLOR: THE FIVE CONCEPTUALIZATIONS, PLUS CIVIC CAPACITY BUILDING

Although there are few recent studies on the problems and barriers of superintendents of color, the overlapping needs of these superintendents identified by Moody (1983), Sizemore (1986), and Scott (1980) are consistent with the needs found in the four-year survey initiated by the CGCS: *Fifth Biennial Survey of America's Great City Schools* (see Appendix D, "CGCS Top 10 Needs of Urban Schools"). Although the CGCS survey of the top 10 needs of urban schools does not represent the needs of superintendents of color solely, three of the four years included in the study reflect a large percentage of superintendents of color. The CGCS survey serves as an approximation of the current needs of superintendents of color used to complement the earlier Jones study on the needs and problems of African American superintendents (cited in Sizemore, 1986). Jones cites the most critical problems for superintendents as follows: instructional, program relevance, accountability, school support (improving educational content), ensuring that goals were met, and adequate financial resources to carry out sound educational programs (Sizemore, 1986, p. 191; see Table 11.1). Additionally, Sizemore found that districts with superintendents of color were faced "with the lack of proper financial support, and the lack of interest on the part of parents, students and teachers" (p. 192).

Six years before Sizemore's report, Scott (1980) found that the critical needs of superintendents of color included improved academic achievement, reorganization of the system, educational accountability, expanded community participation, staff development, staff unity, management improvements, and long-range planning (p. 51). Unsurprisingly, Scott cited the major problems confronting superintendents of color as low academic achievement, recruitment of staff, keeping the public informed, insufficient funds, reorganization of the system, board-superintendent relations, teacher accountability, teacher attitudes, and the image of systems that they lead (p. 51).

Using the findings of Sizemore (1986) and Scott (1980), it might be safe to chart the various needs and problems of superintendents of color. One finds that the problems and needs of superintendents of color fall into five basic categories: (1) *instructional leadership,* (2) *management and finance,* (3) *communication,* (4) *research/problem solving,* and (5) *political leadership.* Together, these categories, which also reflect the role conceptualizations of superintendents, translate into the major overall need and desire for superintendents of color to know and understand the ins and outs of political leadership to develop a civic capacity.

Table 11.1 illustrates the major needs of superintendents of color found in Scott's study. The needs can be framed by the five conceptualizations that have developed over time. However, these conceptualizations are not sufficient for the work that needs to be done by most superintendents of color in their high-poverty, academically challenged urban districts.

As shown in Table 11.1, the major needs and problems of superintendents of color found in Scott's study are reflected by the five conceptualizations recommended as the role expectations developed in the tasks of superintendents. A discussion of the five role conceptualizations and the added conceptualization—civic capacity—as they relate to the needs of superintendents of color supports the relevance of the conceptualizations as skills for today's superintendents of color, as well as superintendents who govern challenged urban districts.

Manager

Of the five role conceptualizations recommended for superintendents, manager is found to be the core essential role that serves as the foundation to remedy the needs that were generated by superintendents of color. Findings from Scott's (1980) research on the needs of African American superintendents (refer to Table 11.1) included reorganization of the system and management improvements. In addition to their survey on needs was their survey of the problems of superintendents of color, which

Table 11.1

Needs of Superintendents of Color	Instruct. Leader	Comm.	Manager	Researcher	Political Leader
Improved academic achievement	√	√	√	√	√
Reorganization of the system	√	√	√	√	√
Educational accountability	√	√	√	√	√
Expanded community participation	√	√	√	√	√
Staff development	√	√	√	√	√
Staff unity	√	√	√	√	√
Management improvements	√	√	√	√	√
Long-range planning	√	√	√	√	√

SOURCE: Needs adapted from Scott, 1980, and charted by author.

listed problems in the areas of reorganization of their systems and insufficient funds. Although a more recent survey of the CGCS (see Appendix D) reveals that of the top 10 needs of urban district superintendents today, finance, principal leadership, and teacher retention/recruitment continue to challenge superintendents—especially those who govern larger districts. Each of these needs and problems emphasizes the importance of management skills to effective district operations and leadership. Moreover, their needs serve as indications that management is a top priority role that affects all components of effective schooling. As Glass stated, in Chapter 6 of this volume, the management role is the underpinning of the superintendency. If district improvements are indeed contingent upon effective and appropriate management, stable leadership strategies can be achieved only through superintendents mastering management skills as a priority task for district leadership. Glass further argues that effective management skills include finance; fiscal planning; budgeting; accounting; debt management; investing; auditing; purchasing and contracting; property management; risk management; salary and wage management; facility management, assessment, and maintenance; human resource management; and other employee-related concerns. Alone, each of these management skills serves as a pivotal component for sound organizational and operational cohesiveness most needed for effective public school leadership. Given the past and present needs of superintendents of color and those who govern crises-laden urban districts, management skills must be a priority requirement.

Instructional Leader

The compounded effects of the social and racial complexities of urban school districts and the challenges these districts experience with the national academic achievement gap (see Education Trust, 2002, and the Harvard Civil Rights Project, 2003) are clear indications that instructional leadership skills are also most needed by superintendents of color to successfully lead their urban and minority-majority school districts. Chapters 4 and 6 of this book reference the importance of superintendents to acquire and implement instructional leadership roles in their districts, as well as support the assumption that current reform initiatives increased public expectations that superintendents should serve as instructional leaders. This assumption supports the notion that instructional leaders enhance academic success for all children. As mentioned previously, federally mandated policies have begun to enforce the accountability requirements on school districts. Some of these accountability requirements necessitate the knowledge of certain skills that fall into the category of "teacher-scholar" expectations of superintendents, as listed by Glass, Björk, and Brunner (2000), which included assessing and testing learner outcomes, providing assistance with the demands for new ways of teaching and operationalizing instructional programs, and negotiating priority modifications in curricula. Thus, the demands for performance accountability have increased the superintendent's role expectations as instructional leader, thereby requiring superintendents to make themselves amenable to acquiring these necessary skills for successful district leadership, especially those who lead academically challenged districts.

Social Scientist

The various authors of this text concur that the role of the superintendent as social scientist remains a core expectation from many school boards. Moreover, the current nature of public school governance and leadership includes the constant reporting of student and staff performance data that shape the public's opinion about the image and success of American schools. The advent of the federally mandated No Child Left Behind policy increased public awareness of school and district achievement and advocated parents' rights to have access to such data. Suddenly, the inner working of school dynamics shifted to the ultimate results of student academic performance and the intersecting variables that affect their performance, including teachers, staff, administrators, and certain connected social agencies. With this increased responsibility of public accountability for student success, the expectation of superintendents to apply knowledge of the social sciences and to use scientific inquiry methods to understand and solve the problems that permeate their practice has become a major asset to their leadership positions (Johnson & Fusarelli, 2003).

Superintendents, particularly those of color, who may have quietly fought isolated battles of injustice for their underserved populations are now given a voice via federal policies to expose injustices that impede student success. For superintendents to be successful at leading the increased numbers of diverse student and staff populations in American public schools, superintendents need to be trained in methods to assist them in identifying and negotiating appropriate advocacy strategies that support the needs of their constituents. This effort is greatly needed by superintendents of color and those who lead in school districts in which their constituents consist of typically underserved populations.

Communicator

Because of the racial barriers and the sociopolitical nature of governing high-poverty urban school districts, one of the most vital roles needed by superintendents of color is that of communicator. As indicated in Table 11.1, among the various concerns of superintendents of color is that of the image of their districts, improved academic achievement, and the need to reorganize their districts. Saddled with the existing challenges that are already inherit in the nature of change, including "replacing norms of bureaucratic, regulated organizations to risk-taking, entrepreneurial organizations" (Kowalski & Keedy, 2003, p. 10), superintendents of color must be prepared to confront these challenges with the additional threat of racial barriers, including possible deficit thinking of stakeholders and key players. In so doing, improved communication skills are some of the major needs of superintendents of color.

Kelleher (2002) concurs that

> [b]ecause of the difficulty in achieving consensus and ensuring a smooth working relationship among the school system's diverse constituencies, including the board of education and the public, the superintendent's ability to clearly articulate and act consistently around a set of core values is critical to the success and stability of the school system. (p. 24)

Consequently, the role of communicator is essential for superintendents of color whose districts are most in need of sustained educational reforms to improve the conditions of the large, high-poverty, predominately minority student populations in their district.

Political Leader

Today's superintendents require a formal political power structure to negotiate sustained reform in their districts, especially large urban districts in which reform is most needed. In that many of these districts are where women and superintendents of color are often appointed, it is essential that these minorities gain access to the *political power* needed to develop and sustain reform for their districts. Björk and Gurley (2003) argue that in the context of the present and future practice of superintendents, political leadership is essential in order to effectively mobilize the students, teachers, administrators, and staff of the school community.

Björk and Gurley (2003) posit that one of the major skills needed for successful superintendency is "higher levels of political acuity," which is negotiated in the context of "participatory politics" (p. 8). They further assert that "participatory politics occurs during periods in which group membership is fluid and alliances are ad hoc with the ebb and flow of interactions among community interest groups on varying issues" (p. 8). Likewise, Cuban (1988) concurs that superintendents need to develop "political leadership" that enables the superintendent to "build coalitions, and negotiate the distribution of resources among multiple and diverse interest groups to gain their support for district initiatives" (Björk & Gurley, 2003, cite Cuban, 1988, p. 9). Both concepts—participatory politics and political leadership—create an expanded platform needed by superintendents of color that leads to the development of civic capacity building, which is recommended as a must for training aspiring superintendents in the contexts of each of the five conceptualizations, particularly for the superintendents of color.

Civic Capacity Building

The previous discussion on political leadership asserts a similar definition to that of civic capacity building. However, civic capacity building, as it relates to superintendents of color in this report, includes more of an elaboration on the need for superintendents of color to develop and become aware of the necessary social and political behaviors that include communication and other socially constructed behaviors. Civic capacity building has been defined as

> [t]he ability to draw together and hold together a viable coalition of public and private stakeholders linked not necessarily by coincident interests, shared visions, or altruistic motives, but by habits of collaboration, a requisite level of trust, and a pragmatic orientation toward making things work. (Henig et al., 1999, p. 27)

As noted in the definition, civic capacity building includes a broader framework than political leadership. Moreover, civic capacity building is an additional conceptualization to the five conceptualizations discussed by others and encompasses the necessary network ties needed to develop the strong reform administration posited by Peterson (in this book). Thus, civic capacity building, in light of the majority of minorities who lead urban districts, is an essential role for effective urban leadership and is of particular benefit for superintendents of color. This, indeed, is a different role conceptualization from the five that have already been discussed. However, these conceptualizations are not sufficient to be effective for the work that needs to be done by most superintendents of color in their high-poverty, academically challenged, urban school districts. It goes without saying that all superintendents are in need of understanding the role conceptualizations. Yet because of the three major barriers discussed earlier, civic capacity is offered as more essential for superintendents of color and those who will lead today's larger districts that suffer from numerous social, political, financial, and academic crises.

These social and political behaviors might be natural assumptions for nonminority superintendents and nonminority aspirants to the superintendency who, because of the "white privilege" (Scheurich & Young, 1997) accorded to nonminorities, have little or no concept of the challenges that minorities face in attempting to gain entrance into social environments in which their platforms might be supported. Of course, this support is contingent upon their (superintendents of color) being given the opportunity for membership, acceptance, and/or platform presentation space. Although political leadership is crucial for superintendents to expand the local constituency for education at large (chambers of commerce, city councils, Rotary clubs, and civic associations), the "one-step-beyond" challenge for minority superintendents is having the social and political savvy and aptitude to "get to the table." According to a

2002 survey conducted by the CGCS—the *Fifth Biennial Survey* of the most helpful groups having the most influence (outside of schools) on urban schools in their districts (see Appendix E, "CGCS Survey on Helpfulness of Groups to Urban Schools")—it found that foundations, business leaders, local public education funds, and colleges/universities ranked as the top four influences during a seven-year period. Followed by these groups were community organizations, mayors, local advocacy groups, state education departments, religious organizations, and the governor (p. 4). Results from this report confirm Björk's and Kowalski's (in this book) assumption that superintendents must be politically savvy leaders of their districts and must also be capable of motivating and mobilizing community organizations and constituents in support of school reform. But in order to promote the success for their high-poverty, minority student populations, it is most crucial for superintendents of color and women to become politically and socially astute, in spite of the possibility of nonacceptance into these formal arenas in which the necessary interactions convene with key power players.

Indeed, getting to the table is critical. Goodman and Zimmerman (2003) concur that "[p]ublic engagement and community mobilization are keys to defining priorities, setting goals, and creating an educational vision, all of which must be tied to quality education for all children" (p. 5). Political leadership, however, does not exist in a vacuum of its own; instead, communication is the crucial component to effectively enact political leadership. But again, racial and gender barriers can inhibit access into the political arena before women and superintendents of color can present their platforms.

An interesting phenomenon that serves as a near-counterpoint to the previous assumption is that of white superintendents who lead minority districts. They, too, are challenged by similar but different communication challenges that are affected by the social environments of urban centers. Their need for capacity building might require border-crossing negotiations to effectively mobilize their diverse constituents, including large populations of minority students, parents, school board trustees, and municipal officials. They (nonminorities) cannot base their previously, and typically limited, assumptions on their knowledge of socially constructed behaviors.

IMPLICATIONS FOR ADMINISTRATIVE PREPARATION PROGRAMS IN PREPARING SUPERINTENDENTS OF COLOR

It is incumbent upon superintendent-preparation programs to incorporate methods and instruction for advancing the five conceptualization skills and civic capacity building in the curriculum for their aspiring superintendents, particularly superintendents of color. This curriculum should include the acknowledgment of (and counteractive strategies to help dissolve) existing barriers (Bonuso & Shakeshaft, 1983; Henig et al., 1999; Marshall, 1984; Metzger, 1985; Payne & Jackson, 1978) that minorities and women experience when attempting to ascend to the superintendency. Consequently, the content of this empowering curriculum is equally as important as the absence of it. In the attempt to create space for helping aspiring superintendents to develop the role conceptualizations, preparation programs must be careful to abandon the traditional "disciplinary practice" approach.

Deficits of the Disciplinary Practice Approach

The disciplinary practice, or discourse practice traditionally used in educational administration-training programs, often supports and models the white, male, middle-class values, behaviors, dispositions, and norms (Scheurich, 1994) that have blocked access of women and minorities in the first place. Admittedly, such norms and behaviors do hold control over "who is" and "who isn't" invited to the table at which powerful decisions are made. Yet it is imperative that these norms be discussed in the context of whether they deserve to be a major focus of preparation programs' disciplinary practice and discourse.

Anderson and Grinberg (1998) define disciplinary practice as a "set of discourses, norms, and routines that shape the ways in which a field of study and its related practices constitute themselves" (p. 330). Traditionally, curricula and instructional delivery methods used in most educational administration preparation and/or certification programs are framed around a disciplinary practice approach that according to Callahan (1962) was colonized by efficiency experts from business and industrial psychology. Moreover, the disciplinary practice approach used in educational administration programs is closely linked to Foucault's (1972, 1980) concept of dividing practices that fragment knowledge and promote a form of rationality that facilitates control, including a sustaining power that is exercised through institutional relations that discipline one's ways of thinking and acting. In other words, if the designers of preparation programs are intent on developing political leadership skills in women and minorities, this curriculum must be framed in a context that meets their realities, including the acknowledgment and analysis of race and gender barriers and the needed methods and behaviors to counteract blocked access.

Counterproductive Curriculum Course Norms

Another concern to bear in mind for preparing minority superintendents is the norm established in the curriculum of general studies. For example, most superintendency programs include courses in school law, finance, governance (board relations), instructional leadership, and other courses taught in isolated curricular strands. These courses, although essential to administrative management and leadership, are often framed in the context of "national norms." This *traditional disciplinary practice* discourse has conflicting implications for the day-to-day realities of superintendents who are appointed to high-poverty, low-performing, "out of the norm" urban and rural districts in which efforts for success are often contradicted by financial and political challenges and conflicts. Unfortunately, shortly after the honeymoon period of their appointments, many of these superintendents are confronted with a reality that becomes a competing discourse between what was presented in the disciplinary practice discourse of their preparation programs and the stark reality of "what is." This experience, also referred to by Foucault (1980) as a "politics of truth," is an additional challenge and barrier for women and minorities in the superintendency. Unsurprisingly, Scott (1980) claims the following:

> Along with the inheritance of school systems that serve large numbers of students with cumulative deficiencies in the basic skills and that are inadequately funded, Black superintendents soon learn that textbook theories in school administration are not relevant to challenges of such magnitude. (p. vii)

Additionally, the norms established in the disciplinary practice approach of most administrator- and superintendent-preparation programs "inculcate a hierarchical structure of gender and race roles that perpetuate the patriarchal system of public school administration" (Anderson & Grinberg, 1998, p. 342). Thus, the disciplinary practice approach serves as the major counterproductive gatekeeper that hinders the success and ascendancy of women and minorities into public school administration and/or appointments as superintendents.

Although the emphasis on effective communication, particularly in civic capacity building, is offered as a crucial need for students of color and females aspiring to the superintendency, this recommendation is not to imply that either of them is deficient in this area. Rather, it is an admission of the status quo and the reality that superintendents of color and females are challenged by the lack of being accepted into social and political power arenas. Yet these power arenas are often the centers in which strategic and powerful decisions are made, including policy, appointments, finance, corporate contracts, community reform planning, acquisition of funds, and other vital issues. Communication skills are crucial to the success of district reform efforts (Chance & Björk, 2004; Kowalski & Keedy, 2003), as are formal and informal relationships.

Thus, recommendations directed toward reconfiguring superintendent-preparation programs to address perspectives of race and ethnicity, as well as the five role conceptualizations and civic capacity building, are as follows:

• Enhance preparation curricula to include empowerment strategies to help aspiring superintendents of color and aspiring female superintendents to negotiate problems precipitated by race and gender. This may be achieved by incorporating a social/political communications component to expose superintendents of color and females to the necessary skills to access political and social platforms that affect sustained reform for their districts. Brunner (1999) found that "superintendents who were successful were those who developed the *personal* connections necessary for support, who understood the interdependence between symbolic and professional expectations, and who enacted a subtle political profile" (p. 100).

• Include a major focus on management, finance, and funds acquisition skills (including how and when to propose school bonds) that incorporates strategic planning for urban crises. Sizemore (1986) alerts educators: "Black superintendents need to know more about financial planning and economic development to understand better how to design developmental strategies that lead to redistribution without negative side effects" (p. 201).

• Establish an open and honest dialogue about race and gender problems in the superintendency. Reject forms of deficit thinking—the belief that the poor and people of color caused their own social, economic, and educational problems.

• Hire and support qualified female and minority practitioners to deliver this sensitive instruction and as preparation-training instructors in general. Too often, attempts by university preparation programs to include race and gender-oriented issues in their administrative preparation curricula fail. This failure results because of several reasons, including the following:

    o Universities and other training programs assign nonminority staff to teach race- and gender-sensitive issues, and these instructors are confronted with social and political fears (e.g., course evaluation ratings, rejection from students, and threats of low enrollment). They water down the curriculum and form key issues into socially acceptable structures. So, the norm continues—omission and dilution.

    o Administrative training programs offer gender- and race-sensitive courses as "nonrequired" courses, electives, or "optional-credited" courses. This sends the message that the status quo exists in the social structures and that challenges to the status quo are irrelevant. This also contributes to the following situation.

    o When administrative training programs hire minorities and women to teach these sensitive courses (courses containing oppressive content), these programs must support women and minorities in their struggles to gain credibility from students. This support must include special provisions for calculating their student evaluation ratings that hold the potential to affect the teacher's tenure and promotion.

• Implement and support human rights training for all aspiring superintendents and their professors who instruct them. Be sure that this training delivers open and honest dialogue about the race and gender discrepancies, especially as these problems exist in civic capacity building and into accessing the position of superintendent.

• Design an aggressive recruitment system for attracting and retaining females and minorities into the superintendent-preparation programs, and provide special provisions for high-poverty urban districts. For example, the Cooperative Superintendency Program at the University of Texas-Austin has been successful at recruiting women and minorities. It established long-term relationships with urban school districts and superintendents for training prospective administrators as an incentive from their districts. One of the major problems for aspiring superintendents of color is that of access. According to the data provided by the NABSE and the CGCS, the number of superintendents of color is declining (see Appendices B and C). Administrative preparation programs must be aware of this deficit and then avidly recruit and support aspiring minorities.

• Create mentorships, networks, and placement assistance to support superintendents of color and females, including assistance and access into nontypical appointment areas (i.e., suburban, ethnically, and economically diverse populations). Concerning the attainment of a superintendency appointment, Moody (1983) argued "[t]raditionally, attainment of this position has depended to an appreciable extent on the help and information an aspirant received from professional contacts—the so-called "old boy network" (p. 383).

• Take responsibility for debunking race and gender myths by admitting and confronting these issues for all to know and understand. This includes advocating superintendent appointments for minority and female aspirants through contacts with other university officials, search firms, school board associations, and so on.

CONCLUSION

The history of the emergence of superintendents of color is a phenomenon that exists outside of the realm of traditional superintendent-preparation programs. Their existence, from early slave beginnings to their re-evolving (revolutionary) presence of the 1960s, has been bounded by conflict and crises. Although today's superintendents of color have needs and problems that are common to all superintendents, superintendents of color experience additional barriers that are precipitated by race, the economic and social deterioration of their minority-populated school districts, and the difficulty of accessing the necessary political and social power relationships (civic capacity building) needed to improve the social and academic performance of their districts.

The five role conceptualizations of superintendents are beneficial for all aspirants to the superintendency, but are particularly valuable for women and minorities whose knowledge and experiences are constantly under scrutiny and observation. Moreover, because of the racial and social complexities inherent in American public school administration, including issues of socially constructed behaviors and race-accorded privilege, an additional conceptualization (civic capacity building) is encouraged in preparation programs for training superintendents of color and their white counterparts, who also lead challenged urban districts.

Access to the position of superintendent continues to be a major concern for students of color who aspire to become superintendents. Strong mentorships, network systems, and sponsorships are needed to support aspiring superintendents, especially women and minorities. According to Glass, Björk, and Brunner (2000), a survey assessing female superintendents showed that many of these women perceived the lack of mentorship experiences to be barriers that limited administrative opportunities for women (p. 88). Likewise, Moody (1983) argues that the mobility of aspiring superintendents of color depended largely on their opportunities for mentorships and sponsorships.

Although the 50 years that have followed the *Brown versus Board of Topeka, Kansas* case (1954) began with hopeful increases in the numbers of superintendents of color who were appointed to school districts, recent data (CGCS, 2003, 2004; NABSE, 2001) indicate a sudden decline in the numbers of superintendents of color. It is thought that with the substantial increase in the salaries of urban superintendents during the past few years, more nonminorities have been motivated to seek superintendencies in the once "undesirable" urban centers. Thus, the urban centers no longer serve as ready options for superintendents of color. With this in mind, aspiring superintendents of color are encouraged to develop the necessary political savvy to transcend the racial and ethnic redlining with social and political organizations that have influence and power. It is essential, also, that these aspirants negotiate diverse social interactions and platforms to establish reform platforms (civic capacity). Thus, aspirants are encouraged to embark upon human rights studies, to share the benefits of such studies and experiences with members of diverse ethnic and gender groups, and to encourage open and honest dialogues about race and gender wherever possible and appropriate. In so doing, others might become inspired by the empowerment of truth.

Last, but not least, preparation programs must become adamant about fairness, including taking the responsibility to debunk race and gender myths, to hire minority practitioners as instructors/professors in their training programs, and to reveal and acknowledge these unfair practices—even in their own institutions. When all superintendent-preparation programs and institutions begin to *model* fairness in their own programs, school board organizations, superintendent search firms, political representatives, agents from community development, and all the "powers that be"(including those who own and control scholarship) will respect and appreciate the sustainability of these efforts.

APPENDIX A

Chronology of the Evolution of the Superintendent of Color: What the History of American Education/Foundations Never Taught You

1833. Ex-slaves established collective schools

- Started in Savannah, GA; extended throughout northeastern South Carolina
  - 4,000+ children of ex-slaves
  - Organized into clusters of 22 schools
  - Established board of "educational collectives, associations, and decision making"
- Secretly grouped; organized by female African American, Deveaux
  - Staffing, facility construction, fundraising, curriculum acquisition and design
  - General managerial responsibilities

1862. Ex-slaves created "native schools"

1863. Abraham Lincoln issued Emancipation Proclamation

1865 (September). John W. Alvord appointed "inspector of schools"

- Freedmen's Bureau sent to organize universal schooling for ex-slaves (sponsored by northern missionary societies and union army)

1865 (July). John W. Alvord named "general superintendent of schools" (first-known use of title)

1930–1950. Sparse number of African American superintendents in rural, minority areas emerge (Glass, Björk, & Brunner, 2000)

- Boley, Clearview, Rentiesville, Redbird, and Taft, OK (Jones, 1985; Moody, 1971; Scott, 1980; Sizemore, 1986)
- Inkster, MI; Lincoln Heights, OH; Macon County, AL (Moody, 1971)

1954. *Brown vs. Board of Topeka, Kansas*

- Birth of "white flight"
- African American community demands representation in politics, education, etc. (NAACP)

Late 1950s–Mid-1960s. Civil rights movements

- Political representation demands continue
- Signs of transition in urban demographics
- Black Panther Party makes aggressive demands, including school leadership representation

1960. Baltimore school enrollment becomes majority African American

1962. Detroit school enrollment becomes majority African American

1963. Atlanta's "white flight" leaves city schools majority African American

1964. Civil Rights Act (televised); major visible transitions in politics

- Representation begins taking effect
- School boards
- Political officials; governing boards

1969. New governing elite takes leadership; urban transformations (see Scott, 1980)

- 1969: Ersel Watson, first African American superintendent appointed to prominent urban system, Trenton, NJ

1970–1971

- 1970: Marcus Foster, superintendent of Oakland, CA (Scott, 1980)
- October 1971: Hugh Scott, superintendent of Washington, DC (Scott, 1980)
- October 1971: Roland Patterson, superintendent of Baltimore, MD (largest public school leadership)
- Transition in school boards

1973. Transitions take major effect (Henig et al., 1999)

- Atlanta: African American superintendent; school board becomes majority African American
- Atlanta: City council becomes majority African American
- Baltimore: School board becomes majority African American
- Detroit: African American mayor

1974. Detroit: African American superintendent

1977. Detroit's school board and city council become majority African American

1987. Atlanta: African American mayor

1992–2000. Larger percentage of African American superintendents appointed to urban areas

1999–2001. Urban superintendents' salaries increase

2000–2001. Number of African American superintendents began declining

- November 2001: NABSE reported 292 African American superintendents (1.8% of national total)
- Leading 14,500,000 students
- In charge of $21 billion budgets

2001–Present

- NABSE reported 271 African American superintendents
- Council of the Great City Schools, 2003 indicates decline in African American superintendents in urban leadership (see Appendix B)

APPENDIX B

States Without Any African American Superintendents

States	NABSE Report Data
Alaska	November 2001
Colorado	November 2001
Hawaii	November 2001
Idaho	November 2001
Iowa	November 2001
Kentucky	November 2001
Maine	November 2001
Nebraska	November 2001
Nevada	November 2001
New Hampshire	November 2001
North Dakota	November 2001
Rhode Island	November 2001
South Dakota	November 2001
Utah	November 2001
Vermont	November 2001
West Virginia	November 2001
Wisconsin	November 2001
Wyoming	November 2001

SOURCE: Permission granted to reprint from the National Alliance of Black School Educators (NABSE), Washington, DC, www.nabse.org

NOTE: Table may not include changes made after NABSE's publication deadline.

Number of African American Superintendents by State (# of AASS)

State	Number of AASS
Alabama	15
Alaska	0
Arizona	1
Arkansas	16
California	15
Colorado	0
Connecticut	5
Delaware	1
District of Columbia	1
Florida	4
Georgia	17
Hawaii	0
Idaho	0

Illinois	13
Indiana	1
Iowa	0
Kansas	2
Kentucky	0
Louisiana	9
Maine	0
Maryland	3
Massachusetts	1
Michigan	12
Minnesota	3
Mississippi	42
Missouri	7
Montana	1
Nebraska	0
Nevada	0
New Hampshire	0
New Jersey	11
New Mexico	1
New York	17
North Carolina	11
North Dakota	0
Ohio	11
Oklahoma	4
Oregon	1
Pennsylvania	4
Rhode Island	0
South Carolina	17
South Dakota	0
Tennessee	5
Texas	15
U.S. Virgin Islands	3
Utah	0
Vermont	0
Virginia	11
Washington	2
West Virginia	0
Wisconsin	0
Wyoming	0

SOURCE: Permission granted to reprint from the National Alliance of Black School Educators (NABSE), Washington, DC, www.nabse.org

NOTE: Table may not include changes made after NABSE's publication deadline.

APPENDIX C

CGCS Superintendents by Race/Ethnicity and Gender:
July 1997, July 1999, July 2001, and July 2003

CGCS Superintendents by Race/Ethnicity and Gender: July 1997, July 1999, July 2001, and July 2003

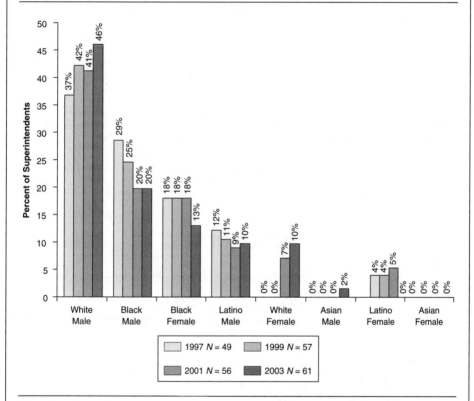

SOURCE: Special permission granted to reprint from the Council of the Great City Schools, 1301 Pennsylvania Ave., NW, Suite #702, Washington, DC 20004; Sharon Lewis, Research Director & Janice Ceperich, Research Specialist.

APPENDIX D

CGCS Top 10 Needs of Urban Schools

Need	01–02	99–00	97–98	95–96	93–94
Academic Achievement	1	1	1	1	8
Closing Achievement Gaps	2	5	9	7	*
Principal Leadership	3	*	*	*	*
Recruiting Teachers	4	2	9	14	*
Teacher Retention	5	*	*	*	*
Professional Development	6	3	3	6	*
School Finance	7	8	4	2	7
Parental Involvement	8	6.5	2	3	2
Reduce Class Size	9	6.5	6	*	*
Public Confidence	10	2	2	4	*

SOURCE: Special permission granted to reprint from the Council of the Great City Schools, 1301 Pennsylvania Ave., NW, Suite #702, Washington, DC 20004; Sharon Lewis, Research Director, & Janice Ceperich, Research Specialist.

*Not rated in given year or presented in a different manner.

APPENDIX E

CGCS Survey on Helpfulness of Groups to Urban Schools

Helpfulness of Groups to Urban Schools (2001–2002)

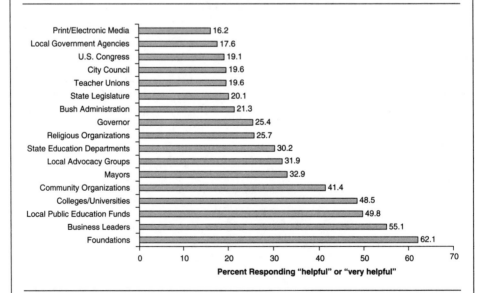

SOURCE: Special permission granted to reprint from the Council of the Great City Schools, 1301 Pennsylvania Ave., NW, Suite #702, Washington, DC 20004; Sharon Lewis, Research Director, & Janice Ceperich, Research Specialist.

REFERENCES

Anderson, G., & Grinberg, J. (1998). Educational administration as a disciplinary practice: Appropriating Foucault's view of power, discourse, and method. *Educational Administration Quarterly, 34*(3), 329–353.

Anderson, J. D. (1988). *The education of blacks in the south, 1860–1935.* Chapel Hill: University of North Carolina Press.

Baker, L. (1996). *The second battle of New Orleans: The hundred-year struggle to integrate schools.* New York: HarperCollins.

Bell, C. (1995). If I weren't involved with schools, I might be radical: Gender consciousness in context. In D. M. Dunlap & P. A. Schmuch (Eds.), *Women leading in education* (pp. 288–312). Albany: State University of New York Press.

Björk, L. G., & Gurley, D. K. (2003, November). *Superintendent as educational statesman, politician and democratic leader: Implications for professional preparation in the 21st century.* Paper presented at the annual meeting of the University Council for Educational Administration, Portland, OR.

Bonuso, C., & Shakeshaft, C. (1983). The gender of secondary school principals. *Integrated Education, 21,* 143–146.

Brown v. Board of Education of Topeka, 347 U.S. 483. (1954) (Brown I).

Brunner, C. C. (1999). *Sacred dreams: Women and the superintendency.* Albany: State University of New York Press.

Callahan, R. (1962). *Education and the cult of efficiency.* Chicago: University of Chicago Press.

Carmichael, S., & Hamilton, C. V. (1976). *Black power.* New York: Vintage.

Chance, P. L., & Björk, L. G. (2004). The social dimension of public relations. In T. J. Kowalski (Ed.), *Public relations in schools* (3rd ed.) (pp. 125–150). Upper Saddle River, NJ: Merrill, Prentice Hall.

Council of the Great City Schools 2003. Urban school superintendents: Characteristics, tenure, and salary—Fourth Biennial Survey. *Urban Indicator, 7*(1), 1–58. Retrieved July 2004 from http://www.cgcs.org/reports/trends.html

Council of the Great City Schools 2004. *Critical trends in urban education: Fifth biennial survey of America's great city schools.* Retrieved August 2, 2004 from http://www.cgcs.org

Civil Rights Project 2003, Harvard University. (n.d.) *Disparity in nation's schools: Race and poverty linked to education and inequality and higher dropout rates.* Retrieved August 5, 2004 from http://www.civilrightsproject.harvard.edu

Cuban, L. (1988). How schools change reforms: Redefining reform success and failure. *Teachers College Record, 99*(3), 453–477.

Education Trust 2002, Federal and State Policy. (n.d.). *Adequate yearly progress under NCLB,* Retrieved August 18, 2004, from http://www.2.edtrust.org

Fairclough, A. (2000). Being in the field of education and also being a Negro . . . seems . . . tragic: Black teachers in the Jim Crow south. *Journal of American History, 87*(1), 1–31.

Foucault, M. (1972). *The archeology of knowledge.* London: Tavistock.

Foucault, M. (1980). Power/knowledge: Selected interviews and other writings by Michel Foucault, 1972–1977 (C. Gorden, Ed.). New York: Pantheon.

Glass, T. E. (1992). *The 1992 study of the American school superintendency.* Arlington, VA: American Association of School Administrators.

Glass, T. E., Björk, L. G., & Brunner, C. C. (2000). *The 2000 study of the American school superintendency.* Arlington, VA: American Association of School Administrators.

Goodman, R., & Zimmerman, W., Jr. (2003). Thinking differently: Recommendations for 21st century school board/superintendent leadership, governance, and teamwork for high student achievement. *American Association of School Administrators—Issues and Insights,* 5–20. Retrieved February 8, 2001, from http://www.aasa.org/issues; http://insights/governance/thinking-differently.htm

Griffiths, D. E., Goldman, S., & McFarland, W. J. (1965). Teacher mobility in New York City. *Educational Administration Quarterly, 1,* 15–31.

Grogan, M. (1996). *Voices of women aspiring to the superintendency*. Albany: State University of New York Press.

Gusfield, J. R. (1957). The problem of generations in an organizational structure. *Social Forces, 35*, 323–330.

Gutman, Herbert G. (1976). *The black family in slavery and freedom, 1750–1925*. New York: Pantheon Books.

Henig, J. R., Hula, R. C., Orr, M., & Pedescleaux, D. S. (1999).*The color of school reform: Race, politics, and the challenge of urban education*. Princeton, NJ: Princeton University Press.

Hill, M., & Ragland, J. (1995). *Women as educational leaders*. Thousand Oaks, CA: Corwin.

Hudson, M. J. (1994). Women and minorities in school administration: Reexamining the role of informal job contact systems. *Urban Education, 28*, 386–397.

Johnson, B. C., & Fusarelli, L. D. (2003, April). *Superintendents as social scientists*. Paper presented at the annual meeting of the American Educational Research Association, Chicago.

Jones, E. (1985). A survey of the problems and characteristics of school districts administered by black superintendents (Doctoral dissertation, George Washington University). *Dissertation Abstracts International, 46*, 35.

Kelleher, P. (2002). Core values of the superintendent. *The School Administrator*, 24–31.

Kowalski, T. J., & Björk, L. (2004). *Role conceptualizations of the district superintendent in the 21st century: Implications for professional preparation*. Paper presented at the annual meeting of the American Education Research Association, San Francisco.

Kowalski, T. J., & Keedy, J. L. (2003, November). *Superintendent as communicator: Implications for professional preparation and licensing*. Paper presented at the annual meeting of the University Council for Educational Administration, Portland, OR.

Lomotey, K. (1993). African-American principals: Bureaucrat/administrators and ethno-humanists. *Urban Education, 27*, 395–412.

Marshall, C. (1984). The crisis in excellence and equity. *Educational Horizons, 63*, 24–30.

Meier, K. J., England, R. E., & Stewart, J., Jr. (1989). *Race, class, and education*. Madison: University of Wisconsin Press.

Metzger, C. (1985). Helping women prepare for principalships. *Phi Delta Kappan, 67*, 292–296.

Moody, C. D. (1971). *Black superintendents in public school districts: Trends and conditions* (Doctoral dissertation, Northwestern University). *Dissertation Abstracts International, 32*, 2965A.

Moody, C. D. (1983). On becoming a superintendent: Contest or sponsored mobility. *Journal of Negro Education, 52*, 383–397.

Murtadha-Watts, K. (1998, April). *Fighting styles: African-American women in urban school leadership*. Paper presented at the annual meeting of the American Educational Research Association, San Diego, CA.

National Alliance of Black School Educators. (2001). *Directory of African-American superintendents*. Washington, DC: Author.

Olson, L., & Jerald, C. (1998). Barriers to success. *Education Week, 17*, 9.

Patton, J. O. (1980). Major Richard Robert Wright Sr. and black higher education in Georgia, 1880–1920. Unpublished doctoral dissertation, University of Chicago.

Payne, N., & Jackson, B. (1978). Status of black women in educational administration. *Emergent Leadership, 2*, 1–17.

Ryan, W. (1976). *Blaming the victim*. New York: Vintage.

Rist, M. C. (1990). Race and politics rip into the urban superintendency. *Executive Educator, 12*, 12–15.

Scheurich, J. J. (1994). Social relativism: A postmodernist epistemology for educational administration. In S. J. Maxcy (Ed.), *Postmodern school leadership: Meeting the crisis in educational administration* (pp. 17–46). Westport, CT: Praeger.

Scheurich, J. J., & Young, M. (1997). Coloring epistemologies: Are our research epistemologies racially biased? *Educational Researcher, 26*(4), 4–16.

Scott, H. J. (1980). *The black school superintendent: Messiah or scapegoat?* Washington, DC: Howard University Press.

Sizemore, B. A. (1986). The limits of the black superintendency: A review of the literature. *Journal of Educational Equity and Leadership, 6,* 180–208.

Smith, J., & Smith, B. M. (1974). Desegregation in the south and the demise of the black educator. *Journal of Social and Behavioral Sciences, 20,* 28–40.

Stone, C. (1968). The National Conference on Black Power. In Floyd B. Barbour, *The black power revolt* (2nd ed.) (pp. 225–237). Boston: Macmillan.

Tsui, A. S., Egan, T. D., & O'Reilly, C. A., III. (1992). Being different: Relational demography and organizational attachment. *Administrative Science Quarterly, 37,* 549–579.

Willer, D., Lovaglia, M. J., & Markovsky, B. (1997). Power and influence: A theoretical bridge. *Pacific Sociological Review, 8,* 52–60.

Index

**CORWIN
PRESS**

The Corwin Press logo—a raven striding across an open book—represents the union of courage and learning. Corwin Press is committed to improving education for all learners by publishing books and other professional development resources for those serving the field of PreK–12 education. By providing practical, hands-on materials, Corwin Press continues to carry out the promise of its motto: **"Helping Educators Do Their Work Better."**